CRACKING HITLER'S ATLANTIC WALL

THE 1ST ASSAULT BRIGADE ROYAL ENGINEERS ON D-DAY

Richard C. Anderson Jr.

STACKPOLE
BOOKS

To my father, Lt. Col. Richard C. Anderson,
USA (Ret.), 1921–2006.
Dad, we miss you.

—————————————————

Published by

STACKPOLE BOOKS
5067 Ritter Road
Mechanicsburg, PA 17055
www.stackpolebooks.com

Printed in the United States of America

10   9   8   7   6   5   4   3   2   1

Library of Congress Cataloging-in-Publication Data

Anderson, Richard C., 1955–
   Cracking Hitler's Atlantic Wall : the 1st Assault Brigade Royal Engineers on D-Day /
Richard C. Anderson, Jr. — 1st ed.
       p. cm.
   Includes bibliographical references and index.
   ISBN 978-0-8117-0589-9
   1. World War, 1939–1945—Campaigns—France—Normandy. 2. Great Britain. Army.
Royal Engineers. Assault Brigade, 1st. 3. World War, 1939–1945—Regimental histories—
Great Britain. 4. Atlantic Wall (France and Belgium) I. Title.
   D756.5.N6A48 2009
   940.54'21421—dc22
                                        2009009486

Contents

Introduction

FOR MORE THAN SIXTY-FIVE YEARS since the Allied invasion of Normandy on 6 June 1944, many misconceptions and flawed assumptions about how that operation was planned and executed have become part of the accepted history of World War II. One of the most misunderstood is the role and accomplishments of "Hobo's Funnies," the 79th Armoured Division, its 1st Assault Brigade, Royal Engineers, and the special-purpose armored assault vehicles, especially the "Armoured Vehicle Royal Engineer" (A.V.R.E.), developed by the British and employed by them on the Commonwealth beaches on D-Day and in Europe.

To understand the role of the 1st Assault Brigade in the invasion, it is necessary first to understand why the Allies planned the Normandy assault as they did. To do that, one must first look at how the German defenses were constructed and organized, then examine the timing and organization of the Allied assault with special focus on the capabilities of the landing craft that were employed. Finally, and perhaps most importantly, to understand the true effectiveness of Hobo's Funnies, it is necessary to explore—albeit somewhat more briefly—what happened on the two American beaches, Omaha and Utah, where the Funnies were absent.

The accounts of the D-Day assault that follow were primarily compiled from the original history of the 1st Assault Brigade, the war diaries of the 5th and 6th Assault Regiment and their assault squadrons, debriefings of the various gapping teams as well as the war diaries of many other formations and units that participated, the reports of the Neptune naval commanders, and postwar accounts by the participants. Many of those accounts are reproduced here in full as they were originally written,

with only minor amendments to correct spelling errors and to clarify the meaning of some of the abbreviated and more esoteric terms used. The official accounts by participants from the 6th Assault Regiment R.E. on Gold Beach are especially vivid, since nearly every surviving A.V.R.E. commander made a report of their activity.

Some may wonder why I have not addressed the flamethrower variant of the Churchill tank that was known as the Crocodile. There is no disputing that it was a ferocious weapon with a terrifying reputation. However, it was not deployed in significant numbers on D-Day (only six were with the assault elements), it is not known to have seen any action on D-Day, and it was not an element of the 1st Assault Brigade Royal Engineers or the 79th Armoured Division on D-Day.

It should be noted that two distinct terms are interspersed throughout the narratives, and their actual meaning is critical to understanding the events. A "lane" was considered to be a passageway cleared of obstacles and mines that extended all the way to the first lateral beach road inland of the assault beach. It could be wide enough for vehicle traffic or so narrow as to be passable only by infantry. On the other hand, an "exit" was a lane that had been well enough developed so as to make it accessible to either wheeled or tracked vehicles and that had a traffic-control system in place sufficient to ensure the orderly procession inland of those vehicles.

In the end, I hope this work helps to fill some of the gaps in the history of that famous "Day of Days." Of course, the conclusions and interpretation of events are my own, as are any errors I may accidentally have made.

CHAPTER 1

Conception

THE ROYAL ENGINEERS (R.E.) have always been inextricably tied to the development of the tank, so it is little wonder that a tank specifically designed for engineer requirements eventually emerged. In World War I, Lt. Col. Ernest Swinton, R.E., directly contributed to the creation of the original tank; his experience in France in 1914 led him to write a report that addressed ways of breaking the tactical deadlock that was created in France by the combination of the machine gun, barbed wire, and trenches. When he returned to England, he was asked to join the Landship Committee that had been formed to develop methods of crossing trenches in armored vehicles. The tank came out of the committee's work, as did a requirement for supply tanks that could carry supplies and engineer stores directly to the front lines.

Another early influential engineer officer was Capt. (later Lt. Gen.) Giffard Le Quesne Martel, who served in France at the headquarters of the nascent British Tank Corps. He was heavily involved, along with yet another engineer, Maj. C. E. Inglis, in the early work to develop a mobile assault bridge that could be carried and laid by a tank and in the creation of three mechanized Royal Engineer "Special" Battalions that were formed at Christchurch in Hants in October 1918. After the war, Martel was promoted to major and given command of the sole special battalion—renamed the Experimental Engineer Establishment—that was maintained after the demobilization of the army.

Martel's Royal Engineer Tank. THE TANK MUSEUM

By the end of the First World War, the Royal Engineers had defined three types of obstacles that could impede a tank assault:

- obstacles, such as natural or man-made ditches or water courses, that required bridging before a tank could pass;
- barricade-type obstacles, such as walls, concrete blocks, and steel posts, that would have to be destroyed by demolitions before a tank could pass; and
- minefields that required removal or destruction before tanks could pass.[1]

Between the wars, Martel and the Experimental Engineer Establishment continued to champion the development of specialized armored vehicles for the engineers and also advocated that an armored engineer vehicle organization should be trained and manned by the sappers of the Royal Engineers rather than by Tank Corps personnel. By the middle of the 1920s, an initial concept vehicle, the R.E. Tank, was completed. By the end of the decade,

however, shrinking budgets resulting from the worldwide Great Depression began to limit development both in the Tank Corps and the Royal Engineers. By the outbreak of war in September 1939, little additional work had been done. Nevertheless, more than twenty-five years of steady development had laid the groundwork. The requirements of defeating the same three classes of obstacles would drive further development during the early years of World War II and become an integral part of the planning for the assault on Hitler's Fortress Europe.

Martel himself continued as an advocate of armor and mechanization, first as the assistant director and then deputy director of mechanization at the War Office from 1936 to 1939 and later as the commander of the Royal Armoured Corps from 1940 to 1943, when he became the head of the military mission to Moscow.[2] In early 1942, a new and younger set of officers took over and brought Martel's work to fruition.

DENOVAN

The most intriguing misunderstanding about the British Army vehicle that would become known as the A.V.R.E. is that in a sense, it was not actually British in origin, but rather Canadian. Little is known about the man whose brainchild it was; even the few references to him frequently misspell his name. He was a very junior Canadian officer, twenty-nine-year-old Lt. John James Denovan of the Royal Canadian Engineers (R.C.E.).[3]

Denovan had been a civilian engineer and joined the Canadian Army early in the war. By the summer of 1942, he was in England, where he was posted to the British Army Department of Tank Design (DTD) as liaison officer between the Canadian and British military engineer establishments. Denovan turned out to be the right person in the right place at the right time following the disaster of Operation Jubilee at Dieppe on 19 August 1942.

During Jubilee, none of the tanks that landed with the 2nd Canadian Division in its assault on Dieppe had managed to get inland from the beaches. All had been destroyed by German fire or had simply gotten bogged down in the sand and shingle of the beaches. As a result, most analyses of the battle recommended abandoning the idea of even attempting to land tanks in future operations before the infantry had secured a firm beachhead. In that prevailing view, tanks had no place in the initial assault. However, Lt. Col. George C. Reeves, assistant director of the DTD, who had participated in Jubilee as an observer, was unconvinced and believed that armor might still have a viable role in an assault, as long as effective ways of getting them onto and off the beach could be developed. Immediately after returning, he met with his staff and discussed his observations and possible solutions for the problems he had seen. Just eight days after the operation, on 27 August 1942, they prepared a report for the War Ministry "exploring the possibility of developing devices to enable obstacles to be surmounted by a tank or destroyed by a tank crew without being exposed to enemy fire."[4]

It is unclear whether Denovan actually attended Reeves's meeting or participated in writing the

Lt. John James Denovan.

report, but it is clear that he was affected by the terrible casualties—some of whom were close friends—suffered by the Canadian forces in Jubilee.[5] Within a few weeks, on 6 October 1942, Lieutenant Denovan, working with Captain Schortinghuis, R.C.E., who commanded the 1st Canadian Mechanical Engineering Company, which was attached to the DTD, had come up with the idea of utilizing a specially adapted tank as a means of carrying the men and stores of an engineer sapper team during an assault and had even completed a preliminary concept drawing for one.[6] Denovan's report summarized the role of his "engineer tank" as

- establishing a route through a minefield by the use of "snake," an explosive mine-clearing device consisting of lengths of pipe filled with explosives that could be pushed into a minefield by a tank or bulldozer and then exploded;
- demolition;
- crossing antitank ditches by the camouflet method, that is, by filling a ditch or crater by placing

explosives along its edge and setting them off so that the edge would collapse into the obstacle;

- destroying bent rail obstacles; and
- laying mines under fire.[7]

Denovan also noted that the list of required engineer stores was to be flexible so that they could be stowed according to the work immediately at hand; that the drivers should be drawn from Royal Armoured Corps personnel; and that three engineer tanks, plus one in reserve, should be issued to each engineer field squadron, the basic engineer unit in the armored division, which had two.

Denovan's, Schortinghuis's, and Reeves's assumptions were supported by Maj. B. Sucharov of the Royal Canadian Engineers, who, in his report on Dieppe, had noted that tanks in an initial assault could be equipped with mechanical devices for placing demolition charges and ramps to enable them to exit the beach more easily. Further support came on 19 October 1942 from Major Hawkins, R.E., the commandant of the Anti-Tank Establishment, who wrote a short paper to the War Office, in which he stated that although the task of breaching obstacles for the passage of tanks and armored vehicles should be that of the Royal Engineers, the currently available equipment was inadequate for the task. He proposed the organization of specialized Royal Engineer troops to address that problem.[8]

Reeves forwarded Denovan's preliminary report to the War Office and urgently recommended development of an engineer tank. He also asked that a Churchill tank be supplied to his team so that a mock-up prototype could be prepared, but since his department was meant only for design and feasibility studies and had no control of acquisition, it quickly became apparent that it would be some time before his request would be acted upon, if ever. Reeves then turned his own attention to a new amphibious tank design proposed by Nicholas Straussler, which became the duplex-drive (DD) tank.[9]

Then Denovan stepped in and somehow managed to get his hands on the necessary requisition documents. According to one rumor, Denovan utilized his charms to convince his girlfriend, who was an Auxiliary Territorial Services clerk in charge of the tank supply paperwork, to turn the tank over to him. Many years later, Denovan offered a less roman-

tic description: "Well, sure I knew the girl; she was in charge of the tank pool. But I very substantially outranked her, so she couldn't get into any trouble. My boss [Colonel Reeves], who knew this work was going on, looked the other way."[10]

Once Denovan had his hands on the tank, he went considerably beyond building a mere mock-up. After carefully hiding the tank from the prying eyes of the Tank Corps, he used the skills of the 1st Canadian Mechanical Engineering Company and went to work. Denovan had them carefully keep the exterior of the tank intact, adding only mock pannier doors. Then, although officially he had no authority to alter the tank beyond that, he had them strip out all the equipment not essential to his needs, including the codriver's seat and dual driving controls, ammunition bins, the turret basket, and other ancillary items. That created a thirty-six-cubic-foot stowage area for engineer stores, demolitions, and tools, with room for a crew of six (commander, gunner, driver, loader, and two sappers). These modifications left the original tank as little more than an armored shell.[11]

The main armament that Denovan planned on using for the vehicle was the Blacker Bombard, invented by Latham Valentine Stewart Blacker, a retired British Army lieutenant colonel. Stewart Blacker was something of a mechanical genius who, in World War I, had helped develop a synchronization mechanism that allowed the machine guns of Royal Flying Corps aircraft to be fired through the propeller, thus ending one of the Germans' significant tactical advantages. His Bombard was a spigot mortar that he had originally designed as a simple antitank weapon during the dark days of 1940. It had been a large and heavy—more than 300 pounds—contraption that used a black-powder charge to propel a 14-pound high-explosive or a 19.5-pound armor-piercing, shaped-charge round to a theoretical maximum range of 450 yards, but it had a practical effective range of about 100 yards. (The design came full circle in 1943 when the spigot mortar principle was utilized in the projector, infantry, anti-tank, which, known as the PIAT, was the standard Commonwealth man-portable infantry antitank weapon during the last years of the war.)

Denovan later claimed that he came up with the idea of developing the Blacker Bombard into a

The Armoured Vehicle Royal Engineer. This photo was taken in Belgium on 18 September 1944. NARA

demolition weapon to replace the ineffective 2-pounder antitank gun that was then mounted in the Churchill tank. Denovan supposedly discovered that Blacker lived nearby and paid him an informal visit to ask for his help. Although that story may be apocryphal, Blacker later confirmed that he had informally met with some Canadian engineers to discuss development of the Bombard. In any case, within a remarkably few short weeks, it had been developed into a demolition mortar capable of accurately firing a forty-pound round filled with twenty-nine pounds of high explosive up to about eighty yards. An experimental model was completed and tested in a Covenanter tank, and then three prototypes of the new weapon were contracted in November 1942.[12]

Luckily for Denovan's future army career, the initial unarmed prototype vehicle worked well in tests, and no questions were apparently ever raised regarding the unorthodox means that had been used to aquire it. On 22 October, the War Office formally issued a Churchill to the 1st Canadian Mechanical Engineering Company to use as a prototype, although it seems likely that the authorization was apparently for the tank that Denovan had already modified. On 12 November 1942, the 1st Canadian Mechanical Engineering Company held a meeting, with Denovan attending, to discuss future requirements for the design. Although Denovan had always championed the Churchill as the basis for conversion, others had focused their attention on the Canadian Ram and the American M4 Sherman. Many favored the Ram for the convenience of its hull-side crew-access doors, but one major problem existed: only the first fifty Rams (known as the Ram I) had the side doors, which had been deleted from the assembly line in January 1942. Worse, it was realized that the tank was simply too small to accommodate the vehicle crew, sappers, and their equipment and stores. The second choice, the Sherman, was in huge demand as a gun tank, was not significantly larger than the Ram, and also did not

The 29-centimeter Petard spigot mortar on a Churchill A.V.R.E. of the 79th Squadron, 5th Assault Regiment, Royal Engineers, under the command of the 3rd Infantry Division, 29 April 1944. A forty-pound bomb can be seen on the right.
IMPERIAL WAR MUSEUM

have side doors, which left the designers with the Churchill as their only practical alternative.

In early 1943, Denovan's initiative continued to gain momentum. The War Office issued a request for complete development of such a vehicle and other engineering devices to the Ministry of Supply on 2 February 1943. At the same time, the DTD was officially tasked with developing means for executing combat engineering tasks while under armor and a Special Devices Section was created to tackle the problem, with Reeves as director and Denovan attached as Canadian liaison. The War Office further agreed that the Royal Engineers should be given tanks to modify and be permitted to study existing tanks—as long as it did "not interfere with current tank production."[13]

A second prototype Churchill was authorized for modification, and by the end of February 1943, the two prototypes—without armament mounted—and one of the Blacker prototype mortars were ready for a demonstration. The trials showed that the vehicles could successfully transport sappers and their equipment and that the prototype mortar—now dubbed a Petard after a French explosive device of the sixteenth century—was capable of demolishing reinforced concrete structures. With twelve rounds, the Petard destroyed a six-foot-high wall, blowing open a hole large enough for the tank to drive through. The Petard was also tested as a mine-

clearing device, with mixed results; it did clear a twenty-eight-foot-wide path, but the method was considered too slow and cumbersome for practical use on the battlefield.[14] As a result of the successful test, nine further Petards were authorized in March 1943, as was a complete set of drawings and instructions for carrying out the conversion of existing Churchill tanks to the newly designated Armoured Vehicle Royal Engineer (A.V.R.E.). On 12 May 1943, a War Office meeting considered how many A.V.R.E.'s were needed, assuming the organization of five Royal Engineer assault squadrons in England, five in the Mediterranean, and two in India and the Far East. The final figure called for for 475, all based upon converting existing Churchills.[15]

The instructions and working drawings were turned over to the Royal Electrical and Mechanical Engineer (R.E.M.E.) units of the 79th Armoured Division so that they could carry out an experimental conversion, a test that was also successful.[16] At that point, the conversion design was also given to two civilian companies—Cockbridge & Company of Ipswich for the manufacture of conversion kits and M. G. Cars of Abingdon to produce the vehicles using the kits. The initial order was for 475 conversion kits, with the 79th Armoured Division R.E.M.E.'s to complete 108 conversions and the balance to be done by M. G.[17]

"HOBO"

In March 1943, Exercise Kruschen was undertaken north of Leiston in order to test various methods of assaulting fortified defensive positions such as might be encountered in a landing in France. The 80th Field Company, R.E., took part as normal sappers, with infantry from the 54th Infantry Division and some tanks and flamethrowers as well. The results of the exercise showed how difficult coordination of such an operation was and led to preliminary acceptance of Denovan's concept of sappers mounted in a specialized armored engineer vehicle.

Luckily, the British had available an officer of extraordinary accomplishments, a man with greater experience than any other general officer in organizing and training an armored division from the ground up. He was Maj. Gen. Percy C. S. Hobart, more commonly known as "Hobo."[18]

In addition to being being one of the most skilled, Hobart was also perhaps one of the most controversial general officers in the British Army. Originally commissioned into the Royal Engineers in 1904, he had served in World War I with distinction in France, where he was awarded the Military Cross, and then in the Mesopotamian campaign, where he received the Distinguished Service Order.

He was also mentioned in dispatches five times. He was captured on 12 December 1916 and held by the Turks until 2 October 1918. Between the wars, he led the push for an independent and powerful tank force, supported by the likes of Martel, B. H. Liddell Hart, and J. F. C. Fuller, and in the process had made numerous enemies in the War Office, partly because of his unconventional thinking, but also because of his acid tongue—he refused to suffer fools or incompetent officers gladly. Nevertheless, on 27 September 1938, he had been given a magnificent opportunity: the task of forming a "Mobile Division" in Egypt that eventually became the 7th Armoured Division of "Desert Rats" fame, Britain's first armored division. There he clashed with his immediate superior, Lt. Gen. Henry Maitland Wilson, who believed Hobart to be "self-opinionated" and "lacking in stability." On 10 November 1938, Wilson recommended Hobart for relief to Gen. Archibald Wavell, commander of British Forces in the Middle East. On 8 December 1939, barely three months into the war, Hobart was summarily relieved and placed into the Regular Army Reserve of Officers, which was effectively a forced retirement.[19]

A Churchill gun tank fitted with a fascine during Exercise Kruschen. THE TANK MUSEUM

Maj. Gen. Percy C. S. Hobart.
THE TANK MUSEUM

Unemployed except by the Home Guard, Hobart spent fourteen quiet months until Churchill, goaded by a timely editorial by Liddell Hart in the *London Sunday Pictorial*, insisted to the War Office that Hobo be given an armored division. So on 14 February 1941, Hobart took command of the newly forming 11th Armoured Division and was also given a position as an advisor to Winston Churchill's "Tank Parliament," a group the prime minister formed to discuss problems associated with tank production, production expansion, and organization.[20]

Unfortunately, just a year later, on 22 February 1942, Hobart was forced to step down because of ill health and was unable to resume his post until 17 May 1942. As a result, when the War Office began to develop plans to send the 11th Armoured Division to Egypt in September 1942 to join Lt. Gen. Bernard Law Montgomery's Eighth Army (few in the army were aware that Montgomery's late wife was Hobart's sister), their plans did not include Hobart.[21] On 10 October, Hobart was told that he was to stay in England and turn command over to Maj. Gen. Montagu Brocas Burrows and that he would again go on the retired list since he was considered too old for field service.[22] However, once again Churchill intervened, and on 16 October 1942, Hobo was instead given command of the 79th Armoured Divi-

sion. Hobart thus commanded, organized, and trained three of the nine British armored divisions that saw service overseas and three of the six that were in existence at war's end. The 11th Armoured Division never went to North Africa.

The 79th Armoured Division had begun forming on 14 August 1942 with the 27th Armoured Brigade, which came from the 9th Armoured Division, and on 8 September with the 185th Infantry Brigade, formerly the 204th Independent Infantry Brigade, which had been engaged in the defense of Britain since the dark days of 1940. Other divisional units included the 142nd and 150th Field Regiments Royal Artillery (R.A.), the 55th Antitank Regiment R.A., and the 119th Light Antiaircraft Regiment, R.A. Initially, the division was commanded by Brig. George McIllree Stanton Bruce, the commander of the 185th Brigade, but he was considered too junior to be given the responsibility of permanent division command, leaving the opportunity open for Hobart.

Hobart threw himself into the work with his customary energy and, in short order, had a functioning organization busily engaged in training for its expected commitment on the continent as part of the long anticipated "Second Front" in Europe. But then, on 11 March 1943, following Exercise Kruschen, Hobo was called to the War Office to meet again with the Chief of the Imperial General Staff, Gen. Sir Alan Brooke. It seems reasonable to suppose that after his previous experiences, Hobart might have experienced some trepidation when going to that meeting, but if so, his anxiety was unfounded. Brooke told him that he was to be given the job of developing doctrine, tactics, and organization for the strange new vehicle that had been developed by Lieutenant Denovan, as well as the rest of the odd menagerie of vehicles and devices that were being developed for the assault on Hitler's Fortress Europe. As Brooke put it, Hobart was to have control of the "flotation tanks, searchlight tanks, anti-mine tanks, and self-propelled guns" for the invasion.[23] As the formal directive Hobart was given said, his object was to "develop a technique for the specialised units which have been placed under your command and to train them to form part of formations assaulting either beach defences or inland defended areas in Western Europe."[24]

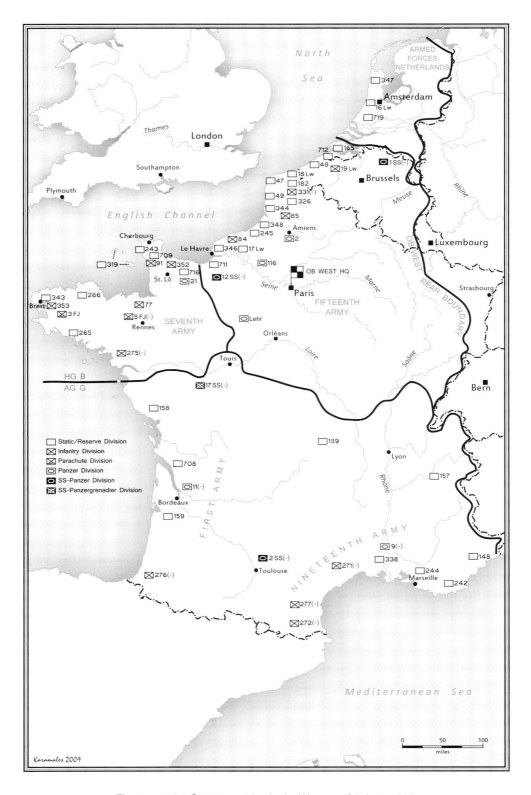

The target: the German armies in the West as of 1 June 1944.

CHAPTER 2

Organization, Training, and Equipping

ORGANIZATION

After Hobart's meeting with the Brooke, things moved rapidly into a period of intense upheaval as the 79th Armoured Division reorganized for its new role. In March and April 1943, the 185th Infantry Brigade and Royal Artillery elements were all detached and left the division for other assignments—the 150th Field Regiment Royal Artillery to the 4th Army Group Royal Artillery (A.G.R.A.); the 185th Infantry Brigade to the 3rd Infantry Division; the 55th Antitank and 119th Light Antiaircraft Regiment R.A. to the 49th and 15th Infantry Divisions, respectively; and the 142nd Field Regiment R.A. to the Eighth Army in the Mediterranean. The 27th Armoured Brigade was retained and began training with the amphibious duplex-drive tank, but otherwise, only the divisional headquarters and some service and support units were left from the original organization.

In exchange, additional troops were assigned to the 79th Armoured Division for its new mission. On 9 April, the 35th Army Tank Brigade—equipped with the top-secret tank-mounted Canal Defence Light (CDL)*—was assigned to the division. It remained until April 1944, when a new CDL unit—the 1st Tank Brigade—was assigned to

---

* The CDL was a powerful searchlight mounted in the turret of a Matilda or Grant tank that was originally intended to blind the enemy but was later used for night operations. Its development was considered so secret that conventional units were never able to practice working with them. They were not actually used until the crossing of the Rhine near the end of the war.

the division and absorbed part of the assets of the 35th Brigade.[2] On 5 May, the 33rd Tank Brigade from the 3rd Infantry Division joined the division, but remained only until 7 August, when it was detached and reformed as a separate armoured brigade. On 9 October, the 27th Armoured Brigade was also detached from the division as a separate armored brigade, although it retained the mission of training for operations with the specialized duplex-drive tanks and continued to exercise with elements of the division. The 30th Armoured Brigade replaced them on 17 October, joining from the 42nd Armoured Division, which had been disbanded on 17 September.

The most significant addition to the division, in terms of the A.V.R.E. that was to become its core, came on 27 April 1943, when the 5th and 6th General Headquarters Troops R.E. arrived. They were headquarters organizations providing command and control for nondivisional support units. The 5th consisted of the 77th, 79th, and 80th Field Companies R.E. and the 6th consisted of the 81st, 82nd,

and 87th Companies R.E. To reflect their new role, the field companies were redesignated as Assault Squadrons R.E.

The 5th and 6th, redesignated on 6 June 1943 as Assault Troops R.E., were joined on 28 September 1943 by the 42nd Assault Troops R.E., which consisted of the 16th and 617th Field Squadrons R.E. and the 149th Field Park Squadron R.E., which were reassigned from the disbanded 42nd Armoured Division. The 16th and 617th Field Squadrons were promptly redesignated as assault squadrons, and on 29 September, the 149th was redesignated as an assault park squadron, withdrawn from 42nd Assault Troops, and placed directly under the command of the 79th Armoured Division. The 149th was intended to man D7 armored bulldozers in support of the assault squadrons.

On 26 October 1943, the 5th, 6th, and 42nd Assault Troops were redesignated yet again, this time as assault regiments. The organization of the regiments was further fleshed out by the additional assignment of the 26th Field Squadron R.E. (from

ORGANIZATION OF THE 79TH ARMOURED DIVISION ON 6 JUNE 1944

79th Armoured Division Headquarters, Maj. Gen. P. C. Hobart

79th Armoured Division Signals
79th Armoured Division R.E.M.E.
79th Armoured Division R.A.S.C.
79th Armoured Division R.A.M.C.
79th Armoured Division R.A.O.C.
79th Armoured Division Provost
264 Special Delivery Squadron

30th Armoured Brigade (Sherman Crabs), Brig. Nigel William Duncan

22nd Dragoons
2nd County of London Yeomanry
    (Queen's Westminster Dragoons)
1st Lothians and Border Horse Yeomanry

1st Assault Brigade R.E., Brig. G. L. Watkinson

149th Assault Park Squadron R.E
5th Assault Regiment R.E.
    26th Assault Squadron R.E.
    77th Assault Squadron R.E.
    79th Assault Squadron R.E.
    80th Assault Squadron R.E.
6th Assault Regiment R.E.
    81st Assault Squadron R.E.
    82nd Assault Squadron R.E.
    87th Assault Squadron R.E.
    284th Assault Squadron R.E.
42nd Assault Regiment R.E.
    16th Assault Squadron R.E.
    222nd Assault Squadron R.E.
    557th Assault Squadron R.E.
    617th Assault Squadron R.E.

1st Tank Brigade (CDL), Brig. Thomas Reginald Price

11th Battalion, Royal Tank Regiment
42nd Battalion, Royal Tank Regiment
49th Battalion, Royal Tank Regiment

33rd Independent Guards Brigade), 222nd Field Company R.E. (from 47th Infantry Division), 284th Field Company R.E. (from 38th Infantry Division), and 557th Field Company R.E. (from 55th Infantry Division), all of which were redesignated as assault squadrons. The 26th Assault Squadron went to the 5th Regiment, the 284th Assault Squadron to the 6th, and the 222nd and 557th to the 42nd Regiment, giving each regiment four squadrons.

The regiments became part of the newly created 1st Assault Brigade R.E. on 26 November 1943, under the command of Brig. Geoffrey Lionel Watkinson, who was designated as Commander Assault Royal Engineers (C.A.R.E.). In turn, the brigade was assigned to the 79th Armoured Division. During the winter of 1943–44 and early spring of 1944, the brigade was fully occupied in organizing, training, and experimenting with its new vehicles and tactics. Then, in a final reorganization just prior to D-Day, the 149th Assault Park Squadron R.E. was relieved from its direct assignment to the 79th Armoured Division and assigned to the headquarters of the 1st Assault Brigade.

ORGANIZATION OF THE 1ST ASSAULT BRIGADE R.E. ON 6 JUNE 1944

1st Assault Brigade R.E. (part), Brig. G. L. Watkinson

Brigade Workshops Company R.E.M.E.	Manned 12 ARV distributed to the various assault squadrons
149th Assault Park Squadron R.E.	Manned 12 D7 armored bulldozers distributed to the various assault squadrons.

I Corps

5th Assault Regiment R.E., Lieutenant Colonel Cocks aboard LCT (Serial 109)

Sword

77th Squadron, Maj. K. du B. Ferguson
1 Troop (Green Gap, Queen Red Sector)
2 Troop (Yellow Gap, Queen Red Sector)
3 Troop (Blue Gap, Queen Red Sector)
4 Troop (Red Gap, Queen Red Sector)
79th Squadron, Maj. J. G. Hanson
1 Troop (Green Gap, Queen White Sector)
2 Troop (Yellow Gap, Queen White Sector)
3 Troop (Blue Gap, Queen White Sector)
4 Troop (Red Gap, Queen White Sector)

Juno

26th Squadron, Major Younger
1 Troop (Green Gap [M1], Mike Green Sector)
2 Troop (Yellow Gap [M2], Mike Red Sector)
3 Troop (Blue Gap [M3], Nan Green Sector)
4 Troop (Red Gap [M4], Nan Green Sector)
80th Squadron, Major Wiltshire
1 Troop (Green Gap, Nan White Sector)
2 Troop (Yellow Gap, Nan White Sector)
3 Troop (Blue Gap, Nan Red Sector)
4 Troop (Green Gap, Nan Red Sector)

XXX Corps

6th Assault Regiment R.E. (part)

Gold

81st Squadron, Maj. R. E. Thompstone
King Green
X Breaching Squadron, Major Sutton (OC, C Squadron, Westminster Dragoons)
Gap 1, Capt. D. A. King
Gap 2, Lt. J. D. Darby
Gap 3, Capt. T. W. Davies
King Red
Z Breaching Squadron, Major Thompstone
Gap 4, Lt. J. C. Skelly
Gap 5, Major Thompstone
Gap 6, Capt. J. M. Birkbeck
82nd Squadron, Maj. H. G. A. Elphinstone
Jig Green West
W Breaching Squadron, Major Elphinstone
Gap 1, Capt. K.M. Wilford
Gap 2, Major Elphinstone
Gap 3, Lt. S.V. Grant
Jig Green East
Y Breaching Squadron, Capt. H. P. Stanyon, (OC, B Squadron, Westminster Dragoons)
Gap 4, Capt. J. M. Leytham
Gap 5, Lt. G. R. Ellis
Gap 6, Capt. F. J. B. Somerset

TRAINING AND EQUIPPING

The training areas for the new organizations were to be Saxmundham in East Anglia, Orfordness in Suffolk, and Linney Head in South Wales. The 79th Division's training area was established at Linney Head and quickly became the primary location for vehicle trials, training exercises, and demonstrations of the new assault techniques for high-ranking officers. Unfortunately, many of these demonstrations "failed ignominiously, and the whole organization was shrouded in a veil of impenetrable secrecy; but it was only by these constant trial-and-error methods that an effective scheme could be arrived at."[1]

At the end of October 1943, the 1st Assault Brigade established the A.R.E. School at the Orford Battle Area at Orfordness. As much training as possible was carried on throughout the winter, but with slender resources—no A.V.R.E.'s yet and some Churchills. The engineers practiced assaults on mock-ups of defenses on the French coast, often failing.[2] As late as December 1943, there were still few A.V.R.E.'s available for the troops of the 1st Assault Brigade. At most, there were perhaps the two originally converted by Denovan, the single one converted by the 79th Armoured Division R.E.M.E., possibly a single conversion prototype by Cockbridge & Company, and at least one conversion completed by M. G. Motor Cars—in total, maybe six more or less completed vehicles.

In May, each squadron received six "decrepit" Churchills, and one officer and about fifty men from the Royal Armoured Corps arrived to give preliminary instruction. Many of the tank troops were not trained on the Churchill, so they and a number of the engineers attended courses together.[3] It appears that the early conversions were mostly utilized as "concept" vehicles for testing the various "devices" that were under development for mounting on the A.V.R.E., thus making them unavailable for training. Nonetheless, some progress was being made in developing the techniques and tactics that would be used on D-Day, but the late delivery of A.V.R.E.'s created frantic haste to complete training and organization in the squadrons prior to D-Day.

Even more revealing of the haste with which the A.V.R.E.'s were sent into battle is the little known fact that none of those deployed on D-Day had actual gun sights mounted for their Petards—quite simply because one had not yet been designed. It was not until August that a proper telescopic sight was designed and available for the Petard; before that, aiming was more or less a matter of "by guess or by God," and the effective range was limited to less than eighty yards. Nor did the gunners have much opportunity to perfect their abilities firing the sightless Petard since most of the A.V.R.E.'s were issued to units within a few weeks of D-Day, and their crews were occupied with courses learning the basic operation of the A.V.R.E., and many A.V.R.E.'s were not fitted with their armament until the day before being loaded into the landing craft for the invasion. The haste with which the A.V.R.E.'s were deployed is also evident from the lack of basic testing done with the vehicle. In September 1944, long after the invasion, it was discovered that the standard 2-pounder gun mount that been used for the Petard was unsafe and simply could not take the recoil stresses of the mortar, which may have contributed to the significant number of failures that occurred when the mortar was fired during the invasion. Thereafter, only Churchill tanks equipped with the sturdier 6-pounder gun mount were accepted for conversion.[4]

In terms of equipment, the 1st Assault Brigade was never able to achieve its planned war establishment. By 1 September 1944, with all twelve squadrons on the continent, the brigade fielded only 217 A.V.R.E.'s—still 95 short of establishment. Partly in response to tactical requirements, but also apparently in response to the limited number of A.V.R.E.'s available, the brigade establishment was changed, so that by V-E Day, it comprised eight assault squadrons with 20 A.V.R.E.'s each and one experimental squadron with 26 A.V.R.E.'s, for a brigade total of 186.

A.V.R.E. DEVICES

The basic A.V.R.E. was configured to carry twenty-six demolition charges for the Petard, as well as bangalore torpedoes[*] and hand-emplaced demolition charges. There were also a large number of innovative—some might call them outlandish—"devices" designed for the vehicle. In general, they were all intended to overcome possible obstacles to the movement of troops and vehicles that the Germans had placed on the beaches of Normandy. The following devices were used with varying degrees of success on D-Day.[5]

Carpet-Laying Devices

Known generically as "bobbins," carpet-layers were devices for laying mats over soft ground. Their development designation was by type (A through D), and production models were referred to by mark (I through III). The Type B was a "twin bobbin" design that deployed two narrow mats directly under each track, but it was not produced in quantity or used in Normandy.

The Mark I—also known as the T.L.C. for tank landing craft—was the oldest and had been designed in March 1939 for Cruiser tanks and then adapted for the Churchill in April 1942. The pilot was tested in July 1942, and at least one was used operationally in the Dieppe raid, Operation Jubilee, on 19 August 1942, where it was lost. As it advanced, the Mark I laid a wire-reinforced nine-foot-one-inch-wide canvas mat in front of the tank from a horizontal roller mounted on fixed arms. The canvas mat was later replaced by an eleven-foot-wide, one-hundred-foot-long canvas carpet reinforced by wire and "chespaling" (chestnut palings). They were intended only for supporting foot and light wheeled vehicle traffic.

The Mark II and III were developed specifically for the circumstances of the invasion, when reconnaissance of the beaches discovered strips of soft blue clay in which vehicles could bog easily. Similar blue clay was found on the beaches of Brancaster in

Churchill A.V.R.E. carpet-layer with bobbin, 79th Armoured Division, 26 April 1944. This is a Mark II or Type C during a pre-invasion exercise. THE TANK MUSEUM

The same Churchill A.V.R.E. Bobbin Mark II with the carpet deployed. THE TANK MUSEUM

---

[*] The Bangalore torpedo was a demolition charge consisting of five-foot lengths of two-inch pipe filled with explosives. The pipes could be joined together and pushed through an obstacle. Intended to clear light obstructions such as barbed wire, it could blow a gap about twelve feet wide.

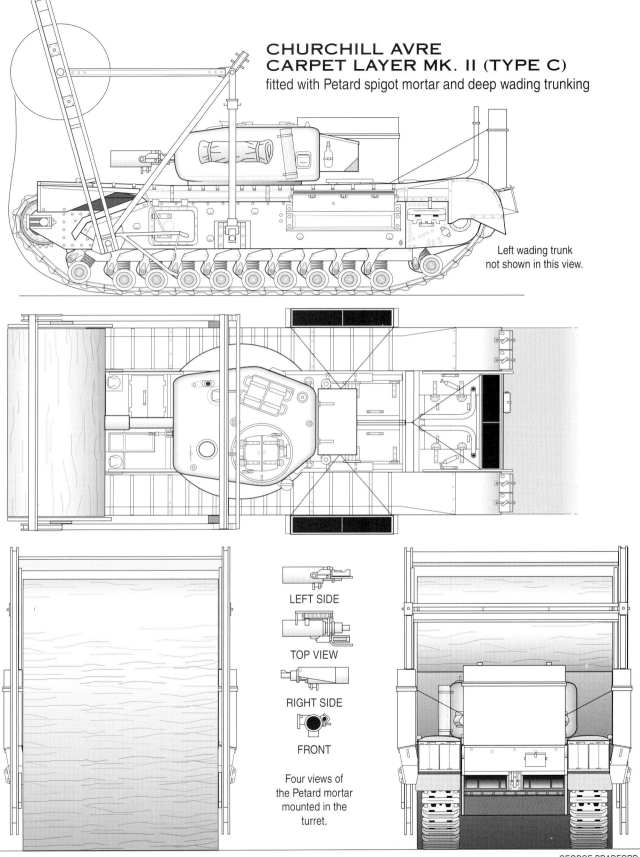

CHURCHILL AVRE
CARPET LAYER MK. II (TYPE C)
fitted with Petard spigot mortar and deep wading trunking

Left wading trunk
not shown in this view.

LEFT SIDE

TOP VIEW

RIGHT SIDE

FRONT

Four views of
the Petard mortar
mounted in the
turret.

A Churchill A.V.R.E. carpet-layer with bobbin, 79th Armoured Division, March or April 1944. This is a Mark III or Type D prototype and does not appear to have a turret mounted. THE TANK MUSEUM

Norfolk, and tests were done there, the solution being a heavier nine-foot-eleven-inch-wide mat of canvas and tubular steel, usually referred to as "shuttering" or "steel shuttering," which required mounting the roller on a girder frame above the turret. In the Mark II, the carpet was 225 feet long. In the Mark III, it was nearly 350 feet long, but the larger roller and its weight made the vehicle clumsier and harder to deploy.

In all of the designs, the carpet was to unroll in front of the A.V.R.E. so that it could drive on the carpet as it unspooled. At least twenty-four carpet-layers of all types sailed in the assault landing craft, tank (LCT), on D-Day.

A similar bobbin carpet-laying device, known as the Roly Poly, was designed to be mounted in the bow of the assault LCT as well, so that the leading A.V.R.E. could push the bobbin onto the beach, the chespale carpet unrolling as it went (the A.V.R.E. was known simply as the Pusher). They were identified explicitly only on Gold, but it is difficult to say exactly how many were mounted in landing craft on D-Day; there is even mention of it being mounted in LCT's of the following waves.[6]

The log carpet device was also intended for soft ground. It consisted of 114-foot-long logs that averaged six to eight inches in diameter and were joined by a two-inch wire cable, and the whole assembly was mounted on a removable steel frame fitted to sockets mounted on the sides of the A.V.R.E. To deploy the log carpet, small charges were blown, cutting cables that secured the logs to the frame, which in theory allowed their weight to pull the entire carpet forward off the frame, with the A.V.R.E. following over it as it unrolled. Eleven were employed on D-Day.

Assault Bridge

The small box girder (S.B.G.) bridge, also known simply as the assault bridge, was a four-ton, thirty-four-foot-long bridge that could span a thirty-foot gap and support a forty-ton load. This was sufficient to convey the heaviest vehicles that the Allies brought to the continent, including the Churchill tank and the A.V.R.E. itself. One end of the bridge was attached to the forward hull of the A.V.R.E., with the other end raised and supported by a kingpost and cables with a quick-release fitting. Twenty were

An S.B.G. photographed during an exercise prior to D-Day. The A.V.R.E. is named *Flint II* and is part of the 81st Assault Squadron, 6th Assault Regiment R.E.
NATIONAL ARCHIVES CANADA

An A.V.R.E. tests the SBG bridge in England prior to D-Day. 1ST ASSAULT BRIGADE HISTORY

planned to be used on D-Day. Only nineteen of them were loaded; the twentieth was damaged while trying to get it onto its LCT in England and was left behind, although its A.V.R.E. did make the assault.

The more sophisticated and probably better known ARK-type bridge-layer was not utilized on D-Day. Twenty-four had been produced by the end of May, but they were not delivered in time for the invasion.

Fascines

The fascine carrier was a simple cradle mounted to the front of an A.V.R.E., allowing it to carry a six- or eight-foot-diameter bundle of brushwood about eleven feet wide. The bundle was intended to fill in craters, ditches, or trenches. Unfortunately, the fascine obscured the driver's vision, which meant that a crewman, usually the commander, had to expose himself outside the A.V.R.E. in order to see and give the driver directions. Eventually, an enormously long periscope was designed for the driver to use, although it was disliked and only one account mentions its use on D-Day. Even then, it was said that it did not work. After the invasion, a redesign shifted the cradle to give the driver vision under it, a more elegant solution. Twenty-four sailed on D-Day.

Mine Plows

The bullshorn plow was one of a number of plow-type mine-clearing devices developed by the 79th Armoured Division independently of the flail-type Crab. It was a simple girder-mounted, furrow-type plow that cleared the area in front of each track and was intended for use in shell craters and other similar areas where the flail chains might not reach. In all, ten were reportedly used on D-Day, including two identified in the loading plans on Juno Beach and four used by the 77th Assault Squadron on Sword.

Miscellaneous Devices

The twin bangalore torpedo, also known as the "Boase" bangalore, consisted of two standard bangalore torpedoes mounted on a light framework on the front of the A.V.R.E. In theory, the framework

Below: A Churchill A.V.R.E. of the 79th Armoured Division with fascine in position, Suffolk, 6 September 1943. This photo was taken during tests of one of the prototypes. Note that the main armament in the turret has not been mounted. IMPERIAL WAR MUSEUM

Above: An A.V.R.E. carrying fascines during an exercise at Orfordness, 9 December 1943. IMPERIAL WAR MUSEUM

Below: One of the few photos of the bullshorn plow. THE TANK MUSEUM

An M4A1 medium tank dozer in use clearing a roadway through a French town after D-Day. NARA

One of the prototype D7 armored bulldozers during tests at Orfordness. IMPERIAL WAR MUSEUM

allowed the torpedoes to be placed and fired while under cover of armor.

The Porpoise was a simple waterproofed sledge that could be towed behind an A.V.R.E. or other armored vehicle for carrying additional equipment and stowage. They could be—and usually were—packed with all manner of equipment; those towed by the A.V.R.E. were generally loaded with additional demolitions and ammunition stores, but those towed by the vehicles of other units carried ammunition, food, fuel, water, and anything else that fit.

The D7 armored bulldozer was a standard bulldozer fitted with a light armored shield around the engine and driver's cab. The D7 seems to have been regarded as too vulnerable for assault operations, and prior to D-Day, Lend-Lease orders were placed for 100 of the newly developed American "tank dozer" kit designed to fit the standard M4 Sherman tank, but only enough arrived in time to equip some American units prior to D-Day.[7]

It is notable that although a large number of mechanical devices for emplacing large explosive charges were designed for the A.V.R.E.—including the rather whimsically named Light Carrot, Onion, Goat, and Elevatable Goat—only the twin bangalore torpedo mounting that was based on Goat was actually used in action on D-Day. Although much effort was spent on the design and fabrication of the mechanical charge-placing devices, it was realized that a single stray bullet had the potential to set off the explosives, so they were all quietly dropped.[8]

The majority of the A.V.R.E.'s on D-Day did not have any devices mounted, beyond their own Petard and the demolitions that could be emplaced by its crew. Such vehicles were generally referred to as "G.P." (General Purpose) A.V.R.E.'s or, occasionally, as "Comd" (Command) A.V.R.E.'s.

Sherman Crabs

Technically not part of the 1st Assault Brigade's organization, but nevertheless a vital part of their organization on D-Day, were the mine-clearing flail tanks known as Sherman Crabs.[*]

Originally developed in the Western Desert by a South African engineer, Maj. A. S. du Toit, as the Scorpion and mounted on a Matilda infantry tank, the flail mine-clearer consisted of a large steel drum, fitted with heavy chains that beat the ground when the drum was rotated by twin auxiliary motors, exploding mines ahead of the tank. In the Mediter-ranean, the Scorpion device was also tested on Grant and Valentine tanks and finally on a Sherman. Unfortunately, in the Scorpion design, the auxiliary motors complicated operations and maintenance since, if one failed or was damaged, the entire vehicle became useless. Thus, in mid-1943, a new design was completed that took power off the vehicle's main engine via a geared shaft running through the right side of the hull. Mounted in an M4A4 Sherman, it was christened the Crab.

The Crab retained the 75-millimeter main armament of the Sherman and so could double as a gun tank—a major advantage. The main armament, however, was normally traversed to the rear when flailing to prevent damage to the gun sight, gun tube, and elevation mechanism from the debris flung up by the flail and exploding mines. It also was not perfect as a mine-clearer: on undulating ground, the rotor boom tended to rise momentarily, missing contact

A Crab of the 1st Lothians and Border Horse Yeomanry in front of the church at Saint Martin de Creully, sometime in July 1944. NATIONAL ARCHIVES CANADA

---

[*] The mine-clearing vehicles were commonly referred to as either Crabs or flails. Technically, the vehicle was a Crab, Mark I, while the mine-clearing device itself was the flail.

SHERMAN V, CRAB II
MINE CLEARANCE DEVICE

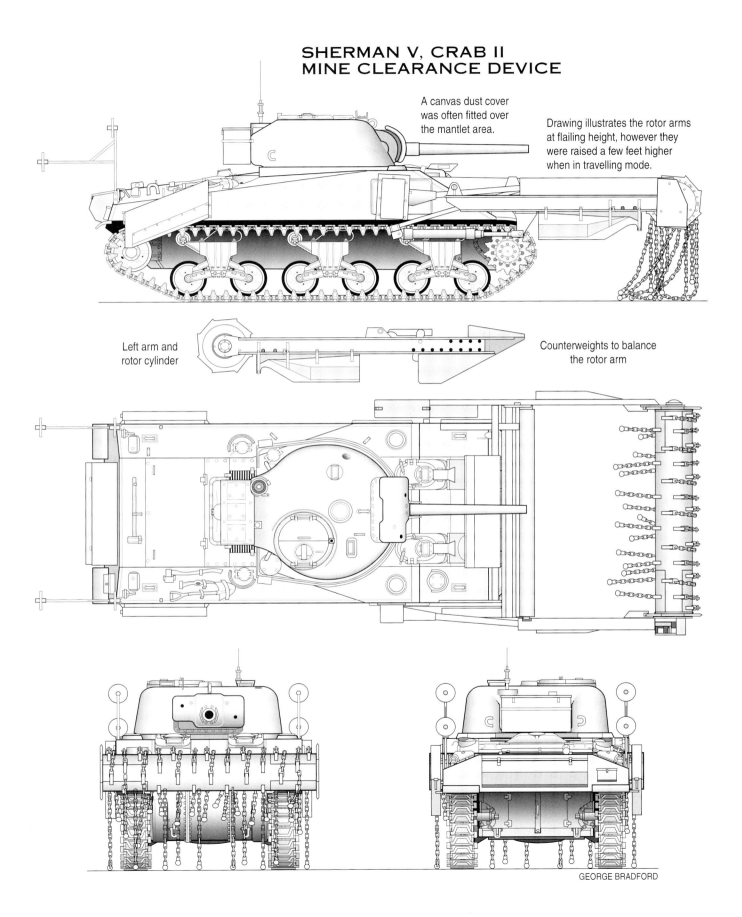

A canvas dust cover was often fitted over the mantlet area.

Drawing illustrates the rotor arms at flailing height, however they were raised a few feet higher when in travelling mode.

Left arm and rotor cylinder

Counterweights to balance the rotor arm

GEORGE BRADFORD

with the ground and thus any mines therein, often with disastrous results. Nonetheless, it was a major improvement over hand-clearing methods of mine removal. Over level ground, a speed of 1 to 1.5 miles per hour could be maintained as the Crab cleared a path eight to nine feet wide.

A total of forty-six Crabs were deployed in eight troops of the 22nd Dragoons, which was attached to the 5th Assault Regiment on D-Day, and twenty-five more were deployed in two squadrons of the West-minster Dragoons (the 2nd County of London Yeomonary, attached to the 6th Assault Regiment) for the initial assault waves. Another five troops of the 22nd Dragoons and A Squadron of the Westminster Dragoons landed with the follow-up waves later in the day. A Squadron had twenty-three Crabs, with ten more in B and C Squadron reserve.[9] Both the 5th and 22nd Westminster Dragoons were assigned to the 30th Armoured Brigade, whose headquarters did not come ashore until 23 June although nearly two-thirds of its operational units had been ashore with other units since D-Day.

Duplex-Drive Tanks

Although, like the Crabs, not technically part of the 79th Armoured Division or 1st Assault Brigade, the amphibious duplex-drive tanks were closely inte-grated with the A.V.R.E.'s and Crabs in the D-Day assault. They were the answer to a question that had vexed the invasion planners from the very outset: how to get armor ashore quickly in the initial assault phase on D-Day and, perhaps just as important, how to get them ashore without exposing what was con-sidered to be the very valuable and highly vulnera-ble LCT to enemy shore batteries.

One method of getting tanks onto the beaches rapidly was the duplex-drive (DD) tank. The Hun-garian-born British automotive engineer Nicholas Straussler developed the DD concept in early 1941. He first tested it on a British Tetrarch light tank in June 1941 and later on a heavier Valentine infantry tank in early 1942. In April 1943, the equipment was adapted to fit the standard U.S.-built M4 Sherman medium tank.

The duplex-drive system consisted of a canvas screen that was fixed to a collapsible boat-shaped plat-form of mild steel tubing, which was in turn welded to the hull of the tank. The screen was erected by

This is a rear quarter view of a duplex-drive tank during testing in England. The platform on the turret rear is for the tank commander to stand on so he could see over the screens when they were raised. NARA

thirty-six rubber air tubes filled from compressed air cylinders carried on the deck of the tank and held in place by lightweight jointed struts. A properly rigged screen brought the turret level with the water and provided about three feet of freeboard.

The tanks were transported in a modified LCT that had an extension mounted to the bow ramp. When in position for launching, the DD tanks would erect their screens and start their engines; then the LCT ramp and extension would be low-ered so that it was well under water. That allowed the tank to be gradually driven into the water, min-imizing the risk of it being swamped by the initial drop into the sea.

Once in the water, the DD tank was capable of speeds of about four miles per hour. It was driven by two propellers that drew power through a simple transfer box from the tracks. Steering was via a hydraulic system that swiveled the propellers and through an auxiliary rudder controlled by the tank commander through a simple manual tiller. The tank commander, standing on a tiny ad hoc platform welded to the turret, had visibility over the screens, while the driver was restricted to a periscope exten-sion to the normal periscope mounted on his hatch.

The advantage of the DD system was that it could be adapted to practically any tank design, and using the DD system meant there was no need to design, prototype, test, and manufacture a purpose-designed amphibious tank. There were also many disadvantages to the system, however, the worst of which was its extreme vulnerability. A puncture in only a few of the air tubes or even a simple tear in the canvas skirt would cause the DD tank to take on water; given the tenuous buoyancy of the vessel, just a minor loss of flotation was sufficient to sink it. Testing of the DD tanks prior to D-Day proved that in anything rougher than a moderate sea, the fragile contraption would sink like a stone and that waves greater than three feet in height could break over the skirt and easily swamp it. As a result, the final recommendation was that DD tanks not be launched in greater than three-foot seas no more than 4,000 yards from the beach.[10]

The standard organization for the British DD tank battalions comprised two reinforced squadrons, each equipped with twenty DD tanks launched from four LST-III's (five per LCT), as well as a "wading" squadron equipped with twenty tanks that had been specially waterproofed and equipped with raised engine exhaust and air intake stacks that theoretically would allow them to traverse water that came up to the top of the turret. The American DD tank battalions were similar, except that two DD companies each consisted of just sixteen tanks launched from four smaller LCT-VI's (four per LCT) and the wading company consisted of sixteen tanks plus eight attached tank dozers. (Six of the tank dozers were

manned by battalion personnel that were intended to man the new 105-millimeter howitzer-armed M4 tank that had not yet arrived in England, and the other two were manned by engineers from the corps engineer light equipment companies.)

Beach Armoured Recovery Vehicle

The Beach Armoured Recovery Vehicle (B.A.R.V.) was yet another specialty vehicle designed for the Neptune assault that was not officially part of the 79th Armoured Division or 1st Assault Brigade menagerie. It was designed for recovering damaged landing craft and vehicles on the beach and was based on the ubiquitous Sherman tank chassis. It featured a specially designed, watertight upper hull and a bilge pump that allowed it to operate safely in nine feet of water with up to a foot and a half surge. It was not fitted with a winch for D-Day so was dependent on straight pulls. A total of fifty-two were completed by D-Day and equipped at least five Royal Electrical and Mechanical Engineer (R.E.M.E.) Beach Recovery Sections on D-Day.[11]

Landing Craft

The success or failure of Neptune ultimately depended on the ability of the Allies to get their assault and follow-on forces—along with the huge quantities of supplies they would require—across the

The B.A.R.V. prototype.
IMPERIAL WAR MUSEUM

SHERMAN B.A.R.V.
(BEACH ARMORED RECOVERY VEHICLE)

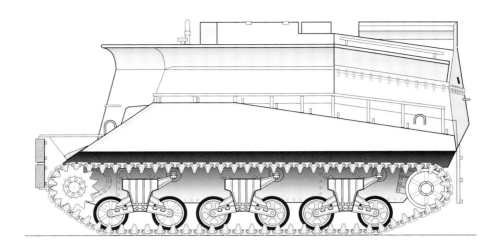

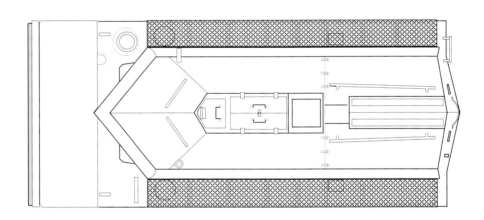

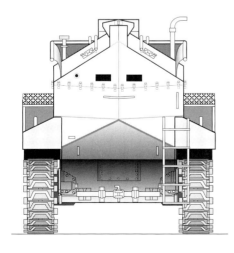

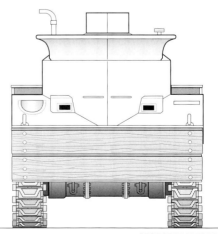

GEORGE BRADFORD

This is LCT-7035 of the 6th Flotilla, H LCT Squadron of Force L, which transported the 22nd Armoured Brigade of the 7th Armoured Division to Jig Beach on 7 June. NARA

English Channel and onto the beaches of Normandy. To do so in the numbers desired required landing craft and ships of all descriptions—in ever-increasing numbers as the invasion plan expanded. The assault phase required, above all else, landing craft, particularly landing craft that could land heavy mechanized vehicles in large numbers. But it also required support craft and craft optimized to land infantry assault teams.[12]

All of the initial elements of the 1st Assault Brigade R.E. arrived on the beach in the ubiquitous landing craft, tank, which was known as an LCT (although it was originally given the name "tank landing craft" or TLC). All featured the conspicuous bow ramp that allowed vehicles to drive off the vessel and directly onto the beach. The first was completed in November 1940 and was given the type designation of TLC Mark I. It was followed by a slightly modified design called the LCT Mark II. Approximately 103 were completed, but these were generally used as training vessels except very early in the war. By D-Day, all were used as training or experimental vessels, and none participated in the D-Day landings.

The first real operational type was the LCT Mark III, of which 235 were built. At 192 feet, it was the longest LCT built. It was 30 feet wide but was limited to a minimum 1/35 slope. It could carry up to 300 tons of cargo or five forty-ton tanks. Like the LCT Mark II, a number were converted to anti-aircraft vessels known as landing craft, flak (LCF), mounting 2-pounder pom-pom and 20-millimeter Oerlikon guns. Others were converted to gunfire support vessels—landing craft, gun, large (LCG[L]), mounting two 4.7-inch guns. Otherwise, the LCT Mark III was largely used on the Commonwealth beaches to transport the DD tanks (apparently under the assumption that the slope limitation was moot for tanks intended to be launched at sea instead of on the beach) and to transport tanks and other vehicles of following waves when the engineers would have had time to prepare the beach.

The LCT Mark IV design solved the problem of the limited beaching capability of the Mark I, II, and III: it could land on as gentle as a 1/150 slope. It was also the last type to be exclusively manufactured in Britain. Slightly shorter than the Mark III, at 187 feet, 3 inches, it was much wider—38 feet, 9 inches—and could carry much more than the Mark III, up to 350 tons or six forty-ton tanks. However, some reports after the invasion indicated that the Mark IV suffered from structural weakness and was unsuitable in operations where it was required to be "dried out," that is, left beached until the tide turned.[22] A total of 731 were built, with some converted to LCF's and LCG's.

The LCT Mark V was based on the British design for production in the U.S., but was shortened to just 117 feet, 6 inches, in length and 32 feet in the beam to make it easier to load aboard larger ships for transport overseas. It was also more limited in the beach gradient it could land on (about 1/120) and could carry only four forty-ton tanks or 150 tons of cargo. Nevertheless, it was sturdy and dependable, and 500 were built.

The LCT Mark VI design was a radical change from the previous ones; it incorporated both a bow and a stern ramp, so it could load directly from the bow ramps of a landing ship, tank (LST), at sea. Otherwise, it had the same load and beaching capabilities as the Mark V.

Aside from the LCF and LCG, there were a number of other variants based on the LCT that played a prominent part in D-Day.

The LCT(R), for rocket, had been modified to mount 1,080 spin-stabilized five-inch rockets that could be ripple-fired as part of the planned "beach drenching" that was intended to suppress the German defenders.* It could be converted from the LCT Mark II, III, or IV, but most of those used in Normandy were the Mark IV type.

The LCT(A), for armored, was an LCT Mark V modified with an armored pilothouse and engine room and an elevated wooden platform in the tank well deck that enabled two tanks to be carried, side by side, where they could fire over the bow ramp at shore targets during the run in to the beach. Unfortunately, the additional top weight made them unstable, and during the D-Day crossing, it was found that the joint between the armor plate and hull was faulty and prone to causing flooding of the engine room.

The LCT(HE), for high explosive, also was based on the LCT Mark V and had the platform of the LCT(A), but not the additional armor. The high-explosive designation was given to them for the rather unnerving reason that they were intended as the primary carrier of the demolitions that were to be used by the obstacle clearance teams.

The LCT(CB), for concrete buster, also was based on the LCT Mark V and was essentially a high-explosive LCT, only it carried two Sherman 17-pounder tanks (Fireflies). They were intended to engage pillboxes from the LCT with direct fire from their high-velocity guns. The Sherman 17-pounder was literally a last-minute addition to the invasion and had only recently become available to British tank units. Initial issue of the tank had started in mid–April 1944, and the decision to put some in the forefront of the invasion appears to have been one of the last modifications to the Neptune landing plan in late May. Typically, regiments equipped with DD tanks for the assault received four Sherman 17-pounder tanks to be issued to the squadron intended to wade ashore since the long barrel of the gun could not fit inside the canvas screen of the DD tank.

In late April, planners decided to employ six of the Sherman 17-pounders as additional support during the run in (accepting the lowered accuracy that would entail) and after beaching. It was hoped that the excellent armor-piercing capability of their guns would be sufficient to defeat the heavy concrete protection of some of the pillboxes—hence the appellation "concrete buster." Two were to support the 13th/18th Hussars on Sword, and four (two per regiment) would support the 6th and 10th Canadian Armoured Regiments on Juno. They were "to be manned by First Reinforcements [cadre personnel meant as a source of immediate replacements in battle] of 27th Armoured Brigade and 2nd Canadian Armoured Brigade."[14] No LCT(CB)'s with 17-pounder Sherman tanks were available for Gold or the American beaches, although, curiously enough, at least one landing craft inventory counted "EX-CB's" along with LCT(A)'s and LCT(HE)'s intended for Omaha Beach.[15]

Complementing the LCT as a bulk infantry transport was the landing craft, infantry, large (LCI[L]). They had a personnel capacity of about 200 men—and so could carry roughly a reinforced company—but they had no vehicle-carrying capac-

---

* The "beach drenching" plan included carpet bombing by heavy bombers, fire from artillery and tank units embarked on the landing craft during the run in to the beach, rocket salvoes from the LCT(R)'s and the LCA(HR)'s, and supporting fire from navy destroyers and gunboats, although most of the heavier naval assets, the cruisers and battleships, were dedicated to suppression of the coast artillery batteries.

LCVP's loading for a journey to their parent landing ships in preparation for D-Day. NARA

ity. The men debarked from two narrow gangway-type ramps that could be lowered on either side of the bow. Because of that and their complete lack of armor, they were considered highly vulnerable to enemy small-arms fire and so were reserved for the follow on waves after the initial assault.

The landing craft, infantry, small (LCI[S]) was a uniquely British craft designed especially for use by the Commandos. Each craft could accommodate a complete Commando troop of three officers and sixty-three other ranks. As in the LCI(L), the men debarked from two gangways that were dropped from the bow. Like the LCI(L), they were unarmored, but they were also equipped with gasoline engines and large unprotected gasoline tanks, which made them potentially deadly in case of an unlucky hit.

Next smaller in size was the landing craft, mechanized (LCM), which was also originally a British design started in the 1920s and perfected in the 1930s. There were various marks, but all the wartime designs were very similar and could carry either a single vehicle (including a thirty-ton tank), sixty men, or thirty tons of cargo. The Neptune planning mostly allocated them for carrying critical vehicles for the infantry assault; often, one or more LCM's were part of the boat complement on the larger attack transport ships, but they were also utilized as support vessels for the obstacle-clearance teams, carrying their demolitions, inflatable boats, and other critical equipment.

The landing craft, personnel, large, (LCP[L]) was the original Higgins-designed Eureka landing boat developed for the U.S. Marine Corps before the war. It could carry thirty-six troops in addition to its crew, but it was not equipped with a debarkation ramp and could not easily accommodate vehicles or equipment. The later LCP(R) and LCV were similar, but they were fitted with a bow ramp. They were all replaced in production by the improved final design, known as the landing craft, vehicle and personnel (LCVP). During Operation Neptune, the LCP(L)'s used on the American beaches were fitted with smoke generators and were usually referred to as "smokers." It was intended that they lay a smoke-screen for the assault craft, but the higher-than-expected and variable wind dispersed the smoke too much on D-Day, and the attempt was abandoned in most cases before the assault waves got to shore. LCP(L)'s were not utilized on the Commonwealth beaches.

The principal small troop-carrying landing craft were the landing craft, assault (LCA), a British design, and the American-designed LCVP. They were similar in capacity: the LCA could carry thirty-three and the LCVP thirty-six personnel in addition to their crews. That accommodated the British infantry platoon very well, but posed problems for the larger American infantry platoon. Worse, unlike the British infantry rifle company, which consisted of a small headquarters and identical rifle platoons, the American infantry company consisted of three rifle platoons and a heavy-weapons platoon consisting of 60-millimeter mor-

LCA's before D-Day. NARA

tars and light machine guns meant to be closely integrated with the rifle platoons in combat. As a result, the American rifle companies were reorganized for the assault into homogenous, but ad hoc teams that integrated elements of the rifle platoon, heavy-weapons platoon, and engineers. Many military analysts and historians have since noted how that decision may have adversely affected the unit integrity of the rifle companies and may have influenced the events on Omaha.[16] It must be assumed, however, that the effect was mitigated by the extensive length of time available for the units to train as part of those assault teams. Possibly more problematic was the difficulty of re-integrating the assault teams back into their doctrinal organization after the initial assault.

LCA's were used on all the beaches, since British-manned attack transport ships were also present on all of them. However, the LCVP was found only on the American beaches.

Finally, three other smaller fire-support craft were the landing craft, support, large (LCS[L]); the landing craft, support, medium (LCS[M]); and the landing craft, support, small (LCS[S]). The LCS(L) was based on the LCI(S) and was armed with a turreted 6-pounder gun, two 20-millimeter Oerlikon guns, a twin .50-caliber machine gun, and two .303-caliber machine guns. The LCS(M) was based on the LCA, but it carried no troops and was armed with two .303-caliber machine guns, one twin .50-caliber machine gun, and a 4-inch smoke mortar. The LCS(S) was based on the LCP(L) and mounted .50-caliber and .30-caliber machine guns. The first two were Royal Navy designs and used only by them while the last was a U.S. Navy design and used only by them.

Overall, the Royal Navy's and U.S. Navy's contributions to Neptune were well integrated, although the Royal Navy's contribution was larger. The Royal Navy provided many of the attack transports carrying the American assault infantry battalions and strong contingents of LCT's of all types for both Omaha and Utah. The Americans contributed flotillas of LCI(L)'s for both Sword and Gold, and U.S. Navy–manned LST's were also a large part of the vessels transporting the Commonwealth follow-on Force L. In general, the different contingents worked very well together, and stories of gun-wielding American army officers "forcing" British crews to land on different beaches are simply apocryphal journalistic inventions.

CHAPTER 3

Allied Planning and Preparation

WHAT'S IN A NAME?

When discussing Operation Neptune, it is important to note one small detail regarding the various "beach" designations normally used in most histories (Sword Beach, Juno Beach, and so on): technically, they are not the names of the beaches at all; they are the designations given to the assault forces and the assault areas they were assigned to. The names of the beaches were actually coded from west to east, according to the phonetic alphabet then in use, as Able, Baker, Charlie, and so on and had long been identified as such in Royal Navy beach-terrain studies.

Under the original plan as conceived by Maj. Gen. Frederick Morgan, Chief of Staff to the Supreme Allied Commander (COSSAC), only three divisions were to assault just three beaches: Lion-sur-Mer–Courseulles, Courseulles–Arromanches-les Bains, and Colleville-sur-Mer–Vierville-sur-Mer, designated as the targets for Forces J, G, and O, respectively. But Eisenhower, who was appointed Supreme Allied Commander (later Supreme Commander Allied Expeditionary Forces) on 6 December 1943, immediately objected to the limited nature of the COSSAC plan. Eisenhower's misgivings may have begun as early as 27 October 1943 in Algiers when he was first briefed on the plan by an American member of the COSSAC staff, Brig. Gen. William E. Chambers.[1] On 27 December 1943, Eisenhower met with Bernard Montgomery, who had been appointed Allied Ground Forces Commander and head of the 21st Army Group on 24 December 1943, to discuss the plan.[2] Both agreed that two additional assault divisions and beaches had to be added. By 21 January 1944, American and British planners

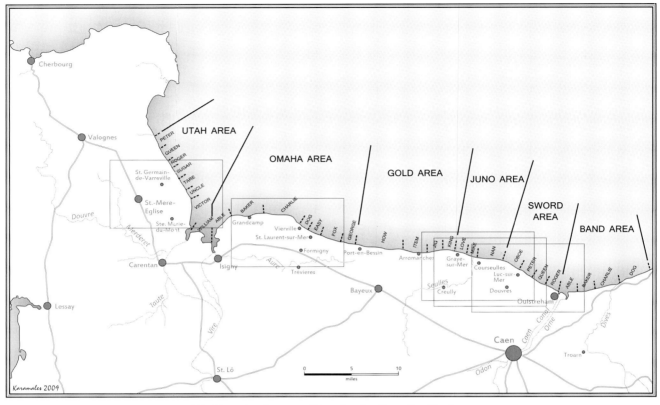

Allied Invasion Areas and Beaches for Operation Neptune.

had agreed to add the beaches at Ouistreham–Lion-sur-Mer and Quinéville–les Dunes-de-Varreville.[3] They became the targets of Force S and Force U.[4]

There remains some confusion about how the assault forces and invasion areas received their code letters and the names that became associated with the beaches. One theory holds that under the original Skyscraper plan that predated COSSAC, the beaches selected for the two-division assault were Oboe and Jig, which were tentatively assigned to an American Force O and a Canadian Force J. It is then supposed that under the three-division COSSAC plan, the American force—retaining its original designation as O—was reoriented westward in order to be more convenient to American bases in England and, later, to shipping traffic from the United States. At the same time, the third division—a British one identified as Force G—was inserted between the Americans and Canadians at George Beach (Arromanches). This theory does not explain Force S,

which was added to the plan and set to land between Oboe and Roger, or Force U, which was originally scheduled in the Initial Joint Plan of 7 February to land on Y Beach (the same document refers to what later became Omaha as X Beach).[5]

At least this theory is somewhat less fanciful than the assumption that the British beaches were assigned fish names—Swordfish, Goldfish, and Jellyfish—but that the Canadians objected to Jellyfish and so insisted their beach be named "Juno" after one of the Canadian officer's mothers.

In any case, the actual force code names appear to have been assigned when the U.S. First Army and British Second Army completed their preliminary planning in March 1944.[6] Other sea areas in the zone of the Eastern Naval Task Force included, from east to west, Scallops, Scallops Plus, and Scallops Minus, which covered the Bay of the Seine and Le Havre; Tunny, which extended the area westward to defense line Trout, a north-south line running from the mouth of the Orne River; and Pike, which was a northward extension of Sword. For the Western Naval Task Force, Omaha was divided from east to west into minesweeping areas code-named Ohio, Oregon, and Kansas; Utah was divided into minesweeping areas from south to north as Vermont and Prairie; and the approaches to Omaha and Utah were from east to west were Elder, Hickory, and Mountain.[7]

Actually, though, the organization of Force J substantially predated its planned use in Neptune. The force was originally set up by Combined Operations Headquarters in the wake of the disaster at Dieppe in August 1942, when it was designated Force J for Jubilee, the code name of the Dieppe operation. Force J was intended to experiment with new assault methods and to be both a training and operational organization that would study and correct the errors that had been made in Jubilee. Since the army component of the staff was drawn from the 3rd Canadian Division, it was only natural that when the division was selected for Neptune, it would retain the landing force designation it had used for more than a year.[8]

Similarly, Force S was actually formed in October 1943, with the British 3rd Division assigned to it in November—well before the Initial Joint Operations Plan was completed, which added the Sword area and the 3rd Division to the Neptune assault force.[9] In truth, it appears that there was no rhyme or reason for the code names, except possibly in the case of Force J. Rather, they were simply drawn from previously prepared code-name lists and had no real meaning of their own at all.

The Commonwealth beaches that were the target of the Eastern Naval Task Force and the British Second Army were assigned to two different corps. The 1 Corps was to the east, with the British 3rd Infantry Division landing as Assault Force Sword on Queen Beach, the 3rd Canadian Infantry Division landing as Assault Force Juno on Mike and Nan Beaches, and the 6th Airborne Division landing east of the Orne River. The 30 Corps was to the west, with a single reinforced assault division, the 50th (Northumberland) Infantry Division, assigned as Assault Force Gold for Jig and King Beaches.

The American beaches that were the target of the Western Naval Task Force and the U.S. First Army were also assigned to two different corps. The V Corps was to the east, with the U.S. 1st Infantry Division and elements of the U.S. 29th Infantry Division assaulting Omaha, and the VII Corps was to the west, with the U.S. 4th Infantry Division assaulting Utah.

THE ALLIED ASSAULT PLAN

What the Allies knew of the German defense preparations was comprehensive and fairly complete. That knowledge was built from numerous sources. They included thousands of aerial reconnaissance photos, signals intelligence like Ultra, human intelligence from Special Operations Executive and French Resistance teams in France, and ground reconnaissance of the beaches themselves by Royal Navy and Royal Marine Combined Operations forces.

One of the most vital decisions made during the Neptune planning was based upon that knowledge. It was the deceptively simple decision whether to make the assault in daylight or at night. The air force commanders of course desired that the operation would occur in full light of day as did, to a certain extent, the naval commanders. Landing exercises and experience had clearly shown that the air and naval bombardment supporting the assault would be most effective if the fire could be clearly observed. At a meeting of the British 1 Corps staff on 6 September 1943, the opinion was that,

> The success of the operation depends on the very early capture of a beach head, which in turn depends on the simultaneous operation of breaching the major obstacles and neutralizing the enemy localities which cover them and then the capture of the localities themselves . . .
>
> If AVREs are to work efficiently they require enough light to see, and if we are to gain the maximum advantage from our available fire support from DD tks, the air, and seaborne craft, some daylight is required. Apart from LCT(R) fire support in a night assault is likely to be of negligible value.
>
> From the Army point of view, therefore, H hour should be as early as possible in the morning, provided there is telescope light, once the DD tks are touched down and ready to shoot. DD tks should therefore touch down at about 20 mins before sunrise, and this time should be selected for H hour.[10]

After considerable discussion, a compromise was reached:

> It has been agreed that H hour shall be so timed that a minimum of 30 minutes of aimed fire can be directed at the defences before the leading craft touch down. This means that at H–30 minutes there must be sufficient daylight for the air observation of Naval fire and for daylight precision bombing to begin. This has been estimated to be about Nautical Twilight plus 70 minutes. The earliest time, therefore, at which H hour is acceptable from the point of view of fire support is at Nautical Twilight plus 100 minutes.[11]

By those assumptions, on 6 June, when nautical twilight occurred at 0555 hours, H-Hour theoretically would have occurred at 0735 hours. However, as in everything associated with Neptune, it did not remain quite that simple.

What the Allies knew, when they knew it, and how they reacted to changes by the Germans also explain many of the decisions made prior to the invasion. The state of Allied knowledge in May and June 1943—when the initial COSSAC plans were being finalized, the A.V.R.E. was being developed, and the 1st Assault Brigade and 79th Armoured Division were being organized for their assault role—is embodied in a number of critical sources. One is a booklet prepared by the U.S. War Department, entitled *German Coastal Defenses*, which was published almost exactly one year prior to the invasion. It succinctly summarized Allied understanding of German coast defense doctrine:

> The Germans well understand that fortifications are truly offensive in character when their employment is based on the military maxim of economy of force. They cannot defend adequately at all points, but by the use of permanent fortifications to maintain an effective defense with a minimum of man power, they hope to keep the bulk of their

force in reserve for offensive action wherever a major attack appears. Consequently, when a landing is made on the shores of Europe, the German High Command will make its major effort against the invading forces with swift, hard-hitting armored and motorized units . . .

Closer inshore, along the landing beaches, the Germans have embedded steel and wooden obstacles just below the water's surface to trap assault boats and tank-landing craft. . . . In the shallow water off beaches with gentle slopes, the Germans have embedded rows of steel stakes and wooden logs. They are set at an angle, their upper ends pointing outward from the beach. Submerged barbed wire and mines may be used in conjunction with these obstacles, which are intended to trap landing boats, or personnel who may be compelled to leave their boats to wade ashore. . . . As obstacles against landing craft, light booms of simple construction are placed by the Germans in front of good landing beaches. They consist, usually, of conical buoys, linked by wire rope that runs through the tops and bases of the buoys. Rafts are similarly employed. Explosives and warning devices may be affixed to these booms.[12]

The War Department also espoused a belief that could only be testable after the fact: "Thorough training in technique, and knowledge of the characteristics of fortifications, will enable an assault force to break through a system of fixed defenses with a minimum loss of men and material, thus conserving its strength for the main task of engaging and destroying the mobile enemy forces behind it."[13] That opinion, with some caveats, was also expressed in a series of lectures at a conference on the subject of assault landings that was held at the nascent U.S. Army Assault Training Center at Wollacombe, from 24 May to 23 June 1943.[14] The lengthy conference was split into four phases that began with orientation and followed with lectures on combined operations (including Dieppe, Exercise Kruschen, and the landings in the Aleutians) and doctrine (civil affairs, intelligence, naval, air, tanks, fortifications, artillery, infantry, signals, chemical warfare, supply, medical, and combined-arms operations).

This is the first in a series of phototgraphs taken on 19 May 1944 by an F-5 photo-reconnaissance aircraft of the Omaha assault area. The cluster of buildings is the beachside houses of Vierville-sur-Mer, some of them concealing the positions of WN 72 while WN 71 is on the crest of the highside. NARA

Dog Green beach with the breakwaters found just east of Vierville that provided shelter for some of the men of the 116th Infantry. NARA

Next in the sequence is the eastern end of Dog Green with the villa of the Hardelay family to left center. WN 70 was on the bluffs just behind it. NARA

The village of Les Moulins and the D-3 Draw leading inland can be clearly seen. WN 68 is in the right foreground while WN 66 is on the bluff to left center behind the buildings. NARA

The E-1 Draw and Easy Red Beach in the Omaha area. The prominent beach house is in front of WN 65. Note the sparseness of the obstacles. The horse teams farther up the beach are hauling poles to be emplaced as obstacles. NARA

The lecturers included Brig. O. M. Wales, who had conducted the armored engineering exercises as part of Kruschen; Cmdre. J. Hughes-Hallett, who later became involved in Neptune planning and the development of the Mulberry artificial harbor; Maj. Gen. Hamilton Roberts, who had participated in Dieppe; and others. The third phase consisted of staff field exercises, and the fourth phase was the preparation of recommendations for adaptations to FM 31–5, *Landing Operations on Hostile Shores*, and a proposed training circular.

Possibly the most intriguing aspect of the conference was the speech on tanks in assault landings that was given by Maj. Gen. P. C. Hobart. Unfortunately, Hobo believed that his information was too sensitive and, for reasons of security, requested that his remarks not be recorded. Instead, Lt. Col. C. R. Kutz of the U.S. Army discussed the use of conventional tanks in a beach assault in very general terms. The ubiquitous Colonel Reeves, now commanding the Special Devices Section, was also present, and in the discussion following Kutz's lecture, he remarked on his experience in developing the DD tank.

The intelligence lecturer, Colonel Zeller, remarked regarding "future developments of fixed defenses" that "improvements in the defense of the shoreline will probably consist of more extensive mining, construction of more and stronger obstacles, and in the concreting of installations already in temporary fashion."[15] With regard to the then-current state of underwater obstacles, he repeated the existing opinion that "to date there has been no evidence of extensive use of underwater obstacles."[16] Colonel Burton, who followed with a lecture specifically on the German fortification effort, also noted little evidence of the placement of underwater obstacles.[17] From the evidence, we may conclude that no great urgency was attached to solving the problem of how to remove underwater and beach obstacles for the simple reason that no such obstacles had been discovered at that point.

CLEARING BEACH OBSTACLES

During 1943, as Allied planning for the invasion accelerated, photo-reconnaissance missions over the beaches still had not revealed any significant German attempts to emplace waterline obstacles. The continued lack of activity on the part of the Germans may have lulled the Allied planners into a false sense of security. As a result, the early engineer planning for Neptune continued to assume that there would be no obstacles underwater or blocking access to the beaches or, at worst, there would be a few hastily emplaced obstacles that could be easily dealt with by naval gunfire and aerial bombardment.

There was some discussion regarding obstacle clearance at the initial U.S. First Army Neptune conference on 21 December 1943. Various methods of clearing the German barbed-wire entanglements were mentioned, including aerial bombing and explosive rockets, but without much detail or even seemingly much interest. Considerable attention was given to finding a way to get men and vehicles over the seawall at Omaha, and Gen. Omar Bradley mentioned British plans for using explosives placed by a Churchill tank to blow a gap in such a wall. But it was Lieutenant Colonel Thompson, commander of the Assault Training Center, who brought up what was to became the most serious concern for the Neptune planners: underwater obstacles along the beach "that would consist of just a lot of 6x6 timber driven as piling and covering the whole beach around 12-foot center, and they [the Germans] could completely block the beach just by driving those piles."[18]

The sudden and massive expansion of beach obstacle construction by the Germans, below the high-water mark, that began in January 1944 presented a considerable headache to the planners. By early February, Eisenhower was sufficiently worried by the development that he sent two senior American engineers, Lt. Col. Arthur H. Davidson Jr. from the staff of the Chief Engineer European Theater of Operations and Lt. Col. John T. O'Neill, commander

Obstacles in Normandy, May 1944. NARA

Another shot of obstacles. This one shows Arromanches west of Jig Green and Le Hamel. NARA

of the 112th Engineer Combat Battalion of the U.S. V Corps, to the Amphibious Training Base at Fort Pierce, Florida, to attend an obstacle-clearance demonstration.* The Amphibious Training Base, a joint army and navy operation, had been experi-

---

* This was just over a month prior to the test of the U.S.-designed, Sherman-based engineer assault vehicle there and occurred at the same time that the American engineer planning staff was developing the 16 February *U.S. Requirements for British Devices* memo. O'Neill commanded the SETF at Omaha on D-Day.

At Arromanches, Element C is placed midway between the low- and high-tide lines while ramps and poles are clustered to obstruct the beach. NARA

menting with methods of clearing underwater obstacles since April 1943 when a specialized underwater obstacle course had been completed.[19]

When Davidson and O'Neill returned to England two weeks later, they found that the German obstacles were proliferating rapidly and, by late March, were present on all the projected beaches in ever-increasing densities. Worse came just six weeks before D-Day when, on 23 April, an errant Allied bomb, intended for one of the coastal batteries, landed on the beach, setting off fourteen secondary explosions, thus confirming that the obstacles were heavily mined as well.[20]

The result was a hasty amendment to the Neptune plan. In mid-March, Montgomery directed his 1 and 30 Corps to prepare plans for clearing the obstacles on Sword, Juno, and Gold, while Bradley gave similar orders to the U.S. V and VII Corps, which were to submit clearing plans for Omaha and Utah by 1 April. By early April, the preliminary plans were in place, and the units had begun to assemble.

The British formed clearing teams based on the Landing Craft Obstruction Clearance Units (L.C.O.C.U.) that comprised Royal Navy and Royal Marine personnel.[21] They also were partnered

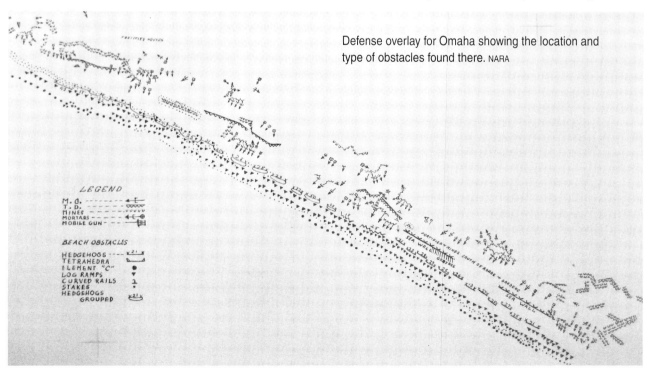

Defense overlay for Omaha showing the location and type of obstacles found there. NARA

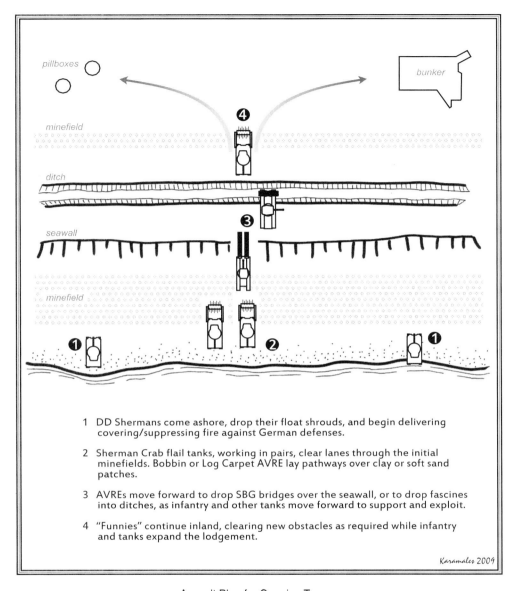

1 DD Shermans come ashore, drop their float shrouds, and begin delivering covering/suppressing fire against German defenses.

2 Sherman Crab flail tanks, working in pairs, clear lanes through the initial minefields. Bobbin or Log Carpet AVRE lay pathways over clay or soft sand patches.

3 AVREs move forward to drop SBG bridges over the seawall, or to drop fascines into ditches, as infantry and other tanks move forward to support and exploit.

4 "Funnies" continue inland, clearing new obstacles as required while infantry and tanks expand the lodgement.

Karamales 2009

Assault Plan for Gapping Teams.

with army engineers and placed under the command of the assault squadrons for the initial phase of the invasion, but they were organizationally part of the beach sub-area commands. On Sword, the beach obstacle clearance was to be done by the 629th Field Squadron R.E. and No. 7 and 8 L.C.O.C.U.; on Juno by 5th Field Company R.C.E., 262nd Field Company R.E., a platoon of the 19th Field Company R.E., and No. 1, 5, 11, and 12 L.C.O.C.U.; and on Gold by the 280th Field Company R.E., 73rd

Field Company R.E., and No. 3, 4, 9, and 10 L.C.O.C.U.

On the Commonwealth beaches, the L.C.O.C.U. were to come in on LCAs that were designed to carry up to thrity-three infantrymen and provide ample room for the teams and their explosives. The supporting Royal Engineers were to come in on the LCT with the A.V.R.E., with each LCT carrying about twenty-five Royal Engineers and two collapsible boats, along with additional demolition charges.

The plan was that the L.C.O.C.U. would concentrate on removing obstacles from the waterline out to sea, while the Royal Engineer teams would support the A.V.R.E.'s in clearing obstacles from the waterline inland.

In outline, then, the organization that was adopted for the Commonwealth beaches was broadly as follows.

Gapping teams—formed from the Royal Engineer assault squadrons and armed with A.V.R.E.'s and Crabs—were to drive forward from the beach to open the initial lanes through the German obstacles and defenses from the beach forward over the dunes and to the inland lateral beach roads. They would be supported by unarmored "foot" demolition teams formed from the Royal Engineer field companies that were assigned to the assault element. They would widen and improve the lanes into complete two-way exits from the beach inland. According to Lt. I. C. B. Dickinson of No. 3 Troop, 77th Assault Squadron R.E., scheduled to land on Sword,

> Obstacles from a depth of ten feet to four feet six inches were the responsibility of the Landing Craft Obstacle Clearance Units of the Royal Navy, and those from four feet six inches to 0 feet were a sapper responsibility. Each Beach White and Red was allotted five AVREs for obstacle clearance. Our latest information before leaving was that the obstacles were laid in four rows in the following order from the dunes to the sea: two rows of Hedgehogs, Stakes, and Ramped Stakes.
>
> The intention was to land with the tide lapping the bottom of the ramped stakes. We were to drive through these, drop our porpoises [loaded with ammunition and explosives] on the beach, and then return, remove such mines as we found on the ramped stakes and then either run them down or tow them away. Having completed Row C we were to go on to B, and so on.[22]

Clearance teams, also formed from the Royal Engineer field companies that were assigned to the assault element, were to widen the cleared gap in the obstacles on the beach from the initial assault lane so as to open more area for the following landing craft—and eventually landing ships, the LSTs—to beach. They were supported in most cases by D4 unarmored bulldozers, manned by personnel of the field park companies assigned to the assault element, and in some cases by D7 armored bulldozers manned by the 149th Assault Park Squadron of the 1st Assault Brigade. It was also intended that some of the A.V.R.E. gapping teams would support the clearance teams after they completed their initial gaps.

Beach sub-areas were the follow-on support echelon for the beach operations. They were comprised of various elements from different services. They were to complete the clearance of the beach obstacles, improve exits from the beach, recover and repair vehicles and landing craft damaged or bogged on the beach, and organize and mark the beach landing areas for the following waves. The beach sub-area included

- Royal Navy Beach Commandos to provide for the organization, marking, and traffic control of the beach landing areas and landing craft, as well as maintenance and recovery of damaged craft;
- Army Royal Engineers to provide for beach exit and road improvement and maintenance, recovery, and maintenance of army vehicles and equipment;
- L.C.O.C.U.'s to clear underwater obstacles and debris as required after the landing;
- army infantry battalions (organized as army beach groups) to provide for unloading the craft and clearing unloaded stores and equipment from the beach and insuring that the stores got forward to units inland, they also were responsible for security on the beach;
- army pioneer corps, who were essentially laborers assisting the army beach groups and were often comprised of "coloured" men from British Colonial Africa, the Mediterranean Levant, or the Caribbean;
- RAF beach units to provide specialized technical knowledge not possessed by army personnel concerning RAF equipment and stores and ensured the expeditious sorting, assembly, and forwarding of equipment, stores, and vehicles peculiar to the RAF; and

ORGANIZATION OF THE 101ST BEACH SUB-AREA

101st Beach Sub-Area

F and R, Royal Navy Beach Commandos
5th Army Beach Group—5th Kings Regiment,
6th Army Beach Group—1st Buckinghamshire Regiment
1st RAF Beach Unit—101st and 102nd Beach Sections
CRE 101 Beach Area (18th GHQ Troops Engineers)
84th Field Company R.E.
91st Field Company R.E.
8th Stores Section R.E.
9th Stores Section R.E.
50th Mechanical Equipment Section R.E.

Attached and in support

205th Workshop Section R.E.
654th Artillery Workshop Company R.E.
722nd Artillery Workshop Company R.E.
Two Advance Park Sections, 176th Workshop and Park
    Company R.E.
49th Bomb Disposal Section R.E.
120th Pioneer Company
129th Pioneer Company

- the beach sub-area headquarters, including joint signals units with personnel and equipment compatible with each of the services, as well as a Corps of Military Police (CMP) provost detachment for maintaining order and discipline on the beach.

To assist in the rapid clearance of the obstacles, the British also developed a specialized landing craft, the LCA(HR), to try to cope with them. "HR" stood for hedgerow, which was the code name for an adaptation of the Hedgehog antisubmarine mortar that had been developed by the Royal Navy. The hedgerow mortar fired twenty-four thirty-pound TNT or thirty-five-pound TORPEX bombs about 400 yards. (TORPEX was an explosive developed by the British as a filler for torpedo warheads. It was about 50 percent more powerful than TNT.) The LCA(HR) was intended to clear the minefields that were expected to be just past the high waterline by sympathetic detonation.

Unfortunately, these were all hasty improvisations at best. In his report after D-Day, the naval commander of Force G specifically mentioned that training in the L.C.O.C.U.'s was excellent but that there was insufficient time for them to practice with the assault squadrons or the Royal Engineers of the field companies assigned to obstacle clearance. The best that was achieved was fourteen days of joint training under the commanding officers of the field companies, rather than a full-scale joint exercise.[23]

On the American beaches, two unique commands were formed, the Special Engineer Task Force (SETF) for Omaha and the Beach Obstacle Demolition Party (BODP) for Utah. The SETF was under the command of the Provisional Engineer Special Brigade Group, comprised of the 5th and 6th Engineer Special Brigades, while the BODP fell under the command of the 1st Engineer Special Brigade. The SETF was formed from the 146th Engineer Combat Battalion of the 1121st Engineer Group, the 299th Engineer Combat Battalion (minus elements that were attached to other commands) of the 1171st Engineer Group, 150 demolition-trained personnel drawn from the 2nd Infantry Division, and Navy Combat Demolition Units (NCDU) 11, 22 to 24, 27, 41 to 46, 127, 128, 130, 131, 133, and 140 to 142. (Each NCDU consisted of an officer or petty officer and five enlisted men. Their strength was augmented to thirteen by the addition of two seamen to handle the rubber assault boats loaded with explosives and five army engineers to assist in placing the explosives.) The smaller BODP for Utah was formed from elements of the 237th Engineer Combat Battalion, the 612th Engineer Light Equipment Company, Company B of the 299th Engineer Combat Battalion, and NCDU 25, 26, 28, 29, 30, 127, 132, 134 to 136, and 139. The army engineers and navy demolition units formed combined gap assault teams and gap support teams, with each gapping team intended to clear an initial fifty-yard-wide gap through the obstacles.[24]

Many of the same organizational and training problems experienced by the British were encountered by the Americans; the men of the NCDU were well trained, but there had been little or no time to integrate the different elements into the close-knit team that was required for such a task. The units were a hastily cobbled together group of men formed from different services and different units, often with unfamiliar commanders.[25]

The appearance of the obstacles also meant the timing of H-Hour had to be adjusted to allow for enough time for the obstacle-clearance operation to occur and also to allow for tidal conditions as well as daylight. The best time for clearing the obstacles was at low tide when they were fully exposed. This also meant, however, that the assault troops would have to cross the greatest expanse of beach while they were exposed to enemy fire. The typical tidal flat at low water on the beaches of Normandy extended 400 yards seaward from the highwater mark. On Utah, it was 900 yards at the planned landing site and 1,700 yards where the landing actually occurred. As a compromise, planners decided to time the landings just as the tide had turned—approximately 0730 hours—giving the engineers twenty to thirty minutes to work in low water.

A further complication was that the tides varied significantly from west to east. At Saint-Vaast-la-Hougue, just north of Utah, low water in the morning on 6 June was at 0504 hours, fifty-one minutes prior to nautical twilight; first high water was at 1004 hours, and the mean high water was 22 feet. At Port-en-Bessin, midway between Omaha and Gold, low water in the morning was at 0521 hours, first high water was at 1036 hours, and the mean depth was 23 feet. Farther east, on Sword, the tides were a full hour later than on Utah. That tidal shift, from west to east, also generated strong currents that generally ran in the same direction, parallel to the coast, and which have been measured at a maximum of 6 knots at Pointe de Barfleur east of Cherbourg and estimated at 2.7 knots off Omaha. That current would make navigation, station keeping, and accurate touchdown for the landing craft waves very problematic on all the beaches and would result in a fortuitous accident on Utah, some calamity on Gold and Sword, and near-disaster on Omaha.[26]

Yet another problem was that the obstacles on Omaha extended farther seaward, while the rocky shallows off Juno created an additional complication on that beach. As a result, planners deemed it "necessary to select five different H hours, ranging over a period of one hour and twenty-five minutes."[27] Ultimately, only three different H-Hours were planned for the main landings: 0735 (100 minutes after nautical twilight) for Sword and Juno; 0720 (85 minutes after nautical twilight) for Gold; and 0630 (35 minutes after nautical twilight) for Omaha and Utah. (In an added complication, the main landing on Utah was to be preceded by two hours with an operation to seize the Isles Saint-Marcouf just offshore.)

ASSAULT FORCE SWORD

The operations order for Assault Force Sword clearly stated the tasks assigned to the leading brigade assaulting the beaches as well as the attached troops, including the 5th Assault Regiment R.E.[28]

Intention

12. The 3rd British Infantry Division will land on QUEEN RED and WHITE beaches and capture Caen, and a bridgehead SOUTH of the R Orne at that place.

Method

13. The Assault Brigade (8 British Infantry Brigade Group)

    (a) 8 British Infantry Brigade with under command 13/18 H, 5 Assault Regt RE (less two squadrons) and 4 and 41 Commando will carry out the assault on QUEEN RED and

WHITE beaches and secure the beach head to include PERIERS-SUR-LE-DAN–ST AUBIN–D'ARQUENAY 0976.

(b) Tasks in Detail

    (i) Assault and clear the beaches of direct fire to enable 5 Assault Regt RE and Divisional RE to construct vehicle exits and clear beach obstacles (see para 26).

    (ii) Relieve 6 Airborne Division at the BENOUVILLE and RANVILLE bridges as soon as possible or should it be necessary, to attack and capture these bridges. The initial force for this task will consist of not less than one rifle company and one squadron of tanks.

    (iii) The destruction as soon as possible of the battery at 102780. [DAIMLER]*

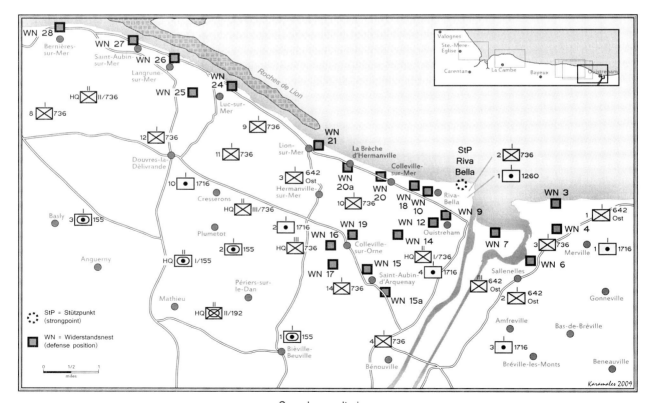

Sword assault plan.

---

* Square brackets indicate comments that were penciled into the original.

(iv) The capture of [high ground about] PERIERS-SUR-LE-DAN and the battery at 0777. [HILLMAN]

(v) The destruction of the Coast Defence battery at OUISTREHAM for which task 4 Commando is specifically allotted.

(vi) The mopping up of the coastal area to LUC-SUR-MER for which task 41 RM Commando is specifically allotted.

(c) The aim of the Assault Brigade must be to establish a firm base quickly with one battalion on the PERIERS-SUR-DAN feature so as to deny this ground to the enemy until the original assault battalions have completed their mopping up tasks and are available to reinforce that position.

(d) As soon as the situation on the Divisional front permits the bridgehead at RANVILLE and BENOUVILLE will be taken over by a Battalion Group from the Assault Brigade. This decision will be made by the Divisional Commander.

14. SS Troops under command

(a) 1 SS Brigade (less 4 Commando) will land under command 8 British Infantry Brigade between H+1 hour 15 minutes and H+1 hour 45 minutes on RED and WHITE beaches and will move as rapidly as possible to cross the R ORNE in the vicinity of the bridge at BENOUVILLE.

Close co-operation will be established with Commander 8 British Infantry Brigade to ensure that 1 SS Brigade is able to move so as to avoid if possible enemy positions still holding out WEST of R ORNE.

(b) 4 Commando reverts to command 1 SS Brigade on completion of its task of mopping up OUISTREHAM.

(c) 41 RM Commando will revert to command of 4 SS Brigade on completion of its task of mopping up LUC-SUR-MER when physical contact is made with 4 SS Brigade. . . .

19. RAC

(b) 22 Dragoons and W Dragoons

(i) Allotment

5 Assault Regt RE for beach exits:

four troops 22 Dragoons

for beach clearance:

three troops 22 Dragoons

Staffs Yeo:

two troops W Dragoons

E Riding Yeo:

one troop W Dragoons

(ii) Dets of 22 Dragoons and Westminster Dragoons on completion of their initial tasks will rally in area 072802 and revert to command 27 Armoured Brigade. . . .

26. Engineers

(a) Allotment to Brigade Groups

8 British Infantry Brigade—

246 Field Company under command

185 Infantry Brigade—

One platoon 17 Field Company under command

9 British Infantry Brigade—

One platoon 253 Field Company under command

Brigade groups are responsible for mine gapping on their own forward routes.

(b) Assault Tasks

(i) The task of constructing beach exits and clearing beach obstacles will be the responsibility of 5 Assault Regt RE. Commander Lt Col D Cooks [sic]

Troops   5 Assault Regt RE less two squadrons
- landing at H Hour
Squadron 22 Dragoons
629 Field Squadron
- landing at H + 20 minutes
263 Field Squadron [sic, Coy]
- landing at H + 30 minutes

(ii) Eight AVRE teams landing at H Hour each in one LCT will be responsible for constructing a minimum of two heavy track exits on each beach and for constructing a beach lateral and inland lateral connecting these track exits.

(iii) Four AVRE teams landing at H Hour in two LCTs will be responsible in construction with 629 Field Company for the clearance of beach obstacles from four zones 225 yards wide.

(iv) 263 Field Company landing at H+30 will form a reserve or second string for the clearance of beach obstacles as described in sub-para (iii) above.

(v) LCOCU land at H+20 to buoy zones which have been cleared of obstacles; to buoy wrecks; and to deal with submerged obstacles which may remain in the zone.

The initial assault force consisted of the 8th Infantry Brigade Group, with the following under its command:*

8th Infantry Brigade Headquarters and Defence Platoon

1st Battalion the South Lancashire Regiment (1st South Lancs)—Queen White

2nd Battalion the East Yorkshire Regiment (2nd East Yorks)—Queen Red

1st Battalion the Suffolk Regiment (1st Suffolks)—Reserve

A Company (MMG), 2nd Battalion the Middlesex Regiment

13th/18th Hussars (DD Tanks) (to revert to command of the 27th Armoured Brigade on reorganization)

67th Antitank Battery R.A. (minus its two 6-pounder antitank gun troops, but plus the M10 self-propelled 3-inch gun troop of the 45th Antitank Battery—i.e., it would have two troops, each with four 3-inch guns)

No. 41 (RM) Commando—Queen White (to revert to command of the 4th Special Service Brigade on completion of its task)

No. 4 Commando—Queen Red (to revert to command of the 1st Special Service Brigade on completion of its task)

1st Special Service Brigade (-)—Queen Red (under the 8th Infantry Brigade for landing only)

No. 45 (RM) Commando—Queen Red

No. 3 Commando—Queen Red

No. 6 Commando—Queen Red

5th Assault Regiment R.E. (-) (to revert to command of 3rd Division on orders from the commander of Royal Engineers)

77th Squadron, 5th Assault Regiment R.E.—Queen White

1st and 3rd Troop, A Squadron, 22nd Dragoons (Crabs)

79th Squadron, 5th Assault Regiment R.E.—Queen Red

3rd and 4th Troop, C Squadron, 22nd Dragoons (Crabs)

629th Field Squadron R.E. (obstacle clearance)

263rd Field Company R.E.

No. 7 L.C.O.C.U. (obstacle clearance)

No. 8 L.C.O.C.U. (obstacle clearance)

246th Field Company R.E. (under command for movement purposes only; it supplied two mine-clearance and four assault-demolition teams to each of the two assaulting infantry battalions)

Platoon, 17th Field Company R.E.

Detachment, 71st Army Field Company R.E.

Detachment, 106th Bridge Company R.A.S.C.

5th (RM) Independent Armoured Support Battery (each troop consisted of four Centaur close-support tanks and one Sherman command and observation post tank)

R, S, T, and V Troop

And in support:

33rd Field Regiment R.A. (self-propelled 105-millimeter M7)

76th (Highland) Field Regiment R.A. (self-propelled 105-millimeter M7)

The landing plan itself was a complicated ballet set to a precise timeline. H-Hour was set at 0735 at Queen Beach. Almost two hours earlier, at H–135

---

* Only the major units are noted here; each of the assault brigades had a multiplicity of minor units attached, such as liaisons from other units and war correspondents. Also not shown here are the initial detachments of the beach sub-areas that landed soon after the assault troops.

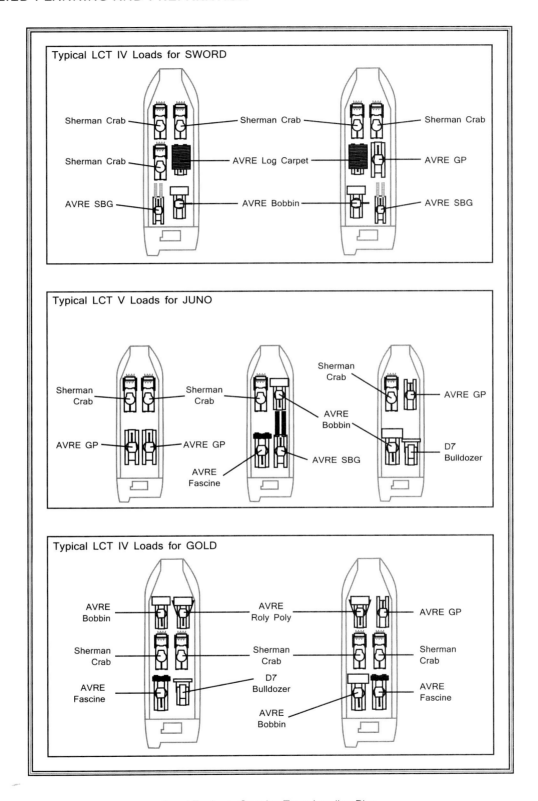

Royal Engineer Gapping Team Loading Plan.

minutes, the first troops—that is, the LCTs loaded with the DD tanks of the 13th/18th Hussars—were to begin to head toward the beach. Forty-five minutes later, at H-90, the LCTs with the A.V.R.E.'s, four LCT(A)'s, and four LCT(HE)'s—along with the supporting tanks of the 5th (RM) Support Battery and the LCAs of the leading infantry companies—were to set off.★ Just three minutes after that, at H-87, the DD tanks were to launch from their LCTs to begin their "swim" into the beach.

If all went according to plan, the DD tanks were to come ashore at H-7.5 minutes, closely following a rocket bombardment from five supporting LCT(R)'s. At H-Hour, the A.V.R.E.'s, Royal Marine tanks, and the first infantry companies were to land, secure an initial foothold, and begin clearing the beach obstacles for the follow-on waves. They then had twenty minutes before the reserve infantry companies, the L.C.O.C.U.'s, and the first elements of the beach groups (combined army, navy, and air force units that were to provide traffic control and other support services in the beachhead) arrived. From that point, things were to become fairly hectic, with masses of craft arriving to disgorge Commandos, infantry, tanks, artillery, and supporting troops and vehicles every ten to thirty-five minutes until

H+270, at which point there was to be a sixty-minute pause when the second tide began to come in, which was to be the signal to begin the beaching and unloading of the even larger LST's.

For the assault itself, the 2nd East Yorks were to land on the left on Queen Red. They were tasked with clearing Cod (WN 20), with the 1st Suffolks landing after them as a reserve to support them if necessary. The 1st South Lancs were to land to the right and drive straight forward. The Commandos were to land between 0755 and 0910 hours, with No. 4 Commando passing through the beachhead to take the coastal guns believed to be at Riva Bella. The rest of 1st Special Service Brigade was to pass through the beachhead and secure the defenses to the east of the Caen Canal, from Franceville-Plage to Cabourg, by crossing at the bridges at Benouville, which by that time would hopefully be in the hands of Major Howard and his gliderborne coup de main force from the 6th Airborne Division. In the meantime, No. 41 (RM) Commando of 4th Special Service Brigade was to pass through, turn right (westward), and clear the area between the British 3rd Division on Sword and the Canadian 3rd Division on Juno.

★ Each LCT(A) carried two Centaur tanks and one Sherman, while each LCT(HE) carried two Centaurs and a Crusader self-propelled antiaircraft tank.

ASSAULT FORCE JUNO

The operational intent for the Canadian 3rd Division of Force J was as succinct as that for the 3rd British Division of Force S: "assault through MIKE and NAN Sectors and seize a covering position on the general line railway crossing 995682."[29] On the left (east) of the 3rd's sector, the Canadian 8th Infantry Brigade Group was to assault Nan White and Nan Red and "overcome resistance on the beaches and gain control from BERNIERES-SUR-MER 9985 to ST AUBIN-SUR-MER 0284, to obtain control of the high ground BASLY 9979 to ANGUERNY 0177."[30]

The initial assault force consisted of the 8th Infantry Brigade, with the following under its command:

8th Canadian Infantry Brigade Headquarters and Defence Platoon

The Queen's Own Rifles of Canada (QOR)— Nan White

The North Shore (New Brunswick) Regiment (the North Shores)—Nan Red

Le Regiment de la Chaudière (the Chaudières)—Reserve

B Company (MMG), Cameron Highlanders of Ottowa

No. 48 (RM) Commando—Nan Red (to revert to command of the 4th Special Service Brigade upon completion of its task)

10th Canadian Armoured Regiment (CAR) (Fort Gary Horse) (DD tanks)

4th Battery, 2nd (RM) Armoured Support Regiment

N, O, P, and Q Troop

105th (Composite) Battery, 3rd Antitank Regiment R.C.A. (M10)[31]

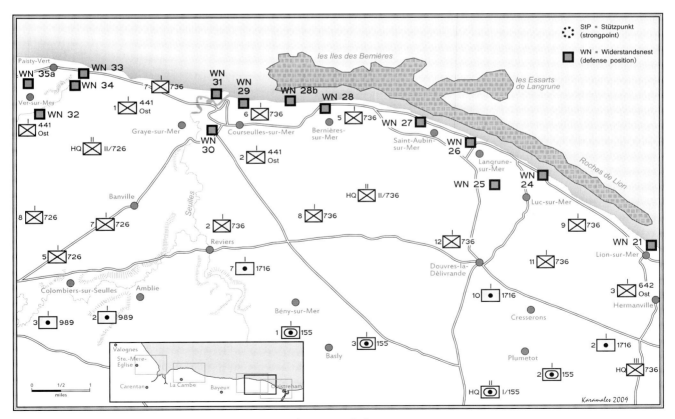

Juno assault plan.

80th Assault Squadron R.E.

1st and 4th Troop, B Squadron, 22nd Dragoons (Crabs)

5th Field Company R.C.E. (part) (obstacle clearance)

No. 1 Platoon, 16th Field Company R.C.E. (obstacle clearance)

No. 11 L.C.O.C.U. (obstacle clearance)

No. 12 L.C.O.C.U. (obstacle clearance)

No. 1 Platoon, 262nd Field Company R.E. (general support)

No. 3 Platoon, 19th Field Company R.C.E.

Detachments, 16th Field Company R.C.E. (sappers)

And in support:

14th Field Regiment R.C.A. (M7 self-propelled 105-millimeter)

19th Army Field Regiment R.C.A. (M7 self-propelled 105-millimeter)

The role of the engineers on Nan was to clear two 400-yard wide gaps in the beach obstacles, one each on Nan White and Nan Red, by H+75 (0800 hours). Sapper detachments from 16th Field Company R.C.E. were assigned to the assault infantry battalions and were to support them in their assault on the German positions. As on the other beaches, while those tasks were being done by the personnel of the field companies, the 80th Assault Squadron would gap forward from the beaches through the German beach position.[32]

On the right (west) of the 3rd Division's sector, the Canadian 7th Infantry Brigade Group was to assault astride the Seulles River on Mike Red and Nan Green and "overcome resistance on the beaches and gain control of area LE BUISSON 9485, GRAYE-SUR-MER 9584, COURSEULLES-SUR-MER 9784, to obtain control of high ground in vicinity PIERREPOINT 9379, and to seize and hold by last light on D-day PUTOT-EN-BESSIN 9072, BRETTEVILLE 9272, and NORREY-EN-BESSIN 9270."[33]

The initial assault force consisted of the 7th Infantry Brigade, with the following under its command:

7th Canadian Infantry Brigade Headquarters and Defence Platoon

The Royal Winnipeg Rifles (the Winnipegs)—Mike Red

The Regina Rifles (the Reginas)—Nan Green

The Canadian Scottish Regiment (C Scot R)-Reserve (less C Company, which was attached to the Winnipeg Rifles for the assault and landed on Mike Green)

A Company (MMG), Cameron Highlanders of Ottawa

6th CAR (1st Hussars) (DD Tanks)

3rd Battery, 2nd (RM) Armoured Support Regiment

J, K, L and M Troop

248th Battery, 62nd Antitank Regiment R.A. (M10)

26th Assault Squadron R.E.

2nd and 3rd Troop, B Squadron, 22nd Dragoons (Crabs)

5th Field Company R.C.E. (part) (obstacle clearance)

No. 1 Platoon, 18th Field Coy R.E. (obstacle clearance)

No. 1 L.C.O.C.U. (obstacle clearance)

No. 5 L.C.O.C.U. (obstacle clearance)

No. 2 Platoon, 6th Field Company R.C.E. (sappers)

262nd Field Company R.E. (No. 2 and No. 3 Platoon) (general support)

And in support:

12th Field Regiment R.C.A. (M7 self-propelled 105-millimeter)

13th Field Regiment R.C.A. (M7 self-propelled 105-millimeter)

The role of the engineers on Mike was given in the 7th Canadian Infantry Brigade Operation Order No. 1: "5 Cdn Fd Coy, landing at H hour and employing bulldozers and explosives will clear gaps through the underwater obstacles. On MIKE sector a gap of 600 yards will be cleared to cover [Gap] M1 95558605 and [Gap] M2 96158590. . . . 262 Fd Coy RE, beaching at about H plus 20 will reinforce the obstacle clearing parties with the alternative tasks of clearing minefields."[34] The two assault brigades would be followed by the Canadian 9th Infantry Brigade as reserve. Later, engineer reinforcements also included the 184th Field Company R.E., which was assigned to the 102nd Beach Sub-Area, which would land at 0810 and contribute to clearing obstacles and mines as necessary.[35]

The timing of Assault Group Juno had been intended to be similar to that of Sword, with H-Hour scheduled for 0735. In the event, problems encountered during the Channel crossing resulted in the landings at Nan Green and Mike Red being delayed until 0745 and those on Nan White and Nan Red until 0755.[36]

ASSAULT FORCE GOLD

The intent for the 50th (Northumberland) Division on Gold was as follows:

> As the spearhead of 30 Corps, 50 (N) Inf Div planned to assault certain sections of JIG and KING sectors. 231 Bde on the right (JIG) on a two battalion front and 69 Bde left (KING) also on a two battalion front, with 56 and 151 Bde in reserve, for extension of the initial beach-head. The final objectives by last light on D-Day for these latter two brigades were BAYEUX (7879), and the high ground to the S.E., SOUTH and SW whilst forward elements of 69 Bde were to hold the high ground in the area of ST. LEGER (8675) astride the road BAYEUX (7879)—CAEN (0368), and 231 Bde were intended to protect the WEST flank and exploit towards MANVIEUX (8286).
>
> Exploitation of the beach-head in the direction of VILLERS BOCAGE (8157) was the role of 7 Armd Div who were to be followed by 49 Inf Div.[37]

On the left (east) of the 50th Division's sector, the 69th Infantry Brigade was assigned to King Beach and was to "overcome resistance on the beaches, gain control of the rising ground from Pt 52 (9085) to Pt 44 (9184), the BAZENVILLE crest 8782 and CREULLY 9180, and to seize and hold by last light on D-day the high ground in area ST LEGER 8675 astride the road BAYEUX-CAEN."[38]

The initial assault force consisted of the 69th Infantry Brigade Group, with the following under its command:

69th Infantry Brigade Headquarters and Defence Platoon

6th Battalion the Green Howards Regiment (6th Green Howards)—King Green

5th Battalion the East Yorkshire Regiment (5th East Yorks)—King Red

7th Battalion the Green Howards Regiment (7th Green Howards)—Reserve

B Company, 2nd Battalion the Cheshire Regiment (MG)

No. 13 Platoon, D Company, 2nd Battalion the Cheshire Regiment (Heavy Mortar)

4th/7th Royal Dragoon Guards (DD tanks)

Troop, C Squadron, 141st R.A.C. (three Crocodiles)

2nd Battery, 1st (RM) Armoured Support Regiment

E, F, G, and H Troop

99th Battery, 102nd (Northumberland Hussars) Antitank Regiment R.A. (with two troops of M10 self-propelled 3-inch and two troops of 6-pounder antitank guns)

81st Squadron, 6th Assault Regiment R.E.

C Squadron, Westminster Dragoons (thirteen Crabs)

280th Field Company R.E. (obstacle clearance)

No. 3 L.C.O.C.U. (obstacle clearance)

No. 4 L.C.O.C.U. (obstacle clearance)

233rd Field Company R.E. (sappers and general support)

89th Field Company R.E. (beach exit clearance)

Detachment, 149th Assault Park Squadron R.E. (armored bulldozers)

Detachment, 235th Field Park Company R.E. (bulldozers)

And in support:

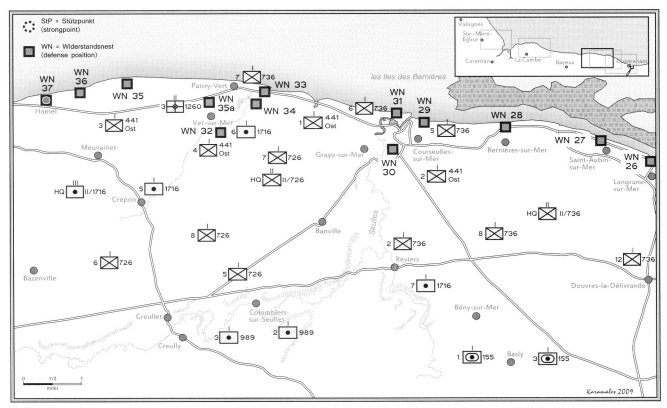

Gold assault plan.

86th (East Anglian) and (Hertfordshire Yeomanry) Field Regiment R.A. (self-propelled 25-pounder Ram*)

On the left (east), the 5th East Yorks were to take WN 33 at La Rivière and WN 34 at Mont Fleury and were then to consolidate, mopping up those positions. On the right (west), the 6th Green Howards were to capture WN 35, then drive inland to seize WN 35a (the Mont Fleury Battery) and the high ground around Meuvaines. The reserve battalion, the 7th Green Howards, would follow up behind the 6th Green Howards and would pass through them to seize the battery position at Ver-sur-Mer.[39]

On the right (west) of the 50th Division sector 231st Infantry Brigade Group was assigned to Jig beach and was to "overcome resistance on the

beaches, gain control of the high ground from WEST OF BUHOT 8685 to MEUVAINES 8884, to protect the WEST flank, and to exploit towards MANVIEUX 8286. 47 Cdo of 4 SS Bde was to land after 231 Bde to capture PORT-EN-BESSIN 7587."[40]

The initial assault force consisted of the 231st Infantry Brigade Group, with the following under its command:

1st Battalion the Hampshire Regiment (1st Hamps)—Jig Green West

1st Battalion the Dorset Regiment (1st Dorsets)—Jig Green East

2nd Battalion the Devonshire Regiment (1st Devons)—Reserve

C Company, D Company, 2nd Battalion the Cheshire Regiment (MG)

---

* The 25-pounder Ram was the self-propelled 25-pounder artillery piece mounted on a Canadian-built Ram tank chassis. It was later named the Sexton.

No. 14 Platoon, 2nd Battalion the Cheshire
Regiment (Heavy Mortar)

No. 47 (RM) Commando

1st Battery, 1st (RM) Armoured Support Regiment
ment

A, B, C, and D Troop

288th Battery, 102nd (Northumberland Hussars)
Antitank Regiment R.A. (with two troops of
M10 self-propelled 3-inch and two troops of
6-pounder antitank guns)

Nottinghamshire (Sherwood Rangers) Yeomanry
(DD tanks)

Troop, C Squadron, 141st R.A.C. (three Crocodiles)
diles)

82nd Squadron, 6th Assault Regiment R.E.

B Squadron, Westminster Dragoons (twelve
Crabs)

73rd Field Company R.E. (obstacle clearance)

No. 9 L.C.O.C.U. (obstacle clearance)

No. 10 L.C.O.C.U. (obstacle clearance)

295th Field Company R.E. (sappers and general
support)

90th Field Company R.E. (beach exit clearance)

Detachment, 235th Field Park Company R.E.
(bulldozers)

And in support:

90th (City of London) Field Regiment R.A.
(self-propelled 25-pounder Ram)

147th (Essex Yeomanry) Field Regiment R.A.
(self-propelled 25-pounder Ram)

On the left (east), the 1st Dorsets was to seize
WN 36 and the village of Meuvaines, then drive
south. On the right (west), the 1st Hamps was to
seize Dart (WN 37 at Le Hamel) and the village of
Asnelles and were then to drive west. The reserve
battalion, the 2nd Devons, was to follow the 1st
Hamps and had as their objectives the villages of
Ryes, La Rosieres, and Fontenailles and the coastal
artillery battery at Longues.[41]

The timing of the assault was again similar to
that on Sword and Juno. H-Hour on Gold was set
for 0725. For the 231st Brigade on Jig, the plan was
to land the DD tanks at H-05, followed at H-Hour
by the breaching teams with the assault squadrons,

Crabs, a Royal Engineer field company, and the
L.C.O.C.U.'s. Then, at H+07, the leading infantry
assault companies would land, followed by the
reserve companies of the assault battalions at H+20,
a second Royal Engineer field company, and the
advance elements of the beach group would arrive
at H+25 to help clear exits from the beach. At
H+35, three Crocodile Churchill flamethrower
tanks would arrive.★ The brigade reserve infantry
battalion would land at H+45 and H+55, artillery
would land at H+60, and the reserve squadron of
the tank battalion and additional vehicles would
land at H+90.

For the 69th Infantry Brigade, the timing was
slightly different. On King, the leading assault
infantry companies were scheduled to land at
H+7.5 minutes and the reserve companies at H+25,
with the reserve battalion and No. 47 (RM) Commando
mando coming in at H+45, along with various battalion
talion vehicles and three Crocodile Churchill
flamethrower tanks. At H+60, the reserve tank
squadrons would land, followed by field and antitank
artillery at H+90 and H+105, with the last elements
of the brigade landing at H+120.

The plan for dealing with the beach obstacles
was again similar to those for Sword and Juno. On
Jig, the 82nd Assault Squadron R.E. formed six
breaching teams, three for the western and three for
the eastern half of the sector. Accompanying them
in each of the six LCT's were two sections of engineers
neers (about twenty-four per LCT) from the 73rd
Field Company R.E., who were to assist in clearing
two 250-yard-wide gaps in the beach obstacles by
H+60. Meanwhile, the L.C.O.C.U.'s would deal
with underwater obstacles during the assault. Following
lowing up the assault were the 90th and 295th Field
Companies R.E. They were to assist in clearing all
the remaining obstacles and in constructing and
improving exits for tracked and wheeled vehicles.

On King, the 81st Assault Squadron R.E. also was
divided into six gapping teams, each accompanied by
two sections from the 280th Field Company R.E.,
but also supported by two D7 armored bulldozers
from the 1st Assault Brigade's own 149th Assault Park
Squadron R.E. They were also to clear two 250-yard

★ On D-Day, the landing of the Crocodiles was delayed by events until the afternoon, and there is no evidence they were engaged on
6 June.

gaps while the L.C.O.C.U.'s cleared the submerged obstacles. Following up the assault teams were the 89th and 233rd Field Companies R.E., which were responsible for completing clearing the beaches, improving the tracked and wheeled vehicle exits, developing the beach and beach maintenance area, and repairing and improving the coast road. In addition, the 233rd Field Company provided sapper detachments for the assault infantry battalions.[42]

A total of about twenty-two infantry battalions made up the assault waves on the three Com-

monwealth beaches, including seven battalion-size Commandos supported by five tank regiments (battalion-size tactical units), nine field artillery regiments (battalion-size tactical units), the assault engineers, and numerous other supporting troops. On a typical brigade front, such as that of 231st Brigade on Jig Beach, the plan expected that more than 3,800 men and 236 tracked vehicles would be ashore within the first hour.

ASSAULT FORCE OMAHA

The landing scheme developed for the American beaches was very similar to that planned for the Commonwealth beaches, but with some significant modifications to the details because of the lack of A.V.R.E.'s and Crabs. Omaha was to be assaulted on a two-regiment front, equivalent to the two-brigade front at Juno and Gold. Unlike the Commonwealth beaches, however, planners decided that each regiment would be drawn from a different division in order to facilitate command and control on D-Day and during the days immediately following as the bridgehead expanded.

The assault echelon consisted of the 16th Infantry Regimental Combat Team (RCT) of the 1st Infantry Division, the 116th Infantry RCT of the 29th Infantry Division, and C Company, 2nd Ranger Battalion. The 1st Battalion, 16th Infantry RCT, and the 3rd Battalion, 116th Infantry RCT, were the immediate reserve for the assault echelon. The 5th Ranger Battalion and two companies of the 2nd Ranger Battalion were a contingent reserve. They were ready for commitment—either with the 2nd Ranger Battalion Headquarters and three companies that were to make the perilous assault on Pointe du Hoc (Charlie Green East and West) or with the 2nd Ranger Battalion's C Company on Charlie Red immediately adjacent to Dog Green. The immediate follow-on to the assault echelon was the 115th Infantry RCT of the 29th Division and the 18th Infantry RCT of the 1st Division. All were initially

under the command of the 1st Infantry Division on D-Day. The total men loaded were recorded as 9,850 with the 16th Infantry RCT, 9,745 with the 116th Infantry RCT, and 752 with the reserve Rangers.[43]

The 29th Infantry Division—with its own 175th Infantry RCT and the remaining divisional troops and the attached 26th Infantry RCT of the 1st Division—was the assault force reserve under the control of the V Corps and was loaded in the initial echelon of Force B, which also included the follow-on 2nd Infantry Division. Thus, the initial deployment was very similar to that planned for Juno and Gold, but with four infantry regiments landing rather than four infantry brigades.

The timing of the assault waves was also very similar. First, two tank battalions, the 741st and 743rd, were to land a total of sixty-four DD tanks in four tank companies. On the left at H-10—again, with slightly different timing because of the tidal variations—sixteen were to land on each of Fox Green and Easy Red, and sixteen more were to land farther west at H-05 on each of Dog Green and Dog White. They were to be followed at H-Hour by the wading tank companies of the two tank battalions in sixteen LCT(A)'s. Each LCT(A) carried two M4 75-millimeter tanks and one M4 75-millimeter tank dozer. In essence, they would substitute for the tasks being fulfilled on Commonwealth beaches by the Royal Marine Armoured Support Batteries and the A.V.R.E.'s of the assault squadrons.

Originally, planners intended to equip the two M4 75-millimeter tanks in the LCT(A) with the same 7.2-inch multiple rocket launcher, the T40 (M17) Whiz Bang, which was also used in the experimental U.S. Army armored engineer vehicle. The massive sixty-one-pound rocket had a 300-yard range, and the thirty-two-pound high-explosive warhead was—in theory—at least as effective as the twenty-nine-pound charge of the Petard.[44] However, experiments by the 70th Tank Battalion (slated to land on Utah) prior to D-Day revealed some significant problems with the equipment.

For one, the heavy launcher and rockets were mounted in a frame that was fixed to the tank turret that raised the center of gravity of the tank and the LCT(A) significantly. And since the center of balance of the vessel had already been raised by the addition of the armored pilothouse and firing ramps, the additional height and weight added by the launcher made an already unstable vessel essentially uncontrollable. For another, the tank crews found that

when the frame was mounted, it was almost impossible for them to escape in an emergency. The idea of placing twenty high-explosive warheads and their solid-fuel rockets—even in an armored launcher—in such a position so exposed to enemy fire was not endearing to the crews either. Finally, the 70th Tank Battalion found that the demolition effect of the rocket on seawalls in England was little different from what the 75-millimeter gun in the tank could achieve. These all evidently played a part in the final decision that eliminated the Whiz-Bang from the inventory of weapons planned for the invasion.[45]

At H+1, one minute after the wading tanks, the leading assault infantry companies were to land to secure an initial beachhead. One company was assigned to each of Dog Green, Dog White, Dog Red, and Easy Green, while two companies were to land on each of Easy Red and Fox Green.

At H+3, the gapping teams were to arrive, two each on Dog Green, Dog White, Dog Red, Easy Green, and Fox Green and six on Easy Red. Each of

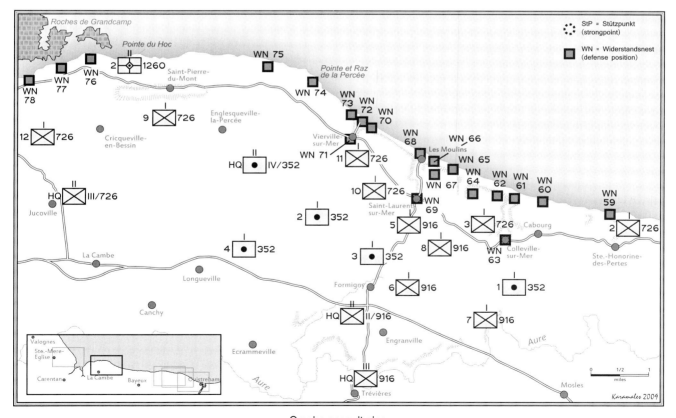

Omaha assault plan.

the sixteen gapping teams was to open a gap fifty yards wide through the beach obstacles to the beach road, supported by sixteen M4 tank dozers. At H+8, eight gapping support teams were to land, one to support each of the gapping teams already landed. The gapping support teams were organized identically to the gapping teams, but carried additional explosives. They were intended to provide additional manpower where it was required. At H+25, four reserve gapping teams and two command teams were to arrive, again with additional explosives. By that time, it was expected that the initial sixteen gaps would be open and the teams were to transition to widening and improving the gaps.

Between H+30 and H+40, the follow-up waves of the initial assault battalions would land with the reserve rifle company, battalion weapons company, and battalion headquarters. In addition, supporting weapons would land, including 4.2-inch heavy mortars[*] from a supporting chemical weapons battalion, a provisional heavy machine-gun battery[**] from a supporting antiaircraft battalion for immediate protection in case of a German air attack, and additional engineers. At the end of that stage, two battalions were to be ashore on Dog Green, Dog White, Dog Red, and Easy Green and two on Fox Green and Easy Red.

Between H+50 and H+60, the two reserve battalions and regimental headquarters of the two assault regiments were to land, along with additional engineers and other supporting troops. At H+90, two armored field artillery battalions, each with eighteen M7 105-millimeter howitzers, were to land in support of the two assault regiments. Additional engineers, artillery, and beach-support units were to arrive about every ten minutes after that, with the last major combat elements, the reserve infantry regiment, landing beginning at H+195.

The force broke down as follows:
Assault Group O-1, 16th RCT (Reinforced)

16th Infantry
    3rd Battalion—Fox Green
    2nd Battalion—Easy Red
    1st Battalion—Easy Red(Reserve)
    Cannon Company (M3 towed 105-millimeter)
    Antitank Company
741st Tank Battalion
197th Antiaircraft Automatic Weapons Battalion (self-propelled)
Provisional Machinegun Battery, 197th AAA (AW) Battalion
A and C Company, 81st Chemical Weapons Battalion (4.2-inch mortars)
62nd Armored Field Artillery Battalion (M7 self-propelled 105-millimeter)
7th Field Artillery Battalion (M2 towed 105-millimeter)
1st Engineer Combat Battalion
20th Engineer Combat Battalion
Elements, 5th Engineer Special Brigade
Elements, Engineer Special Task Force
    Demolition Section Command Team No. 2 (299th Engineer Combat Battalion)
    Gapping Teams No. 9, 10, 11, 12, 13, 14, 15, and 16
    Gapping Support Teams E, F, G, and H
Assault Group O-2, 116th RCT (Reinforced)
116th Infantry
    2nd Battalion—Dog White, Dog Red, Easy Green
    1st Battalion—Dog Green
    3rd Battalion (Reserve)
    Cannon Company (M3 105-millimeter Towed)
    Antitank Company
5th Ranger Battalion—Dog Green
C Company, 2nd Ranger Battalion—Charlie Red
743rd Tank Battalion

---

[*] In the U.S. Army, the 4.2-inch heavy mortar had been developed prior to the war as a weapon for dispensing chemical agents, including poison gases and chemical smoke. Early in the war, a high-explosive round was also developed to make the mortar highly effective in an infantry-support role.

[**] The provisional battery consisted of sixteen water-cooled, tripod-mounted .50-caliber antiaircraft machine guns. Each gun weighed 100 pounds, while the tripod weighed 139 pounds. With the ammunition and cooling water, these guns would be a backbreaking load to carry ashore under fire.

467th Antiaircraft Automatic Weapons
    Battalion (self-propelled)
Provisional Machinegun Battery, 397th AAA
    (AW) Battalion
B and D Company, 81st Chemical Weapons
    Battalion (4.2-inch mortars)
58th Armored Field Artillery Battalion (M7
    self-propelled 105-millimeter)
111th Field Artillery Battalion (M2 towed
    105-millimeter)
112th Engineer Combat Battalion
121st Engineer Combat Battalion
Elements, 6th Engineer Special Brigade
Elements, Special Engineer Task Force
    SETF Command Section
    Demolition Section Command Team No.
        1 (146th Engineer Combat Battalion)
    Gapping Teams No. 1, 2, 3, 4, 5, 6, 7, and 8
    Gapping Support Teams A, B, C, and D

It is immediately apparent that the order of battle for the American forces on Omaha was quite similar in outline and intent to those found on the Commonwealth beaches. Each assault group on Omaha was based upon a three-battalion infantry regiment, quite similar to the three-battalion infantry brigade employed on Sword, Juno, and Gold. The Omaha assault groups were reinforced with a tank battalion, heavy mortars, engineers, field artillery, antiaircraft artillery, and engineers, just as the Commonwealth assault brigades were, and in similar proportions. Even the American engineer special brigade mirrored the organization, strength, equipment, and purpose of the Commonwealth beach sub-areas, as did the improvised engineer obstacle-clearance teams.

There were also major differences between the American and Commonwealth beaches. On Omaha, because of the limitied availability of LCT's, only half the artillery battalions were equipped with self-propelled gun carriages, a distinct disadvantage for getting them off the beach and inland. Worse, lack of the appropriate landing craft meant that the towed howitzers had to be brought into the beach on amphibious trucks, a risky endeavor. On American beaches, the tank battalions were forced to assume the many tasks spread among the A.V.R.E.'s, Royal Marine Centaurs, and tanks on the Commonwealth beaches. D-Day would reveal if that was asking too much of the American tankers.

ASSAULT FORCE UTAH

Utah was planned to be assaulted in Tare Sector, Beach Green (Tare Green), and in Uncle Sector, Beach Red (Uncle Red). However, various events caused the landings to slip south of where they were intended. Despite that, the original beach names were retained. Two battalions of the 8th Infantry, 4th Infantry Division, were in the assault echelon, with the third in reserve. The Utah assault plan was broadly similar to Omaha, except that the engineers and NCDUs of the beach obstacle demolition parties relied on LCM's and LCVP's for transport instead of just LCM's. Another interesting variation from the planning for Omaha—and indeed the Commonwealth beaches—was that the aerial bombardment preceeding the assault was to be by low-flying medium bombers of the U.S. Ninth Tactical Air Force rather than the heavy bombers of the Eighth Air Force. Furthermore, it was planned that

just prior to the assault waves' landing, a group of medium bombers would attempt to blast four lanes through the beach obstacles by flying at very low level using delayed-action fuzed bombs so that the aircraft could clear the area before the bombs exploded.[46]

The force broke down as follows:
Assault Group U, 8th Infantry RCT
    (Reinforced)
    8th Infantry
        2nd Battalion—Uncle Red
        1st Battalion—Tare Green
        3rd Battalion (Reserve)
        Cannon Company
        Antitank Company
    70th Tank Battalion
    Provisional Machinegun Battery, 474th AAA
        (AW) Battalion

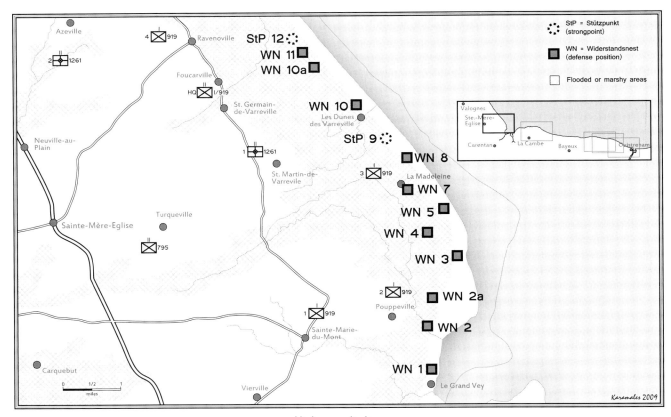

Utah assault plan.

A, B, and C Company, 87th Chemical
Weapons Battalion (4.2-inch mortars)
65th Armored Field Artillery Battalion (M7
self-propelled 105-millimeter)
29th Field Artillery Battalion (M7 self-
propeleld 105-millimeter)
42nd Field Artillery Battalion (M7 self-
propelled 105-millimeter)
Elements, 1st Engineer Special Brigade
Beach Obstacle Demolition Party

Assault Force Utah was organized nearly identically to the force at Omaha, although Utah had one
possible advantage. Assault Force Utah had been allocated 160 LCT's by the Neptune planners, while
Assault Force Omaha, for reasons that remain
unclear, had been allocated only 147—despite the
fact that the Omaha assault was on a two-regiment
front while the Utah assault was on a single-regiment
front. That anomaly allowed the 4th Infantry Division to allocate a critical few additional LCT's to the
assault echelon, which were used to bring in additional self-propelled artillery pieces. That is also
apparently what enabled them to convert the 29th
and 42nd Field Artillery Battalions from towed to
self-propelled, like the field artillery regiments in the
Commonwealth assault divisions.

Soldiers exiting an LCI(L) during Exercise
Fabius in May 1944. NARA

A tank destroyer battalion practices a landing at
Slapton Sands, England, prior to D-Day. In the
background is an LCT and, behind it, and LST.
NARA

SUMMARY

Thus, a total of nine infantry and two Ranger battalions made up the assault waves on the American beaches, along with three tank battalions, three self-propelled armored field artillery battalions, and two field artillery battalions equipped with self-propelled carriages for the invasion. They were supported by strong contingents of engineers, and each of the three regimental sectors was allocated eight M4 medium tanks with bulldozer blades as the closest available substitute for an American armored engineer vehicle.

Numerically, at least in terms of infantry deployed in the assault, the planning of the American beaches was actually quite similar to those of the Commonwealth. Each of the brigades and regiments assaulted with two battalions "up front" and one in reserve and each were supported in some cases by Commandos or Rangers.

Nor was there a huge difference in the number of tanks deployed: roughly sixty-eight medium tanks per brigade on the Commonwealth beaches and fifty-four medium tanks per regiment on the American beaches.

However, there were two glaring differences between the Commonwealth and American beaches. There were about sixty-four self-propelled artillery pieces per brigade deployed in the assault echelon on the Commonwealth beaches, including the Centaurs of the Royal Marine Armoured Support batteries, but only eighteen per regiment on Omaha and forty-two on Utah. In terms of engineering vehicles, the difference was even greater: there were an average of more than thirty-eight A.V.R.E.'s and Crabs per brigade for the Commonwealth assault forces, compared to just eight tank dozers for the Americans. On the other hand, no tank dozers were employed in the assault on the Commonwealth beaches, while the American engineers did plan on bringing in large numbers of D4 unarmored bulldozers following the initial assault waves.

The lack of self-propelled artillery in the American contingent appears to have been partly because of the limited number of LCT's available. There was no lack of armored field artillery battalions in England and no lack of spare self-propelled howitzers; at least two of the battalions of the 4th Division, the 29th and 42nd, each received twelve M7 self-propelled 105-millimeter howitzers to replace their M2 towed 105-millimeter howitzers. However, the best evidence is that the lack of enough LCT's meant that there simply was not enough shipping space to do the same with all the assault divisions. Why the Commonwealth divisions received such a priority remains unexplained. Instead, the 1st and 29th Divisions were forced to load the M2 105-millimeter howitzers of the 7th and 111th Field Artillery and the slightly lighter M3 105-millimeter howitzers of the two regimental cannon companies precariously atop DUKW's (amphibious trucks), which were expected to drive them up off the beaches inland where they could be offloaded and begin firing. (The howitzers could have been brought in on LCVP's, but would have required a separate lift for their prime movers. It was reasoned that once unloaded they could have been towed inland by the DUKW's.) The results turned out to be nearly catastrophic on D-Day; the 7th Field Artillery lost seven of twelve, the 111th Field Artillery eleven of twelve, and the 16th Infantry Cannon Company all six howitzers when the overloaded DUKW's foundered in the heavy seas.

The thirty "missing" A.V.R.E.'s were potentially an even more serious problem than the shortage of artillery on the beach. After all, naval gunfire support was supposed to fill in for the field artillery until the guns were ashore anyway. Only after the landing was over would it be known if that was a significant shortcoming.

CHAPTER 4

German Planning and Preparation

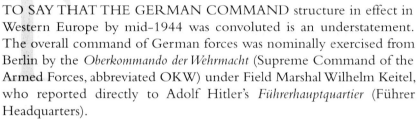

TO SAY THAT THE GERMAN COMMAND structure in effect in Western Europe by mid-1944 was convoluted is an understatement. The overall command of German forces was nominally exercised from Berlin by the *Oberkommando der Wehrmacht* (Supreme Command of the Armed Forces, abbreviated OKW) under Field Marshal Wilhelm Keitel, who reported directly to Adolf Hitler's *Führerhauptquartier* (Führer Headquarters).

Under OKW responsibility for the defense of the Belgian and French coastline was *Oberbefehlshaber West* (High Command West, abbreviated OB West), commanded by Field Marshal Gerd von Rundstedt, who had direct command and control only of the army (*Heer*) units in his zone of responsibility. The navy (*Kriegsmarine*) and air force (*Luftwaffe*) units in the area were not under his tactical control, except in certain limited circumstances, and were otherwise required to cooperate and provide support to OB West only as they saw fit. Nor did he have complete control of all the *Luftwaffe* ground forces or *Waffen-SS* deployed in OB West. The *Waffen-SS* and parachute army forces were only tactically subordinated to OB West, while their administrative chain of command ran to Berlin and Reich Marshal Hermann Goering's High Command of the *Luftwaffe* and Heinrich Himmler's SS Head Office. Rundstedt also had no direct control over the German forces in Holland or the military governors of the occupied territories, including France and Belgium, and their occupation troops; they reported directly to OKW and were to come under direct command of OB West only in the event of an invasion.

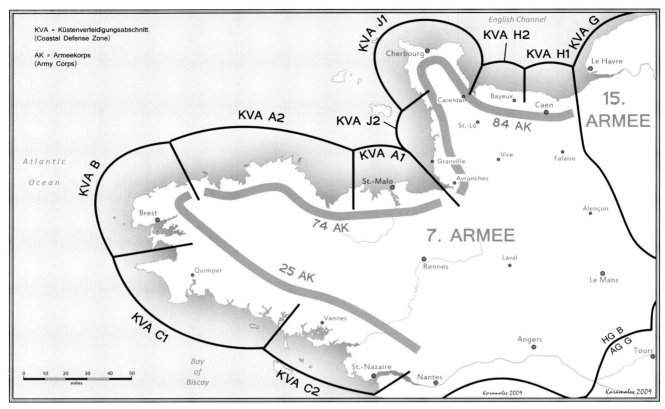

The German 7th Army defense scheme.

The army troops of OB West were responsible for the defense of the coastline, essentially from the waterline inland to a depth of just over six miles, whereupon the military governors had control. The navy was responsible from the coastline seaward, utilizing small naval units (destroyers, torpedo boats, motor torpedo boats, minesweepers, and small patrol boats); long-range, large-caliber coastal defense artillery; and land-based fire-control and early-warning radar sites. Similarly, the *Luftwaffe* was to provide general support for the army and navy, including short-range tactical reconnaissance, long-range strategic and operational reconnaissance, attacks on invasion shipping, and close air support of the coastal defense line; in addition, it also manned a large number of coastal and inland radar sites that were part of the air raid early-warning and fighter-interceptor system defending the Reich and its occupied territories against the Allied combined bomber offensive.

Early in 1944, while the Allies were completing their Neptune planning, OB West and its commander, Field Marshal Rundstedt, doubled as both a theater command and an operational army group command, Army Group D. In turn, Army Group D had command of four armies, the 1st, 7th, 15th, and 19th. But on 15 January 1944, the decision was made to place the two strongest armies, the 7th and 15th—which were responsible for the most critical areas in the west, the Channel coast area opposite England extending from Holland to the Brittany peninsula—under the command of Field Marshal Erwin Rommel and Army Group B. Rommel had been acting as inspector of the coastal fortifications in Holland, Belgium, and France since December 1943, with his staff subordinated to OB West. An ad hoc army group headquarters, Army Group G, under Col. Gen. Johannes Blaskowitz, was eventually formed on 1 May 1944 to command the 1st and

19th Armies, which were responsible for the Biscay coast and the French Riviera.

OB West divided the various regional army commands into coastal defense zones (KVA), each of which was the responsibility of a single division. The KVA was in turn then subdivided into coastal defense groups (KVGr) and coastal defense sub-groups (KVUGr). For example, in the area of the 7th Army, the 716th Infantry Division was assigned to KVA Caen and in turn was responsible for two coastal defense groups, Riva Bella and Courseulles. KVGr Riva Bella was divided into two sub-groups, Orne and Lion, and KVGr Courseulles was also divided into two sub-groups, Seulles and Normandy. In effect, the KVA was a division-size zone, the KVGr was a regiment-size zone, and the KVUGr was a battalion-size zone.

The actual defenses consisted of a combination of five types of fortified positions: the fortress (*Festung*), the defense area (*Verteidigungsbereich*, or VB), the strongpoint (*Stützpunkt*, or StP), the strongpoint group (*Stützpunktgruppe*), and the resistance nest (*Widerstandsnest*, or WN). On D-Day, however, the 1st Assault Brigade R.E. was concerned only with the strongpoint, the strongpoint group, and the resistance nest; it was not until later in the campaign that they were required to deal with any fortresses or defense areas.

Strongpoint groups were generally occupied by a reinforced company or even a battalion, while strongpoints were as large as company-size and resistance nests were platoon-size or even smaller, about twenty-five officers and men. The strongpoint group normally incorporated one or more interlinked strongpoints and restance nests, and the strongpoint interlinked resistance nests. It was also common for a coastal defense sub-group to consist solely of resistance nests. For example, KVGr Riva Bella included KVUGr Orne on the eastern bank of the Orne River, which contained Strongpoint 02 (Franceville East) and Strongpoint 05 (Franceville West) as well as Resistance Nests 01, 03, 04, and 06. Its counterpart on the western side of the Orne River was KVUGr Lion-sur-Mer, with Strongpoint 08 (Riva Bella) and Strongpoint 18 (La Brèche) as well as Resistance Nests 07, 09, 10, 11, 12, 14, 15, 15a, 16, 17, 19, 20, and 21.

On 19 January 1944, Adolf Hitler designated fourteen areas in OB West as fortresses, adding the Channel Islands on 3 March. Each was to be fortified, manned, equipped, and provisioned in order to be capable of withstanding an assault independently for some weeks. A fortress consisted of a permanent security garrison that was typically regiment-size and always stationed within the area of the fortress. They were comprised of troops detailed from units throughout an entire corps area and were in addition to the general garrison comprised of the troops assigned to the KVA it was situated in. Thus, the nominal strength of a KVA containing a fortress would be a reinforced division. The fortresses replaced many of the earlier defense areas. By June 1944, VB Den Helder was one of the few remaining defense areas that had not been upgraded.

The fortresses were Ijmuiden, Hoek van Holland, and Vlissingen in the Netherlands and Dunkirk, Calais, Boulogne, Le Havre, Cherbourg, Channel Islands, St. Malo, Brest, Lorient, St. Nazaire, La Rochelle, and Royan in France. This meant that none were directly encountered by the 1st Assault Brigade on D-Day, but they later became intimately familiar with some of them since the Funnies were heavily engaged at Le Havre, Boulogne, and Calais, and participated in the assaults on Brest and Vlissingen (Walcheren Island).

The actual fortifications that made up these defenses were quite variable in size, strength, and design. Initial construction was carried out according to designs originally meant for the West Wall (known to the Allies as the Siegfried Line), the German frontier defenses begun in 1936. They were known as the standard-type design and consisted of more than 200 different types built to six different strength standards in reinforced concrete. Additional types were added to accommodate larger weapons and specialized designs for *Luftwaffe* and navy requirements. By 1944, some 15,000 fortification structures had been completed or were being built for the Atlantic Wall.

A typical resistance nest in the Neptune invasion area consisted of a combination of prepared concrete positions and simpler and less permanent field works. Normally there were one or two concrete ammunition bunkers, a half-dozen or so concrete personnel

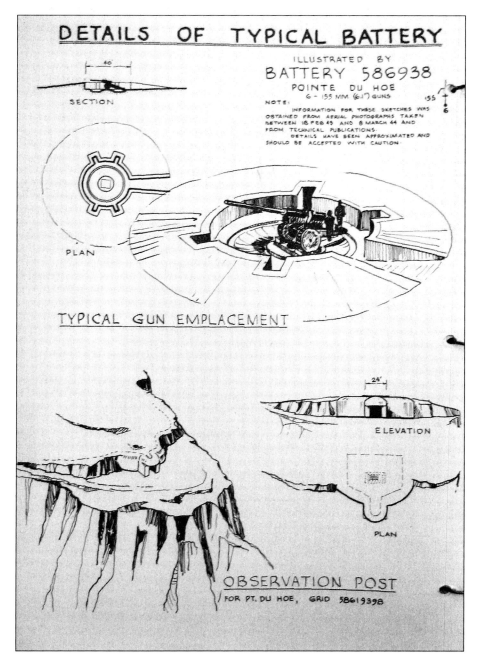

DETAILS OF TYPICAL BATTERY

ILLUSTRATED BY
BATTERY 586938
POINTE DU HOE
6 - 155 M.M. (6.1") GUNS

NOTE:
INFORMATION FOR THESE SKETCHES WAS
OBTAINED FROM AERIAL PHOTOGRAPHS TAKEN
BETWEEN 18 FEB 44 AND 8 MARCH 44 AND
FROM TECHNICAL PUBLICATIONS.
DETAILS HAVE BEEN APPROXIMATED AND
SHOULD BE ACCEPTED WITH CAUTION.

SECTION

PLAN

TYPICAL GUN EMPLACEMENT

OBSERVATION POST
FOR PT. DU HOE, GRID 58619398

ELEVATION

PLAN

Typical open coastal battery construction as viewed by the Allies. This is Pointe du Hoc. NARA

shelter bunkers, three or four small concrete fortifications for machine guns and mortars (which the Germans called *Ringstände* and the Allies knew as Tobruks, having encountered similar structures in the Italian fortifications around Tobruk in Libya), and possibly one or two concrete positions for heavier weapons such as medium and heavy antitank guns or light artillery pieces, while the rest of the position consisted of simple trenches, dugouts, and open firing pits. Any buildings within the perimeter were usually prepared for defense, often with interior walls and roofs reinforced and windows and doors bricked up or sand-bagged closed and loop-holed. The whole position was normally prepared for all-round defense, surrounded by a heavy belt of barbed wire, perimeter minefields, and other obstacles.

ROMMEL'S BEACH-OBSTACLE PROGRAM

On 21 November 1943, Field Marshal Erwin Rommel left Villafranca airfield in Italy for a special assignment given to him by Adolf Hitler: Inspector General of Coastal Defenses.[1] His initial inspection tour began in Denmark on 2 December, working there until 14 December when he arrived at his new headquarters in the Château at Fontainebleau. He then continued his inspection, traveling along the Belgian and northern French coast until 19 January 1944, when he returned to his headquarters.

In the meantime, Rommel had been given another task: reconstituting his Army Group B headquarters in France and taking command of the German armies in France and Belgium. But he continued to fulfill his duties inspecting the coastal defenses as well, traveling to Brittany and southern France in February. His final report on the coastal defenses was not completed until 22 April 1944, but the recommendations and comments on the state of the defenses began to take effect much earlier.

The two principal shortfalls that Rommel found in his inspections were a lack of mines emplaced in sufficient quantities and a lack of density and strength in beach obstacles. Mine emplacement was limited

Element C on Omaha after the invasion. The piles of small smooth stones that make up the beach shingle in so many areas of Normandy can also be seen. JULIUS SHOULARS

Below: Germans install obstacles off a French beach, using hoses from the local fire engine. NARA

Below: Low tide on the invasion coast at Grandcamp-les-Bains shows German Teller mines affixed to posts and planted several hundred feet from the beach. This area was not assaulted on D-Day, but it accurately shows how the beams appeared to approaching craft. NARA

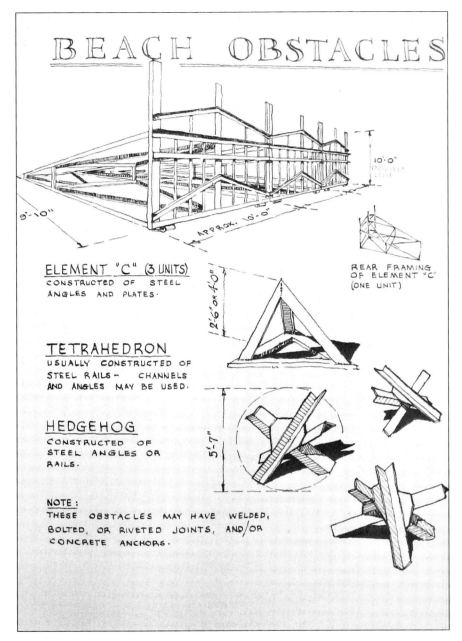

The most common German obstacle types as outlined in a secret Allied report from April 1944.
NARA

partly by the munitions production capacity of German industry, but beach obstacles were only limited by the ingenuity and amount of labor expended by the troops on the effort. Rommel exhorted his commanders and men to work nearly round-the-clock placing obstacles. (He rewarded a particularly industrious unit with the gift of an accordion.)

These obstacles included a multitude of purpose-built types, from the large Belgian gates (so-called since they originated as a Belgian fortification obstacle and looked vaguely like farmyard gates; also known as Element C for their French inventor, Colonel Cointet) to the smaller Czech hedgehogs (three or more steel rails crossed and bolted or welded together) and concrete or steel tetrahedrons. More improvised, but also effective, were the break beams, log tripod ramps designed so that landing craft would ride up on them and be capsized or

A German Teller antitank mine mounted in the typical fashion at Omaha. Note that the other poles that can be seen do not appear to have any mines mounted on them. The simple wire fastening rusted easily in the sea, and many fell off. NARA

A pile of Teller mines and artillery shells as they were dumped on Omaha by engineers after D-Day. NARA

Below: Unexploded German artillery shells wired together as extemporaneous mines. These and others were found and photographed by Colonel Reeves on King Beach, 6 June 1944. TNA

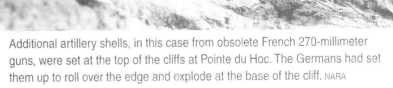

Additional artillery shells, in this case from obsolete French 270-millimeter guns, were set at the top of the cliffs at Pointe du Hoc. The Germans had set them up to roll over the edge and explode at the base of the cliff. NARA

holed. Possibly the simplest of all were the wooden poles, which were simply that—heavy wooden poles driven deep into the sand so that they protruded just a foot or so below water at high tide. After initial backbreaking work attempting to plant them using a pile-driver, the Germans began using a high-pressure water stream from a fire-engine pump and hose to burrow a hole to slide the poles into. The poles frequently had mines mounted on them, but it was expected that at the least, a landing craft driving onto them at any speed would have had a large hole put in it. Finally, a more regularly manufactured extemporaneous obstacle was the "nutcracker mine," which consisted of protruding wooden poles or steel I-beams hinged to a steel or concrete base; it was designed so that a landing craft striking and moving the beam would set off a fused artillery shell mounted on the base.

TYPES AND NUMBERS OF OBSTACLES FOUND ON THE BEACHES

Obstacle Type	Utah	Omaha	Sword	Gold
Ramps	12	450	76	112
Stakes	2,400	2,000	267	228
Hedgehogs	1,350	1,050	522	655
Tetrahedrons	150	0	0	45
Element C	0	200	46	66
Nutcracker Mines	?	?	?	10
Width (Yards)	9,600	7,500	3,000	2,700

WIDTH OF BEACHES AND NUMBERS OF OBSTACLES

Beach	Width (Yards)	Total Number of Obstacles
Jig (Gold)	3,200	1,413
King (Gold)	2,500	1,042
Mike (Juno)	2,220	915
Nan (Juno)	5,500	2,701
Queen (Sword)	3,000	911

DENSITY AND WEIGHT OF THE OBSTACLES

Area	Obstacles-per-Yard	Average Weight per Obstacle (lbs.)
Sword	0.30	217
Juno	0.47	340
Gold	0.43	394
Omaha	0.49	401
Utah	0.41	250
Average	0.42	320.4

Prior to the invasion, the Allies had constructed duplicates of the obstacles that had been observed in analysis of reconnaissance photos for use at the various assault centers in England. Shortly after the end of the war in Europe, British analysts investigating the German defenses attempted to gauge the density and strength of the actual obstacles that were encountered on each of the beaches. Perhaps the most interesting component of their analysis was the actual obstacle count given for some of the beaches, drawn from engineer reports compiled shortly after D-Day. The information is compiled in the tables above.[2]

In 1946, Maj. Gen. John D. Inglis, the chief engineer of the 21st Army Group, described the obstacles found on Juno, which was typical for all the beaches:

Extending across the whole of MIKE and NAN Sectors, hedgehog defences have been erected from 80 to 250 yards from the coast. These obstacles consist of three 6-inch angle irons, approximately 6 feet 6 inches long joined at their centres with gusset plates to form a double tripod. . . . Individual obstacles are placed 12–15 feet apart with 25–30 yards between rows. . . . All obstacles are below high water mark. From the location and distribution of these obstacles it seems that they are intended to be anti-craft rather than anti-vehicle.[3]

THE GERMAN DEFENSES

The German defenses in the sector assaulted by the Commonwealth forces on D-Day were part of the 716th Infantry Division, commanded by Lt. Gen. Wilhelm Richter.[4] His command sector, known as KVA Caen, was part of the 7th Army's LXXXIV Corps and extended from the Dives River (the boundary with the 15th Army) in the east to just east of Le Hamel (the boundary with the 352nd Infantry Division) in the west. The German defenses in the sector assaulted by the American forces on D-Day were also part of the LXXXIV Corps. Facing the assault on Omaha was the 352nd Infantry Division, commanded by Maj. Gen. Dietrich Kraiss. His command sector, known as KVA Bayeux, extended from the juncture with KVA Caen to the Merderet River. Facing the assault on Utah was the 709th Infantry Division, commanded by Lt. Gen. Karl-Wilhelm von Schlieben. Uniquely, the 709th "shared" a coastal defense zone with the 243rd Infantry Division farther north at Cherbourg, each commanding three sub-groups. The sector that was assaulted by the U.S. 4th Infantry Division was KVUGr Marcouf.

The Defenses in the Sword Area

The Sword area extended from the mouth of the Orne River, just east of Ouistreham, to just west of St. Aubin-sur-Mer, where it adjoined the Juno area. From east to west, it was further subdivided into Roger, Queen, Peter, and Oboe Beaches and extended a total of about 11,700 meters. The shoreline actually assaulted by the British 3rd Infantry Division covered a contiguous front from just east of Lion-sur-Mer to the western outskirts of the resort village of Riva Bella, a distance of about 1,800 meters that constituted Queen Beach. The beaches were gentle, backed by low dunes. Inland of Her-

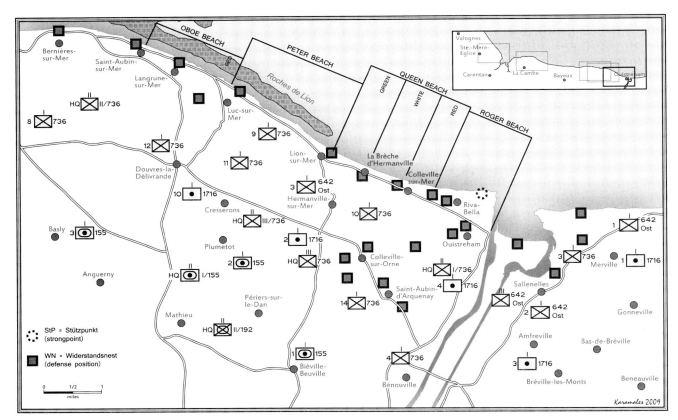

The defenses in the Sword area.

German pillbox construction with wing wall to protect the embrasure from naval fire. This one appears to mount a 50-millimeter or 75-millimeter gun. NARA

manville-la Brèche, there was an extensive area of marshy inundation and another between La Brèche and Riva Bella. Farther inland, the ground rose gently to a low ridge running generally from St. Aubin to Colleville.

The German defenses in this area were part of KVGr Riva Bella, with its sub-groups KVUGr Orne controlling StP 08 and seven resistance nests numbered roughly from east-to-west (WN 09, 10, 11, 12, 14, 15, and 15a) and KVUGr Lion controlling fourteen more positions (WN 16 and 17, Stp 18, WN 19, 20, 20a, 21, 22, 23, 23a, 24, 25, 26, and 27).* Not included in that count are the six resistance nests of KVUGr Orne that were on the eastern side of the river covering the beaches at Franceville Plage since they were effectively not part of the battle for Sword Beach on D-Day.

Overlooking Queen Beach from the east was StP 08, which was a critical objective in the early-morning landing plan. Consisting of several inter-

locking defensive positions, it was one of the larger and more powerful army coast artillery positions found on the Norman coast. Overall, it extended about 1,000 meters west of the Orne estuary and as much as 350 meters inland.

StP 08 itself contained six open gun pits for the 15.5-centimeter K418(f) guns** of the 1st Company of the 1260th Army Coastal Artillery Battalion. But because its positions were under construction on D-Day (the Germans were building massive concrete casemates to house four of the guns), the battery was actually in camouflaged field positions about 4,000 meters inland, east of Saint-Aubin-d'Arquenay. Otherwise, StP 08 included a 5-centimeter gun*** in an open pit guarding the approaches from the south, a casemated 5-centimeter gun facing east across the estuary, a casemate mounting an ex–French Army tank turret with a 3.7-centimeter gun and coaxial machine gun, and two 2-centimeter antiaircraft guns, one of which was mounted on the roof of the

---

* Apparently superstitious, the Germans did not designate any of the positions as WN 13.

** Many of the weapons utilized by the Germans in the fortifications were war booty. Most were Czech, French, Belgian, and Soviet guns. The Germans designated captured weapons for the country of their origin as "t" for Czech, "f" for French, and "r" for Russian.[5]

*** The 5-centimeter guns had been taken from obsolescent Panzer III tanks and mounted on simple utilitarian pivot mountings for coastal defense. A few were 5-centimeter PaK 38s. Most of the 7.5-centimeter guns were war booty; in many cases, they were 7.5-centimeter FK231(f), the famous "French 75." The 5-centimeter guns were still very effective as antitank guns at close range or when firing from the flank, and the 7.5-centimeter guns were highly effective as antiboat, antitank, and antipersonnel weapons.

massive seventeen-meter-tall coastal artillery fire-control bunker and the other on a slightly raised concrete emplacement in the southwest corner of the position.

Adjoining the western end of StP 08 and extending it about 200 meters farther west was WN 10, which was also known as StP Casino since it was partly built into the foundations of a demolished seaside casino. It included a casemated 7.5-centimeter FK38 field gun, an open position with a 5-centimeter gun, a 2-centimeter antiaircraft gun, and at least three machine-gun positions. A small minefield was also placed between WN 10 and Riva Bella.

The primary responsibility of the Riva Bella complex was in the hands of a single infantry company, the 2nd Company of the 736th Grenadier Regiment. All told, there were probably about 200 officers, NCOs, and enlisted men in the Riva Bella complex, not including the men of the absent 1st Company, 1260th Army Coastal Artillery Battalion. The position was enclosed by barbed-wire entanglements, and the southern landward approach was obstructed by an antitank ditch extending from the Orne inland about 500 meters.

West of Riva Bella, WN 18, WN 20, and WN 20a ran east to west from Hermanville-la Brèche to La Brèche. Along with WN 19, a smaller position inland, they were collectively known as StP La Brèche. The positions were directly opposite the planned British beaches that were known as Queen White and Queen Red. WN 20, located in the center of the complex, was given the code name Cod by the British. WN 18 at the eastern end of the position contained a powerful 8.8-centimeter PaK 43/41 antitank gun in a casemate, mounted in order to enfilade the entire beachfront eastward to the mouth of the Orne; two 5-centimeter guns in casemates covering the beach; another 5-centimeter gun in an open pit covering the inland approach; and at least three machine-gun posts. WN 20 had a second 8.8-centimeter PaK 43/41, mounted to enfilade the

beachfront to the west; a casemated 5-centimeter gun that could fire in a 180-degree arc from west to south to east but that was completely protected against gunfire from the sea (most of the casemated 5-centimeter mountings on the Commonwealth beaches were of this type); a casemated 4.7-centimeter gun (probably an ex-French PaK 183a); a 5-centimeter gun in an open pit; two 5-centimeter mortar positions; and at least six machine-gun positions, including one coaxial with a 3.7-centimeter gun in a an ex-French tank turret mounted on a beachfront casemate. Supporting the beachfront positions was WN 20a with three 8-centimeter mortar pits and at least one machine-gun post. The perimeter of StP La Brèche was surrounded by barbed-wire entanglements, but there were no antitank ditches or seawalls to block access inland. However, there was an extensive minefield extending from just west of WN 10 almost to WN 20 and scattered minefields that extended west of WN 20 all the way to Bernières.

The defense of the sector from La Brèche-d'Hermanville to Lion-sur-Mer—including WN 20, 20a, and 21 on the coast and WN 19 inland—was in the hands of two infantry companies, the 10th Company of the 736th Grenadier Regiment's 3rd Battalion and the unwilling soldiers of the 3rd Company of the 642nd East Battalion, which apparently occupied the small position at WN 19 on the road leading inland from the beaches to Colleville-sur-Orne.[*] Together, the two companies probably numbered fewer than 240 officers, NCOs, and enlisted men to defend about 3,800 meters of beach front.

To the west of Hermanville and Queen Beach, the coast began to rise to twelve-meter-high bluffs, with a rocky shallows and narrow beaches. Along the cliffs were three small positions—WN 21, with one 7.5-centimeter and two 5-centimeter guns and a 5-centimeter mortar at Lion-sur-Mer; WN 24, with two 5-centimeter guns and a mortar at Luc-sur-Mer; and WN 26, with a single 7.5-centimeter gun in an open field emplacement at Langrune-sur

---

[*] *Osttruppen*, or "eastern troops," were former Soviet prisoners of war who had been recruited into the German Army. They were mainly ethnic Poles, Ukrainians, Lithuanians, Latvians, Tatars, Azerbaijanis, and others, but also included ethnic Russians, all of whom the Germans believed would participate in their anti-Communist crusade. In practice, their combat effectiveness was spotty, although a few initially fought with some determination. They were usually interspersed with more reliable German troops to provide "stiffening."

Mer. Most of these positions had only limited visibility of the British landings and played little part in the morning's events on Sword, except for WN 21, code-named Trout, which was a troublesome early-morning objective for No. 41 Royal Marine Commando.

The western half of the Sword area (Oboe and Peter), extending from Saint Aubin to Lion-sur-Mer, was part of KVUGr Grand Luc. It included the previously mentioned positions at WN 24 and WN 26 as well as WN 22, WN 23, WN 23a, and WN 25, which were inland and manned by the rest of the 736th Grenadier Regiment's third battalion. The battalion headquarters was just outside of Cresserons. The 9th Company manned WN 24 and WN 26; the 11th Company was in reserve south of Luc-sur-Mer at WN 25; and the 12th Company was in reserve at WN 22 and WN 23a, just east of Douvres-la-Délivrande. Together, they probably numbered another 500 officers, NCOs, and enlisted men.

Inland, there was a second line of reserve and artillery positions. South of Riva Bella were WN 09, a simple infantry outpost that guarded the approaches to WN 14, code-named Sole, which was the headquarters of the 1st Battalion, 736th Grenadier Regiment, and WN 12, known as the "Chateau d'eau" to the Germans because of the prominent water tower nearby and code-named Daimler by the British. It contained an artillery battery (the 4th Company of the 1716th Artillery Regiment) that included four ex-French 15-centimeter s.F.H. 414 (f) howitzers, as well as a 5-centimeter mortar and two 2-centimeter Flak guns. Farther south was WN 11, code-named Rover, which guarded the approaches to the Bénouville bridges across the Caen Canal and Orne River from any attacker approaching them from the beaches. In addition to the artillerymen and the battalion headquarters personnel, this area was occupied by the 736th's 4th Company, which was nominally the battalion reserve for the sector west of the Orne River and Caen Canal; it probably had about 350 officers, NCOs, and enlisted men.

Farther to the southwest, at Saint Aubin-d'Arquenay on the northern outskirts of Caen, were two positions, WN 15 and WN 15a, which appear primarily to have provided troop billeting for miscellaneous divisional units. As noted earlier, the 1st

Company of the 1260th Army Coastal Artillery Battalion was also placed there temporarily while its casemates were being constructed in the Riva Bella position. Just to the northwest at Colleville-sur-Orne were WN 16 and WN 17, which formed StP Höhe. WN 16, code-named Morris, was another artillery battery position, with four ex-Czech 10-centimeter le.F.H. 14/19(t) light field howitzers of the 2nd Company of the 1716th Artillery Regiment, and also an artillery battalion headquarters (the 1st Battalion, 1716th Artillery Regiment). WN 17, code-named Hillman by the British, was the headquarters of the 736th Grenadier Regiment, which commanded KVGr Riva Bella. WN 17 mounted two antitank guns (probably 4.7 or 5 centimeters), and a number of machine-gun positions. These positions probably included another 500 officers, NCOs, and enlisted men.

Altogether, the German forces immediately available in the sector probably totaled fewer than 1,800 officers, NCOs, and enlisted men. In addition to the armament of the fixed positions, they were probably equipped with at least another eighty-three machine guns, six 8-centimeter mortars, and six 5-centimeter mortars.[6] Most of the inland strongpoints were protected by associated minefields. There were various-size fields surrounding WN 12, WN 14, and WN 17 and an extensive field around WN 16.

The Defenses in the Juno Area

The Juno area encompassed a front from St. Aubin-sur-Mer, where it adjoined the Sword area, to Ruisseau de La Provence, just east of Ver-sur-Mer, where it adjoined the Gold area. From east to west, it was further divided into Nan, Mike, and Love Beaches, and extended an overall distance of just under 9,000 meters. Two beaches, Nan and Mike, were actually assaulted, one on either side of the mouth of the Seulles River at Courseulles. To the east, Nan Beach extended for about 1,900 meters between Berniéres-sur-Mer and Saint Aubin-sur-Mer while, to the west, Mike Beach extended about 2,200 meters opposite Graye-sur-Mer. The German defenses here were also part of the 716th Infantry Division and KVGr Courseulles, with KVUGr Seulles commanding seven resistance nests (WN 27, WN 28, WN 28a, 28b, WN 29, WN 30, WN 31, and WN 33a).

Nan Beach faced four rather small positions: WN 27 at Saint Aubin, WN 28 and WN 28b at Berniéres, and WN 29 at Courseulles. WN 27 had a single 5-centimeter gun in a Typ SK casemate, apparently two 8-centimeter mortars, and two or three machine-gun positions. There was little in the way of concrete reinforcement, but building openings had been bricked up and loop-holed for defense.[7] WN 28 was more substantial and included a 7.5-centimeter PaK 40 antitank gun in a casemate, a pillbox mounting an ex–French Army tank turret with a 3.7-centimeter gun and coaxial machine gun, a partly completed casemate mounting an aging World War I–era MG 08/15 machine gun, and an 8-centimeter mortar. It was protected by the typical extensive barbed-wire entanglements, and the landward side was partially enclosed by a strong antitank ditch and a number of substantial minefields. Just to the west, WN 28b was a field fortification, with a 5-centimeter PaK 38 antitank gun mounted in a log and sandbag emplacement and a similar but smaller position for a machine gun. Scattered in positions throughout the village were at least another five machine-gun position and an 8-centimeter mortar pit. WN 29 (Courseulles East) was the most substantial position the Canadians faced on Nan Beach. It included an 8.8-centimeter PaK 43/41 antitank gun, a German 7.5-centimeter FK 16 n.A. field gun, and an ex–French 7.5cm FK 231 (f) field gun—all mounted in concrete casemates facing east and sweeping the entire beachfront from Courseulles to Saint Aubin. In addition, there was a 5-centimeter gun in an open pit, a pillbox mounting an ex–French Army tank turret with a 3.7-centimeter gun and coaxial machine gun, three 5-centimeter mortar emplacements, and at least five machine guns. Inland was a substantial antitank ditch. In the center of Courseulles was WN 30 whose armament is uncertain, but which probably consisted of a few machine guns and possibly a 5-centimeter mortar. Another obstacle found intermittently in this sector was a seawall, built by the French before the war to control erosion, extending across most of Nan Beach from Saint Aubin to Courseulles. It varied

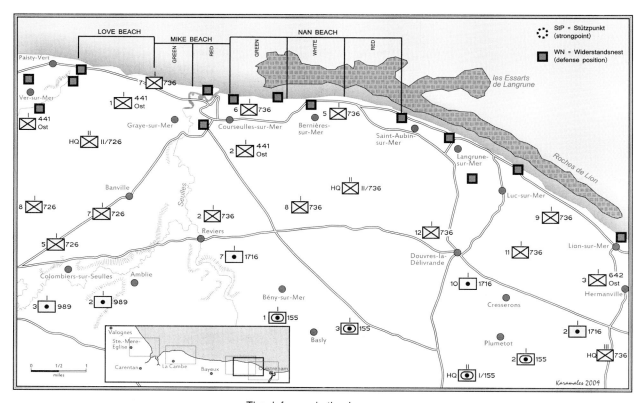

The defenses in the Juno area.

The view of the beach from the gun embrasure of the 88-millimeter gun position at WN 29. NATIONAL ARCHIVES CANADA

from six to ten feet in height and in some spots severely limited access inland.[8]

The Canadians assaulting Mike Beach faced just two German positions, but WN 31 (Courseulles West) was nearly as strong as its partner across the estuary. It mounted another 7.5-centimeter FK 16 n.A. field gun in a flanking casemate facing westwards, a 5-centimeter gun in a casemate and another in an open pit emplacement at the western end of the position and a second in a double-embrasure casemate that could fire east or west at the eastern end of the position overlooking the harbor. They were supported by at least six machine guns and two 5-centimeter mortars. Access to the strongpoint from landward was almost entirely blocked by a bend in the River Seulle, and as usual, extensive barbed-wire entanglements obstructed it. On the other hand, WN 33a, adjoining it, consisted mostly of field fortifications that extended from the outskirts of Graye, west to La Riviere. It too was surrounded by barbed-wire, and there were extensive minefields covering the landward side.

Inland near Tailleville was WN 23, which was the headquarters of the 2nd Battalion of the 736th Grenadier Regiment, which commanded KVUGr

Seulles. A few hundred meters to the west was a small antiaircraft gun position, with six ex-French 7.5-centimeter antiaircraft guns (probably Canon de 7.5 cm D.C.A. Mle 1938), manned by personnel of the 3rd (Flak) Company of the 716th Tank Destroyer Battalion. (Curiously, the Canadians later reported finding only five guns.[9]) Nearby was a multiple rocket launcher battery, consisting of about twenty 32-centimeter *Wurfgerät*, a simple, fixed, rack-type launcher that doubled as its packing crate and contained four of the large demolition rockets. Also scattered in positions covering the exits from the beaches were the static guns of the 2nd Company, 716th Tank Destroyer Battalion, headquartered at Reviers. It had three 8.8-centimeter PaK 43/41 antitank guns on the ridge south of Berniéres, three 7.5-centimeter PaK 40 antitank guns slightly to the northwest overlooking Courseulles, another three 7.5-centimeter PaK 40 west of the Seulle overlooking Graye, and finally one 7.5-centimeter PaK 40 overlooking the eastern and two the western beach exits at La Rivière.

The troops defending KVUGr Seulles included all of the 736th Grenadier Regiment's 2nd Battalion, under Captain Deptolla. The sector from Saint Aubin to Bernières was held by the 5th Company in WN 17, 28, and 28b; StP Courseulles (WN 29 and 30) was held by the 6th Company; and Graye-sur-Mer and La Rivière (WN 31 and 33a) were held by the 7th Company. In reserve was the 8th Company around Tailleville and the eastern troops of the 2nd Company of the 441st East Battalion at Reviers. Artillery support for the sector was provided by two batteries from the 1716th Artillery Regiment: the 7th Company at WN 28a near Bény-sur-Mer with four 10-centimeter le.F.H. 14/19(t) and the 10th Company with four 15-centimeter s.F.H. 414(f) near Douvres in a field position. Altogether, with the gun crews of the 716th Tank Destroyer Battalion's 2nd Company, they may have numbered about 1,100 officers, NCOs, and men and were equipped with thirty-three machine guns, two 5-centimeter mortars, and two 8-centimeter mortars in addition to those in the fixed defenses.

The last position in the area was not actually under army control; rather, it was a *Luftwaffe* radar station complex that straddled the Beny-sur-

Mer–Douvres-la-Délivrande road just west of Douvres and south of Tailleville. It consisted of two positions, a smaller one mounting a single radar aerial north of the road protected by three 2-centimeter Flak guns and four machine-gun positions. The larger position south of the road mounted four more radar aerials, a 7.5-centimeter gun, five 5-centimeter guns, three 2-centimeter antiaircraft guns, eight machine guns, and a 5-centimeter mortar. The massive fortified position was ringed by barbed wire and some of the densest minefields in the area and was manned by about 230 officers, NCOs, and men of the 8th Company of the 53rd *Luftwaffe* Signal Regiment.

The Germans had emplaced a large number of mines in the area. In addition to those strung along the cliffs from WN 21 to Berniéres and those around the radar station, there were additional fields scattered between Berniéres and Courseulles.

The Defenses in the Gold Area

The Gold area encompassed a front from Ruisseau de La Provence, where it adjoined the Juno area, to Port-en-Bessin, where it adjoined the Omaha area. From east to west, it was further divided into King, Jig, Item, and How Beaches and extended an overall distance of 17,900 meters. The area actually assaulted extended from slightly west of Le Hamel to Grey-sur-Mer, a distance of about 6,400 meters, covering King and Jig Beaches. The beaches were gentle and were backed by large dunes in places. Inland the ground rose to a low ridge, running from La Rivière to Crépon. However, along the western edge of the landing zone the slope rises more abruptly to the plateau around Arromanches.

The German defenses facing King and Jig included the second half of KVGr Courseulles, KVUGr Meuvaines, with seven resistance nests from east to west (WN 32, 33, 34, 35, 35a, 35b, and 36) and three others along the beach (WN 37, 38, and 39), as well as three small positions inland (WN 40, 40a, and 40b), defended by elements of the neighboring 352nd Infantry Division on the extreme western edge of Jig.

Of these, a total of five (WN 33, 34, 35, 36, and 37) could observe and bring direct fire on Jig and King, where the assault took place. WN 33 had an

The 88-millimeter gun bunker at WN 29 east of the Seulles River in Courseulles. NATIONAL ARCHIVES CANADA

8.8-centimeter PaK 43/41 antitank gun in a casemate sited to fire in enfilade west along the beach, a 5-centimeter gun in a Typ SK casemate, two mortar positions, and two machine-gun posts. WN 34 stood on a bluff with the Mont Fleury lighthouse, overlooking the beaches. It mounted a 5-centimeter gun in an open emplacement, along with an unknown number of machine-gun positions. Below it, on the beach, WN 35 at Hable de Heurlot had another 5-centimeter gun in a Typ SK casemate and three machine guns. WN 36 near Asnelles was at the Cabane des douanes (the Custom Hut) and included a 5-centimeter gun in an open pit emplacement, a 3.7-centimeter antitank gun, and three machine-gun positions. WN 37, on the beachfront at Le Hamel, mounted a 7.5-centimeter gun (possibly Czech) and a 5-centimeter gun in a casemate, both enfilading the beach eastward, and at least five machine-gun positions.[10]

There were three artillery batteries supporting those positions: the 6th Company of the 1716th Artillery Regiment at WN 32 (the Mare Fontaine Battery) with four 10-centimeter le.F.H. 14/19(t); the 3rd Company of the 1260th Army Coastal

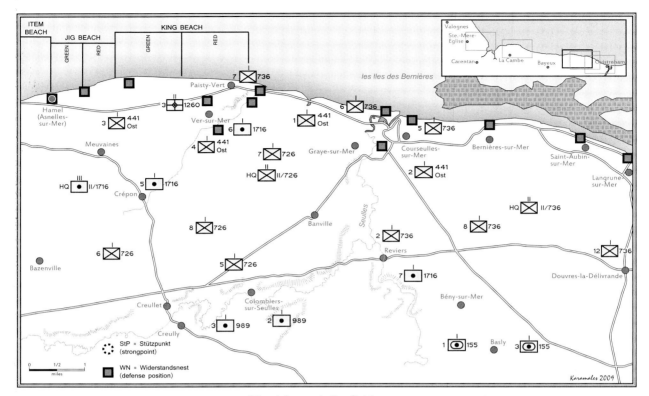

The defenses in the Gold area.

Artillery Regiment at WN 35a (the Mont Fleury Battery) with four ex-Soviet 12.2-centimeter K390(r); and the 5th Company of the 1716th Artillery Regiment at WN 35b (the Crépon Battery) with four 10-centimeter le.F.H. 14/19(t).

Farther to the west, WN 38 and 39 at St. Come-de-Fresne mounted two 7.5-centimeter FK 231(f), two 5-centimeter PaK, and one 5-centimeter mortar, with perhaps as many as eight machine guns. The two 5-centimeter PaK at WN 38 (Le Hamel West) had a limited field of fire partly covering the western edge of WN 37 (Le Hamel East), but it and WN 39 were primarily designed to defend the seaward and eastern landward approaches to the harbor at Arromanches.

A great weakness to the sector was the lack of reliable infantry to defend it. Located with the artillery at WN 35b near Crépon was a headquarters unit of the 441st East Battalion, which had four infantry companies. Of them, the 2nd, based at Reviers, was not engaged at Gold and spent D-Day

fighting the Canadians at June. The 1st and 3rd made up the garrison of WN 33, 34, 35, and 36, "stiffened" by elements from the 7th Company of the 726th Grenadier Regiment. Adjoining them were the elements of the 7th that occupied WN 33a at La Riviere, while the rest of the company was in field fortifications in Graye-sur-Mer. Finally, the 4th Company of the 441st East Battalion occupied field fortifications along the low ridge overlooking Ver-sur-Mer.

The second infantry element defending in the Gold sector was the 2nd Battalion of the 726th Grenadier Regiment. The headquarters and 7th Company were at Sainte-Croix-sur-Mer, with the 7th providing "stiffening" for the eastern troops in the resistance nest. The 6th Company, based at Bazenville, occupied WN 36 and 38, while the 5th and 8th Companies formed a reserve for KVGr Courseulles at Creully about five kilometers inland.

The last infantry elements on Gold were parts of the 916th Grenadier Regiment of the 352nd

Infantry Division, which was present in the form of a single company occupying WN 37 (Le Hamel East), 38 (Le Hamel West), and 39. The rest of the battalion was deployed to the west between Arromanches and Le Hamel (the regimental and divisional boundary ran through Le Hamel (inclusive of the 916th Grenadier Regiment and 352nd Infantry Division) and Bazenville (inclusive of the 726th Grenadier Regiment and 716th Infantry Division), occupying WN 40, 40a, and 40b.

The defenders of the positions assaulted at Gold (WN 33, 33a, 35, 36, and 37) consisted of the 6th and 7th Companies of the 726th Grenadier Regiment; the 1st, 3rd, and 4th Companies of the 441st East Battalion; and a platoon of the 2nd Battalion of the 916th Grenadier Regiment—a total of about five and a third companies of infantry. Another two infantry companies, three artillery batteries, and two battalion headquarters companies supported them. All told, these may have amounted to about 1,500 men equipped with approximately fifty-nine machine guns and nine 5-centimeter and nine 8-centimeter mortars in addition to those weapons in the fixed positions.

Minefields were fairly extensively used by the Germans in the Gold area in an attempt to compensate for the lack of natural barriers. One ran in an almost continuous belt from Courseulles to La Rivière and then on to Le Hamel. WN 34 and 35, Le Hamel, and Asnelles were also heavily mined.

German Reserves for KVA Caen

In theory, the German forces defending the beaches at Sword, Juno, and Gold had available some highly effective mobile forces that were intended to react and counterattack an invader coming across the beaches.

Inland from Sword, the first were the few fully mobile elements of the 716th Infantry Division, including a mixed force of combat engineers (2nd Company of the 716th Engineer Battalion), eight self-propelled 2-centimeter antiaircraft guns of the 3rd Company, 716th Tank Destroyer Battalion, at Anisy (one platoon of the battery was on the eastern side of the Orne with an additional four guns), and the division mobile antitank element, ten self-propelled antitank guns (7.5-centimeter s.PaK Sfl. auf Lorraine Schlepper) with the headquarters and 1st

Company of the 716th Tank Destroyer Battalion at Biéville.

The second and much more powerful element available for Sword was a battalion of motorized infantry (the 2nd Battalion of the 192nd Panzer Grenadier Regiment) from the 21st Panzer Division and its supporting artillery from the 1st Battalion, 155th Panzer Artillery Regiment. The infantry battalion was headquartered at Le Mesnil with its various elements dispersed at Villons-les-Buissons, the Château de la Londe (northeast of Epron), Buron, Périers-sur-le-Dan (overlooking Hermanville-sur-Mer), and Cairon. The headquarters of the supporting artillery battalion was at Mathieu under Captain Feckler, with the 1st Battery at Beuville with four ex-Soviet 12.2-centimeter le.FH 396(r) howitzers; the 2nd Battery at Périers-sur-le-Dan, also with four 12.2-centimeter le.FH 396(r); and the 3rd Battery at Colomby-sur-Thaon with four German 10-centimeter sK18 guns. Also in support was an antitank platoon from the 5th Company of the 200th Tank Destroyer Battalion with four 8.8-centimeter PaK 43/41 antitank guns.

Farther west and in positions that could support Sword, Juno, or Gold was most of the rest of the 200th Tank Destroyer Battalion. The 1st Company and its headquarters were at Le Fresne-Camilly and had one platoon of four more 8.8-centimeter PaK 43/41 guns each at Sainte-Croix-Grand-Tonne (1st Platoon), Château de Mesnil-Patry (2nd Platoon), and Basly (3rd Platoon). At Creully was the 3rd (Mototorized) Company of the 21st Panzer Division's engineer battalion, the 220th Panzer Engineer Battalion. Finally, powerful additional artillery support was provided by an attached partly motorized heavy artillery battalion, the 989th Heavy Artillery Battalion, with its headquarters at Reviers and three batteries each of four 12.2-centimeter s.F.H. 396(r) at Basly (1st Battery.), Amblie (2nd Battery), and Creully (3rd Battery).

On D-Day, however, the German reaction was sluggish, and few of these reserve forces had an influence on the actions of the 1st Assault Brigade on the beaches.

The Defenses in the Omaha Area

The Omaha area encompassed a front from Port-en-Bessin, where it adjoined the Gold area, to the

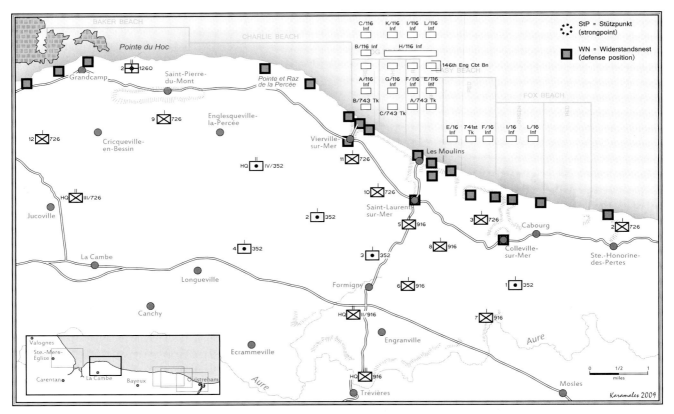

The defenses in the Omaha area.

mouth of the Vire River, where it adjoined the Utah area.★ From east to west, it was further divided into George, Fox, Easy, Dog, Charlie, Baker, and Able Beaches and extended a total of about 29,200 meters. The area actually assaulted extended from just west of St. Honorine-des-Pertes to just west of Pointe de la Percée, a distance of about 6,800 meters, covering parts of Fox, Easy, Dog, and Charlie Beaches. The German defenses facing that sector included fourteen resistance nests (WN 60, 61, 62, 63, 64, 65, 66, 67, 68, 69, 70, 71, 72, and 73). A prominent feature of the area was the high bluffs that overlooked the beaches. East of Colleville and west of Vierville, these bluffs became virtual cliffs that came right down to the sea except for a thin strip of

beach at low tide. They were impassable for vehicles and heavy equipment. However, the bluffs for the most part were impassable to even tracked vehicles, although men on foot could get up them with some effort. Otherwise, the only routes available for vehicle movement were the five valleys that were called "draws" in the American V Corps plans.

Farthest east was a powerful German strongpoint. It covered Fox, the eastern edge of Easy Red, and two valleys that led inland from the beach, the Number 5 (F-1) Draw—really little better than a footpath—and the Colleville (E-3) Draw, which was suitable for vehicles and led to Colleville-sur-Mer. The positions included WN 60, with two 7.5-centimeter FK 231(f)'s (one casemated and the other in

---

★ Between the Gold and Omaha landing sites were WN 40, 41, 42, 43, 44, and 45, which constituted StP Arromanches and protected that small port; WN 46, 47, 48, 49, 50, 51, and 52, which defended the Longues plateau and the coast artillery battery there; and WN 53, 54, 55, 56, 57, 58, and 59, which constituted StP Port-en-Bessin and protected that small port. They were not attacked directly on D-Day.

The antitank ditch in front of WN 62 blocking the E-3 Draw (Colleville Exit). NARA

Below: Another common position was a standard field fortification, in this case another 5-centimeter KwK. It is dug into the side of the bluff in WN 62, with little overhead cover, but it was well camouflaged. This gun had excellent visibility and fields of fire onto Fox Green and Fox Red and caused considerable havoc to the troops landing there. NARA

an open field emplacement), a casemate guarding the landward approach armed with an ex–French Army tank turret with a 3.7-centimeter gun and coaxial machine gun, three mortars, and a 2-centimeter anti-aircraft gun. Next was WN 61 with an 8.8-centimeter PaK 43/41 in a casemate flanking the entire beachfront from east to west, two 5-centimeter guns in open gun pits, another casemate-mounted ex–French Army tank turret with 3.7-centimeter gun and machine gun, and at least three machine-gun positions. WN 62 included two 7.5-centimeter FK 235 (b)'s mounted in casemates that flanked the beach to the west, two 5-centimeter guns covering the eastward approaches, two mortars, and five machine guns. Inland at Colleville-sur-Mer was a small position for the company command post.

In addition to the array of beach obstacles, the area between WN 60 and WN 61 leading to the

Number 5 Draw was blocked by three ruined seaside houses and a dense mixed antitank and antipersonnel minefield, while the Colleville Draw was blocked by an antitank ditch and a thin belt of antitank mines. Antipersonnel mines were scattered heavily along the slopes south of WN 61.

Next, to the west, were the positions covering Easy Red, Easy Green, Dog Red, the St. Laurent (E-1) Draw, and the Les Moulins (D-3) Draw, both leading inland to St. Laurent-sur-Mer. On the east side of the St. Laurent Draw was WN 64, which was only partially completed, with a 7.62-centimeter le.K.H. 290(r) light gun howitzer in an unfinished casemate facing west and a 2-centimeter antiaircraft gun. Otherwise, its only real defense was a trenchline overlooking the beach. On the opposite side of the St. Laurent Draw was WN 65, which was "two-tiered" with an open gun pit on the bluff with a 3.7-centimeter antitank gun, and a casemated 5-centimeter gun, a 5-centimeter gun in an open pit, and two mortars. Inland was a field fortification with a 7.5-centimeter PaK 40 antitank gun covering the exit from the draw.

On the east side of the Les Moulins Draw was WN 66, with a casemate-mounted ex–French tank turret with 3.7-centimeter and machine gun on the bluff covering the landward approach, a partially completed machine-gun casemate covering the draw,

One of the partly completed casemates at WN 64. NARA

The 50-millimeter gun bunker at WN 65. NARA

and a lower complex that was still under construction. The lower area included a 5-centimeter antitank gun in an open pit and two mortar pits. Opposite it was WN 68, another "two-tiered" posi-

tion with a 4.7-centimeter PaK 181(f) in an open pit and a machine-gun casemate that covered the draw from the bluff. On the beach was a 5-centimeter gun in an open pit and two 7.5-centimeter turreted guns mounted on casemates that had been taken from a tank prototype, the VK3001, that had never been put into full production. WN 67 was at the head of the Moulins Draw, where it split into two narrower valleys. It was a simple position designed to accommodate the firing position of a multiple rocket launcher battery and was similar to that near Tailleville in WN 23 on Juno. It was armed with thirty-eight 32-centimeter *Wurfgerät*.[11] WN 69, also inland near St. Laurent-sur-Mer, was an unimproved field fortification with a single 2-centimeter antiaircraft gun.

The St. Laurent Draw was blocked by antitank and antipersonnel mines, but apparently of no great density. The Les Moulins Draw, though, was sealed by a strong antitank ditch on the beach and what appeared to be a massive, steel-reinforced concrete antitank wall farther south. However, the wall was

One of the partly completed casemates at WN 66 displays the typical German construction methods. NARA

Below: One of the prototype tank turrets mounted on a bunker at WN 68. NARA

actually something of a sham: it had been quickly poured without reinforcements of any kind and was actually very weak. It was easily cleared with a few bulldozer passes after the defenses had been subdued on the evening of D-Day, although the American planners were not aware of that before the fact.

The final group of positions covered Dog White, Dog Green, Charlie Red, and the Vierville (D-1) Draw, leading inland to Vierville-sur-Mer. WN 70 was on the bluffs between the St. Laurent and Vierville Draw. It included a 7.5-centimeter FK 17(t) in a casemate on the bluff sited to fire eastward along the beachfront, a 7.5-centimeter gun of unknown type in an open pit facing northwest, two mortars, five casemated machine-gun positions, and

a 2-centimeter antiaircraft gun. Farther west, WN 71 was on the bluff overlooking the Vierville Draw. It does not appear to have contained any heavy anti-tank guns, but it had at least nine machine-gun positions in casemates, Tobruk mounts and trenches that could sweep the beaches, and two mortars. Across from it was WN 72 with a casemated 8.8-centimeter PaK 43/41 that enfiladed the beach to the east. Attached to the casemate was a massive, steel-reinforced concrete antitank wall that closed vehicle access to the road leading from the beach into Vierville. The position also had a 7.5-centimeter PaK 97/38 (the barrel of a French 75-millimeter Mle 1897 gun mounted on the carriage of a German 5-centimeter PaK 38[12]) in an open pit, a 5-centimeter gun in a double-embrasure casemate farther west that could fire either to the east or west, and five machine guns. WN 73 was placed on the cliffs overlooking the Vierville Draw. Its casemated 7.5-centimeter FK 23(f) could fire the length of the entire beach eastward to the Colleville Draw. It was protected by at least eight machine-gun positions and three mortars and was accessible only from seaward via a small crescent-shaped beach and a narrow footpath. Finally, the *Luftwaffe* radar station at WN 74 included a 7.5-centimeter Czech field gun that

Above: This photo was taken from the 5-centimeter double-embrasure casemate of WN 72 looking east at the juncture of Charlie and Dog Green Beaches. In the foreground is the massive casemate for the 88-centimeter gun. NARA

The double-embrasure casemate of WN72 looking west at the steep bluffs at the Vierville exit. NARA

could bear on the extreme western edge of Charlie and Dog Beaches.

All of the positions were protected by masses of barbed wire, and the walking paths leading up the bluffs inland were liberally laced with antipersonnel mines and blocked by more barbed wire. However, except for the cases noted, it does not appear that a large number of mines were emplaced around the positions. The usual estimate is that about 17,000 were used between Colleville and Vierville, which is not a significant density for such an extended front.[13] In addition to the antitank ditches, much of the paved coast road extending from Vierville to Les Moulins was paralleled by another antitank ditch, while the road itself was obstructed in a number of places by transverse ditches.

However, in addition to those man-made obstacles, the Germans could also depend on a number of terrain features other than to the bluffs that acted as natural obstacles. First, the beachfront along Omaha was comprised mostly of shingle, masses of small rounded stones piled up on the beach by wave action. The shingle provided little traction and proved difficult for men as well as wheeled and tracked vehicles to move through. Second, a strong masonry seawall extended the entire length of the western half of the beach, from a point just west of Les Moulins all the way to the cliffs west of WN 73. It varied from four to eight feet high through most of its length and was even higher west of Vierville. Third, inland from the beach road was a low-lying, flat, sandy marshland that at its widest, between Les

The 75-millimeter Czech gun at WN 74, Pointe de la Percée. This is a standard field fortification and is well camouflaged.
STUART BRANDELCOLLECTION/THOMAS LANE

Below: This is the most common type of German gun position encountered by the Allies on D-Day. It is a 5-centimeter KwK that has been converted into a field piece by mounting it on a simple ring mount in an open concrete pit. The position offers some protection from small-arms fire but is otherwise completely open. This one was at the base of the bluff at WN 66 and is looking onto Easy Red and Dog Green.
NARA

Moulins and Colleville, extended about 200 yards to the base of the bluffs, although it was much narrower at either end of the beach.

All of the resistance nests on Omaha—except three, WN 63, 67, and 69—could engage targets on the beach with direct fire. In addition to the weapons identified in the fixed positions, the defenders' armament included one additional mortar (in total there were seventeen mortars, at least two of which were 8 centimeters while the others were 5 centimeters), another forty-eight machine guns, and the *Wurfgerät*.[14] Four artillery batteries from the 1st and 4th Battalions of the 352nd Artillery Regiment, with one more at Pointe du Hoc, backed the position up with a total of twelve 10.5-centimeter le.F.H., four 15-centimeter s.F.H., and five 15.5-centimeter K 418(f) guns.

Curiously enough, there is no mention in the historical record of how the sector of the 352nd Infantry Division (KVA Bayeux) was divided into KVGr's or KVUGr's. Instead, when the 352nd moved up on 15 March to take command of the former KVGr Bayeux, the previous KVUGr's were apparently renamed as regimental sectors, using the regimental designations or the regimental commanders names. The eastern sector was that of the 726th Grenadier Regiment (attached from the 716th Infantry Division) and was also known as *Kampfgruppe* (combat group, usually abbreviated KG) Korfes for regimental commander Col. Walter Korfes. The center sector was that of the 916th Grenadier Regiment and was also known as KG Goth for regimental commander Col. Ernst Goth. The western sector was that of the 714th Grenadier Regiment and was also known as KG Heyna for regimental commander Lt. Col. Ernst Heyna.[15]

The American assault primarily struck in the sector of KG Goth, although it also overlapped slightly the extreme left (western) edge of the zone of KG Korfes. Infantry units in the defenses included the 3rd Company of the 726th Grenadier Regiment based at Colleville-sur-Mer and occupying WN 60, 61, and 62. Next in line to the west, the 10th Company of the 726th Grenadier Regiment occupied WN 64, 65, 66, and 68. Then the 11th Company, based at Vierville, occupied WN 70, 71, 72, and 73. The headquarters of the 726th's 1st Battalion was at Maisons; that of the 726th's 3rd Battalion was at Chateau du Jucoville; and that of the 916th Grenadier Regiment's 2nd Battalion was at Formigny. The 916th's 5th (based at St. Laurent-sur-Mer) and 8th (based at Colleville-sur-Mer) Companies "stiffened" the 726th's 3rd, 10th, and 11th Companies in the coastal positions.

In addition, possible immediate reserves included the 726th's 9th Company at Château Englesqueville, the 916th's 6th Company at Formigny, and the 916th's 7th Comapny at Surrain, under control of the headquarters of the 916th's 2nd Battalion. They constituted the division reserve. Altogether, five infantry companies occupied the positions, supported by another three infantry companies in reserve and four artillery batteries—a total of about 2,440 officers, NCOs, and men.

German Reserves for KVA Bayeux

Additional German reserves were available in the sector of the 352nd Infantry Division, but they constituted the reserve of the LXXXIV Corps and were not under the immediate control of the divisional commander, Maj. Gen. Dietrich Kraiss. That reserve

The concrete antitank wall that closed the St. Laurent Draw after it was demolished on D-Day. Note the complete absence of steel reinforcing rods in the construction. STUART BRANDEL COLLECTION/THOMAS LANE

included the 915th Grenadier Regiment, with the 1st Battalion and regimental elements motorized with requisitioned French civilian trucks and the 2nd Battalion mounted on bicycles. Attached to the regiment was the divisional "light" infantry battalion, the 352nd Fusilier Battalion, also mounted on bicycles, and the 352nd Tank Destroyer Battalion, including its 1st Company with fourteen self-propelled 7.5-centimeter PaK's and its 2nd Company with ten assault guns. All told, they probably numbered about 3,600 officers and men. The powerful reserve, known as KG Meyer after the commander of the 915th Grenadier Regiment, Lt. Col. Karl Meyer, was deployed south and southeast of Bayeux, within easy marching distance of either Gold or Omaha.

The Defenses in the Utah Area

The Utah area encompassed a front from the mouth of the Vire River, where it adjoined the Omaha area, to Quinéville. From south to north, it was further divided into William, Victor, Uncle, Tare, Sugar, Roger, Queen, and Peter Beaches and extended a distance of about 20,200 meters. As originally intended, the beaches that were to be assaulted, Uncle Red and Tare Green, lay between the tiny seafront villages of La Madeleine and Les Dunes-de-Varreville, a distance of about 1,900 meters. However, as will be seen, the beach that was actually landed upon was not the one that was planned; the assault troops landed about 1,800 meters south of the planned location, well south of La Madeleine. Thus, for clarity, all discussion of the German defenses is based upon where the troops actually landed, rather than where it was planned they land.

The entire eastern shore of the Cotentin Peninsula was flat and featureless. The beaches were extraordinarily flat and were backed by low dunes that averaged twelve to sixteen feet in height. Inland, the Germans had reversed the ancient system of drainage canals and locks meant to allow runoff from the pastureland to the sea and had dammed some of the streams running to the beach. The result was extensive areas of marshy inundation that extended almost uninterruptedly from Pouppeville to Quineville behind the beaches and running as much as 1,500 to 3,000 meters inland. The inundations left just a few passable routes inland from the beaches. Four of these routes were critical to the VII Corps plan and were designated, from south to north, Exit 1, running from the lateral beach road through Pouppeville; Exit 2, running from La Grand Dune to Houdienville and St., Marie-du-Mont; Exit 3, from le Mesnilde to Audouville-la-Hubert; and Exit 4, from les Dunes-de-Varreville to St. Martin-de-Varreville.

The German defenses were part of KVUGr Marcouf. Facing the American forces where they actually landed were just three resistance nests—WN 4 (La Dune), WN 5 (La Grand Dune), and WN 7 (La Madeleine). They were garrisoned by elements of the 709th Infantry Division: the 2nd and 3rd Companies of the 919th Grenadier Regiment, under the command of 1st Lietuenant Matz, who had his company command post in WN 7. Of the three, only WN 5 was heavily armed, with a casemated 5-centimeter gun and two 5-centimeter guns and one 4.7-centimeter PaK 183a(f) antitank gun in open

pits. It also contained at least five machine guns, including one in an ex–French Army tank turret with a 37-millimeter gun, an 8-centimeter mortar, and—uniquely—a dozen Goliath remote-controlled, tracked demolitions carriers. The garrison at WN 5 totaled about twenty-five officers and men, under Lt. Artur Jahnke. The other positions were small clusters of bombproof concrete shelters and trenches; each had a few machine guns as their heaviest weapons.

South of the left boundary of the actual landing, and barely within extreme small-arms range, was WN 3 (Beau Guillot), also garrisoned by elements of the 2nd Company of the 919th, under the command of Lieutenant Rohweder. The other positions farther south held by that company—WN 1 (Le Grand Vey); WN 2 (Pouppeville), the command post for the 2nd Company; and WN 2a—were all out of sight and range of the landing.

North of the actual landing site, where it had been intended to land, were actually the strongest

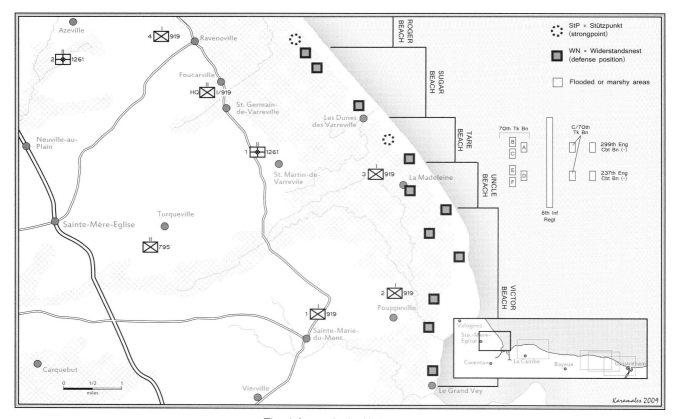

The defenses in the Utah area.

German defenses in the sector. They were also garrisoned by the 3rd Company and consisted of a powerful complex, WN 8 and StP 9 at Audouville-la-Hubert and WN 10 at Les Dunes-de-Varreville. However, only WN 8 had line of sight on the actual landings and was again barely within range.

Artillery support for the defenders was not provided by their own divisional artillery, which was located farther north defending the approaches to Cherbourg, but rather by elements of a coastal artillery regiment, the 1261st. One battalion of the regiment was headquartered at Foucarville, with the 1st Battery at Sainte-Martin-de-Varreville with four 10.5-centimeter K331(f) guns, the 2nd Battery at Azzeville with another four 10.5-centimeter K331(f)'s, and the 3rd Battery at Fontenay-sur-Mer with six 15.5-centimeter K418(f) guns. Inland was a *Wurfgerät* position with reportedly six to eight six-barrel launchers.[16]

Other than the beach obstacles, which were relatively few in number, there was a substantial seawall that extended the entire length of Uncle Red, Tare Green, Sugar Red, and Roger Beaches, but it was generally fairly low—65 inches high through most its length—but was up to 100 inches high along Roger Beach. The Germans had extensively mined the areas of the dunes around the resistance nests and along the approaches to and verges of the exit roads, but no Teller mines were encountered on the obstacles in the area actually assaulted, although the obstacles in the area that was intended to be assaulted turned out to be heavily mined.[17] Since trafficable routes were so limited by the inundations, it resulted in very high, but localized, mine densities that were to prove to be a serious problem for the American engineers on D-Day.

SUMMARY

The defenses of the the five beaches are summarized in the table below. The number of weapons only counts those direct-fire heavy weapons that could reasonably bear upon the landing beaches (the 4.7-centimeter guns are included with the similar 5-centimeter weapons). In the case of the mortars and machine guns, it counts all those in the fixed positions capable of firing on the beaches as well as those assigned to the infantry units in the area.[18] The number of resistance nests also only includes those more or less directly opposite the landing beaches.

What stands out is the similarity between Omaha and Sword. Both had more direct-fire heavy weapons emplaced than did the other beaches. In terms of 4.7-centimeter and heavier direct-fire weapons, there were twenty-three on Omaha and sixteen on Sword capable of firing on the beaches that were assaulted. There were eleven on Gold, ten on Juno, and three on Utah. Omaha and Sword were also the strongest defended in terms of machine guns, closely followed by Gold, then Juno, and finally Utah. Only in terms of mortars were Gold and Juno better defended than Omaha and Sword.

Beach	Width of the beach assaulted	Number of WN	Width/ WN	Weapons						
				88mm	75mm	50mm	37mm	20mm	MG	Mortars
Sword	1,800	2	900	2	2	12	2	3	97	16
Juno	4,100	4	820	1	4	5	2	0	58	18
Gold	6,400	5	1,280	1	3	7	1	0	75	21
Omaha	6,800	10	680	2	11	10	3	4	88	17
Utah	1,900	3	633	0	0	3	1	0	17	3

SUMMARY OF THE BEACH DEFENSES

CHAPTER 5

Assault Force Sword: The British 3rd Infantry Division

UNIQUELY FOR THE COMMONWEALTH BEACHES, on Sword the assault was made in a column of brigades instead of by two brigades assaulting abreast, largely due to a lack of assault landing craft and a lack of suitable beaches—the coastline from Lion-sur-Mer to St.,-Aubin-sur-Mer featured rocky offshore shallows, steep bluffs, and narrow beaches, while Roger was considered too close to the coast artillery positions in Ouistreham.[1] Partly to make up for that, the 8th Infantry Brigade was allotted twice the A.V.R.E. support given the brigades on Gold and Juno, under the apparent assumption that the additional lanes opened would facilitate the rapid landing of the following brigades, while the large allotment of Crabs was based on intelligence estimates that anticipated extensive minefields inland of Sword.

Two squadrons of the 5th Assault Regiment, the 77th and 79th, with twenty-six Crabs from A and C Squadron of the 22nd Dragoons, were assigned to support the 3rd British Division assault in the Sword area.[2] They were carried in ten LCT-IV's of the 45th LCT Flotilla. Overall commander of the breaching teams was Lt. Col. Arthur Denis Bradford Cocks, the commander of the 5th Assault Regiment.

Because of the sea conditions, the decision was made to bring the DD tanks closer inshore and launch them at 5,000 yards instead of the planned 7,000 yards. Of the thirty-eight DD tanks embarked, thirty-two were successfully launched, and twenty-nine made it ashore, where they provided welcome support for the A.V.R.E.'s, infantry, and engineers.[3] However, the delay in launching meant the DD tanks touched down between five and twelve minutes late, well after the LCT-IV's with the A.V.R.E.'s and the LCA's with the leading infantry waves. In

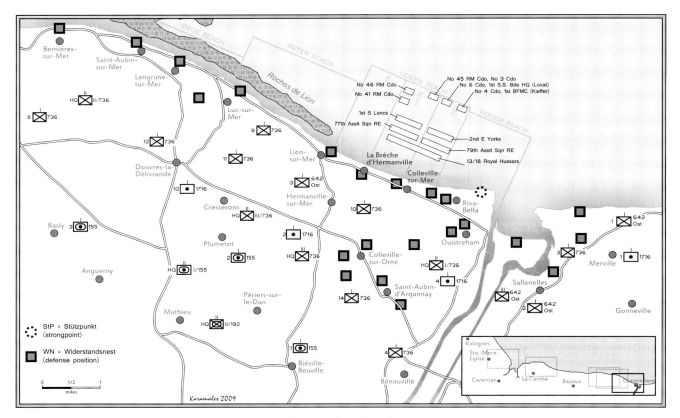

The assault on Sword.

fact, it was reported that one of the DD tanks lost was actually overrun by one of the LCT's carrying the A.V.R.E.'s in to shore (the other two lost sank immediately on launching).[4] Despite the last-minute change, the actual timing of the rest of the assault craft was quite accurate, with the initial touchdowns occurring as planned.

The heavy seas also caused problems with some of the craft that were intended to be towed across the Channel by larger vessels. The worst affected were the nine small landing craft of the 592nd LCA(HR) Flotilla with their heavy load of hedgerow projectors and mortar bombs. Only one, LCA(HR)-976, made the passage; five others foundered, two broke their tows and were presumed to have foundered, and one broke its tow but was found and recovered after D-Day. The single survivor gallantly fired her mortar bombs, with no noticeable effect.[5]

Another major problem caused by the heavy seas was found after the landing: the A.V.R.E.'s, DD's,

Centaurs, and Shermans, as well as other tracked vehicles, were all highly susceptible to having their engines drowned by the heavy surf once they were on the beach. Of the sixteen tanks of the 5th (RM) Support Battery, for example—including twelve Centaurs, two Shermans, and two Sherman 17-pounders that were landed on D-Day—four were lost to the surf. Of the remainder, one LCT(A) with two Centaurs and one Sherman was forced to return to England, and one LCT(A) with two Centaurs and one Sherman was delayed in the passage and landed on D+1. Of the thirty-one DD tanks successfully landed, nine were swamped, although many of their crews continued to fight from their vehicles as they were slowly submerged by the rising tide.

The heavy surf and rapidly turning tide also made the work of the L.C.O.C.U.'s nearly impossible. They were able to mark a single buoyed channel each on Queen Red and White Beaches, but between the strong seas and the many craft approaching the beach, it was simply too risky to attempt to clear any of the submerged obstacles. Instead, both teams came ashore and assisted the dismounted engineers and A.V.R.E.'s in clearing the beach obstacles.

However, it was found that the worries generated by the appearance of the German obstacles were partly unfounded. On Sword and the other beaches, it was discovered that the careful briefing of landing craft crews that instructed them to "drive their craft in at full speed for the last mile of the approach" was sound.[6] It was reported that the momentum of the heavily laden craft took them "over and through covered or partially submerged obstacles."[7] Many were damaged and unable to retract from the beach without risking sinking, but their cargo was gotten ashore more or less intact, which was what counted at this early stage of the invasion. Another risk was friendly fire: "As [LCT(HE)]2433 made her approach, a rocket-firing LCT(R), stationed at the rear, released her salvo. One of the rockets fell short and hit 2433's bow door, rendering it useless. After a struggle, the craft disgorged its tanks and returned to seaward its downed ramp dragging in the sea."[8]

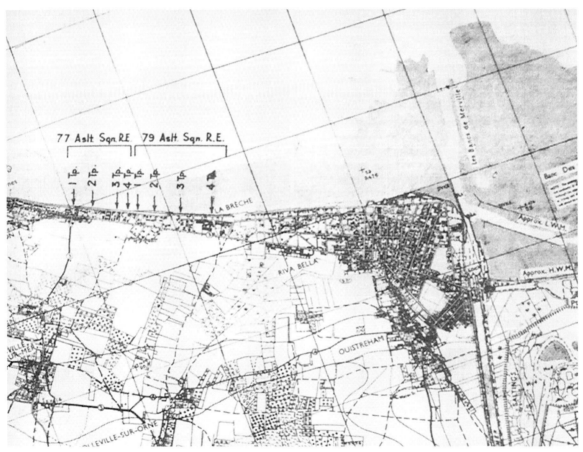

This map was prepared by the 5th Assault Regiment RE after D-Day to show where the squadrons and troops landed. TNA

79TH ASSAULT SQUADRON

The squadron strength was 10 officers and 169 other ranks, including a 65-man detachment consisting of 3rd and 4th Troop, C Squadron, 22nd Dragoons, with thirteen Crabs. Maj. John Glanville Hanson commanded the 79th Squadron, while Capt. Humphrey Forester "Tim" Wheway of C Squadron, 22nd Dragoons, was in overall command of the Crab detachments on both Red and White Beaches.[9] In addition to the A.V.R.E.'s and Crabs of the gapping teams, the 79th Squadron also had two D7 bulldozers, two A.V.R.E.'s, and one Crab in reserve, which it carried on three LCT(A)'s assigned to the 5th Royal Marine Independent Armoured Support Battery.[10]

Queen Red Beach, Red Gap: 4th Troop— Successful

LCT-(116)* carried three Crabs and three A.V.R.E.'s (Log Carpet, SBG, and Bobbin) under Capt. E. B. Pollard, the commander of the 4th Troop, 79th Squadron, who was wounded; 2nd Lt. P. R. R. Phillips, also of the 4th Troop; and Lt. J. Allen of the

3rd Troop, C Squadron, 22nd Dragoons. The war diary summarizes the troop's activities: "Beached at H [H-Hour, 0735]. Flails cleared up to low dunes. Log carpet and chespals were laid and rd [road] clearance began. One Flail knocked out and the other completed clearance to lateral. Bangalore hit side of craft on disembarkation and had to be jettisoned. Tp [Troop] rallied. Total Tp casualties, Killed nil and 1, wounded one and 3."[11]

The troop's story is taken up in the account in the 22nd Dragoons' history:

> Gaps on the left of Red beach were made by teams of 3rd Troop, "C" Squadron. Flails on the outer lane, commanded by Lieutenant J. Allen and Corporal Johnson, were met by heavy fire from an emplaced 75 mm. gun as soon as the ramps went down. Before it was clear of the waterline Lieutenant Allen's tank was hit three times, and he and three good men of his crew (Lance-Corporal James and

Red Beach shortly after 0805. A Crab is burning while a Bobbin A.V.R.E. is to the left waiting to move up the lane.
THE TANK MUSEUM

---

* The designation of the LCT as given in the reports was by their landing table identification number (LTIN) rather than by their navy pennant number. For clarity, I have used the LTIN number throughout in parenthesis, although if the pennant number is known, I have placed it before the parenthetical number, as in: LCT-(115) and LCT(CB)-2337 (548).

This is La Brèche d'Hermanville, probably around 0800 on D-Day. The landing craft are clustered in front of WN 18 at center, where the three short, parallel diagonal roads can be seen just inland of the position. The road running inland farther to the left leads to Colleville-sur-Orne, which is at the edge of the frame. At the lower left is the edge of Riva Bella, with WN 10 just out of frame. NARA

Trooper Thomas and McShand) were killed. Only the gunner, Lance Corporal Pummell, escaped from the burning tank; wounded and with his clothing alight, he managed to throw himself into the sea, from which he was picked up by an assault craft and was shortly on his way back to hospital in England. Corporal Johnson's tank was left to make good the lane, task that was successfully carried out.[12]

Queen Red Beach, Blue Gap: 3rd Troop—Successful

LCT-(115) carried two Crabs and four A.V.R.E.'s (GP, Log Carpet, SBG, and Bobbin), under Lt. William Haynes Hilton Hutchinson, who was

wounded. The squadron assault reserve followed in LCT-(114a) with two Crabs, two A.V.R.E.'s (GP), and two D7 armored bulldozers, under the troop commander Capt. William H. B. Ayers, who was killed. According to the war diary, the troop "landed at H. Both Flails knocked out. Mines were cleared by hand by dismounted crews. Br [SBG bridge] was dropped and later blocked by DD falling off the side of it. A second gap was made by D7. Tp rallied. Total casualties, killed one and nil, wounded one and 4."[13]

Again, the 22nd Dragoons' history fills in some of the gaps in the story:

On the inner lane, too, there was plenty of trouble. Sergeant "Timber" Wood (one of the original cadre of professional soldiers at Blundellsands) took on a pill-box which was laying down mortar fire and silenced it; while his second tank, commanded by Corporal Rains, closed with the gun that had knocked out his troop leader and wiped it out. This was fierce shooting at close range; like so much of the fighting on this beach, tanks ran for the gun emplacements in a grim race to put their shells almost point-blank through the mouths of the concrete "boxes" before they themselves were put out of action. The team was thus able to complete its breach and shoot in the assault infantry before moving up to sweep its lateral communications.[14]

Queen Red Beach, Yellow Gap: 2nd Troop— Failed

LCT-(114) carried three Crabs and three A.V.R.E.'s (Log Carpet, SBG, and Bobbin), under the troop commander Capt. Geoffrey C. Desanges, who was killed, and Lt. A. J. Nicholson, who was mortally wounded. The war diary recounts the troops activities:

Tp landed at H and Flails began to clear lane to top of beach. They were both knocked out. Bomb release on br was hit prematurely and br fell. Gap was made with hand placed charges and improved by D7. Bobbin was damaged and had to be jettisoned. Capt Desanges killed and 2/Lt Nicholson wounded. All AVRE knocked out, remainder of crews rallied on foot. Total Tp casualties, Killed one and nil, wounded one and 3, missing nil and 2.[15]

The account from the point of view of the 22nd Dragoons was again less laconic, but no less violent. Yellow Gap was evidently one of the deadliest spots on Queen Red.

[The Flail] tanks commanded by Sergeant Cochran and Corporal Agnew took bitter punishment. The flails grounded on time, but in a few minutes Corporal Agnew's tank was hit three times in the engine compartment by armour-piercing shell and burst into flames. The crew escaped, and by good fortune only

one—Trooper Jennings—was wounded as he struggled out of the river's hatch. An 88 mm. shell also hit the turret of Sergeant Cochran's tank, wounding the commander and his gunner, Trooper McKinnon, and killing the operator, Trooper Kemp. Behind them all the A.V.R.E.s were knocked out, and the gap was completed by an armoured bulldozer and through the gallantry of members of the breaching team who ran forward with their explosive charges and succeeded in lighting the fuses under intense small-arms fire which caused many casualties. The gap was made, at heavy sacrifice on the part of the breaching team.[16]

Queen Red Beach, Green Gap: 1st Troop— Successful

LCT-(113) carried two Crabs and four A.V.R.E.'s (GP, Log Carpet, SBG, and Bobbin), under the 1st Troop commander, Capt. Redmond C. Cunningham, and Lt. Victor W. Boal of 4th Troop, C Squadron, 22nd Dragoons. It also had the 79th Squadron's commander, Major Hanson, aboard. According to the war diary, the troop

landed at H and Flails flogged up beach until one Flail was knocked out. Second Flail continued lane. Br was dropped but badly placed. Second lane was started and carpet laid, lane completed. Eventually both lanes made good. Bangalore was jettisoned. Tp rallied. Tp was later ordered fwd [forward] to hold lock gates at Ouistreham which it did until relieved by 2 Bns Beach Gp [5th Kings Regiment and 1st Buckinghamshire Regiment, which were designated the 5th and 6th Beach Group, respectively, of 101st Beach Sub-area] the following morning. Tp returned to Sqn [Squadron] rally. Total Tp casualties, killed nil and 7.[17]

The 79th Assault Squadron had been successful but had suffered fairly heavy losses; six Crabs and three A.V.R.E.'s were knocked out, three Crabs and one A.V.R.E. damaged, and twenty-five men were lost—the heaviest personnel loss of any of the six

This photo was taken as the 185th Infantry Brigade landed, but it gives a good idea of the confusion and congestion on the beaches. A Crab can be seen to the right. A swamped LCA is in the center and another just beyond it, while just beyond that and to the right is an A.V.R.E. JOE LOGAN

assault squadrons that landed on D-Day. It appears that all were lost in the assault phase, although that was not the end of the squadron's actions on D-Day. They went on to assist the Commandos at Ouistreham:

> At 1500 hrs CO [commanding officer] 4 Commando reports to Sqn Ldr [the Squadron Leader, Major Hanson] that lock gates and br [bridge] at Ouistreham held by enemy. CO 4 Commando asks Sqn Ldr for assistance. Sqn Ldr promises to take over since CO is badly injured. Sqn asks for inf [infantry] and gets none. Sqn with 10 AVREs moves off at 1530. Enemy is surprised and W [west] Bank is taken but enemy blew E [east] Span of br. After intense Besa and Petard fire enemy surrenders at 1630. 6 offrs and 51 ORs taken prisoner with 3 A-Tk [antitank] guns and eqpt [equipment]. Sqn deployed and took up position on W Bank with Bren posts on E Bank. Locks and remainder of br inspected for demolition charges and are made safe. Four AVRE move off at 2200 to sp [support] 2 RURs [2nd Battalion, Royal Ulster Rifles] at Benouville. Remainder held lock gates until relieved by inf the following morning.[18]

77TH ASSAULT SQUADRON

The squadron strength was 13 officers and 166 other ranks, including a 65-man detachment consisting of 1st and 3rd Troop, A Squadron, 22nd Dragoons with 13 Crabs. Maj. Kenneth du Blois Ferguson, commanding the 77th Squadron, was on LCT-(111). Two more D7 bulldozers and one Crab were also carried in reserve on two of the LCT(A)'s assigned to the 5th Royal Marine Independent Armoured Support Battery, but it is unclear when or if those landed.[19]

Queen White Beach, Red Gap: 4th Troop—Failed

LCT-947 (109) carried two Crabs and four A.V.R.E.'s (Plow, Log Carpet, SBG, and Bobbin) under the troop commander, Capt. Thomas Fairie; Lt. J. G. Charlton, also of 4th Troop; and Lt. Donald Robertson, commanding 1st Troop, A Squadron, 22nd Dragoons. Also aboard was the commander of the 5th Assault Regiment, Lt. Col. Arthur D. B. Cocks, and his headquarters signals sergeant. According to the war diary, the troop "beached on previously chosen exit [at about H-Hour, 0735]. Leading Flail disembarked, second Flail was hit by A-tk gun and jammed in doorway of LCT. Craft was hit by A-tk fire and the remainder could not disembark. An explosion occurred on board killing Lt-Col Cocks and wounding Lt. J.G. Charlton. Total casualties unknown. LCT was ordered back to UK."[20]

The explosion on board LCT-947 (109) was reported in the Royal Navy account of the landings as having been caused by a German mortar round that hit one of the A.V.R.E.'s and ignited its twin bangalore torpedoes. However, a more complete account of what happened was written shortly after the war by Lambton Burn, a Royal Navy Volunteer Reserve lieutenant who was aboard LCT-947 (109).

> Shells are bursting all round. They are not friendly shorts from bombardment warships, but vicious stabs from an enemy who has held his fire until the final two hundred yards. He is shooting well—shooting often. Mortar shells whine and burst with sickening

inevitability. An L.C.T. to port goes up in flames.

> There is a sudden jerk as our bows hit the beach. Down goes the ramp, with Sub-Lieutenant Monty Glengarry, R.N.Z.N.V.R. [Royal New Zealand Navy Volunteer Reserve] and his party working like madmen at the bows. There is a roar of acceleration and Donald Robertson in "Stornoway" [the first Crab, which managed to disembark] is away like a relay runner . . .

> "Dunbar" [the second Crab, with Colonel Cocks aboard as commander] moves forward. Colonel Cocks leans from his turret and motions the other tank-commanders to follow. But enemy fire is now concentrated on us. There are bursts on both sides and then—snap—two direct hits on our bows followed by a third snap like a whip cracking over the tank hold. The First Lieutenant is flung sideways against a bulkhead and lies stunned. "Dunbar" stops in her tracks—slews sideways—blocks the door. Another and greater explosion as the bangalore shafts of "Barbarian" [the Log Carpet A.V.R.E., with Captain Fairie in command] explode with a flash of red. Colonel Cocks is killed as he stands, and there is a scream from within his tank. Cold with anger, Tom Fairie moves "Barbarian" forward—tries to edge "Dunbar" to the ramp—but fails. He vaults from his turret and is joined by other tank-men who strain furiously to bring chain and tackle to bear.[21]

The other casualties were Cpl. Ernest "Bob" Brotherton, 22nd Dragoons, commanding *Dunbar*, who was killed, as was Sgt. James "Jock" Wingate, who was Cocks's signals sergeant. The wounded were Trooper Raby, 22nd Dragoons, who was also in *Dunbar*; Trooper Winstanley, the driver of the Plough; Tpr. Fred Linsell, commander of the Bobbin; and Lt. Jock Charlton, commanding the SBG, who suffered a face wound.[22] Thus, the 5th Assault Regiment's headquarters suffered losses of one officer

U.S. Navy LCI(L) 9 and 14 land troops of the 185th Brigade. A Crab can be seen on the left while other vehicles burn in the background. JOE LOGAN

Infantry and armor on Sword Beach. Medics are attending to wounded in the shelter of a Churchill A.V.R.E. (named *Cheetah*) from the 5th Assault Regiment. In the background is an M10 Wolverine tank destroyer, probably from the 20th Anti-Tank Regiment. THE TANK MUSEUM

and one other rank killed; No. 4 Troop, one officer and two other ranks wounded; and the 22nd Dragoons, one other ranks killed and one wounded.

It seems likely that at least the first two hits—and possibly all three—were from an antitank gun. Apparently, both *Dunbar* and *Barbarian* suffered penetrating hits by a heavy antitank gun, *Barbarian* reportedly being penetrated "fore and aft."[23] That would indicate, given the heavy armor protection of the A.V.R.E., that the offending German gun was either a 75-millimeter or 88-millimeter since the 5-centimeter guns simply did not have the power to do such damage. However, Burn also remarked that Wingate was killed by a "stray rocket," which might lead to the conclusion that a mortar or rocket was responsible for setting off the bangalore torpedoes as the navy account said. The badly damaged LCT-947 (109) made a difficult return to England where the troop vehicles and survivors were transferred to another LCT, eventually reaching Normandy later in the month.[24]

Queen White Beach, Blue Gap: 3rd Troop—Successful

LCT-(110) carried the assault team, under the command of the 3rd Troop commander, Capt. William Charles Sinclair Carruthers, and Lt. I. C. B. Dickinson, both of whom were wounded. It was loaded with three Crabs of the 1st Troop, A Squadron, 22nd Dragoons, and three A.V.R.E.'s (Log Carpet, SBG, and Bobbin). The squadron assault reserve in LCT-(110a) followed them with two Crabs, two A.V.R.E.'s (GP), and one D7 armored bulldozer. According to the war diary, the troop "grounded [at about H-Hour, 0735] on top of a DD, after clearing and beached to the left instead of right of 4 Tp. Flails cleared tracks, carpet was laid and br was dropped on attacked exit which was cleared to lateral. Bobbin hit by mine and A-tk fire and was drowned. D7 hit mine. Capt Carruthers wounded in hand by grenade. Total Tp casualties, Killed NIL and 1, wounded 2 and 2."[25]

The 22nd Dragoons continued to have a hard fight: "1st Troop of 'A' Squadron ran into harder trouble. On the right, Sergeant Turner and Corporal Aird (both of them killed by snipers' bullets an hour or two later) made an excellent lane with the utmost determination under heavy fire, and after an unexpectedly deep 'drop' from their assault craft, which had grounded short of the beach on a sunk D.D. tank."[26]

Queen White Beach, Yellow Gap: 2nd Troop—Successful

LCT-(111) carried two Crabs of the 3rd Troop, A Squadron, 22nd Dragoons, with four A.V.R.E.'s (GP, Log Carpet, SBG, and Bobbin), under the 2nd Troop commander, Capt. A. Low, and the 77th Squadron commander, Maj. K. du B. Ferguson, aboard. The war diary recounts:

Beached [at about H-Hour, 0735] to the right of 1 Tp instead of to left due to drift whilst LCT lay off to allow DD to go in. Bangalore was placed in dunes but was blown prematurely by enemy fire. Gap was made and Flails surmounted dunes. One Flail blew tracks on mines but route was cleared round it. The br was dropped right on top of gun position. The bobbin was damaged and jettisoned. D7 was not used. Tp rallied with 1 Tp, and later, assisted in attack on LION-SUR-MER. Total Tp casualties, killed NIL and 4, wounded NIL and 6.[27]

In an account written after the war, Low gave some additional details:

About 1,200 yards out the house known to us all as "Sad Sack Villa" was spotted and the LCT commander set course to land 10 yards to port of the house. We were ahead of the DDs due to touch down before us. All craft were ordered to stop to allow them through. Approximately 1,000 yards off shore the LCT(R) opened up. Rockets collided in mid-air and rained down on craft waiting to go in. One landed immediately under our starboard bow, showering the bridge with pieces of casing. LCT were then ordered to beach at full speed. Our gaps were hidden by dust showered by the barrage on the beach, but at 300 yards the building was again visible a bit to port. Twenty yards from the beach, the craft were attacked by four planes with British markings, two bombs landing very close to our doorway. We climbed onto my tank as the ramp dropped. Ahead of us was a gun apparently concentrating on the troop on our left. One flail flailed straight for the gun. I followed out with the Boase carpet. Another Crab flailed a second path up to the sand dunes and this I used to push the Boase Bangalore into a sand dune about six feet high. I had trouble cutting the receptacle on the Boase which had pushed easily into the dunes, as snipers kept up a steady hail of lead wherever I appeared.

Queen White Beach, Green Gap: 1st Troop—Successful

LCT-(112) carried three Crabs and three A.V.R.E.'s (Log Carpet, SBG, and Bobbin), under the troop commander, Capt. George Alaistair McLennan, who was killed. After McLennan was killed, command was shared by Lt. C. J. P. Tennent of the 77th Squadron and Lt. D. Knapp, commanding the 3rd Troop, A Squadron, 22nd Dragoons. According to the war diary, the troop landed at place previously chosen at H hr. Obstacles were 6' to 8' high sand dunes. The flails flogged up the beaches and crossed the dunes unaided. The Bangalore was jettisoned. Mines were cleared from lateral rds by Flails and hand clearing teams. One AVRE hit by A-tk gun broke track and drowned. Crew dismounted and forced their way into Hermanville, killing many enemy and holding the village until followed by inf. Br was jetti-

One of the SBG emplaced on Queen White. THE TANK MUSEUM

Another of the SBG emplaced on Queen White. These were probably those of the 2nd and 3rd Troop, but the exact location is not known. 79TH ARMOURED DIVISION MEMORIAL ALBUM/DANNY LOVELL

soned. Tp rallied and was sent in sp 41 RM Commando to mop up Lion-sur-Mer. Capt McLennan killed. Total Tp casualties, Killed 1 and 1, missing nil and two.[28]

Sgt. Thomas Reginald Kilvert commanded the Bobbin A.V.R.E. that was knocked out and then the dismounted party that stormed Hermanville. He left the following account of the landing:

We stood to at dawn on board the LCT 100A [it is unclear which he was referring to since there was no such designation used on Sword; it is possible that it is a garbled rendition of LCT-1009 of the 43rd LCT Flotilla] at 0500 hours. Breakfast was on but nobody really wanted it, being more or less seasick. I had AVRE 1c started up, all guns loaded and a last minute check over the tank. It was now about 0610 hours and the coastline stood out in the haze; we were coming in fast. About a half mile out everyone mounted their tanks. Almost in, 400 yards to go when 1c had a violent shake, we had been hit. Damage not known because the LCT had also sustained damage a bit forward and we had to get off at once.

The LCT stopped . . . going down the ramp now and the water was almost up to our cupola. Again we were hit but on our Bobbin, it being at a crazy angle. Coming out of the water, hit again and at last dry land and following the 1a [the Troop Leader's AVRE] up to sand. Hit a mine, one bogie gone, but, following in the 1a's track, we were ordered to put up a windsock [to mark the route], 1a having lost his. Struck a second mine, two bogies and left track gone.

L/Corporal Fairlie and Sapper Vaughan jumped out to put up a windsock. L/Corporal Fairlie was blown up by a mine as he came round the tank. I ordered abandon tank, take all arms, and jumped out myself, destroyed "slidex and code papers". We were all out now, petrol was pouring out of 1c and filling the mine crater. Everyone lay down whilst I looked for the L/Corporal's remains.

None found so I returned and organised the crew into a fighting patrol. Just then L/Sergeant Freer from 3 Troop joined us; he had swum ashore from his tank which had been on our LCT. Moving up the beach we passed Captain McLennan in 1a, stood on the gap top. I ordered defensive position and to consolidate in front of 1a on the crossroads.

Asking the troop leader to cover us, we moved forward behind the leading flail, until he reported no more mines in the road ahead. Again we consolidated. I went back to the beach to bring up the troop. Captain McLennan had now advanced through the gap and was followed by 1b, who stood in the exit a little to one side. I collected L/Sergeant Freer's crew and a couple of infantrymen and brought them forward to our advanced position.

Again we moved forward (we thought) until a bend in the road cut them, by 1a and 1b, from view.

We advanced in short bounds to the high wall of the large farm. Here we split into three parties, one covering the main road or killing zone, another as rear protection and another as house clearance.

It was then that fire came at us from three sides, but bursts from our two Brens brought a lull. Shooting open the garden door, I advanced covered by my L/Sergeant and Sappers Lewis and Hand, up the two paths and raked the whole front of the house and part of the farm with fire killing, we later found eleven of the enemy.

We rushed the house with hand grenades, and searched it from top to bottom. Going out into the yard we found the air raid shelter and the civilian occupants of the farm.

Sapper Hand, who spoke the lingo, obtained the information that the big house (on the corner of Hermanville itself) housed about 200 of the enemy. I then reorganized the party, sending two runners back to Captain McLennan. Using the road ditch and the garden wall as vantage points we advanced about sixty yards when Sapper Vaughan opened fire with a Sten gun on an enemy party coming down the road towards us. Immediately everyone of us opened fire, and with the two Sergeants with 199 round magazines with their Bren guns this scattered the enemy. An SP [self-propelled] gun then came up, followed shortly after by the infantry and Lieutenant Tennent on foot. We then handed over to a RA major, and moved to our RV (rendezvous] in a field opposite. On Captain McLennan's instructions we used a detector and tested for mines.[29]

The 77th Squadron had also suffered heavily; seven killed, thirteen wounded and two missing, just slightly fewer that the 79th Squadron. They also had lost two A.V.R.E.'s and four damaged, along with one Crab damaged.

Overall, the accomplishments of the A.V.R.E. gapping teams on Queen White and Red may be summarized by the following table. It shows the time when the team was reported to have touched down, when they cleared their first obstacle, and when they had cleared a practicable gap free of mines and obstacles to the first lateral road. As can

be seen, on White Beach, except for the mishap in Red Gap, the basic job of the A.V.R.E.'s had been completed between 0810 and 0900 hours, just an hour and a half from the first touchdown to the three gaps opening, a very credible accomplishment. On Red Beach, three gaps were also cleared, but not as quickly; it was 0940 before all three were done, some two hours and fifteen minutes after the first touchdown.[30]

Unfortunately, those gaps cleared were all considered to be lanes, rather than the more complete exits that would have allowed easy passage of vehicle traffic. It appears that the first two exits for tracked vehicles were not completed until sometime between 0906 (according to the Royal Navy) and 0930 hours (according to the army) and the first two wheeled vehicle exits were not open until 1130 hours. The result was that the multitude of vehicles, especially the self-propelled artillery regiments and the tanks of the 27th Armoured Brigade that were landing at that time, began to pile up on the beach as the delay in getting through the limited exits stretched from twenty minutes to an hour. It was not until 1700 hours that the traffic jam began to ease; by that time, four exits were open on White and five on Red.[31]

GAP CLEARANCE ON SWORD

	77th Assault Squadron—White				79th Assault Squadron—Red			
Lane	Green	Yellow	Blue	Red	Green	Yellow	Blue	Red
Touched Down	0730	0731	0740	Not Landed	0725	0725	0725	0730
1st Obstacle	0750	0800–0830	0800		0730	Crabs	0815	0800
1st Gap	0810	0830–0900	0820		0905	Knocked Out	0940	0940

THE ASSAULT BY 8TH INFANTRY BRIGADE GROUP

The landing of the clearance teams and the landing of the assault battalions of the 8th Infantry Brigade on Queen Red (2nd East Yorks) and Queen White (1st South Lancs) occurred nearly simultaneously instead of in neat succession, with the infantry following the clearance teams, as had been planned. On Queen Red, the infantry actually landed first by about five minutes, while on Queen White the clearance teams landed about five minutes before the infantry. The war diary describes the troop's actions:

> Landed at H [actually between 0725 and 0740 hours] and began work of clearance. Incoming tide and congestion of vehs [vehicles] on beach stopped work. Beach was cleared later. Mines and shells on obstacles were neutralized by hand and wooden obstacles towed away or crushed.
>
> At 0720 hrs the two leading company's of 1 S LAN R touched down on the beaches, and although met by MG and mortar fire made satisfactory progress. At 0725 hrs the two leading company's of 2 E YORKS touched down on the left of 1 S LAN R, also encountering some opposition.[32]

Queen Red

The two leading companies of the 2nd East Yorks, A and B, came under heavy mortar and small-arms fire as they approached the beach, but suffered only six casualties. Once on the beach, though, casualties began to mount; by the end of the day, the 2nd East Yorks had lost a total of 5 officers and 60 men killed and 4 officers and 137 men wounded.[33]

About five minutes later, the A.V.R.E.'s of the 79th Assault Squadron landed. At nearly the same time, two troops of the 5th Royal Marine Independent Armoured Support Battery came ashore, carried in LCT(A)'s and LCT(HE)'s. Two of the LCT(A)'s landed on the extreme left (eastern) side of Queen Red beach, LCT(A)-2191 on the left and LCT(A)-2052 on the right. Both managed to disgorge their tanks—a total of four Centaurs and two Shermans—but were both then hit repeatedly. LCT(A)-2191 was disabled and lost five crewmen killed and four wounded, and LCT(A)-2052 lost one killed and three wounded.[34] The two LCT(HE)'s, carrying four more Centaurs, beached farther to the right (west), but at least one of them was hit as well. Seven of the Centaurs were swamped while attempting to get to the beach. That of Lt. A. C. Badenoch, apparently the same that Tear was in, managed to get ashore and provided some covering fire, as apparently did the two Sherman OP tanks of the troop.[35]

Also about that time, the DD tanks of B Squadron, 13th/18th Hussars, came ashore, but there is some confusion about their number. Five of the original nineteen got stuck on LCT-467 when the lead tank tore its skirt before exiting; the LCT commander elected to beach his craft rather than jettison the damaged tank, but he did not succeed in getting to shore until H+40. Of the remaining fourteen, it appears that all successfully swam in, but five were quickly knocked out, and two were swamped by the rising tide on the beach. The remaining seven supported the 2nd East Yorks and were later joined by the five on LCT-467, along with one 17-pounder Sherman, commanded by Lieutenant Knowles, which had landed off LCT(CB)-2337 (545) on Queen White.*

The underwater obstacles were densely enough placed that the men and tanks had a hard time maneuvering around them in the heavy seas. The

---

* The various accounts conflict badly about the number of tanks that landed; many accounts report that only twenty-four tanks of A and B Squadron were launched. However, it is clear that thirty-four were launched, with three sinking on the run in. At least ten appear to have been knocked out and nine swamped on the beach. The clearest account is that of the 13th/18th Hussars, which reports that by the end of D-Day, B Squadron had eight operational, including Knowles's 17-pounder Sherman, while A Squadron had six, including the second 17-pounder Sherman, under the command of Sergeant Ellis, from LCT(CB)-2337.

The 2nd East Yorks had been given the difficult assignment of capturing Cod (WN 20), then Sole (WN 14) and Daimler (WN 12), followed by clearing St. Aubin-d'Arquenay, before finally taking over the defense of the canal and river bridges at Benouville and Ranville from the 6th Airborne Division. Nevertheless, they had accomplished nearly all their D-Day assignments, despite suffering 137 casualties, including their commander Lt. Col. G. F. Hutchinson, who was wounded—a remarkable achievement.

Advance by the 2nd Battalion, East Yorkshire Regiment, with B Squadron, 13th/18th Hussars, on WN 12. THE TANK MUSEUM

Below: The town center of La Brèche on the morning of D-Day. Waterproofed carriers can be seen moving up on the right, and an A.V.R.E. is at center. THE TANK MUSEUM

Above: Support troops of the British 3rd Infantry Division assemble on Queen Red at 0830 under intermittent enemy mortar and shell fire. In the foreground and on the right, identified by the white bands around their helmets, are sappers of the 84th Field Company RE. Behind them, medical orderlies prepare to move off the beach. In the background are men of the 1st Battalion, the Suffolk Regiment, and Lord Lovat's No. 4 Army Commando landing from LCI(S)'s of Naval Force S. NARA

regimental history of the 2nd East Yorks remarked that the Germans maintained a heavy crossfire that continued to cause casualties to the regiment, which by 0800 had landed their two reserve companies. D Company was dispersed when a German mortar round landed in the midst of its company headquarters party, killing the company commander, Major Barber, and killing or wounding a number of others. Nevertheless, by 0830 hours, when the follow-up waves began landing, the 2nd East Yorks had moved inland and were out of sight of the beach. According to the 2nd East Yorks' unit history,

> After emerging from the houses and beach defences and into the lane behind, there was a fair amount of stuff coming down (i.e., shells and mortar bombs). Two very large and very frightened cart horses came galloping down the lane. A Lance Corporal with a small party of men told them [the men, not the horses!] to get out of the way and take cover behind a low wall, as they might otherwise get hurt. To take cover to avoid getting hurt by shells and mortar bombs had never occurred to him![36]

C Company of the 2nd East Yorks advanced, and supported by the self-propelled 25-pounders of the 76th Field Regiment, it took Sole after a sharp fight. A Company joined them in clearing the beach and helped them consolidate. Once B Company arrived a little later, the battalion advanced on Daimler. Lieutenant Colonel Hutchinson was wounded by mortar or artillery fire while reconnoitering, but Daimler was seized with little loss with the help of a few tanks from the 13th/18th Hussars and the artillery of the 76th Field Regiment. Seventy Germans were captured.

After seizing Daimler, the 2nd East Yorks continued, along with the tanks of 13th/18th Hussars, to St. Aubin-d'Arquenay. It was in ruins and devoid of defenders, so the exhausted battalion settled in to defend it against a possible German counterattack. They remained there until later in the afternoon when they were relieved by the 1st Battalion of the King's Own Scottish Borderer Regiment of the 9th Infantry Brigade. The weary men of the 2nd East

Yorks then withdrew to a cornfield west of Hermanville, where they spent the night.

The 2nd East Yorks had been given the difficult assignment of capturing Cod (WN 20), then Sole (WN 14) and Daimler (WN 12), followed by clearing St. Aubin-d'Arquenay, before finally taking over the defense of the canal and river bridges at Benouville and Ranville from the 6th Airborne Division. Nevertheless, they had accomplished nearly all of their D-Day assignments, despite suffering 137 casualties, including their commander—a remarkable achievement.

Queen White

Farther west, the two leading companies, A and C, of the 1st South Lancs on Queen White touched down more or less simultaneously, shortly after the gapping teams of the 79th Assault Squadron and at about the same time as the fifteen surviving DD tanks from A Squadron of the 13th/18th Hussars. T Troop of the 5th Marine Support Battery was landed from LCT(A)'s at about 0728; apparently, all four Centaur tanks made it safely ashore.

Also at that time, LCT(CB)-2337 (545), carrying the two Sherman 17-pounder "Concrete Buster" tanks under the command of Lieutenant Knowles and Sergeant Ellis of the 13th/18th Hussars, landed on Queen White. Sergeant Ellis remained with A Squadron, but Lieutenant Knowles worked his way east to join with B Squadron. What happened to the reserve Crab and A.V.R.E. that were aboard is unknown.

A Squadron, 13th/18th Hussars, had suffered a particularly hazardous journey. Of the nineteen DD tanks in the squadron, one had gotten stuck on LCT-465 when its ramp collapsed after launching four DD tanks. Two others had sunk almost immediately after launching, although both crews were saved. One was run down by one of the LCT's carrying the A.V.R.E. to the beach with the loss of all but its commander. Then of the fifteen that managed to get ashore, three were quickly knocked out, and seven more were soon swamped by the rising tide. The last five, joined by Sergeant Ellis in the 17-pounder Sherman, did the best they could in supporting the 1st South Lancs. Lance Corporal Hennessey of A Squadron, 13th/18th

Hussars, left a vivid account of the landing from the point of view of one of the DD tanks:

We heard the order over the ship's tannoy, "down door, no 1", and we knew this was our cue. The ramp on the bow of our LCT was lowered into the sea, the ship hove to, tank engines started, and Sergeant Rattle's tank moved forward down the ramp and nosed into the waves. We followed, and as we righted in the water I could just see the shore line some 5,000 yards away; it seemed a very long distance and in a DD Tank, in that sea, it certainly was!

Slowly we began to make headway. The crew were all on deck apart from Harry Bone who was crouched in the driving compartment, intent on keeping the engine running because, as we all knew, if that stopped we stood no chance of survival. The noise seemed to increase and the sea appeared even rougher from this low point of view, with only a flimsy canvas screen between us and the waves. We shipped a certain amount of water over the top of the screen from time to time, so Trooper Joe Gallagher, the co-driver, whose task it was to man the bilge pump, was kept hard at work. . . .

We battled on towards the shore through the rough sea. We were buffeted about unmercifully, plunging into the troughs of the waves and somehow wallowing up again to the crests. The noise continued and by now the shells and rockets were passing over our heads, also, we were aware that we were under fire from the shore. The Germans had woken up to the fact that they were under attack and had brought their own guns into action. It was a struggle to keep the tank on course, but gradually the shoreline became more distinct and before long we could see the line of houses, which were our targets. Seasickness was now forgotten. It took over an hour of hard work to reach the beach and it was a miracle that most of us did. As we approached, we felt the tracks meet the shelving sand of the shore, and slowly we

began to rise out of the water. We took post to deflate the screen, one man standing to each strut. When the base of the screen was clear of the water, the struts were broken, the air released and the screen collapsed. We leapt into the tank and were ready for action.

"75, HE, action-traverse right, steady, on. 300 white fronted house first floor window, centre", "On". "Fire!" Within a minute of dropping our screen we had fired our first shot in anger. There was a puff of smoke and brick dust from the house we aimed at, and we continued to engage our targets. Other DD Tanks were coming in on both sides of us and by now we were under enemy fire from several positions, which we identified and to which we replied with 75mm and Browning machine gun fire. The beach, which had been practically deserted when we had arrived, was beginning to fill up fast. The infantry were wading through the surf and advancing against a hail of small arms fire and mortar bombs. We gave covering fire wherever we could, and all the time the build-up of men and vehicles continued.

Harry Bone's voice came over the intercom: "Let's move up the beach a bit I'm getting bloody wet down here!" We had landed on a fast incoming tide, so the longer we stood still the deeper the water became. As we had dropped our screen, the sea was beginning to come in over the top of the driver's hatch and by now he was sitting in a pool of water. The problem was that the promised mine clearance had not yet taken place so we had to decide whether to press on through a known mine field, or wait until a path had been cleared and marked.

Suddenly the problem was solved for us. One particularly large wave broke over the stern of the tank and swamped the engine, which sputtered to a halt. Now, with power gone, we could not move, even if we wanted to. Harry Bone and Joe Gallagher emerged from the driving compartment soaking wet and swearing.

Above: La Brèche d'Hermanville later in the morning when the tide has come in. On the left, a column of vehicles is moving south through Lane 8, a second column is moving through Lane 7 at left center, and a third through Lane 6, which is just to the left of the dark shadow caused by the aircraft's propeller. NARA

A close-up view of the same location from the sea taken after the war. DANNY LOVELL

More infantry were coming ashore, their small landing craft driving past us and up to the edge of the beach. There was quite a heavy firefight in progress so we kept our guns going for as long as possible, but the water in the tank was getting deeper and we were becoming flooded. At last we had to give up. We took out the browning machine guns and several cases of .3 inch belted ammunition, inflated the rubber dinghy and, using the map boards as a paddle, began to make our way to the beach. We had not gone far when a burst of machine gun fire hit us. Gallagher received a bullet in the ankle, the dinghy collapsed and turned over, and we were all tumbled into the sea, losing our guns and ammunition.

Somehow, we managed to drag Gallagher and ourselves ashore. We got clear of the water and collapsed onto the sand, soaking wet cold and shivering. A DD tank drove up and stopped beside with Sergeant Hepper grinning at us out of the turret "can't stop" he said, and threw us a tin can. It was a self-heating tin of soup, one of the emergency rations with which we had been issued. One pulled a ring on top of the tin, and miraculously it started to heat itself up. We were very grateful for this, and as we lay there on the sand, in the middle of the battle taking turns to swig down the hot soup, we were approached by an irate captain of Royal Engineers who said to me: "Get up, corporal—that is no way to win the second front!" He was absolutely right of course. Rather shame-facedly we got up, moved further up the beach and found some medical orderlies into whose care we delivered Joe Gallagher who cheered up considerable when someone told him he would be returning to Blighty as a wounded "D-Day hero."[36]

Maj. Adrian R. Rouse of the 1st South Lancs gave just as vivid an account from the infantryman's point of view of the run-in to the beach.

The boat crews had been ordered to go in at 4 knots and hit the beach hard. During the last

100 yards of the run-in everything seemed to happen at once. Out of the haze of smoke the underwater obstacles loomed up. We had studied them on air photographs and knew exactly what to expect but somehow we had never realized the vertical height of them, and as we weaved in between iron rails and ramps and pickets with tellamines [sic, Teller mines, the standard German antitank mines] on top like gigantic mushrooms we seemed to be groping through a grotesque petrified forest.

The noise was so continuous that it seemed almost like a siren. The seamanship was magnificent. The LCAs weaved in and out of the obstacles and we almost had a dry landing. I have very little recollection of wading ashore, there was too much going on above and around to notice it. It was however, apparent from the beginning that it was by no means an unopposed landing. Mortar fire was coming down on the sands, an 88mm gun was firing along the line of the beach and there was continuous machine-gun and rifle fire. Immediately ahead of us a DD tank, its rear end enveloped in flames, unable to get off the beach, continued to fire its guns.[37]

C Company of the 1st South Lancs had a much easier time than A Compnay. It landed correctly on the western edge of Queen White and immediately began its assault. A Company unfortunately was scattered; two platoons landed correctly to the right of C Company, where they suffered some casualties. However, the third platoon and company headquarters were swept eastward directly in front of Cod (WN 20) and suffered heavily.

About twenty-five minutes later, the reserve companies, B and D, and battalion headquarters landed. They were also supposed to land on the western edge of Queen White, but were swept eastward by the current under the guns at Cod (WN 20) and suffered heavily. The commander of B Company, Major Harrison, was killed, and the commander of D Company, Major Egglinton, was wounded. Shortly afterward, the battalion commander, Lt. Col. Richard Burbury, who was carrying a small regimental flag to mark his position, was killed by a sniper, leaving his second-in-command, Maj. Jack Stone, and Maj. Eric Johnson of C Company as the two senior officers on the beach.

The remnants of company headquarters and the single rifle platoon of A Company in front of Cod (WN 20) managed, with the assistance of an A.V.R.E. (probably from No. 3 or No. 4 Troop of the 79th Assault Squadron, the record is unclear), to breach the wire entanglement blocking the beach exit. Under the leadership of the platoon commander, Lt. Eddie Jones, they began to clear the fortified houses on the beach, capturing a large number of Poles and Russians and meeting up with the remnants of the other two platoons under Lt. Bob Pearce. The reunited company then joined some tanks and began clearing the outskirts of Lion-sur-Mer. Meanwhile, Major Stone and Major Johnson led battalion headquarters and C and D Companies off the beach toward Hermanville-sur-Mer.

A good deal of confused fighting followed, with platoons and sections taking on their own targets. There are many acts of individual heroism. The orders were that as soon as the beach task had been completed the battalion should rendezvous at Hermanville. The silencing of the concrete pillbox at the western end of "Cod" by Bob Bell-Walker enabled battalion headquarters to work round to the right and begin to move towards Hermanville. The confused fighting on the beaches lasted for a considerable time. The anti-tank platoon coming in at H+30 even had their share with a corporal bringing one of the battalion six-pounders into action on the sand to deal effectively with a machine-gun post.[38]

THE ASSAULT RESERVE LANDS

Thirty minutes after the leading assault waves had landed, fourteen LCA's with No. 4 Commando approached the shore. They were led into the beach by two LCI(S)'s carrying Capitan de Corvette Philippe Kieffer and the Free French Commandos of No. 1, No. 8, and K Troops of No. 10 (Inter-Allied) Commando.[39] Unfortunately, although on time at 0755, the Commandos had actually managed to get ahead of the follow-on waves of the 2nd East Yorks Battalion Headquarters and C and D Companies. As a result, the following companies of the 2nd East Yorks came in fifteen minutes late at 0805 hours, causing some congestion and confusion on the beach.[40]

Lt. Col. Robert Dawson, commanding No. 4 Commando, was among the wounded, once in the leg upon landing and then again in the head as they formed up and prepared to turn left toward Riva Bella and Ouistreham. He was forced to relinquish control to his second in command. According to the Commandos' war diary,

'C' Tp waited for the remainder of the Commando to position itself, and then moved on behind 1 and 8 (Fighting French) Tps along

the OUISTREHAM road to the Check Pt, being harassed by snipers and machine gunners in houses. Tanks greatly helped in clearing this opposition. From the Check Pt, 'C' Tp again took the lead and established a route to the Battery—the Commandos main task. Invaluable assistance was given to the leading Tp by a French Gendarme member of the Underground Movement, who helped the Commando to bypass other enemy strongpoints and reach their objective without unnecessary delay. Great help was also afforded the Unit by 4 Centaurs which gave cover from snipers. On arrival at major tank obstacles covering the inland side of the Battery strongpoint, and still under enemy fire, a search was made and two suitable bridges made. Here, a machine gun post and mortar position were silenced by PIAT fire.

Together with 'A' Tp, under command of Capt A. M. Thorburn, 'C' Tp then gave covering fire to enable 'D' Tp, (commanded by Major P. A. Porteous VC) to pass through 'E' Tp, (commanded by Capt. H. Burt) and 'F' Tp (commanded by Capt. L. N. Coulson), were then covered across. Continued sniping and mortar fire inflicted further casualties.

The heavy ruck-sacks carried by the Commando had been dumped under HQ and the Mortar Section.

Under orders by Unit wireless, mortar fire was brought to bear on the Flak Tower at the EAST of the Gun Battery and covering the whole area. The French Detachment, commanded by Capt. P. Kieffer, who was later evacuated severely wounded, over-ran the Cassino area on the WEST of the strong-point.

Then the assault went in on the Battery, all Tps moving according to plan. Heavy casualties were inflicted on the enemy who put up a very stiff resistance from their strong fortifications and cunningly camouflaged block houses commanding excellent field's of fire. The concrete emplacements had withstood severe Naval bombardment exceedingly well, and although out numbered, the Germans were in excellent defensive positions and had advantages of emplacements which had successfully withstood a terrific pounding from the sea and air. Several prisoners were taken when the Germans surrendered after their position had become untenable. Casualties on both sides had been high and after the engagement medical orderlies from opposing sides worked side by side succoring the wounded.

One of the outstanding features of the defence of the Battery by the enemy was the careful sighting of their positions, and from the Commando's view point, the difficulty of finding points of enemy fire power during the mopping up stages, so well had the emplacements been prepared. But at least one point of Hitler's Western Wall had proved vulnerable under determined enough attack.[50]

The Free French had landed 185 strong, but at the end of the day mustered only 114 officers and men, implying that they lost 71 casualties, although only 39 were killed or wounded; the rest were apparently stragglers.[51] The casualties in No. 4 Com-

mando are unknown, but were probably severe as well. Following the action at Riva Bella and Ouistreham, No. 4 Commando turned south and marched to rejoin the rest of the 1st Special Service Brigade at Benouville.

Meanwhile, at 0810 hours, reinforcements for the beachhead continued to stream in; two troops of self-propelled M10 antitank guns of the 20th Antitank Regiment R.A. landed along with two troops of self-propelled light antiaircraft guns of the 73rd Light Antiaircraft Regiment R.A. Fifteen minutes later, the reserve battalion, the 1st Suffolks, under the command of Lt. Col. R. E. Goodwin, landed, suffering only two men wounded. More serious was a shell that hit one of the LCA's coming in, killing the naval forward bombardment officer and his entire party, negating any naval gunfire support for the battalion for the rest of the day.[52]

With the Suffolks came C Squadron and regimental headquarters of 13th/18th Hussars, with twenty-four more Sherman tanks, including four more 17-pounder Shermans, along with four additional mine-clearing teams of the 246th Field Company R.E. The entire group assembled in an apple orchard and by 0900 hours was ready to move on to its multiple objectives of Colleville-sur-Orne, Morris (WN 16), Hillman (WN 17) and finally the Periers Ridge.

The rest of the 1st SS Brigade Signal Troop landed at 0835 hours, losing three men wounded to the random mortar and artillery fire. Five minutes after that, at 0840 hours, No. 6 Commando, under Lt. Col. Derek Mills-Roberts, landed and immediately moved out toward the Caen Canal and Orne River. They apparently suffered fewer than ten men wounded from the ongoing shelling. Mills-Roberts recounted the events after the war in his memoir:

> It was full daylight as we approached the shore and prepared to land. . . . Away to our right a destroyer was on fire from stem to stern, but I had no time to look at her as I had to keep my eyes glued on where our landmark should be. As I leant on the forward edge of the bridge there was a shattering explosion, and the craft in line with us and to our right went up with a full-blooded roar. A shell had pierced her petrol tanks—several

thousand gallons of high octane fuel can cause quite a bang.

I had got our landmark now but it was still indistinct in the smoke haze. The heavy swell had lessened inshore, but our way was barred by huge iron stakes and on the end of each was a live mine. . . . The shell fire was now more intense and the splashes round us more frequent. Our men were lying flat on the deck behind the cover of their bullet-proof casings. We would strike the beach any second now. On these occasions the officer always goes first. I took up my position on the port bow with Alan Pyman in a similar position on the starboard bow. As the landing-craft touched, the two light gangways were slammed ashore, but almost immediately the sea took the stern of the vessel and my gangway swung adrift. There was no time for delay and I jumped into the sea, followed by Corporal Smith and those on the port side of the ship. We were about waist deep and I turned to Corporal Smith and said, "It seems ages since we've had a dry landing. D'you find the sea cold?" "Not as cold as the west coast of Scotland, sir," he replied, thinking of our numerous immersions during training.

We doubled up the beach, with the water pouring from our battledress and rucksacks. As I ran I tore the water-proof bandages from the breech of my automatic rifle and checked the mechanism. Looking back, I saw that our gangway had been rigged again but almost immediately both of them were hit by an anti-tank gun sited just beyond the beach. By this time most of the men were ashore, but three of them were wounded on the gangways. The beach was littered with equipment and dead. One poor devil floated in the shallow water supported by his Mae West: he was quite dead but the swell gave him grotesque lifelike movements—he was only one of many.

It looked as if the Allied air bombardment had done its work well. The beach was not now under small-arms fire but there was plenty of mortaring and shelling. . . . The beach was still getting a pounding but we were assembled, according to plan, on the side of the road beyond the beach. David Powell reported that 6 Commando was now ashore complete and we turned off inland to cut through the German defences as we had so carefully planned. It was curiously quiet as we left the noisy beach and cut inland along our ordinary-looking hedgerow which led towards the enemy defensive positions. We had two hundred yards to go across a flat salt marsh before we hit the first pill-box. Suddenly to our left fell six thermite bombs from a thing called a Nebelwerfer; as the bombs touched the ground and exploded they also burst into flames. The Nebelwerfer fired again—it made a low moaning sound like a cow in labour—and I hoped that the Germans had not noticed our stealthy but rapid advance along the hedgerow. There was no time for careful concealment or caution.

We came to a hedge junction, and Alan Pyman's troop pulled off to attack a position of three small pill-boxes which could be seen from where we were. The following troop pushed on to the next objective—we had no time to lose. It was our intention to outflank the village of Colville-sur-Orne and then enter a patch of well-grown woodland beyond. I got a signal from Alan Pyman: he had destroyed his enemy position and had given the occupants of the pill-boxes a taste of his portable flame-throwing apparatus. I knew they had been bursting to use it.[53]

Also landing at 0835 were the self-propelled 105-millimeter M7 Priests of the 76th Field Regiment R.A. (a reconnaissance and forward observer team of the regiment had landed earlier at 0745), which immediately "deployed in shallow water in the beaches, firing continuously at short range in support of the Assault Bde attacks for over six hours under incessant enemy artillery fire and some sniping."[54]

No. 41 (RM) Commando, under the command of Lt. Col. T. M. Gray, touched down at 0845 hours, but on Red Beach instead of White Beach as had been planned. Unfortunately, their craft grounded well out to sea, forcing the men to wade through 200 yards of water before reaching the beach. Worse, their "proper beach White 300 yards away . . . was in fact drawing less fire than Red."[55] By the time the Commando was assembled and on its way to Lion-sur-Mer, it had lost three officers and twenty-five other ranks. They were followed at 0855 by No. 3 Commando, under Lt. Col. Peter Young, which had two of its landing craft hit by shell fire as they came in, but with few casualties.

By 0900 hours, it was reported that the 13th/18th Hussars were off the beach and were helping the infantry "to mop up enemy defense after considerable shelling and sniping from the houses."[56] Also at about that time, the 1st South Lancs had finished mopping up Hermanville and were about 2,000 yards inland.

The last major infantry element in the assault echelon, No. 45 (RM) Commando, under Lt. Col. N. C. Ries, and a second self-propelled artillery unit, the 33rd Field Regiment R.A., landed at 0910. The marines' war diary noted, "Intention—push inland contact Airborne Div holding bridges across CAEN CANAL and R ORNE." They suffered a few casualties in landing, although by the end of the day the toll had mounted to forty-one, including four killed, sixteen wounded, and twenty-one missing. Joining up with No. 3 and No. 6 Commando and Brig. Simon Fraser, Lord Lovat, commanding the 1st Special Service Brigade, they did just what they had intended, heading for Colleville-sur-Orne at about 0940, led by Lovat's piper Bill Millin.[57]

It was just after noon when No. 6 Commando reached the orne bridges. It is reported that Lovat's first words to Pine-Coffin were an apology to him for being late—by some two and a half minutes; the plan had envisaged the Commandos and Airborne troops linking up at noon! No. 3 Commando crossed the river at 1230 hours, followed by No. 45 (RM) Commando and then, after a grueling nine-mile march from Ouistreham, No. 4 Commando. They had secured one of the most important objectives on Sword.

Meanwhile, at about 1000 hours, the 2nd East Yorks completed clearing Cod (WN 20), effectively ending the beach assault for 8th Infantry Brigade. All units assigned to the brigade for the assault had been put ashore, along with the leading elements of the 101st Beach Sub-area who were responsible for beach maintenance—completing the tasks begun by the assault engineers, clearing the obstacles and minefields, completing and improving the beach exits, and assisting in the landing of additional troops, equipment, and supplies.*

By the time the final German resistance in Cod (WN 20) ended, most of the units that had landed as part of the initial assault had either completed their mission and were reorganizing—like the hard-hit 1st South Lancs and 2nd East Yorks—or were well on their way to their objectives. The 1st Suffolks had just reported Colleville-sur-Orne cleared and were on their way to Hillman (WN 17). The two Free French Commando Troops, No. 4 Commando, A Company of the 1st South Lancs, some Centaur tanks of the 5th (RM) Support Battery, and a few lost tanks from 13th/18th Hussars were busily beginning the reduction of Riva Bella and Ouistreham, where they were later joined by the ten A.V.R.E.'s of the 79th Assault Squadron. To the west, No. 41 (RM) Commando had begun its assault on Lion-sur-Mer, only to be temporarily thrown back by a counterattack by part of the 736th Grenadier Regiment's 3rd Battalion sallying out of Cresserons. Captain McLennan, the commander of 1st Troop of the 77th Assault Squadron was killed there attempting to support the Royal Marines with three of his A.V.R.E.'s. And as already was related, Lord Lovat, with No. 6 and No. 45 (RM) Commando, and some errant tanks of B Squadron 13th/18th Hussars (they had turned the wrong way en route to join up with the rest of their squadron and the 1st Suffolks) were on their way to relieve the airborne troopers defending the Caen Canal and Orne River bridges at Bénouville and Ranville.

---

* The leading elements of 101st Beach Sub-area—reconnaissance parties from the 5th Battalion, the King's Own Regiment (5th King's)—landed at H-Hour and began work at improving the beaches at 0815. They were followed by the 84th and 91st Field Companies R.E., the 241st Headquarters Provost Company, Corps of Military Police, and the 53rd Company, Pioneer Corps. After landing, No. 7 and No. 8 L.C.O.C.U. and 629th Field Squadron R.E. also came under the sub-area's command.

THE INTERMEDIATE AND RESERVE BRIGADES LAND

Between H+150 and H+250, roughly from 0955 to 1135 hours, the "intermediate brigade" (the 185th Infantry Brigade) of the 3rd Division began to land on Queen. In the Neptune plan, it was Montgomery's intent that the 185th Brigade, with strong armored support from the 27th Armoured Brigade, would dash into Caen and seize that vital town before the Germans could react to the Allied landing. Unfortunately, although much of the initial landing had gone according to plan, slight delays and the higher than normal tides had played havoc with unloading the tanks and other vehicles, and in getting them off the beach. Maj. J. P. Asher, commanding the 253rd Field Company R.E., left a vivid account of conditions on Queen at even that late an hour:

> Soon I could pick out the silhouette of houses on the low flat skyline and I tried to identify the house with a tower which showed on my panorama this was Lion sur Mer. It was my responsibility to get all these men and their vehicles clear of the beach, but from where I was standing on the bridge of this LCT emblazoned with the red and black triangle of 3rd Division, I could not see

This photograph was taken by Stanley Galik of LCI(L) 35 landing at La Brèche at about 0955 hours. The bow of the craft is in the foreground, while the first troops debarking are moving up the beach to the right. STANLEY GALIK

enough room on the beach for a dinghy to pull in. However, to my intense relief our skipper touched down perfectly full marks to the Royal Navy as he dropped his ramp without mishap just at this moment a shell landed forward on our immediate neighbor and removed his ramp before he reached the beach, and I saw a sapper jump for it and swim loaded like a Christmas tree with assault jerkin and mine detector.

Now I began to get very impatient because although our ramp was down there was so much traffic in front of the mouth of our craft that none of our vehicles could move. Visions of another shell hitting us amidships and cooking our goose! So I walked off the craft and trudged along the beach to see what the hold up was.

I never found the cause of the stoppages, but slowly things began to move, terribly slowly it seemed to me; occasionally over the din of the shelling I heard the unmistakable "woomph" of a mine going off and a stretcher passed me with a badly wounded man with his face knocked about and I realised with a jolt that this was the real thing again. When I had walked as far as the road behind the beach, I saw that mines in the verges had already taken their toll and went back along the column warning every driver including my own, to stick to the crown of the road; then I got aboard and we drove off the beach in a column that was still bonnet to tail.

This movement was very short lived, for soon there was another inexplicable hold up and again I got out and walked forward to try to clear the block this time I got as far as the crossroads which lead to Hermanville and as I walked back one of my hussar friend shouted "your truck's had it, sir". It had two rear wheels blown clean away and the center of the truck ripped up like so much paper—there were seven men aboard but only one

This mass of wreckage on Queen White Beach at Lion-sur-Mer was photographed on 14 June. Two knocked-out DD tanks can be seen, as well as a Porpoise sledge on the left and a number of landing craft. 79TH ARMOURED DIVISION MEMORIAL ALBUM/DANNY LOVELL

was wounded and that not serious, and the track marks of dozens of trucks had crossed this mine before us.

The contents of the truck were vital and included two wireless sets the company control and the rear link to the CRE [Commander, Royal Engineers of the 3rd Division]. We all got busy and unloaded the essentials on to the dusty road in a matter of minutes. How to get all this to our RV was my next problem![58]

At about noon, the last element of the 3rd British Division, the 9th Infantry Brigade, and its supporting units, began to arrive. Intended as a reserve and to protect the right flank of the planned thrust by 185th Brigade on Caen, it was instead diverted to help the 6th Airborne Division contain counterattacks by the 21st Panzer Division and the 711th Infantry Division on the east bank of the Orne River and Caen Canal. Then at 1245 hours, the Royal Navy decided to close the beach to further landings so as to have time to clear more debris from the beach. The closure affected the last element of the 27th Armoured Brigade, the 1st East Riding Yeomanry Regiment, which did not begin landing until 1550 hours, over three hours late.[59]

The traffic jams, troop diversions, and the temporary closure of the beach to further landings turned the rapid coup de main that had been intended into a fitful start and stop. The advance finally came to a halt late in the afternoon when the major German reaction to the landings at Sword, a counterattack by the 21st Panzer Division, belatedly began at 1620 hours. The ensuing tank battle, which was handily won by the British, ended any attempt to seize Caen, which did not fall until over a month later (and even then the industrial suburbs of the city on the south bank of the Orne River and Caen Canal did not fall until 18 July).[60]

Worse followed. Shortly after receiving the change of orders from Major General Rennie and the I Corps commander, Lt. Gen. John Crocker, who had also just landed, Brig. J. C. Cunningham, commanding the 9th Infantry Brigade, and six members of his brigade battle staff were wounded, and another six of the staff were killed by German mortar fire, paralyzing the brigade movement. Only one battalion of the brigade, the 1st Battalion of the King's Own Scottish Borderer Regiment (1st KOSB), moved to help the airborne troopers, while the other two battalions and their supporting tank battalion remained in their concentration area near Hermanville-sur-Mer for the rest of the day.

SWORD ASSESSED

The total losses incurred by the 8th Brigade and the other units of the I Corps, 3rd British Division, and 101st Beach Sub-area that supported them on D-Day are fairly complete and are staggeringly higher than has generally been supposed. They totaled at least 1,062 officers and other ranks killed, wounded, and missing, which is much higher than previous estimates that are popularly accepted (630 being the number that is usually reported). However, 630 was actually the "best estimate" derived in the post-battle

CASUALTIES IN THE SWORD ASSAULT, 8TH BRIGADE AND ATTACHED UNITS[61]

Unit	Killed Off.	OR	Wounded Off.	OR	Missing Off.	OR	Total
1st South Lancs	5	13	6	83	0	19	126
2nd East Yorks	5	60	4	137	0	3	209
1st Suffolks	2	5	0	25	0	0	32
13th/18th Hussars	0	12	0	12	5	78[a]	107
5th Assault Regiment	4	15	6	20	0	4	49
22nd Dragoons	1	8	8[b]		25[b]		42
1st SS Bde HQ	0	0	0	7	0	0	7
4th SS Bde HQ		1					1
No. 3 Commando	0	3	4	27	1	20[c]	55
No. 4 Commando[d]							154
No. 6 Commando[68]	1	4	2	28			35
No. 41 (RM) Commando	1	26[e]				1	28
No. 45 (RM) Commando	1	3[f]	2	14	1	20	41
5th (RM) Spt Bty	0	1	3	3	0	0	7
No. 1 and 8 Trp. FF Commando	2	6	4	27	0	0	39
5th Kings	2	9	2	25	0	0	38
84th Fd Coy RE	1	5	0	12	0	1	19
629th Fd Co RE	2	8	2	13	0	8	33
241st HQ Prov Coy CMP	0	2	0	6	0	0	8
53rd Coy Pnr Corps	0	1	0	11	0	9	21
76th Fd Regt RA	1	2	0	2	0	0	5
33rd Fd Regt RA	1	1	0	5	0	0	7
Total	29	185	35	457	7	163	1,063

a. The cause of the large number of missing was that so many crews had been left on the beach with their bogged or damaged tanks and so were unable to respond to the roll called that evening. Most returned to the unit within a day or two.

b. Wounded and missing figures combine officers and other ranks. It appears that all twenty-five missing returned safe to the regiment.[63]

c. Of the missing, it was later confirmed that one officer and fourteen other ranks were killed.[64]

d. No. 4 Commando and the attached Free French reportedly landed with a total of 35 officers and 650 other ranks and ended the day with 9 officers and 420 other ranks unhurt, implying that 26 officers and 230 other ranks were casualties. Given that the known casualties of the French were 6 officers and 33 other ranks, the implication is that No. 4 Commando's casualties were 20 officers and 197 other ranks. However, only 15 casualties in the 1st SS Brigade are unaccounted for after the totals for the other units are deducted from the brigade total of 289, so the total casualties were probably 154, with the other 58 simply being stragglers.

e. Postwar Royal Navy casualty reports give 1 officer and 26 other ranks killed and 1 other rank missing/presumed killed. The number of wounded is unknown but could easily have been 100 or more.

f. Postwar Royal Navy casualty lists report that 6 other ranks were killed, 2 died of wounds, and 1 was missing/presumed killed. It appears that the initial report of 1 officer killed was incorrect and that probably 2 other missing men were found to be killed.

operations research study, *Opposition Encountered on the British Beaches in Normandy on D-Day*, which attempted to strictly apply that measure only to those casualties counted as having been incurred "on the beach," rather than those lost in the later fighting inland. The actual range of the estimate they made was 573 at the lowest end and 730 at the highest.[65] That stricture meant that many casualties were simply not included. Some of that was due to simple error—such as missing the large number of casualties incurred by No. 3 Commando, which lost twenty missing of sixty-three embarked on LCI(S)-509 when it was hit by gunfire on the run in,[66] and the losses of the Free French Commandos, which were simply overlooked. Some, though, were excluded by intent—such as the losses incurred by many units once they were "off the beach." For example, the total loss of the 1st Special Service Brigade was recorded on the morning of 7 June as 13 killed, 189 wounded, and 87 missing, a total of 289. And yet the total of the individual unit casualties of the 1st Special Service Brigade as given in *Opposition Encountered on the British Beaches in Normandy on D-Day* total only 57, a shortfall of 232.[67]

Thus, the higher figure given here seems to be more accurate than the accepted one and indicates that the battle for Sword was much fiercer and less easy than is usually supposed. The heavy losses in the two DD tanks squadrons—at least three tanks sunk, nine swamped, and ten knocked out (55 percent); five A.V.R.E.'s knocked out and five damaged (29 percent); and six Crabs knocked out and four damaged (38 percent)—are another indicator of the intensity of the fighting on Sword.

Losses of landing craft on Sword were also severe and are something of a measure of the effectiveness of the obstacle-clearing program. Note, however, that these figures are also somewhat deceptive, since they include both lost and damaged craft. For example, total losses (sunk or damaged so badly as to be irreparable) of Royal Navy LCT's for D-Day on all three of the Commonwealth beaches were just nine—six LCT-IV's and three LCT(A)'s. Of those, only two can be identified on Sword, LCT(IV)-750 and LCT(IV)-947 (109), although the location of loss for two others, LCT(IV)-524 and LCT(IV)-715, is unknown. LCT(IV)-750 was recorded as lost off La Brèche-de-Hermanville, but the cause is unknown. LCT(IV)-947 (109) was the one that Colonel Cocks was killed in off Queen White.[68] The tables give additional details of loss and damage to landing craft at Sword.[69]

LANDING CRAFT IN THE SWORD ASSAULT			
Total Craft Engaged in Assault	Number Known Sunk	Number Lost or Damaged	Percentage Lost or Damaged
110 LCA		29	26
Unknown LCM		7	Unknown
12 LCP(L)		1	8
28 LCI(L)		9	32
27 LCI(S)		15	56
81 LCT, LCT(A)	2	18	22

CHAPTER 6

Assault Force Juno: The Canadian 3rd Infantry Division

THE 5TH ASSAULT REGIMENT DEPLOYED another two of its squadrons for the assault on Juno, the 26th and 80th, supported by twenty Crabs of B and C Squadron of the 22nd Dragoons. Overall commander of the breaching teams was Brig. Geoffrey Lionel Watkinson, commanding the 1st Assault Brigade. One distinct difference between Juno and the other beaches was that instead of the British-designed LCT-IV, the assault squadrons were transported in the American-designed LCT-V. Because of their smaller vehicle-carrying capacity, more of the LCT-V were required than the LCT-IV, so each troop was allotted two LCT-V's instead of one LCT-IV, while two more LCT-V's were made available as reserves. The 102nd LCT Flotilla carried the 26th Squadron and the 106th LCT Flotilla the 80th Squadron.

Although all the task forces of Neptune had problems keeping their place in the complicated timetable, usually because of the difficult conditions at sea, Assault Force Juno had to overcome some of the most difficult timing problems encountered by any of the task forces. The first occurred just prior to sailing when "last minute intelligence" indicated that the shoals lying off Nan, Les Iles de Berniéres, were two feet shallower than expected. That meant that H-Hour would have to be postponed past the turn of the tide so as to allow sufficient clearance for the landing craft over the rocks. As a result, the landings at Nan Green and Mike Red and Green were delayed until 0745, and those on Nan White and Nan Red were delayed until 0755.[1] Many of the obstacles were nearly submerged when the landings began, making the job of the engineers that much more difficult.

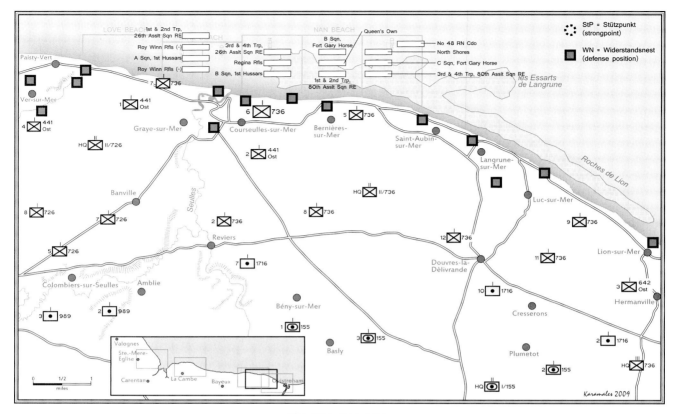

The assault on Juno.

Then, to make matters worse, a number of the assault convoys intended for Juno, including that carrying the 26th Assault Squadron to Mike Red and Green and Nan Green, became lost and managed to enter one of the swept channels intended for the convoys of Group G. It took some time to get the muddle sorted out and the convoy ships back to their proper position. The upshot of these last-minute confusions was that the first landings were delayed even later than the adjusted H-Hour.

On Nan White and Nan Red, the A.V.R.E.'s of the 80th Squadron actually touched down first, at 0805, but only because the decision was made to delay the infantry waves by thirty minutes so as to allow the A.V.R.E.'s to get ashore. As a result, the landing of the 80th Assault Squadron was closely followed by the infantry and L.C.O.C.U.'s at 0811 and the DD tanks at 0821.[2]

On Mike Red and Green and Nan Green, the first DD tanks landed at 0750. The infantry on Mike

Red and Green officially landed at 0749, in theory slightly before the DD tanks, although it is obvious the landings were somewhat intermixed in timing. Meanwhile, on Nan Green, it was apparently twenty minutes before the first infantry landed at 0810. The A.V.R.E.'s of the 26th Squadron, delayed by their errant passage, landed with the infantry and L.C.O.C.U.'s, beginning at about 0800 on Mike and over a half hour after the infantry on Nan Green.

The L.C.O.C.U.'s immediately turned to clearing the seaward obstacles, but found the rising tide was swiftly covering them. The seas also proved too rough for them to work underwater, so the attempt was abandoned until the next low tide, and an attempt was made to clear some of the inshore obstacles, but again with little success. Worse, the naval report scathingly commented that No. 11 L.C.O.C.U. on Nan Red had "showed lack of determination and failed to achieve any result."[3] However, the landing craft proved to have few trou-

A magnificently detailed reconnaissance photo of Courseulles on D-Day.
NATIONAL ARCHIVES CANADA

bles beaching, but that success was tempered by another problem noted in the naval report: the Teller mines attached to obstacles were taking a heavy toll of the landing craft on both Mike and Nan, usually when they were retracting after unloading on the beach.

The clearance teams from 5th, 6th, and 16th Canadian Field Companies R.C.E. and 19th and 262nd Field Companies R.E. had little better luck in the rising tide. On Nan Red, the engineers landed in five feet of water, reporting that

> The 5 Cdn Fd Coy bulldozers were useless owing to the depth of water so I attempted to blow a gap 200 yards in width and as deep as my men could go without drowning. This was quite successful, but as the charges were under water only about 80% of them were effective . . .
>
> Having done all we could on the beach we went on to mine clearing along the promenade and round the houses and across the 160 yard gap which was formed by a field running down to the shore from the first lateral road.[4]

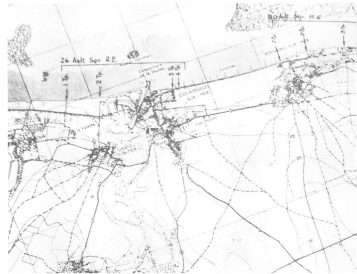

This map prepared by the 5th Assault Regiment after D-Day shows where the squadrons and troops landed. TNA

80TH ASSAULT SQUADRON

The 80th Squadron, under the command of Major Wiltshire along with eleven Crabs of the 1st and 4th Troop, B Squadron, 22nd Dragoons, was to clear two lanes on Nan White and two on Nan Red for the 8th Canadian Infantry Brigade. The squadron strength, including the 55-man detachment of the 22nd Dragoons, was 11 officers and 180 other ranks. The officers and men of the 80th Squadron complained vehemently of the difficult Channel passage: "A bad crossing which caused most men to be seasick. Station keeping by RN [Royal Navy] was poor. Craft touched down far from simultaneously and in most cases, due to the tide, well to the left of their planned gaps."[5]

At least here the LCA(HR)'s apparently had some effect. All nine of the 2nd Division of the 590th LCA(HR) Flotilla managed to arrive off Nan White and Red, despite the heavy seas. All fired without problem, and although the exact effect isn't known, the Royal Navy observers reported that they "fired their bombs with very good effect."[6]

Nan Red Beach, Green Gap: 4th Troop— Successful

LCT-(1414) carried half the assault team, under the command of Lt. Jack H. Hornby, who was killed. It consisted of two Crabs and two GP A.V.R.E.'s. After Hornby was killed, Lt. Peter d'Arcy Burbidge, commander of the 4th Troop, B Squadron, 22nd Dragoons, took over. LCT-(1415) carried the other half of the assault team, under the 4th Troop, 80th Assault Squadron commander, Captain Bellingham-Smith, who was wounded. It consisted of one Crab and three A.V.R.E.'s (Bobbin, Fascine, and SBG). They landed just after 0745 hours (within a few minutes of 3rd Troop). The war diary describes their actions:

> Touch down 150 yds to left of target. Craft serial 1415 in 7' of water. Collision between LCT(A) HE and AVRE carrying br [bridge]. Dismounted crew sniped and attacked with grenades in the water. Flails turned right and cleared second path across the same gap in the dunes as No. 3 Tp. Tubular and coir carpet bobbin laid on soft sand in flailed track, but did NOT stand up to tracked traffic. Fascine NOT used. Lt Hornsby dismounted to direct traffic through the gap while it was being marked and fatally injured between a tk [tank] and D7. Gaps widened by hand methods. Casualties Killed 1 offr and 1 [Other Rank], wounded 3 [Other Ranks].[7]

Nan Red early in the morning, with troops of the 80th Assault Squadron and the North Shore (New Brunswick) Regiment. On the far left is a D9 armored bulldozer, and in the center can be seen a DD tank and two universal carriers. On the right is a B.A.R.V. and a truck, another DD tank, and (closest to the photographer) an A.V.R.E. NATIONAL ARCHIVES CANADA

An A.V.R.E. of either the 3rd or 4th Troop, 80th Assault Regiment, on the outskirts of St. Aubin-sur-Mer on the morning of 6 June. NATIONAL ARCHIVES CANADA/GEORGE BRADFORD

Nan Red Beach, Blue Gap: 3rd Troop— Successful

LCT-(1412) carried half the assault team, under the troop commander, Captain Essery, with one Crab and three A.V.R.E.'s (GP, Fascine, and SBG). LCT-(1413), with the other half of the assault team, under the command of Lieutenant Gloyn, carried one Crab, two A.V.R.E.'s (GP and Bobbin), and one D7 armored bulldozer. The reserve LCT-(1413a) carried two B.A.R.V.'s of the 23rd Beach Recovery Section R.E.M.E., one Crab, one D7 armored bulldozer, and Brig. G. L. Watkinson, commanding the 1st Assault Brigade R.E. with a small advance head-quarters section. They landed at 0745 hours. The war diary recorded: "Craft serial 1413 out of sight and reported sinking at touch down, which was 200 yards left of the target gap.* Flailed up to 10' sea wall followed by SBG which was placed in position. Flail then sent to the lateral over dunes to the left where mines were blown. Reserve Flail used to widen gap to the lateral. AVRE crossed br [bridge] but all other traffic preferred the route over the dunes. No DDs until H+60. Casualties: Personnel nil, AVRE nil."[8]

Nan White Beach, Yellow Gap: 2nd Troop— Successful

LCT-(1410) carried half the assault team, under Lt. Ian Charles Hammerton, commander of 1st Troop, B Squadron, 22nd Dragoons, with two Crabs and two A.V.R.E.'s (GP and Fascine). LCT-(1411) carried the other half, under the 2nd Troop, 80th Assault Squadron commander, Capt. Sir Francis Grant, with one Crab and three A.V.R.E.'s (GP, Fascine, and SBG). Both LCT's landed together at 0805. According to the war diary, the troop

touched down 500 yds E of planned gap. High tide and mined obstacles forced gap to be made opposite point of landing—wall 12' high. Flails start flailing to the wall but br [bridge] shot away as it left the craft (comd cas [the A.V.R.E. commander was a casualty]). Second comd [commander] killed by MG fire. Two Petards out of action due to enemy fire. Ten dustbins [fired] at lip of wall but crater too steep and soft. Inf then began landing some way to right. Moved down beach towards ramp blocked by element C (10 shots). Flailed up ramp with two Flails. One Flail caught up in wire. Eventually clear after some hand clearance under smoke. Fascine dropped in A-tk ditch and ramped by hand. Second path made to by-pass Bernieres.[9]

---

* LCT-(1413) was not actually sunk; it had broken down during the passage and lost contact with the rest of 3rd Troop. It landed Brigadier Watkinson, Lieutenant Gloyn, their men, and equipment some time later in the morning.

Bernières, with WN 28 at left center and Nan White on the right.
NATIONAL ARCHIVES CANADA

Below: Two elderly French civilians evacuating Berniéres-sur-Mer on the morning of 6 June. Behind them is an A.V.R.E. of the 80th Assault Squadron, probably from the 1st or 2nd Troop.
NATIONAL ARCHIVES CANADA

Sgt. Frank Weightman commanded the A.V.R.E. (GP) on LCT-(1411) and left this account after the war, beginning with the Channel crossing:

We all groaned with sheer misery, sickness and the cold. There was only the AVRE for shelter packed as it was with equipment, ammunition, explosives, rations for weeks and the five of us. Myself, Claud [*sic*] Raynes (Driver, a staunch-hearted Jewish lad from Manchester with poor eyesight), R. G. Swabey (Wireless Operator, a good one, always keeping his nervousness under firm control), George Raines (Gunner or Mortar-man, a cheery young Geordie) and H.A. Meads as co-driver (exchanged a few days later for Arthur Turner, from Staffs). But no corporal to squeeze in as 2 i/c and Demolition NCO.[10]

Then, on arriving off the beach, the Royal Navy crew broke out the rum, and after a mug, Weightman and his crew were

feeling better now and were so hungry that we were munching ration biscuits as drove clearly off into about four feet of water. . . . The tide was early, high and choppy with the following wind. Only 60 yards of beach from

the water's edge to the solid masonry at the foot of the sea wall, crowded with various ruined steel obstacles, reached through a mass of beached and washed up landing craft, stranded, wrecked, or smashed. Captain Grant and [Troop Sergeant] Bill Reed preceded by two flails dropped off wall and tried to blast an exit with Petard bombs. No success, they were impeded by the Canadian infantry who were taking cover. Jock Martine (fascine) and Sam King (SBG Bridge) both met deep trouble.

On Nan White, the two teams succeeded in clearing lanes through to the first lateral road, but both routes were narrow, and it seems to have taken considerable time to get them through. As late as 0850 to 0920 hours, elements of the 114th Light Antiaircraft Regiment R.A. reported that only a single exit was open and that the beach was packed solid with vehicles waiting to get inland. It was 1040 before three exits were complete, but by that time, it

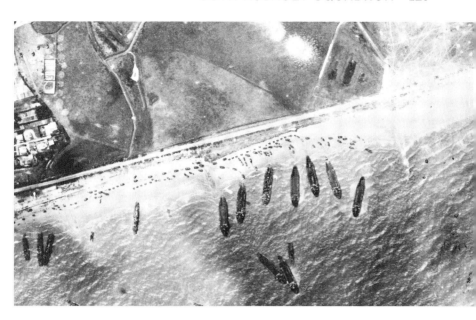

East edge of Bernières and right edge of Nan White. NATIONAL ARCHIVES CANADA

was too late—the early traffic jam had created chaos on the beach. As late as 1400, it was reported that "the beach itself was in terrible confusion. There were only about 25 yards of beach in front of the promenade which was heavily wired, so there were only the exits put up by the beach group. The beaches were jammed with troops with bicycles, vehicles and tanks all trying to move towards the exits. It was an awful shambles."[11]

Nan White Beach, Green Gap: 1st Troop— Successful

LCT-(1408) carried half the assault team, under the command of Lieutenant Saunders of the 1st Troop, with one Crab and three A.V.R.E.'s (Log Carpet, Fascine, and SBG). LCT-(1409) carried the other half, under the command of Lieutenant Oxtoby, also of the 1st Troop, with one Crab, two A.V.R.E.'s (GP and Fascine), and one D7 armored bulldozer. The reserve LCT-(1409a), under the 1st Troop commander, Captain Tracy, carried one A.V.R.E. (Plow), one B.A.R.V. of the 23rd Beach Recovery Section R.E.M.E., and one D7 armored bulldozer. LCT-(1408) landed at 0815 and LCT-(1409) at 0820, after the infantry and DD tanks. The war diary reported:

> Touched down opposite planned gap among the beach obstacles att [attached] to which were fused shells. First Flail flailed to a sea wall followed by aslt br [assault bridge]. First AVRE over the br hit a mine and blocked the exit. Two Flails then cleared a second path to a place where the sea wall was broken down and managed to mount it. Flailed to the first lateral and joined the two exits. Flails then flailed lateral to 2 Tp gap. Fascine dropped in A-tk ditch crossing the lateral. Meanwhile D7 used to push the br tank clear of the br. Remainder of exit to lateral cleared of mines by hand. Porpoise jammed on br and moved by D7. Dvr [Driver] of D7 dismounted and killed by S mine. Later second fascine dropped into ditch and good crossing bulldozed.
>
> Inf arrived before AVRE but were still on the beach, limiting Petard operations. No mines on beach but very dense between top of beach and lateral. Mainly S mines and Tellermines. DD tanks arrived after AVREs.
>
> Casualties, Killed 1, wounded 1, AVRE nil.[12]

The 80th Squadron had been completely successful despite the muddled timing of the landings. Three of the A.V.R.E.'s had been damaged and one lost, but personnel casualties remained low, totaling just nine, including only three killed.

THE ASSAULT BY 8TH CANADIAN INFANTRY BRIGADE GROUP

Nan Red

On Nan Red, opposition to the engineer obstacle-clearance teams was strong:

> During the whole operation (i.e. attempted obstacle clearance in deep water) we came under LMG, shell and mortar fire. Snipers were also active by this time as the armour had pushed inland followed by the infantry, and many men were being hit. Due to the strong current and heavy kits, many men were drowning so we set to work pulling them ashore and saving as many as we could. . . . During one bad spell of sniping, Cpl Muddle made good use of a Bren gun in silencing a few snipers and enabling the work of clearing to carry on. (19th Field Company R.E.)[13]

Armored support on Nan Red came from the twenty DD tanks of C Squadron, 10th CAR (they were also known by their traditional "cavalry" title as the Fort Gary Horse). They were brought in directly to shore and landed at about 0805 hours and found that the beach defenses "had not been touched . . . [and] soon came to life. . . . [They] found the beach fairly quiet on landing except for sniping and the occasional shells on their left."[14]

It was about five minutes later, at 0810 hours, when the assault infantry began to land—A and B Companies of the North Shore Regiment. "But by the time the infantry assault companies got in the situation had become much more lively and the tanks were giving supporting fire in all directions. The Tanks had now lost 4 and were down to 16; crew commanders directing fire were subjected to sniping and several were lost here."[15]

The 558th LCA Flotilla reported that landing them was a torturous exercise by that time; the LCA's had to pick their way through the partly submerged obstacles—mostly Element C and stakes. "Troops were put down into 1 foot 6 inches to 2 feet of water. All troops were put ashore and although looking very green went off in good order, the majority calmly walking up the beach and getting under the shelter of the sea wall."[16]

It appears that the infantry were barely opposed at that time; only one officer and "several" other ranks were reported wounded, mostly to mines and booby traps in houses along the beach. By 0948 hours, A Company had reached its initial beachhead objectives after having incurred twenty-four casualties. B Company found that its objective, WN 27 in St. Aubin-sur-Mer, had been untouched—"no damage to the defenses of the strongpoint had been caused by the air and naval bombardment previously arranged. It appeared not to have been touched. Nevertheless the company proceeded to clear the village."[17]

The assault sapper detachments from the 16th Field Company R.C.E. advanced with B Company through St. Aubin-sur-Mer and found some tanks of C Squadron held up by steel-rail roadblocks and cut them while under fire, allowing the tanks to advance. "No 1 Section of No 1 Platoon landed in two parts at H plus 20 mins. They assembled at a rendezvous some 200 yards from the beaches without casualties, despite enemy MGs, mortars and snipers. They proceeded inland behind the leading infantry through ST AUBIN-SUR-MER, checking the roads and verges for mines."[18]

B Company, with the tanks and some of the A.V.R.E.'s, continued to clear German resistance from the town throughout the early-morning hours. "The cooperation of infantry and tanks was excellent and the strongpoint was gradually reduced. At 1115 hrs, 4 hours and 5 minutes after landing the area was cleared. 48 prisoners were taken and it is estimated that the same number were killed."[19]

Brigadier Watkinson, who landed on Nan Red, witnessed the clearance of St. Aubin and remarked, "This fire, mortar MG and rifle, continued for an hour or more with some intensity from houses and a pillbox in the cliff. It was not possible to see flashes of weapons and when it was suppressed it broke out again from another direction. Later it continued as sniping throughout D-day. . . . The pillbox and the

St. Aubin looking east from one of the 5-centimeter gun positions in WN 27. The wreckage is a P-47. NARA

The seawall at St. Aubin with an LCT broached to on the left, another in the distance, and what is probably Green Gap to the right. NATIONAL ARCHIVES CANADA

compartment beneath it in the cliff were destroyed by petard and some houses were silenced by both petard and 75 mm gun fire."[20]

The fighting in St. Aubin went on for some time, and the last strongpoint did not surrender until 2000 hours that night.

Commando Landing

At 0843 hours No. 48 (RM) Commando of the 4th Special Service Brigade began landing from LSI(S)'s.

Their mission was to pass through the North Shores and seize Langrune-sur-Mer, east of St. Aubin-sur-Mer, linking up with No. 41 (RM) Commando (also part of the 4th Special Service Brigade), which was attacking west from Sword.

About 0730 hrs the flotilla moved in towards the shore [note that the transit to shore from the anchorage took nearly an hour and fifteen minutes]. At first it appeared that the landing would be unopposed and most craft dismounted the 2 in mortars which were prepared to cover the landing with smoke. Then MGs opened up from the strongpoint at ST AUBIN, which was almost opposite the Easternmost landing craft and perhaps 200 yards from the Westernmost and the craft was subjected to mortar and shell fire. The 2nd Troop craft received a direct hit amidships. The Oerlikons [20-millimeter guns mounted on the LSI(S)] replied and HQ craft put down smoke on the beach with 2 in mortars.

0843 hrs. Beach obstacles had not been cleared and were well below the water when the Commando landed. Two craft (Y and Z Troops) struck obstacles and were unable to beach. HQ craft struck an obstacle but was fairly close inshore. A, B, X and HQ troops were able to wade ashore in about 3 feet of water by Y and Z troops could only get ashore by swimming. Many officers and men attempted to swim ashore from these craft and a high proportion of these were lost from drowning in a strong undertow. On reaching shore troops made for the cover of the earth cliff and seawall. Here they found a confused situation. The cliff and seawall gave some protection from SA [small arms] fire but any movement away from them was under MG fire. The whole area was under heavy mortar and shell fire. Under the seawall was a jumble of men from other units including many wounded and dead. The beach was congested with tanks, SP guns and other vehicles, some out of action, other attempting to move from the beaches in the very confused space between the water's edge and the seawall. LCTs were arriving all the time and attempted to land their loads, adding to the general confusion.

A quick recce showed that the beach exit to the right of the isolated houses was free from aimed SA fire except for an occasional shot and that a gap had been cleared through the mines. As this was the quickest way to the assembly area, orders were immediately passed for troops to move out to the assembly

area by this route. B Troop led, followed by A Troop, HQ and X Troop. The assembly area was much quieter. The CO returned to the beach to contact X and Z Troops. A considerable number of men of mixed troops were found still under the cliff and those were moved off to the right. He found Y Troop attempting to get ashore from an LCT in which they had transferred from their LCI. However the landing of Y Troop was very slow and few men managed to get ashore before the LCT shoved off, taking with her about 50 men of the Commando to England, despite their energetic protests. Z Troop was more fortunate and about 40 men were eventually collected in the assembly area. In the assembly area it was found on calling for reports that A, B, and X Troops each had about 50 to 55 men available. HQ had had about 20 casualties but was working satisfactorily. The five men of Y Troop present were joined with Z Troop (about 40).[21]

Altogether, No. 48 (RM) Commando reported four killed, 90 wounded, and 55 missing on D-Day. Their landing was followed shortly after, at 0900 hours, by the headquarters of 4th Special Service Brigade.

As the craft closed the beach a group of men could be seen standing in the shelter of the seawall and it appeared that there was little enemy activity. The width of the beach was only about 15 yards instead of 150 yards as expected, due to the rough weather. As the first men came ashore an MG opened up from the window of a house on top of the seawall, causing a few casualties and thereafter there was sniping until after about 4 to 5 minutes. Oerlikon fire from the craft silenced the enemy.

Owing to bad conditions, brigade HQ took 10–12 minutes to off load all its equipment as opposed to 4 to 5 minutes "under best circumstances". . . . Had the landing been opposed by determined MG fire from even a pair of MGs it would not have been possible to land the equipment required for communication within the brigade.[22]

However, the problem clearing the obstacles at Nan Red was coming to a head. More and more landing craft were being damaged by the mined obstacles, some seriously, and many more were either hung up on an obstacle or were trying to pick a way through the congested waters. Starting at about 1030 hours, craft at Nan Red were diverted to Nan White, and at 1400 hours, Nan Red was closed to landing. After that, all the engineer obstacle-clearance teams were diverted to Nan White.[23]

Nan White

The first infantry ashore on Nan White were A and B Company of the Queen's Own Regiment of Canada (QOR) at 0815, after the 2nd Troop but almost simultaneous with the 1st Troop of the 80th Assault Squadron. The account given by the 556th LCA Flotilla, which lifted the QOR to the beach, reported,

> [The Germans] had made a rapid recovery from the very heavy bombardment, and were firing very actively, though the firing to start

with was hesitant and spasmodic, but mortars were already ranging and machineguns were firing concentrated bursts.

All the Canadians were disembarked on the beaches and none, as far as I can ascertain, was lost before we touched down.[24]

The QOR view of what happened after touch-down was quite different:

> 0805 hours. The assault companies get the word to go in. As yet no DD tanks or AVsRE can be seen, which looks rather ominous.
> 0815 hours. A and B Coy touch down. B Coy immediately catch a packet of trouble as they are landed in front of a very heavily defended position at MR 998855 [WN 28]. Several of the LCAs of both coys are blown up by mines, but only the front two or three men are injured. A Coy are a little better off than B, for they at least were able to get off the beach at MR 989855 [just west of Berniéres]. However, as soon as they hit the railway they come under very heavy mortar fire and are pinned down. Their casualties here begin to mount up. The balance of A

This is the incomplete (note the rough wooden shuttering for the concrete roof, which has not been poured yet) emplacement for the MG 08/15 on the seawall in WN 28, Bernières, 6 June 1944. The view is from the beach looking east-southeast.
NATIONAL ARCHIVES CANADA

German prisoners being searched by men of the 3rd Canadian Division Provost (Military Police) Company later in the morning at St. Aubin. NATIONAL ARCHIVES CANADA

The German prisoners collected in front of the seawall at Bernières. They are from the 5th Company, 736th Grenadier Regiment. The machine-gun pillbox of WN 28 is to the left center. NATIONAL ARCHIVES CANADA

More German prisoners guarded by the provost company at St. Aubin. In the background is one of the troublesome Typ SK 5-centimeter gun positions of WN 27. NATIONAL ARCHIVES CANADA

Coy managed to get through and to carry on with the job. B Coy meanwhile have really got quite a packet, but they outflanked the enemy position, and finally the remnants of the enemy surrendered. The coy has suffered very heavily, three officers and one warrant officer wounded and two sergeants killed.[25]

The battalion war diary noted that later on 8 June, a total of thirty-six other ranks were buried who had been killed in the initial assault. B Company suffered "very heavily" while landing directly into the heart of WN 28. Later, the war diary recorded that "B Coy casualties being so heavy they gather just off the beach and try to sort themselves out." A Company, landing farther west, suffered less in the initial landing, but then came under very heavy mortar fire as they advanced inland.[26]

Ten minutes after the QOR, at about 0825, the first of their supporting armor, the DD tanks of B Squadron, 10th CAR, began to land. Because of the rough seas, it had been decided to bring them "close inshore" before they were launched; although their skirts were inflated, they had little more than a deep wade to get ashore, and all twenty tanks made it to the beach without a problem. "It was found that several centres of resistance along the beach had not been touched by the preliminary air or support artillery bombardment and soon came to life. AVsRE came in late, though the assault infantry were in [*sic*] time on the beach. The beach defences were found to be very much as foreseen by Intelligence."[27]

The tanks were followed five minutes later by the reserve of the QOR; C and D Companies.

The casualties among the LCAs are quite heavy, almost half of them being blown up by underwater mines. However, the personnel get ashore without too much trouble and pass through the assault companies on the way to their positions. By now the DDs and AVsRE are on the beach, but do not seem to be getting any place. The support all round has been very disappointing so far as we are concerned, for none of the beach defences have been touched, and this has caused very high casualties among the assaulting companies.[28]

The war diary of 10th CAR also remarked upon the sudden resurgence in the German defenses:

After the infantry landed enemy fire opened up and one company of the QOR of C [either C or D Company] suffered severely before B Sqn could support it. The tanks remained on the beach until almost 0930 hrs. No gaps were made at all till then as the RE

This fortified beach villa was part of WN 28. Nicknamed "Denise and Roger," it was captured by men of the Queen's Own Rifles of Canada. NATIONAL ARCHIVES CANADA

Low oblique photo of Bernières, with the landing of the Queen's Own of Canada on Nan White.
NATIONAL ARCHIVES CANADA

company were late on the beach also. Considerable sniping took place and sporadic shelling came down.

When they were able B Sqn moved up through Bernieres-sur-Mer near headquarters of QOR of C. This squadron undoubtedly proved a valuable service in supporting the QOR of C from the beach and later took out several MGs and two 76 mms to the SW of town.[29]

The Assault Reserve Lands
The reserve battalion of the 8th Canadian Brigade, the Francophone Le Regiment de la Chaudière (Chaudières), landed at 0830.

Disembarked at BERNIERES-SUR-MER where fighting is already taking place between Boche defences and QOR of C. The beach is infested with mines and most LCAs are blown up and many men are wounded by German mortars. The regiment is formed to wait an hour on the beach under artillery fire because QOR of C has not yet succeeded in capturing the village. As soon as the village is captured the regiment moves through the breaches made in the notorious "West Wall" [the seawall] and passed through the village, followed by tanks, artillery and MMGs. BERNIERES-SUR-MER is almost totally destroyed and many houses are in flames. In the assembly area, a small wood south of the village, we come under heavy artillery and MG fire for two hours: one officer and several other ranks killed and wounded.[30]

It is unknown what Chaudière losses were on 6 June, but on the evening of 7 June, the battalion war diary recorded losses of thirty-two killed and eighty-three wounded or missing to date.

Between 0850 and 0920 hours, it appears that at least six of the eight LCT(A)'s and LCT(HE)'s carrying the 4th Battery, 2nd (RM) Armoured Support Regiment, landed. They brought twelve Centaur tanks and probably three Sherman OP tanks. Nothing is known of the two 17-pounder Sherman tanks on the LCT(CB) that should have been with them. Their craft, LCT(CB)-2338, survived the landings, but when they landed and what happened to the tanks are unknown. Given that the 2nd Canadian Armoured Brigade reported the loss of six 17-pounder Shermans on D-Day, it is possible they were lost or damaged.[31]

Intermixed among the LCT's of the 4th (RM) Armoured Support Battery were six LCT-V's carrying the 19th Army Field Regiment R.C.A., which was an army asset attached to the 3rd Canadian Division for the landing. They were equipped with twenty-four self-propelled M7 105-millimeter howitzers and began firing in support of the infantry immediately after landing. "The first LCT beaches at approximately 0910 hrs, and though heavily mortared got off the beach and have their first SP in action in prepared position at 0920 hrs. A troop had two vehicles, one SP and one half track receive direct hits. RHQ craft beached under heavy mortar fire, two OR killed, one officer and two OR severely wounded."[32]

The regimental forward observation officers and reconnaissance parties, landing with the assaulting infantry, had already had one officer wounded and one other rank killed. All told, the regimental casualties for D-Day were finally tallied as two officers and seven other ranks killed, and four officers and nine other ranks wounded, a fairly stiff price for an artillery unit to pay in a single day.

Also landing at the same time as the 19th Army Field Regiment was the headquarters groups of the 8th Canadian Infantry Brigade. They too mentioned the heavy fire that was still incoming: "The actual beach had been cleared of enemy at this time but Bernieres itself still contained enemy snipers and machine guns whose fire together with some artillery was directed on to the beach and the seaward side of the town. The clearances of the latter enemy caused some slight delay before the two brigade command posts [8th Canadian and 4th Special Service] were established at the southern edge of Bernieres."[33]

However, it turned out that Berniéres was not the only remaining hotbed of German resistance on Nan. A Company, 5th Battalion of the Royal Berkshire Regiment (5th Royal Berkshires) of the 102nd

The Chaudières advancing through Bernières toward Bény-sur-Mer. The vehicle to the left is a D7 bulldozer. NATIONAL ARCHIVES CANADA

Beach Sub-area that had landed on Nan Green, attempted to move to Nan White at 1200 hours to begin preparing the beaches for the LST landings later in the day. In the process, they ran into a number of positions in the dunes that hadn't been reduced and suffered three men wounded from grenade splinters while killing two Germans, wounding six, and taking twenty-five prisoners.[34]

Inland from Nan
While the QOR continued to hunt down snipers in Bernières and the 5th Royal Berkshires cleaned out the beach defenses, at about 1000 hours the Chaudières passed through and continued south, supported by the 14th Field Regiment, which had landed at 0925 hours, and A Squadron, 10th CAR. Just north of the Tailleville-Reviers road they encountered a minefield, covered by an 88-millimeter antitank gun, probably one of those of the 2nd Company, 716th Tank Destroyer Battalion.

The Germans knocked out three of the self-propelled howitzers of the 14th Field Regiment and temporarily halted the advance. The Chaudières reported they were "under heavy artillery and MG fire for two hours, losing 1 officer killed and several OR wounded," before A Company was able to outflank the guns.[35] They reported capturing the gun with three prisoners and somewhat further on a "battery of 88 mms" (probably the other two guns of the 716th's 2nd Company), while losing one officer wounded themselves in the attack.[36] Luckily for them, the pre-assault bombing had cut all the control cables to the launchers of the nearby *Wurfgerät* battery so they were useless.

Overall, the 8th Canadian Brigade's operations were a success, despite the massive confusion. By the end of the day, they reported that enemy casualties had been high and that units of the brigade had captured 250 Germans.[37]

26TH ASSAULT SQUADRON

At about 0800, the first of the LCT's with the A.V.R.E.'s of the 26th Assault Squadron finally began to arrive on Mike Beach, about fifteen minutes late. The task of the 26th Squadron, under the command of Maj. Allan Elton Younger, with nine Crabs of the 2nd and 3rd Troop, B Squadron, 22nd Dragoons, was to clear two lanes on Mike Beach and two lanes on Nan Beach for the assault troops of the 7th Canadian Infantry Brigade. The squadron strength, including the 45-man detachment of the 22nd Dragoons, was 11 officers and 201 other ranks.

It was noted that all troops had a "rough passage, high proportion of crews seasick." [38]

Nan Green Beach, Red Gap (M4): 4th Troop—Successful

LCT-(1024) carried half the assault team, under the 4th Troop commander, Capt. Raymond John Mare, with one Crab and three A.V.R.E.'s (Fascine, Log Carpet, and SBG), and LCT-(1025) carried the other half, under the command of Lieutenant David, with one D7 armored bulldozer and two A.V.R.E.'s (Fascine and SBG). They arrived some time after the 3rd Troop at 0831 hours, but at the correct location at M4 Gap, where the 3rd Troop had already begun working. Its actions were recorded as follows:

> 3 Tp Flails fired at Hitler emplacement. Flail from reserve craft (1023a) and half sqn comd land with fascine from 3 Tp, mounted dunes easily and opened way across A-tk ditch for AVRE but NOT for the Flail owing to the width of the ditch. 3 Tp dropped a fascine in their gap with similar results. 4 Tp having arrived flailed a second route to the fascine

Above: Two Canadian soldiers examine a terrain relief model of Courseulles after the battle, probably in the headquarters of the 2nd Battalion, 736th Grenadier Regiment, at Tailleville. Nan Green is on the far side while Mike is closest to the camera.
NATIONAL ARCHIVES CANADA

Nan Green Beach at Courseulles. On the left is the eastern edge of WN 29. NARA on their gap and placed a further fascine alongside the other. Both were improved by armd D7s and route open to the first lateral by 0900. No mines, since both gaps were straight into the defended post within its perimeter. 81mm mortar between the two gaps was unmanned.

Improvement of gap carried out by D7s. AVREs used in half tps or singly with inf in the town. No opposition and little work. 3 Tp gap made fit for wheels by bobbin being laid over bulldozed ramp. AVREs tow vehs to entrance of gaps when tide up to soft sand.

4 Tp gap blocked at about 0915 by the trailer of a bulldozer overturning at the ditch. SBG aslt br dropped over ditch—24' wide with vertical sides. One br fell off sideways in crossing the dunes. Second br very successful, ready by about 0945 and carried traffic all day. A further fascine was dropped in 4 Tps' gap, the crossing improved by logs and a whld [wheeled] crossing 20' wide resulted.

Six AVREs and two D7s on beach clearance when tide fell—hedgehogs, element C and ramps booby trapped with Tellermines or Shell fitted with DZ 35 push igniters.[39]

Nan Green Beach, Blue Gap (M3): 3rd Troop—Successful

LCT-(1022) carried half the assault team under the command of Lieutenant Ash, with one Crab and three A.V.R.E.'s (Fascine, Log Carpet, and SBG), and LCT-(1023) carried the other half, under the command of Capt. Richard B. O. Boase, the 3rd Troop commander, with one Crab and three A.V.R.E.'s (one Bobbin and two GP). LCT-(1023a) was in reserve with one D7 armored bulldozer and two A.V.R.E.'s (Fascine and SBG), under Lt. W. G. Shaw, commander of the 3rd Troop, B Squadron, 22nd Dragoons. They landed at 0815 hours: "Touch down 40 mins late, 150 yds east of proposed gaps. 100 yds of beach only. Element C submerged. Infantry have arrived but still on the beach. Some DDs out of the water. Little fire except for sniping and mortar fire."[40]

The Crabs on Nan were also successful:

On the left of Mike sector, east of the Seulles estuary, 3rd Troop (Lieutenant W. G. Shaw) made a remarkable landing. Of all 22nd Dragoons' troops engaged in the assault, 3rd Troop was, perhaps, the most anxious to get at the enemy. It was tough, it was aggressive, and it was prepared, if need be, to mix it with a complete armoured division. The assault craft carrying these restless men (whose appetite for action had, it is true, been diminished by the miseries of an extremely bad crossing) swept in towards Courseulles as if on exercise, almost dead on time. As they rode straight over the Element C there was no opposition from the beaches. The ramps went down at half-past seven, the tanks rolled out through the doors in drill order, and the chains began to beat a way up the beach. There was practically nothing to stop them. A few Germans went through the motions of firing their rifles and machine guns—and that was the end. Half an hour after landing the flails were over the dunes, across fascines laid in the ditch by the A.V.R.E.s, and were turning methodically to clear the lateral communications. By nine o'clock the assault task was complete. In the best of spirits, crews settled down behind their tanks to brew their first pans of "compo" tea on French soil and watched, with the complacent air of proprietors, the unending streams of men and equipment that were pouring through their lanes.[41]

Mike Red Beach, Yellow Gap (M2): 2nd Troop—Successful

LCT-(1020) carried half the assault team, with the 26th Assault Squadron commander, Major Younger, and Lieutenant Pratt, with one Crab, three A.V.R.E.'s (Plow, Cmd, SBG), and one D7 armored bulldozer. LCT-(1021) carried the other half, under the command of Captain Hendry, the 2nd Troop commander, with one Crab and three A.V.R.E.'s (Cmd, Fascine, and SBG). In reserve, and landing later, was LCT-(1019a) with three A.V.R.E.'s (GP) and one B.A.R.V. of the Beach Recovery Section.

Mike Red Beach at the loop of the Seulles River. The devastated area is WN 31. The vehicles are exiting via Lane M2 (Yellow Gap) opened by the 2nd Troop, 26th Assault Regiment. NARA

They touched down at 0810 at the correct spot and found the 1st Troop already there and at work.

> Correct touch down. Br dropped on dunes immediately to the right of M2. Flail crossed but hit mine and blocked route. Fascine dropped into water and bulldozed.
>
> Opened weir to allow culvert to drain. 30 prisoners taken during this operation. SBG taken inland to crossing near REVIERES but NOT required.
>
> OC recc'd route into COURSEULLES, removed mines and charges from the bridges

and declared lateral between M and N open at 1200 hours.[42]

Mike Green Beach, Green Gap (M1): 1st Troop—Successful

LCT-(1018) carried half the assault team, under Lt. Michael Charles Barraclough, 2nd Troop, B Squadron, 22nd Dragoons, with two Crabs, one A.V.R.E. (Bobbin), one D7 armored bulldozer, and one B.A.R.V. (attached from the Beach Recovery Section). The other half of the assault team, under Captain Hewitt of the 1st Troop, 26th Assault Squadron, was on LCT-(1019) carrying one Crab and two A.V.R.E.'s (Fascine and SBG). They beached at 0800, but in the wrong location.

Touch down opposite M2, 2 Tps' gap which at the time was assumed to be M1. Two Flails in echelon. No mines other than those fixed to obstacles. Crater 20' X 9' on landward side of dunes. Two Flails blew tracks whilst by-passing the crater. Third Flail cleared the route forward to the culvert 150 yds inland which had been cratered to form an obstacle 60' wide and over 12' deep surrounded by sheet flooding. Remaining Flail backing to clear track ditched itself for the remainder of the day, but continued to fire its guns. Fascine AVRE owing to sheet flooding overran the crater and became submerged. The crew returning to the beach came under mortar fire killing three and wounding the remainder.

Fascines dropped in first water by 2 Tp now arrived, and bulldozed to allow SBG to be brought up to the damaged culvert. The br pushed the fascine from the submerged AVRE and then placed onto its turret. Tanks used this bridge from 1030 to 1330 hrs. Later br replaced by filling in by hand.[43]

The operations of the Crabs on Mike were also detailed by Birt. They worked together as a single team with the A.V.R.E.'s after being put down in the wrong location.

With one flail of use only as a gun tank (its rotor had been blown off just before touching down), the teams ran hard to the high dunes beyond the beach under considerable mortar and sniper fire. The opposition from the beach itself was, however, negligible. Some Canadian D.D. tanks had managed to land and had silenced the emplaced guns that faced the sea. By half-past eight both teams were passing through the dunes; where, half turning, two flails touched off heavy mines and were put out of action for the time being with broken tracks. It was an unpleasant time in which to repair the damage, for mortar fire

was falling steadily on the dunes and a persistent 75 mm. gun was giving trouble from the flank. This gun was quickly disposed of, however, and the troop leader pushed his lane inland until, attempting to sweep a path for the A.V.R.Es. to the edge of a large crater, his tank settled firmly in the mud. The A.V.R.E. that followed him carrying a fascine also bogged down, and three of its crew were killed and three wounded by mortar fire as they dismounted to get a bridge in place over the crater. For the next hour the breaching team divided their time between dodging mortar shells and snipers' bullets and, dismounted, filling in the crater with rubble. Meanwhile the gunners were on the watch for targets, one of which, alas, was the tower of the church in Graye-sur-Mer, which was harbouring a nest of snipers, and was accordingly brought down by fire from Lieutenant Barraclough's ditched tank.[44]

At half-past ten, the only 2nd Troop tank still capable of flailing moved off to clear a lane on the right of its sector. It met little trouble, cleared its lane of mines, and was shortly able to report "lane clear." The tank remained on duty in this area, widening its lane and sweeping lateral communications, until at half-past one it was hit by an antitank gun and knocked out. The whole troop was thus, for the time being, immobilized. But the breaches had been made good, and the opposition—though unpleasant—had been surprisingly lighter than could have been expected.

In terms of completing their mission, the 26th Squadron had been very successful and had suffered only seven casualties, of which three were fatal, almost all from the fascine carrier submerged in the flooded crater that was used as a support for the SBG. Four Crabs had run onto mines or gotten bogged, but only one A.V.R.E. had been lost, the fascine carrier. It later became well known to the brigade and had a prominent mention in the brigade history, as "Le Pont A.V.R.E.," and many years later, in 1976, it was finally excavated, partly restored, and put on display in Graye-sur-Mer.

THE ASSAULT BY 7TH CANADIAN INFANTRY BRIGADE GROUP

As already noted, the first troops to land on Nan Green were actually some of the DD tanks of 6th CAR (they were also known by their traditional "cavalry" title as the 1st Canadian Hussars). Because of the continuing bad weather and heavy seas, it had been decided to land them directly on the beach as had been done with the 10th CAR on Nan Red and White. However, the senior officer in charge changed his mind and decided to launch the DD tanks during the run in to the beach. They began to land between 0740 and 0759 hours.[45]

The tanks of A Squadron were intended to support the Winnipegs on Mike. However, only eleven tanks were actually launched. On two of the four LCT's, all ten DD tanks successfully launched, but on the third, LCT-413, a shell cut the chains holding the ramp, preventing the remaining four from exiting, and then a mine exploded, badly damaging the LCT and causing it to list. For some reason, the other LCT did not launch its tanks either and instead decided to accompany the damaged one into shore.

Of the eleven launched, one was lost in the run in after being run down by an LCT(R); one crewman was killed by machine-gun fire as he tried to escape. Ten managed to beach, but two were swamped by the unexpectedly high water and three crewmen were wounded attempting to reach shore. Two of those wounded later died. The first of the remaining eight tanks apparently touched down just a few minutes after the initial infantry waves of the Royal Winnipeg Rifles. They began engaging targets on the beach while awaiting the following waves, reportedly destroying two 75-millimeter guns and six machine-gun positions. In turn one was knocked out by a 5-centimeter gun and all five crewmen were killed trying to escape. Later, the tank commanded by the squadron second in command, Capt. J. W. Powell, had its gun disabled by a hit from a 5-centimeter gun, but unfazed, he continued to engage the Germans with his machine guns.[46]

The damaged LCT-413 eventually landed, but continued to suffer misfortunes, striking another mine on the way in. One tank managed to get ashore, but another damaged its screens and sank. The remaining two in the damaged LCT were trapped and were unable to get ashore until the afternoon.[47]

B Squadron was to support the Reginas on Nan Green and launched nineteen DD tanks, of which fifteen reached the shore (apparently the twentieth tank could not be started and was landed in the afternoon). One was lost almost immediately after its engine stalled, two more had their screens collapse in the rough seas and sank, and the tank of the squadron commander, Major Duncan, was hit on the way in and also sank; one of his crew drowned. At least three more tanks were drowned out on the beach after landing by the rapidly rising tide or were knocked out, which left twelve operational.[48] The survivors immediately went to work and silenced a number of the beach positions before the infantry battalion they were to support, the Reginas, arrived.

Here, at least, the DD tanks were said to have had a great effect on the defenders: "A very noticeable event was that very shortly after the tanks deflated back of the underwater obstacles and commenced firing on the beach fortifications, the enemy manning these casemates surrendered. It has since been learned from some of their prisoners that the presence of tanks at this stage of the attack came as a complete surprise and were the main factor in their decision to surrender instead of fighting."[49]

No. 5 L.C.O.C.U. followed the tanks and the first of the engineer parties, landing at 0805 on Nan Green, while No. 1 L.C.O.C.U. reached the shore at Mike Red a little later at 0810. Both found the same insuperable obstacle on Mike Red and Nan Green that had been found on Nan Red and White; the rapidly rising tide and rough surf made it impossible for them to operate effectively, and the obstacles were already in three feet of water. They then tried to divert landing craft to Nan Green, but without success. Fortunately, both No. 1 and No. 5 L.C.O.C.U.'s noted that the "obstacles were less formidable and more widely spaced than had been expected," which did at least allow landing craft to touch down with few problems.

Also landing ahead of the A.V.R.E.'s of the 26th Assault Squadron were the LCA's of the leading companies of the 7th Canadian Brigade Group. They were hard on the heels of the L.C.O.C.U.'s and began coming ashore at about 0810.

Nan Green

The assault on the far left (east) of the 7th Brigade sector was by the Reginas on Nan Green. On the run-in to the beach, the 505th LCA Flotilla of the Royal Navy noted that "[t]he only opposition encountered whilst approaching the beach was rather desultory fire from the strong point at Courseulles. As soon as the ramps were let down a considerable amount of MG fire was directed at us from the right and far ahead." The account given by the 3rd Canadian Infantry Division of the Reginas assault is more detailed:

> The two assaulting companies of Regina Rifles touched down on Nan Green beach before Courseulles, 969855 to 984855 [note that is not indicating where the two companies touched down, those are the boundaries of Nan Green, which ran from the mouth of the Seulles River to a point 1,500 meters to the east]. A Coy on the right was to assault the pillboxes from the mouth of the R SEULLES to about half-way along the beach. Both companies were slightly late and unfavourable weather conditions denied any effective support whatsoever to A Coy. . . . While B Coy met with little trouble, A on the other hand, found their first task a long and arduous one. They eventually executed a left flanking attack which succeeded in breaking through the defences.

> For purposes of assault the town of Courseulles had been partitioned into blocks numbered 1 to 12, each to be cleared by designated companies. Careful study of enlarged aerial photos and maps showing the sites of enemy strong points had made the ground itself easily recognizable. At the sane time, training in street fighting had been carried out in anticipation of resistance in the town.

The strongpoint engaged by A Coy was contained in Block 1, and A was held up here while B Coy cleared Blocks, 2, 3, and 4. The reserve Coys now commenced to come ashore. C Coy touched down without mishap and moved through the town to clear Block 8. D Coy's craft were blown up in the water by mines and only 49 survivors reached land. These reorganized within Courseulles and set out for Reviers, 9681, as planned.

C Coy next reported Block 8 clear and then within a short time, Blocks 9, 10, and 11. A Coy now reported Block 1 in their hands and were ordered to take on 5, 6, and 7 on the lock bank. Shortly afterwards B Coy had cleared 4 and was sent on to 12.

Now came a report from A Coy that they were being fired on from Block 1, only just mopped up. They had neglected to leave there a small force to prevent re-occupation and the enemy had swiftly returned to the SW corner of the strong point, by tunnel and trenches. It was, therefore, necessary to return to this corner and begin the disheartening work once again. Matters progressed so slowly that another troop of tanks was assigned to them for assistance. Meanwhile, C Coy, having finished with Block 11, set out for REVIERS, following the remnants of D, whose leading elements had arrived there about 1100 hrs.

Comms between Bn HQ and A Coy now broke down and the second in command set out to find them. He returned with the report that they had now gone on to Block 5 and would remain in Courseulles to complete its clearance (Blocks 6 and 7).

Bn HQ followed C Coy to Reviers and established itself there about 1500 hours. Lt Col Matheson pointed out here that exact reconstruction of time was impossible and references to the hour of the day could only be vague. B Coy next arrived in Reviers, followed after an interval by A Coy, and then the bn rested there, awaiting brigade orders to move on. Many prisoners had been taken there by surprise.

Lt Col Matheson (OC) was of the opinion that Courseulles contained more troops than had been expected from the Intelligence Reports. In any event about 80 Germans were taken in the town, and many more had been killed or had escaped south.

The battalion's training in street fighting stood them in good stead even though the clearing of Courseulles did not involve house-to-house battles (as is apparent from the comparatively short time required to take it).

The infantry were assisted in clearing up the town by S Tp, 2nd RM Armd Sp Regt, equipped with Centaurs.[50]

Luckily, at least two of the LCT(A)'s with S Troop of the 3rd (RM) Support Battery had arrived to support the Reginas, apparently at about H+10. Of the LCT(A)'s that did not arrive, one had sunk en route, four landed about two hours late, while the last didn't land until D+1, 7 June. However, the LCT(CB) attached to the Royal Marine LCT group also arrived with its two powerful Sherman 17-pounder tanks. "During the actual landing operations two 17 pdr. Shermans, commanded by Lieut. F.L. Irving and Sgt. Lamb, were to engage and destroy specific forts from their LCT. The scheme was carried out according to plan, but while proceeding inland Lieut. Irving was killed when his tank was hit by a 50 mm. The tank, however, was repaired by the unit fitters and put back into action two days later."[51]

Mike Green and Red

To the right (west) of the Reginas, the Winnipegs assaulted with D Company on the left (east) on Mike Green and B Company on the right (west) on Mike Red. The remarks that were recorded in their war diary regarding the value of the "beach drenching" fire plan were somewhat jaundiced, but apparently were accurate:

RN and arty bombardment opens up with SP guns afloat firing short as usual.

0749 hrs. In spite of the air bombardment failing to materialize, RN bombardment being spotty, the rockets falling short and the DDs and AVsRE being late, D Coy R WPG RIF with under command 1 Pnr Sec [Pioneer Section] landed to the left of Nan Green and B Coy, with under command No 15 Platoon and two secs No 6 Fd Coy RCE landed on Mike Red—all within seven minutes of one another.

The bombardment having failed to kill a single German or silence one weapon, those companies had to storm their positions "cold" and did so without hesitation.

D Coy (Mike Green) landed at the junction of Green and Red beaches and encountered some mortar and MG fire. Two men were killed crossing the beach.

B Coy (Mike Red) was engaged by heavy MG fire, 75mm and mortar fire, starting when the LCAs were 700 yards from shore. This fire continued steadily as we touched down and on "doors down" craft was being badly hit but the men cleared the craft without hesitation. A large percent were hit while chest-high in water. The sand dunes were reached and the pillboxes taken by sheer guts and initiative of the individual.[52]

On the other hand, they were greatly appreciative of the help given them by the tanks of A Squadron, 6th CAR:

In the assault on the beach defense of Mike sector, A Sqn literally made possible the overwhelming of the defences. It will be recalled that the pre-assault bombardment had been either ineffective or non-existent and had it not been for the gallantry, determination, dash and skilful use of fire-power on the part of Maj Brooks and squadron, it is conceivable that this battalion's casualties and those of C Coy 1st C SCOT R would have been much heavier and the capture of the beachhead greatly delayed.[53]

On Mike Green, D Company was also joined by A Company, 8th Battalion of the Kings Own Regiment (8th Kings), which was part of the 7th Beach

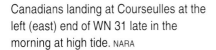

Canadians landing at Courseulles at the left (east) end of WN 31 late in the morning at high tide. NARA

The right (west) end of WN 31 and WN 33a. Troops and vehicles are exiting the beach via Yellow Gap. NARA

Group. They were supposed to be reconnoitering and securing the beach for the main body of the 7th Beach Group, which was responsible for command and control of the beach-unloading operation. Instead, they found themselves under sporadically heavy small-arms fire as they tried to assist in clearing the beach, preparing it for the reserve waves. Later, the 8th Kings helped to clear out pockets of resistance around Vaux and La Buisson that had been bypassed, but were unable to clear the Germans from the villages; it wasn't until mid-afternoon that they declared the beaches secure, and it was the next day before the two villages were liberated.

On Mike Beach, the tanks and infantry were at last also joined at 0800 by two sections of the 5th

Field Company R.C.E. and three sections of the 18th Field Company R.C.E., perhaps some fifty engineers in all, and No. 1 Troop, 26th Assault Squadron R.E. They found the tide higher than expected and "considerable difficulty was experienced in landing due to the high water."[54] Nevertheless, in about thirty minutes, they were able to clear a gap fifty yards wide before the water got too deep and ended work until the next tide. Unfortunately, somewhat later, two LCT's coming in to the beach missed the gap and were disabled by mines on other obstacles; they then drifted into the gap, completely blocking it.[55]

To the right (west) of the Winnipegs, C Company, 1st C Scot R, landed on the extreme edge of

Mike Beach Sector on 6 June with the mouth of the Seulles River in the center. On the right, elements of the 7th Canadian Brigade Group are landing opposite WN 31, while to the left, where the burning buildings are marked, is WN 29. NATIONAL ARCHIVES CANADA

Centaur tank of the Royal Marine armored support group coming ashore at Courseulles. It is towing a Porpoise waterproof supply sledge. NATIONAL ARCHIVES CANADA

Mike on the boundary with Love. They reported, "As we moved towards the shore the tremendous preparatory bombardment was going on all around us. No enemy fire was noticed. We landed in about three feet of water just short of the beach obstacles. At first there was no fire but as we moved forward

the odd mortar bomb landed amongst us and MG fire started to come from our left flank, causing several minor casualties."[56] They moved quickly to the position they were to assault, only to find it wrecked by naval gunfire and devoid of Germans.

The worst problem on Mike had been the delays. P Troop of the 2nd (RM) Armoured Support Regiment, which had also arrived two hours late, commented, "Things were chaotic on the beach; as yet there were no exits for vehicles tracked or otherwise. The tide was in and an enormous amount of equipment was jammed in a narrow strip of sandy beach. The Troop Commander made a recce of several exits during the course of the day but was unable to get the troop off the beach."[57]

The assessment by the 2nd Platoon, 262nd Field Company R.E., confirms that "at this stage (0930 hrs) the beach was choc-a-block with vehicles of all types and no exits were available from the beach to the first lateral."[58]

At about 1030, the 262nd Field Company R.E. finished clearing mines from a track running inland from the M2 gap, and then shortly after, a second was cleared to the right from the M1 gap, as was the inland lateral track connecting the two.

The combination of delays in landing, clearing the beach obstacles and the gaps inland, and wrecked landing craft fouling the exits caused many units to land hours after they had been planned to. For example, Battery Headquarters, 375th Light Antiaircraft Regiment R.A., scheduled for 1025 hours, landed more than five hours late, at 1530. Other units landed three or more hours late. It was not until 1530 hours that the 262nd Field Company R.E. declared Mike sector clear of obstacles.[59]

Inland from Mike

The late arrival of the A.V.R.E.'s at 0816 led to some grumbling; the 6th CAR war diary later caustically remarked that "from 1 to 1.5 hrs elapsed before the DDs were able to move off the beach."[60] Nonetheless, as the engineers began to clear the gaps, troops started moving inland. A Squadron, 6th CAR, noted, "As soon as exits were cleared the tanks split in 3 groups for Phase I, as follows, 2 going to support C Coy C SCOT R and 2 groups of 4 each moving up with left and right leading coys of R WPG RIF. The two tanks which went with the C SCOT R later joined up with the group of the squadron."[61]

The Reginas had already begun moving to Reviers, their next objective, even before Courseulles had been completely cleared. By about 1700 hours, they had consolidated on Reviers and were advancing southward along with the ten DD tanks of B Squadron, 6th CAR. Together, they ran into one of the German 88-millimeter antitank batteries and lost five of the tanks before overrunning the battery, but effectively ending the days advance for B Squadron.[62] However, the Reginas continued to press on, supported by two troops of C Squadron, 6th CAR, which had finally managed to clear the congestion off the beachhead, and eventually made the farthest advance by the Canadians on D-Day, reaching Bretteville L'Orgueilleuse before withdrawing slightly.

When battalion headquarters, A and C Company, of the Winnipegs landed in the second wave, they found the beach still under heavy fire. Nonetheless they joined with B and D, the two assault companies, and accompanied by eight tanks of A Squadron, 6th CAR, they advanced to Banville and then Colombiers-sur-Seulles, where they joined up with the 1st Canadian Scottish and continued the advance.

The jammed beachfront at Courseulles late in the morning. To the left is a deep-wading Sherman while a long column of tanks, led by a Stuart, await their turn to get off the beach. At the center can be seen an SBG that was laid from the beach onto the promenade. NATIONAL ARCHIVES CANADA

Nan Green from the sea on D-Day. The LCT is from the 31st Flotilla of K LCT Squadron, which brought the 12th and 13th Field Regiments ashore. NATIONAL ARCHIVES CANADA

C Company, 1st C Scot R, moved inland with little difficulty, clearing out snipers and a machine-gun nest and capturing an artillery piece and sixty-five Germans. They were joined by the rest of the battalion, which landed about 0930, and moved west to Ste Croix-sur-Mer, assisted by the two DD tanks of A Squadron, 6th CAR. As noted above, they met up with the Winnipegs at Colombiers-sur-Seulles and then continued the advance abreast with them, ending south of Pierrepont. One officer and two other ranks were killed and about twenty-seven were wounded.

Landing of the Reserve Brigade

By 1140 hours, the first reconnaissance parties of the 3rd Canadian Division reserve, the 9th Canadian Infantry Brigade Group, began to arrive, landing on Nan White and Red. At that time, there apparently was little hostile fire still being received on those beaches, but the chaos of wrecked landing craft, a legacy of the delayed landing and the confusion that had ensued, proved to be just as much an impediment. "Bernieres was jammed with vehicles and tanks of all sorts. . . . Into this mass the 9 Cdn Inf Bde began landing. . . . The roads were plugged with zealous soldiers, impatient to get on; fortunately the enemy did not shell the town."[63]

The North Nova Scotia Highlanders took nearly an hour and a half to complete their landing. "At 1235 hrs after finding the beach blocked by craft of the 8 Cdn Inf Bde we were able to land. Only one mortar carrier and crew were casualties when they ran over a mine after landing. By 1400 hrs all our troops were ashore, but as 8 Bde had not found the going as easy as anticipated we were unable to get through the town and assemble near Beny-sur-Mer as planned." They finally managed to complete their assembly in Beny-sur-Mer at 1700 hours, having suffered losses of four other ranks killed and six wounded, mostly to mines and sporadic mortar fire; half the casualties were suffered after reaching Beny.

The Stormont, Dundas, and Glengarry Highlanders managed to do no better, despite their beginning to land at 1220 hours on Nan White. It was not until 1830 that they completed assembly at Beny, although they also suffered very light casualties, just one other rank killed and thirteen wounded.[64]

The last battalion of the brigade, the Highland Light Infantry of Canada, landed at 1400 hours, suffered no casualties at all, and gave a concise account of the problems encountered:

Approaches to beaches were sown with obstacles such as hedgehogs, Element C and poles. A number of LCAs from the assault wave were lying under water where they had hit these mines.

The eastern end of Nan White shortly after 1140. A D9 armored bulldozer is working on the right, with another in the distance at left center, while engineers lay timbers, probably to reinforce the carpet already laid on the sand. A Sherman tank is moving up the lane. At least four LCI(L)'s are unloading in the background. They are from Group J.331, carrying the reserve 9th Canadian Brigade Group. NATIONAL ARCHIVES CANADA

Canadian troops of the Stormont, Dundas and Glengarry Highlanders land on Nan White at 1220. The fortified beach villa nicknamed "Denise and Roger" captured by men of the Queen's Own Rifles of Canada is at center right. A DD tank, with its screens still raised, is to the left of "Denise and Roger" while a D7 works the beach just to the right of the bow of LCI(L) 299. NATIONAL ARCHIVES CANADA

To the right, along the seawall, is a cluster of vehicles, including an A.V.R.E., a Crusader antiaircraft tank, and a jeep. Just above them, driving through Nan White Green Gap, is another A.V.R.E. At center is the SBG that spanned the seawall. NATIONAL ARCHIVES CANADA

The beach itself was in a terrible confusion. There was only about 25 yards of beach in front of the promenade which was heavily wired, so there were only the exits put up by the Beach Group. The beaches were jammed, troops, with bicycles, vehicles and tanks all trying to move towards the exits. It was an awful shambles. One gun ranged on the beach would have done untold damage, but the 9 Cdn Inf Bde landed without a shot fired on them. We had not gone many yards inland when we met the rear elements of the 8 Cdn Inf Bde. The streets of the village were blocked with rubble from the heavy prepara-

tory shelling and bombing. Well-placed MG posts and snipers had caused the QOR of C to deploy and attack them.

Thus ended D-Day—not a shot fired by our battalion as yet.[65]

The 9th Brigade War Diary summed up the day as follows: "Strange as it may seem, we have attained complete surprise in the assault as we did not encounter any mines or booby traps back of the beach area and evidence that Jerry pulled out in a hurry is apparent when kit and equipment left in houses is examined. D-day ended with all the brigade well established ashore and very few casualties incurred."[66]

JUNO ASSESSED

The table on the opposite page gives the timing of the various A.V.R.E. gapping teams on Juno. It shows the time of initial touchdown by the LCT's, when the first obstacle was cleared, and when the first complete gap was declared open. In those cases where two times are given, they distinguish between the times given for the different LCT's carrying elements of the same gapping team (for simplicity the time of landing for the reserve LCT is not given).

However, it is unclear if the generally good performance obtained clearing the obstacles and opening gaps on Juno actually contributed to the relatively small number of craft lost and damaged there. Nor is it clear why the accounts of Juno appear to be full of dire comments about the number of landing craft that were wrecked. But the data reveals that only in the case of the LCI(S)'s were the losses significantly different than on Sword. And that was the result, even though, on Sword, two of eight planned gaps failed and all but one of the six others were opened later than those on Juno. The better gapping performance on Juno seemed to result in little relief for the congestion on the beach, which

by some accounts was the worst of the three Commonwealth landings.

Using the casualties that were suffered by the assault brigades as a measure, it seems clear that neither brigade's assault at Juno was as strongly opposed as that on Sword. For example, of the 704 total casualties calculated to have been incurred by the 8th Canadian Brigade and attached units (including those of the 102nd Beach Sub-area) on D-Day, about 433 were estimated to have occurred "on the beach," and furthermore, a large number of those, perhaps as many as 35, were caused by drowning in No. 48 (RM) Commando. However, on Sword, the total loss for the British 8th Brigade and attached units was 1,062, while the median estimate of their casualties "on the beach" was 630. Thus, both the losses "on the beach" and the total losses on Sword were about 31 percent higher than those sustained by the 8th Canadian Brigade on Juno, the worst hit of the two brigades assaulting there.

Of course, that is not conclusive, but it seems to be a good general indicator that resistance on Juno was perhaps less—although other factors played

Courseulles on 6 June.
NARA

GAP CLEARANCE ON JUNO

	80th Assault Squadron—Nan				26th Assault Squadron—Mike			
Lane	Red	Blue	Yellow	Green	Red	Blue	Yellow	Green
Touched Down	0805	0750/ Did not Arrive	0805	0815/0820	0831	0815	0810/0815	0800
1st Obstacle	0815	0820	0818	0840	0840	0840	0815/0820	0805
1st Gap	0820	0825	0830	0845	0900	0900	1030	0930

CASUALTIES IN THE JUNO ASSAULT, 8TH CANADIAN INFANTRY BRIGADE AND ATTACHED UNITS

Unit	Killed		Wounded		Missing		Total
	Off.	OR	Off.	OR	Off.	OR	
Brigade Headquarters	0[a]		1		0		1
N Shore R	34[b]		90		0		124
QOR	56[c]		78		0		134
Chaudière	18[c]		48		38		104
10th CAR	14		12		0		26
80th Assault Squadron	1	0	2	6	0	0	9
22nd Dragoons				1			1
No. 48 (RM) Commando	4[d]		90		55		149
5th Fd Coy. R.C.E.[e]							12
16th Fd. Coy. R.C.E.							12
184th Fd. Coy. R.E.[f]							5
14th Fd. Regt. R.C.A.	10		12		0		22
19th A. Fd. Regt. R.C.A.	3		17		0		20
114th LAA Regt. R.A.							5
22nd Fd. Amb. R.C.A.M.C.							7
Miscellaneous							73[g]
Total	136		265		38		704

a. Except for the 80th Assault Squadron and the 22nd Dragoons, casualty figures are not broken down by officers and other ranks and include both categories.

b. Includes 6 who died of wounds.

c. Includes 1 who died of wounds.

d. Postwar Royal Navy casualty reports give losses of 3 officers and 36 other ranks killed, 1 officer and 3 other ranks died of wounds. It seems clear that 35 of the missing initially reported had died, quite possibly by drowning.

e. Losses to all Royal Canadian Engineer personnel totaled 19 killed, including 2 who died of wounds, and 42 wounded, but the numbers were not further subdivided by unit.

f. Part of the 102nd Beach Sub-area

g. Sixty-nine of those were suffered by units of the 102nd Beach Sub-area in the afternoon.

a part. Certainly, the defenses on Nan at St. Aubin, Berniéres, and Courseulles were somewhat weaker than those on Queen at La Brèche and Hermanville in terms of firepower; there was only a single 88 and many fewer 50-millimeter guns on Nan, for example. In terms of manpower, however, there appears to have been little advantage at either beach—except

that on Sword there wasn't a second brigade landing farther west to distract the Germans. Casualty details for Nan Beach are given in the table above.[67]

Of the 462 casualties estimated to have been incurred by the 7th Canadian Brigade and attached units (including those of the 102nd Beach Sub-Area) on D-Day, about 288 were calculated to have occurred on the beach. The worst hit was the Royal Winnipeg Rifles, which may have lost as many as 80 men in the initial assault on Nan Green and 129 men for the day. However, even those losses were much less than on Sword or even those suffered by the 8th Canadian Brigade on Nan Red and White. Overall, the total casualties of the 7th Canadian Brigade on Juno were just 44 percent of those suffered by the British 8th Brigade in their assault on Sword. The table below gives additional casualty details for Mike.[68]

Losses in landing craft on Juno were not nearly as heavy as on Sword. Furthermore, on Juno, the number of craft actually sunk was much better defined—just three LCT(A)'s. Yet even that, as in so many things on D-Day, was not what it seemed. The two LCT(A)'s lost on Juno were identified by the Royal Navy as LCT(A)-2263 and 2428. Both were part of the 105th LCT(A) Flotilla that carried the

3rd (RM) Armoured Support Battery to Nan Green, 2428 having sunk the evening before en route.[69] Of course, it is possible that the third LCT lost was actually one of the two LCT(IV)'s, pennant numbers 524 and 715, that were recorded lost, but without any indication of where.

In any case, it seems certain that although as many as ninety craft were lost and damaged, and perhaps thirty-seven were badly damaged, only two or three actually sank, which was a remarkable achievement. Compared to Sword, where seventy-nine were lost or damaged on a single brigade front, only forty-five per brigade front were lost and damaged on Juno.[70] It seems that the perception was considerably different from the reality, a phenomena that is quite common in the reporting of combat operations.

Overall, in terms of timeliness, the Juno landing suffered from some severe problems. The naval assessment reported:

CASUALTIES IN THE JUNO ASSAULT, 7TH CANADIAN INFANTRY BRIGADE AND ATTACHED UNITS							
Unit	Killed		Wounded		Missing		Total
	Off.	OR	Off.	OR	Off.	OR	
1 C Scot R	1[a]	21[b]	3	60	0	1	85
R Wpg RIF	58[c]		66		5		129
Regina Rifles	46[d]		55		1		102
6th CAR	22		17		4		43
26th Assault Squadron	1	2	1	3	0	0	7
6th Fd. Coy. C.R.E.							25
18th Fd. Coy. R.E.							2
85th Fd. Coy. R.E.[e]							5
262nd Fd. Coy. R.E.							10
22nd Fld. Amb.							5
12th Fld. Regt. R.C.A.	1		7		0		8
13th Fld. Regt. R.C.A.	6[d]		4		2		12
Inns of Court[f]							1
8th Kings							13
Miscellaneous							15[g]
Total	158		216		13		462

a. Except for the 1 C Scot R and 26th Assault Squadron, casualty figures are not broken down by officers and other ranks and include both categories.

b. Includes 5 who died of wounds.

c. Includes 43 who died of wounds.

d. Includes 1 who died of wounds.

e. Part of the 102nd Beach Sub-area.

f. A reconnaissance detachment of the I Corps armored car regiment. It had been intended that they make a dash for the Orne River bridges in Caen on the morning of D-Day, but they became entangled in minefields on the beach and failed to make it inland.

g. All suffered by units of the 102nd Beach Sub-area in the afternoon.

LANDING CRAFT IN THE JUNO ASSAULT

Total Craft engaged in Assault	Number lost	Number lost or damaged	Percentage lost or damaged
144 LCA	0	36	25
8 LCS(M)	0	2	25
8 LCI(S)	0	7	87
146 LCT, LCT(A), etc.	3	45	31

7th Brigade

Up to 0858 no exits had been established on Mike beaches or Nan Green, and at 0941 Mike Red reported landing of vehicles was held up by lack of exits and flooding inland.

At 1022 the exit situation on Mike Sector was reported to be hopeful, and this was followed at 1112 by a report that one exit was working on Mike with difficulty, and that the land inshore was flooded.

At 1148 the exit on Mike Red was reported to be satisfactory.

8th Brigade

The sea wall was bridged at Nan White at 0850.

At 0940 beach exits on Nan Red were reported to be choked and under small arms fire, but on Nan White vehicles were proceeding over the bridge.

By 1040 there were two exits working on Nan Red and three on Nan White. . . .

Situation at Dusk on D-Day

At dusk it was clear that the unloading of LST was badly behind the planned timetable and unless the weather and the state of beaches improved, unloading of build-up convoys expected at daylight on D+1 would not be satisfactorily completed.[71]

Nevertheless, progress was being made inland. The Royal Navy report noted:

At 1100 the leading elements were reported to be halfway to the divisional intermediate objective.

8th Brigade reported at 1120 that Tailleville, Banville, and St. Croix-sur-Mer had been captured and that they were advancing.

No. 48 R.M. Commando had by this time taken the LANGRUNE coastal strip.

The General Officer Commanding, 3rd Canadian Infantry Division landed on Nan White beach at 1310.

The first hundred German prisoners were ready for evacuation from the beaches at 1400.

At 1436 8 Brigade reported that they were mopping up Tailleville.

The forward elements of the division were reported to be on line "Mallet" at 1510.

9th Brigade [the division reserve brigade] were established on line "Rim" by 2146 with Main Division H.Q. set up half-way between lines "Rim" and "Ale". [Mallet was the final phase-line of the division on D-Day; Rim, and Ale were the intermediate phase lines.]

This, with the information that the troops were continuing to advance against opposition, was the final picture of the military situation before nightfall.[72]

Despite all the problems—the last-minute change in H-Hour, the faulty intelligence, the scrambled landing sequence, and the chronic congestion—by the end of the day, the Canadians had been remarkably successful and had made a substantial penetration inland. However, the attempt to link up Juno and Sword had been a failure, leaving a significant salient in the I Corps' beachhead line. That, though, was a minor failure—and an ultimately meaningless one—compared to the success that was gained.

CHAPTER 7

Assault Force Gold: The British 50th Infantry Division

THE REPORT OF NAVAL COMMANDER FORCE G makes it clear just how difficult the passage was for many of the assault convoys. As at Juno, the careful timing and organization began to unravel slightly under the stresses of weather, darkness, and exhaustion. En route, they encountered errant convoys from both Force O and Force J; in the latter case, they were the A.V.R.E. group that had gotten into the wrong swept channel and, as the Naval Commander Force G dryly noted, "stoutly maintained that they were in number seven, their correct channel."[1]

The poor weather and heavy seas eventually forced a major change—the DD tanks, instead of swimming in before the initial assault waves, were now to be carried in all the way to the beach on their LCT.

> The weather was bad for an assault. A wind force 4 from west by north made the beaches a lee shore and raised a considerable sea in the anchorage . . . [It was decided by the LCT Flotilla and Tanks Squadron commanders] that the weather was too rough for the successful launching of their D.D. tanks, a decision in which I fully concurred, and on both sectors the tanks were landed behind the AVRE. This resulted in the LCOCU being the first to set foot ashore and they worked on obstacle clearance for a considerable time virtually unsupported. Their work is deserving of the highest praise.[2]

Despite those problems, perseverance and good seamanship paid off; most of the initial landings were within a few minutes of their planned time and—except on Jig—were at least reasonably close to their planned location.

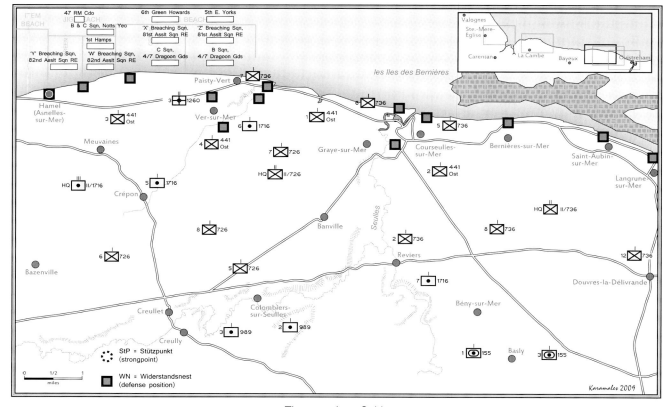

The assault on Gold.

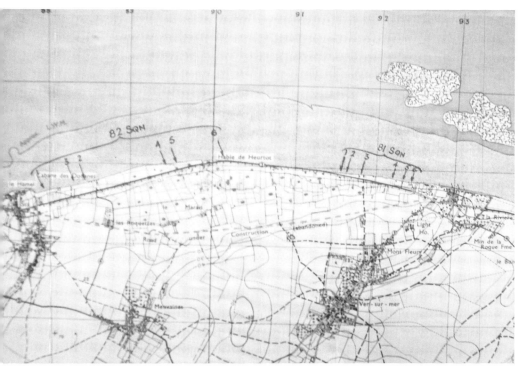

This map was prepared by the 6th Assault Regiment after D-Day to show where the squadrons and troops landed.
TNA

On Gold, the 6th Assault Regiment provided the 81st and 82nd Squadrons and 30th Armoured Brigade twenty-five Crabs from B and C Squadrons of the Westminster Dragoons for the assault on Jig and King Beaches. Each lane gapping team normally consisted of three or four A.V.R.E.'s and two Crabs—the lead A.V.R.E. in each team was a Pusher for the Roly Poly carpet-layer mounted in the bow of the LCT. Each of the Gold assault squadrons had six LCT's available for transport; thus, there was only one LCT per lane. The twelve LCT's used at Gold were assigned to the 28th LCT Flotilla and were British-built LCT Mark IV's.

Note that because it was decided to open six lanes each on Jig and King, it was impossible to assign one troop to each exit as was done on Sword and Juno. Instead, the assault squadron troops were intermixed with those of the Westminster Dragoons and allocated evenly between the gaps. They were then split into two breaching teams per beach, each responsible for three gaps. Each breaching team also alternated command between the assault squadron and the Westminster Dragoons.

Again, the LCA(HR)'s proved to be only marginally effective. Of the eighteen (nine each for Jig and King) planned, seven foundered in the heavy weather, one parted its tow and then had the towline foul its screw before leaving Portsmouth, one failed to fire because of the water that had been shipped aboard, and one arrived an hour late and partly swamped, so did not fire. Of the eight that did fire, only one was at King and seven at Jig, and it was reported that "due to the flatness of the beaches and the state of the tide, it was a physical impossibility for the bombs with a range of about 400 yards to reach the beach minefields. The patterns instead fell on the beach obstructions and are definitely stated to have set off mines etc., attached to them."[3]

So it may be said that at least in this case, the LCA(HR)'s had some positive effect, even if it was not exactly the effect that had been planned for.

King Beach. The Mont Fleury Battery (WN35a) is the heavily bombed white area just to the right of the apex of the distinctive V of the antitank ditch. At the upper right, along the coast, can be seen WN 33, with the heavily bombed area of the "Lighthouse" position (WN 34), while at left center is WN 35. NARA

81ST ASSAULT SQUADRON

The task of the 81st Assault Squadron on King Beach, under Maj. Robert Edward Thompstone, and the Crabs of C Squadron, Westminster Dragoons, was to clear six lanes for the assault troops of the 69th Infantry Brigade on the beaches west of La Rivière. Major Thompstone was commanding officer of Z Breaching Squadron on King Red while Major Sutton, commanding C Squadron, Westminster Dragoons, was the commanding officer of X Breaching Squadron on King Green.

The decision to land the DD tanks directly onto the beach meant that the LCT's with the 81st Squadron and the LCA's with No. 3 and No. 4 L.C.O.C.U.'s were the first to approach King, and the men of the L.C.O.C.U.'s were the first to set foot on the beach, about five minutes before the first A.V.R.E.'s and the Royal Engineers of 280th Field Company. However, they were not fired upon for some time and had five to ten minutes to work on the first row of hedgehogs, demolishing quite a few, before sporadic German fire opened up. The greatest problem became the tide, which quickly began covering obstacles, delaying much of the work until the next ebb.[4]

King Red: Lane 6—Successful

LCT-(2425), with the assault team under the command of Capt. J. M. Birkbeck, carried two Crabs and three A.V.R.E.'s (Pusher, Bobbin, and Fascine), along with a D7 armored bulldozer. It landed in the correct place, but it is not known if it was at the correct time. Birkbeck reported:

> On craft Bobbin had to be wedged as sway would have been too much for it.
>
> We beached very accurately on the right part of the beach. The shore defences were active and fire was coming heavily from all positions in LA RIVIERE.
>
> The wade was about 100 yds in about 4' of water.
>
> The Roly Poly was pushed sideways by the current so that L sjt [Lance Sergeant] Simp-

son's AVRE had to mount it with one track and was nearly turned over. It was not possible to see where the carpet had been laid or follow it more than 10 yds from the craft. A heavy steel shuttering roller might be more stable and less liable to float away.

> The Bobbin AVRE followed and had to rely on the driver for direction owing to very limited visibility for Comd. Driver had to look through triplex block as periscopes were wet. So finally a way through beach obstacles to the top of the beach was a matter of luck. Looking sideways out of the top of the turret I was able to see the 88mm firing some 6 shots. Many more must have been fired but I did not see.
>
> The beach presented no difficulties of going and all the rest of the team got up it and through the first minefield.
>
> The Bobbin AVRE made for the wall to drop its unneeded Bobbin out of the way in order to use its weapons. The blowplates went but the Bobbin only fell halfway—it may be that the pistons were damaged by shell fire. Only one puff charge worked. I was ordered to move to avoid being shot at and still being unable to see we arrived about 50 yds in front of the 88—but it did not fire at us. We must have been hit at some time by an 88 which jammed the turret, hit the corner of the turret and set the nets on fire. I got out and pulled the other holding pin out—after 5 minutes maneuvering we got free of the Bobbin and went down the beach to help the Field Coy [Company].
>
> One of their boats had got damaged as the Bobbin left the craft. There were very few on the beach and most had been wounded: the tide had covered the spikes and was round the hedgehogs.
>
> There were so few that I returned to the top of the beach, where the infantry were collecting under the wall. As my turret was

jammed I could not load Petard. I contacted the OC and L sjt Wharton (Bobbin of 4 team).

L sjt Young came and reported to me what had happened to his tank and what the situation was and after he had recovered a bit he went off to get treatment.

The OC and I then left the beach. I eventually freed my turret and we employed a route for tracked vehicles into VER SUR MER.

All my men behaved well and coolly, particularly the driver who had great difficulty and responsibility while I could not see, and the Dem NCO and Co-driver who had to get out to help free the turret.[5]

King Red: Lane 5—Partially Successful

LCT-(2424), with the assault team under the command of Major Thompstone and Capt. T. F. Croxall, carried two Crabs and four A.V.R.E.'s (Command, Pusher, Bobbin, and Fascine). It arrived five minutes early, but it is unclear if it was in the correct place or not. Croxall reported:

I was in command of two Roly Poly AVREs, my own and one commanded by Sjt Simpson in Lane 6.

Sjt Simpson touched down at 0725 hrs, his Roly Poly was released, he pushed it approx 10 yards, it failed to unroll any further: on trying to climb over it, he fell off the right had side, but managed to keep going: the ducts fell off and water came into the engine compartment, affecting the steering brakes such that he was unable to steer.

He moved up to the beach and attempted to dry out the brakes: when the brakes dried out he was jammed in by traffic on the beach—the time was now 0815.

A lane had been made along the beach towards the "88" gun and Sjt Simpson took his AVRE along this lane, passed the gun, on to the lateral road, turned left and moved towards the first cross-roads in the village of LA RIVIERE: on the way, he demolished a pillbox, which was reputed to still be occupied by the enemy, with a petard round, using a 289 Fuze at short range.

He then moved towards the RV.

My AVRE touched down at 0730: the Roly Poly rolled to the bottom of the ramp and as soon as we touched it with our pusher, the AVRE climbed it and we carried on the beach threading our way through the obstacles following a flail which had landed East of us.

This flail eventually became stuck a few feet from the lateral road: another flail passed by on my right, so I reversed by [sic, my] AVRE and then came forward down the new lane and out on to the road, turned left and moved into the village: time of arrival 0740 hrs.

We could not contact the infantry when we first arrived as the Royal Navy was still shelling the village. At approx 0815 hrs we contacted B Coy of the 5th EY [5th East Yorks] and we commanced [sic, commenced] mopping up all the small posts still in the village.

The village was cleared completely and we returned to the main cross-roads in LA RIVIERE at approx 1100 hrs.

Damaged houses in La Rivière after the landing showing damage from the Petards of the 81st Assault Squadron. 79TH ARMOURED DIVISION MEMORIAL ALBUM/DANNY LOVELL

The journey up to the Harbour Area was slow due to mines and a large stream of traffic.[6]

The Bobbin A.V.R.E. was hit after it successfully lay its shuttering. It reportedly blew up just fifteen to twenty seconds after being hit and may have been the victim of the 8.8-centimeter PaK 43/41 in WN 33, which appears to have been responsible for losses in Lanes 3, 4, and 5. Both Crabs bogged before they finished clearing the lane.

King Red: Lane 4—Partly Successful

LCT-(2423), with the assault team under the command of Lt. J. C. Skelly, carried two Crabs and three A.V.R.E.'s (Pusher, Bobbin, and Fascine), along with a D4 bulldozer. It is not recorded when it arrived or if it was the correct spot. Skelly reported:

All vehicles cleared the craft OK but the last four had to make a sharp LH [lefthand] turn as the LCT swung round to the left on the tide.

Just as we passed through the first line of obstacles, wooden inclined rails with shells on top, I noticed through the periscope that the

Feeves's photo of the Churchill Crocodile *Sinner*, which illustrates how tanks lost tracks in the rough shingle of the beach. TNA

first AVRE out, the Roly Poly, was on fire and almost immediately after it exploded. I did not see if any of the crew got out. We made our way through the other obstacles, mostly hedgehogs and then I noticed that the Bobbin AVRE was not with me. I had no report on the R/T from him.

Just on the shingle the first flail, Sjt Webb, turned right followed now by the second flail, Cpl Wild and my own AVRE (fascine). Sjt Webb selected a spot on the dunes lower than the rest and commenced flailing followed by Cpl Wild. When I arrived at the sand dunes I stopped and my Dem NCO placed the Sock on the left of the gap and dumped the Gap marking signs alongside it. At the same time the Driver threw a Green smoke canister out of the RH panniers. I dumped off the Ironmongery before following the flails. About halfway through the minefield I noticed that the flail in front was stopped, Sjt Webb reported he was bogged just across the coast road. Cpl Wild swung left and followed by me made along the coast road towards the main cross roads in LA RIVIERE. About fifty yards down the road we came across a crater in the centre about 8' deep and 20' across.

I told Cpl Wild to turn right here and try to flail up the Westside of the N-S [north-south] minefield but he also bogged. I then dropped my fascine in the crater but it fell too awkwardly to cross. I tried to detour the crater to the right just on the edge of the minefield which stretched on both sides of the road but I also bogged. L sjt Kerwin whose two flails had bogged came along then and towed me out with his AVRE. I towed out Cpl Wild's flail and L sjt Kerwin towed out Sjt Webb's and I set the two flails to flail a path to the left of the crater but Cpl Wild, in front, was bogged again.

I had instructions to proceed to RV immediately so I left Sjt Webb to pull out Cpl Wild and L sjt Kerwin to fix his track which was riding off the sprocket, and went back onto the beach. I went along to the casemate at the end of the wall and from there back onto the coast road where I met Capt Noxall [Croxall].

We made our way with difficulty past a line of carriers until we came to a crater in the centre of the road. A DD tried to detour and had a track blown off. We waited until the Div RE cleared a detour and proceeded to the Sqn RV which we reached without any other incident.[7]

The Pusher A.V.R.E. had been hit by an 88, quite possibly the 8.8-centimeter PaK 43/41 in WN 33, just west of La Rivière. Like the Bobbin A.V.R.E. in Lane 5, it was set on fire and reportedly blew up within fifteen to twenty seconds.

King Green: Lane 3—Partially Successful

LCT-(2414), with the assault team under the command of Capt. T. W. Davies and Lt. E. H. Boulter, carried two Crabs and four A.V.R.E.'s (Pusher, Bobbin, Fascine, and SBG). It arrived on time and at the correct spot. Davies reported:

1st AVRE—(Roly Poly) Serjeant Teanby

Landing craft touched down at approx 0730 hrs at the right place. The Roly Poly came off the LCT alright but a strong current washed it to port side as soon as it entered the water with the result that the 1st AVRE landed in 5' water with one track on the matting drum and one track in a crater.

It then proceeded towards "Lav. Pan" [Lavatory Pan, the lateral road inland that led to a beachfront house nicknamed the "Lavatory Pan Villa" because of the shape of its circular driveway[8]] road as planned, picked a way through beach obstacles and reached the mud belt when it got through with difficulty. Here it turned towards "RUG" position and joined Capt King in supporting the 6 Green Howards. It sustained one hit from medium caliber A-tk antitank gun on the left of turret.

2nd AVRE—(Bobbin) Lt Boulter

Just before touching down the wireless of this AVRE went dis. It came off about 30 yards behind the 1st AVRE but by this time the LCT had been swung round by the current with its stern to port (approx 35°).

It followed the first AVRE up the beach in its tracks and through the obstacles until the dvr reported that the 1st AVRE tracks were sinking into mud. It then turned left and right and continued parallel to tracks of leading AVRE and laid steel shuttering [this indicates it was probably a Bobbin Mark II or III designed for the soft clay beds] across mud. Once it was off the shuttering it turned left to join 280 Fd Coy in beach clearance role.

While waiting for Fd Coy personnel it came under fire from the 88mm gun at LA RIVIERE.

It was unable to contact 280 Fd Coy so it joined the Landing Craft Obstacle Clearance Unit in clearing obstacles until the tide was at full ebb when it joined 280 Fd Coy who by this time were able to start clearing beach obstacles.

3rd & 4th Tanks (Crabs) Serjeant Burch & Corporal Ryder, Westminster Dragoons

Both Crabs followed 2nd AVRE off LCT and proceeded to top edge of beach satisfactorily. The steel shuttering enabled them to cross the mud belt.

Just as the leading Crab started to flail it sustained a frontal hit which blew off the flail but crew was unhurt. [This again may have been from the 8.8-centimeter PaK 43/41 in WN 33, just west of La Rivière.]

The second Crab was following in echelon but had a bogie blown off just as it was entering the minefield.

The result was that no gap was made in the minefield by these two flails.

5th Tank (Fascine AVRE) Serjeant Houghton & Lance Corporal Mather

By the time this AVRE came off, the LCT had swung further round almost parallel to the shore with the result that the fascine AVRE did not go straight for the beach but continued in same direction as it came off

LCT. (NOTE: Driver who is the only man who can see forward in fascine tk was well below water level.)

It then appeared to go into deeper water and stop while another LCT came in with its ramp partly lowered on top of the fascine.

Meanwhile on enquiry I received a report from them by wireless that their engine had flooded and had stopped and that they could not move. I then told them to bale out. Afterwards some members of the crew were seen getting out of the turret.

It was reported to me afterwards that Sjt Houghton did not go ashore in his tank. He had been hit in the jaw by shrapnel from a nearby shell burst and went aft for attention by naval personnel.

Bridge AVRE—6th Tank (Capt Davies)

After fascine AVRE had put off the craft comd pulled out from the beach and came in again square on. By this time the landmarks were obscured by smoke and the Br AVRE came ashore to the left of the "Lavatory Pan" road.

It negotiated the beach obstacles and although there was no steel shuttering it got through the mud patch after some difficulty.

On reaching the top of the beach the comd stopped and looked for a gap in the minefield on to the lateral road without result. He then got on to the Breaching Sqn comd who told him where a gap had been made.

He then proceeded about 500 [yards] along the beach to the right and crossed minefield on to the road, turned left until he reached "Lavatory Pan" road when he was instructed to drop the bridge across a large crater about 200 [yards] inland from "Lavatory Pan" house.

The dropping was satisfactory but the release hooks had to be disengaged by dismounting and using a pick head.

After a short interval a request was received to move a road making machine obstructing the road to VER SUR LE MER. This was moved satisfactorily.[9]

King Green: Lane 2—Successful

LCT-(2413), with the assault team under the command of Lt. J. D. Darby, carried two Crabs and three A.V.R.E.'s (Pusher, Bobbin, and Fascine). It touched down five minutes early but at the correct place. Darby reported:

1. LCT touched down at approx 0725 hrs at the correct place.

2. Roly Poly AVRE

Roly Poly rolled down the ramp when the craft touched down but the current carried it over to the left, with the result that the AVRE mounted the roll with one track, the other being in the mud. The AVRE then carried on up the beach avoiding the obstacles and negotiating the mud. It then turned off to the right and joined Capt King as planned.

3. Bobbin AVRE

Came off after the Roly Poly AVRE, the roll by this time having been carried out of the way to the left by the current. No trouble was found in going in over the mud, so it was decided to lay the carpet right up to the head of the beach. In blowing the release of the roll the charge on the balloon cable failed to work and a member of the crew got out and fixed a No 27 det[onator] and safety fuze in the PHE and so set it off. The carpet was rolled successfully (but it was not used before the tide covered it, after which it was impossible to see it. When the tide went down it was found that the carpet had been ruined by an LCT touching down on it).

The AVRE comd then reported to the beach clearing party which consisted of two men—the rest not having been able to get off the craft. Six hedgehogs [German beach obstacles] were towed away in pairs and then the two 15'6" strops [towing lines] broke. By then operations had to cease until the tide went down. Afterwards operations proceeded under the direction of Major Clayton (280 Fd Coy [Field Company RE] to clear the beach, towing hedgehogs, drowned veh, etc.

4. Flails

They were not seen after leaving the craft.

5. Fascine AVRE

By the time this AVRE came off, the craft had swung off the beach and was lying parallel to the shore. Also it was found impossible to steer to the left (i.e. towards the shore). It took about 10 mins to get onto dry land and the AVRE was then about 250 [yards] further down to the beach. The flails were not in sight and the W/T [radio] was dis[abled]. The AVRE moved up to near the start of the Lavatory Pan Rd. The AVRE comd then got out to look for a flail. One belonging to No 1 team was eventually found. The two vehicles then proceeded to carry out the task of No 2 team which was to make a lane from the beach up to the village of VER SUR MER. This included a flog of approx 800 [yards] and the dropping of a fascine in the antitank ditch.

6. All vehs eventually rallied at the appointed RV [rendezvous].

Lance Sergeant Miller, in a Pusher A.V.R.E., reported:

Performance of Roly Poly

It failed to unroll on ramp of craft, therefore I had to push it down. A strong wave then swept it away from the tank and as it still refused to unroll I climbed over it.

It was very hard going for the tank up the beach, and avoiding as much mud and obstacles as possible made increasing difficulties. I had to halt in the sea as two LCAs were swept in front of me by heavy waves.

On reaching beach 2 platoons A Coy 6th Green Howards followed behind me. It was here that we first met mortar and small arms fire, also occasional grenades were thrown.

I fired the Petard at pillbox—hit target but failed to explode. I then covered inf[antry] advance by Besa fire and continued over sea wall—a drop of about 5 feet.

A few prisoners were taken and eventually at approx 1100 hrs I followed flails to first rally position without further interference from enemy.

Lance Sergeant Kerwin, in a Fascine A.V.R.E., reported:

I have to report that I left the LCT closed down and my driver followed the flail (in front of him on the craft). I found that I could not use the periscope extension, and used my own judgment as to when we were clear of the water, and opened up the turret, and found the fascine I was carrying was lying to one side of the AVRE. During my journey from the LCT to the beach I had lost touch with the remainder of the team and had gone over to one side (the right) so made my way between the obstacles and made my way onto the beach road. On that journey my fascine was removed, so I cleared the cradle which obstructed the driver's vision port and carried on. On reaching the road I assisted 3 flails and one AVRE to get on the road again after they had got "bogged". My own tracks had to be broken for while assisting these other people my own left track had come off its sprocket. [When a tanks track "came off its sprocket" it meant that the track had been forced off the drive sprocket, immobilizing the tank. "Breaking the track" was an arduous procedure where the pins holding the track links together were hammered out so that the heavy track could be pulled back into place and then pinned together again.] At approximately 1500 hrs I made my way to the rendezvous and reported to the OC.[10]

King Green: Lane 1—Successful

LCT-(2412), with the assault team under the command of Capt. Dennis Aubrey King, carried two Crabs and three A.V.R.E.'s (Pusher, Bobbin, and Fascine). It touched down on time and in more or less its correct place. King reported:

King Red, west of La Rivière. NARA

The sea was very choppy and when the LCT touched down the depth of water was four feet. The roly poly rolled down the ramp as soon as this was lowered and I followed it into the water. The distance of the wade was about 250 [yards] but on leaving the craft the roly poly was swept to one side by the current and began to wrap itself around the AVRE. I made two more attempts to push the roly but in each case it began to wrap itself round the tracks. I backed clear of the debris and proceeded ashore without it.

As soon as I reached the beach I was joined by two other AVRE under my command to attack the position [probably WN 35], and proceeded to thread my way through the beach obstacles. There was still fire coming from all four pillboxes [and] also

from German inf[antry] behind the seawall. We fired one round of Petard at the left hand pillbox and the fire from here ceased, we then fired at the pillbox containing the 50mm. The round got stuck in the barrel [of the Petard] and had to be removed, also the turret became jammed as a result of a hit, but these we managed to cure by dismounting.

By this time the in[fantry] had got onto the beaches and all the pillboxes were silenced. Boche were behind the sea wall with Spandau and stick bombs. We turned our Besas onto the top of the wall but could not get at the Boche satisfactorily. My other two AVREs which had also arrived joined in and one of my serjeants blew the front out of a house inside the position, I then decided to climb over the wall and ordered my other

AVRE to follow me. This was completed successfully and enabled the infantry to get into the position and mop up. As soon as we could get through we then proceeded up the road to the quarry where we met Major Sutton OC [Officer Commanding] X Breaching Sqn and rallied under his orders.[11]

Both Crabs were successful in flailing a lane through to the lateral road.

The 81st Squadron had lost four of its twenty A.V.R.E.'s; its personnel losses were heavy and included fourteen other ranks, of which one was killed, eight were wounded, and five were missing.[12] All six of the breaching teams had cleared the beach, but the Crabs in four teams were bogged—and in one team were damaged—before they reached the lateral beach road. Only a single Crab, in Team 1, had managed to complete its tasks. By 1400 hours, only five Crabs had reached the rally point, but no casualties were mentioned by C Squadron, Westminster Dragoons: "At one time all AVRE and Crabs in lanes 4, 5, and 6 were either out of action, bogged or employed in trying to recover bogged Flails which it was anticipated might be badly required to push in a lane somewhere."[13]

The report by the 104th Beach Sub-area stated that "in spite of incredible gallantry the Assault Division did not manage to <u>complete</u> many exits. Flails are unreliable on soft or very hard ground."[14] In all fairness, the 88-millimeter antitank gun at WN 33 in La Rivière had caused considerable damage before it was silenced. The report by the Westminster Dragoons highlights that and a number of other problems with the assault planning:

(a) The 88 mm gun (in the sea wall at La Riviere) was active when we touched down on the beach. It was silenced by the C Sqn tank commanded by Capt Bell [Lane 6].

(b) Information regarding minefields was inaccurate, there were far more minefields than we had been told about. They were, however, well marked by signs.

(c) Information about the marsh was even more inaccurate; the only way off the beach on the front in which we were put down was along the roads.[15]

THE ASSAULT BY 69TH INFANTRY BRIGADE GROUP

On King Beach, the order of assault that had been planned was actually very similar to what occurred—a rarity on 6 June. The DD tanks were landed directly instead of swimming in, but here at least that did not cause a delay. Both B and C Squadron, 4th/7th Royal Dragoon Guards (4th/7th RDG), landed promptly at 0720 hours, five to ten minutes before the A.V.R.E.'s and the leading assault infantry companies. They actually recorded little or no opposition. "The assault went well and after some trouble getting off the beach B and C pushed on with their infantry inland."[16]

However, as the LCT with the gapping teams of the 81st Assault Squadron arrived, the Germans opened a heavy fire, particularly from the 88-millimeter gun in WN 33 at La Rivière. As we have seen, it caused some serious casualties and considerable confusion before it was finally silenced.

It had been planned to land a total of fourteen supporting demolition teams onto King Beach, simultaneously with the arrival of the A.V.R.E. gapping teams. Twelve of those were from the 280th Field Company R.E.; two sections landed in each of the six 81st Squadron LCT's. The remaining two were No. 3 and No. 4 L.C.O.C.U., which in the event landed about five minutes before the LCT's arrived.

0730 hrs. All LCT touch down and AVRE tanks proceed ashore. LCOCU beach and commence demolishing obstacles on King Red and King Green beaches. The folding boats in which stores were being towed ashore by AVsRE prove too flimsy for the heavy seas, and most of them capsize. Heavy enemy opposition encountered from MGs, mortars and 88 mm gun. No flank protection from DD tanks owing to heavy seas. In spite of this all ranks carried on with the job and two 200 yard gaps were cleared for craft in the underwater obstacles before the advancing tide made further work impossible.

The enemy was still very active and several men fell about this time as a result of hand grenades lobbed over the sea wall. After about half an hour, however, an assault party succeeded in disposing of all the enemy with the exception of a few snipers operating from inland.

0830 hrs. Further work being impossible for the time being owing to the tide, etc., roll was called and it was found that 8 men were killed and 26 wounded. 1 officer was seriously wounded. 1 naval rating was killed and 4 wounded from LCOCUs under command.[17]

The gapping teams were quickly followed by the assault infantry battalions and the attached sapper teams of the 233rd Field Company R.E.

King Red
No. 2 Platoon, 233rd Field Company R.E., landed on King Red. One sapper team, apparently organized as a small demolition party of five or six sappers—also called "thug parties" in the reports—was with each of the leading assault companies of the 5th East Yorks. They were followed by two assault sections and a reserve section with the reserve companies.

One of the thug parties had 2 casualties, 1 killed and 1 wounded. . . . The assault section on the left beach was pinned to the beach by accurate SA fire, while the other succeeded in clearing two personnel exits from the beach—casualties 2 wounded. One track exit was developed left of the north-south minefield, as far as the coast road, but it was not until 1100 hours that it was declared open to vehicles. Following the initial assault the platoon proceeded inland clearing debris and creating diversions along the route La Rivière–Mont Fleury–Ver-sur-Mer.[18]

D Company, 5th East Yorks, was the left assault company of the battalion and landed at 0725 hours, closest to WN 33 at La Rivière. Again the trouble-

King Red, where the 6th Green Howards landed, as well as the 151st Brigade around noon. WN 35 is where the road runs inland from the beach. NARA

some 88 millimeters there caused problems. D Company "met strong opposition from LA RIVIERE and were pinned on the beach by MGs and one 88 mm gun firing from strong points to the EAST [left]. D Company suffered heavy casualties."[19]

Their losses included the officer commanding and two men from the FOO party attached from the 86th Field Regiment R.A. Eventually, fire support from the LCG's and LCS(L)'s standing just offshore

engaged the pillbox on the wall-front, destroyed the 37 mm gun [probably the 5cm gun in WN33] and joined in to destroy all houses overlooking the infantry, and drive off a tank [which cannot be correct, unless they were accidentally targeting one of the Crabs or one of the tanks of 4th/7th RDG; the Germans had no tanks] and displace mortar detachments. The infantry were enabled to proceed inshore and attack an A tk gun [the 88-millimeter] from the rear.[20]

However, B Company, 5th East Yorks, the left reserve company, landed at 0750 hours, supposedly after the position had been silenced, and found that the opposition was still heavy. "Troops wading ashore through deep water were picked off by small arms fire and were unable to reach shore."[21]

It was not actually until about 1000 hours that La Rivière was silenced by a combined assault by C Company, 5th East Yorks, with A.V.R.E.'s, Crabs, and DD tanks. "The enemy posts were neutralised and heavy casualties were inflicted. 45 PW were taken from LA RIVIERE locality."[22]

Meanwhile, A Company, 5th East Yorks, had landed at 0725 hours as the right assault company and had a much different experience. The company met "spasmodic opposition and went on to take their objective, a battery at Mont Fleury with the loss of 8 casualties. A Coy took 30 PW. The Commander of the enemy battery committed suicide."[23]

Total casualties to the 5th East Yorks on D-Day were six officers and eighty-five other ranks.

In one of Reeves's photos, an LCT-IV of the 24th Flotilla, D LCT Squadron, runs onto a disabled DD tank on King Beach. TNA

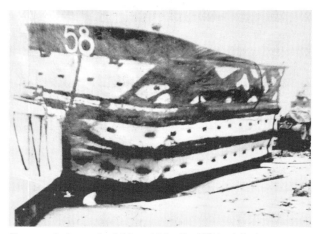

Reeves photographed this vehicle, the DD tank that was run down by LCT 883. TNA

This is an unexploded "flying dustbin" found by Reeves on Gold. TNA

King Green

The second assault battalion, the 6th Green Howards, landed to the right of 5th East Yorks on King Green. They encountered much less opposition and suffered relatively few casualties. A Company on the right attacked WN 35, but the defense put up by the Russian "volunteers" of the 3rd Company of the 441st East Battalion collapsed almost immediately. To their left, D Company landed without opposition, drove inland, and seized the Mont Fleury Battery, WN 35a, led by their redoubtable company sergeant major, Stan Hollis. Hollis personally cleared two of the pillboxes at WN 35a with Sten gun and grenades and then later at Crépon again almost single-handedly wrecked another German battery position, saving the lives of two of his men in the process. CSM Stan Hollis was awarded the Victoria Cross for his actions, the only one presented for actions on D-Day.[24]

> The reserve Coys (C and B) followed the landing of A and B Coys. B Coy moved to area 908863 [about 1,000 meters west of Ver-sur-Mer on the Route d'Asnelles] and attacked enemy positions clearing a quarry on route occupied by the enemy. C Coy moved with little opposition to area P 52 (904850) [about 1,400 meters east of Meuvaines on the road to Ver-sur-Mer] the bn reorganizing area.[25]

By 1000 hours, the battalion reported that the enemy was falling back rapidly, but that the many snipers they left behind were delaying the advance.

No. 3 Platoon, 233rd Field Company R.E., landed with the 6th Green Howards:

> 1 and 4 sections, 3 Platoon landed at H plus 5 (0730 hrs) on King Green beach with the assault waves. They were landed well out to sea below the obstacles and waded ashore. As the last men were leaving, the mortar bombs began to fall on the beach causing casualties. Although the grass in the minefields covering the beach had caught fire and was giving off considerable smoke, the assaulting infantry was taken through the minefields by the

Above: King Beach to the right (west) of WN 33. The road leads inland to Mont Fleury and is the boundary of King Red on the left (east) and King Green on the right (west). NARA

These British tanks are unloading on King on the afternoon of 6 June 1944. NARA

"thug" parties. Casualties sustained during the initial stage made further gapping impossible until all sections were connected together when a further personnel gap was made to the left of the central road: here a Schu mine and two French A tk mines were lifted.

At H plus 25 approx No 2 and 3 sections landed under similar conditions with Pl Sjt and recce L Sjt in command. The latter was wounded and unable to carry out his task; 3 men in the same LCA were also reported missing—all four have since been recorded as killed in action. The LCA carrying the Plt Sjt and 4 men broke down and was very late in landing.

2 and 3 sections proceeded along the road, running SOUTH to VER-SUR-MER, and near the OP house where the crater had been bridged by the AVRE [the SBG from Lane 3, the crater was the one "200 yards inland from the "Lavatory Pan" house], the flanking minefield was cleared as a further diversion.

Total casualties for the day [in No. 3 Platoon] were 6 killed, 6 wounded, 1 missing.[26]

The 89th Field Company R.E. began to land reconnaissance parties with the assault troops at 0730. Their task was to improve the inland exits opened by the gapping teams. They suffered just four casualties on D-Day, one man wounded by mortar fragments and three wounded by exploding mines while clearing the minefields. "0730 hrs first elements of unit landed at LA RIVIERE. By the end of the first tide 7 offrs and 196 OR landed. Gaps were made through defensive minefields and exits from beaches for tracked and wheeled vehicles constructed."[27]

The Assault Reserve Lands
No. 1 Platoon, 233rd Field Company R.E., landed with the reserve battalion of the 7th Green Howards, some 800 yards west of its planned position between 0810 and 0815 hours. They cleared a gap through an 80-yard-deep minefield from the beach lateral road to the road running inland to Ver-sur-Mer. Neither they nor the 7th Green Howards

reported suffering a single casualty during the landing although mortar fire was still landing sporadically. Their first casualties were apparently not incurred until they reached Crépon, nearly two miles inland.[28]

Jig Green: 82nd Assault Squadron
The task of the 82nd Squadron on Jig Beach, under the command of Maj. Harold G. A. Elphinstone, and B Squadron, Westminster Dragoons, was to create six lanes for the assault troops of the 231st Infantry Brigade through the German obstacle belt on the beaches east of the village of Le Hamel. In this sector, all the LCT's touched down more or less simultaneously although three different timings of the landing are given, but all were within five minutes after the scheduled H-Hour.[29] Major Elphinstone was in command of Y Breaching Squadron on Jig Green West while Capt. Harold Percy Stanyon, commanding B Squadron, Westminster Dragoons, was in command of W Breaching Squadron on Jig Green East. Each had three of the breaching teams under his command. Capt. John Michael Leytham reported:

At 0200 hrs Saturday 3 Jun 44, the Sqn commenced to embark on LCT of Flotilla 28 at Q2 Hard Stanswood. The embarkation proceeded without incident.

The bridge carried by AVRE 68932 u/c L sjt Pinka had to be jettisoned before embarkation owing to the right hand jib breaking away from the anchor, and both members bending. [Oddly enough, losing the bridge apparently wasn't considered an "incident."]

On Sunday 4 Jun 44 sailing orders were cancelled due to the weather conditions. On Monday 5 Jun the flotilla shipped at approx 0730 hrs the weather still being bad and sea rough and choppy.

Whilst at sea the men's accommodation was extremely poor, owing to the weight of cargo the hold deck was constantly 6–12" underwater leaving little sleeping space for the 60 men (approx) embarked on each craft.

The men thus suffered for two days through loss of sleep and lack of hot food. In

Above: King Red, where the 6th Green Howards landed and probably shows the landing of the 151st Brigade around noon. WN 35 is where the road runs inland from the beach. NARA

Another view of King Red, where the 6th Green Howards landed and probably shows the landing of the 151st Brigade around noon. WN 36 and Jig Beach is just out of frame to the left. NARA

spite of this they disembarked with very high morale.

On the morning of June 6, 1944, the craft touched down at approx 0720 hours in a somewhat disorganized condition.

LCT Serial No 2025 touched down on the correct spot.

LCT Serial No 2026 touched down on the left of lane 3.

LCT Serial No 2027 touched down opposite lane 3.

LCT Serial No 2028 touched down 200—300 yards EAST of lane 4.

LCT Serial No 2029 [and] 2030 touched down to the left of the wreck which marked our left boundary.[30]

Because of the decision not to launch the DD tanks, the LCT's with the A.V.R.E.'s approached the beaches first, but the L.C.O.C.U.'s in the shallower-draft LCA's were actually the first to touch down and the first to set foot on the beach.[31] On Jig, No. 9 and No. 10 L.C.O.C.U.'s immediately came under heavy fire and suffered some casualties. As a result, they were forced to take cover in the water until some of the tanks and A.V.R.E.'s had successfully landed and begun to suppress the defenses. But by that time, the windblown tide, generating deeper water than expected, left them with just 100 yards of dry beach below the high water mark, instead of the 300 yards that had been planned for. With most of the obstacles already under water, work proceeded slowly, and most of it was eventually done at the next low tide. The summary assessment of their role was that they were "unsuccessful in clearing a gap during the assault phase."[32] That left nearly all the initial clearance work on Jig to the A.V.R.E.'s and Royal Engineers, and they were to encounter some problems of their own.[33]

Perhaps worse, the rough seas made station keeping for the various craft as they approached shore a problematic exercise; many of the craft touched down in the wrong order, in the wrong place on their beach, or even on a completely different beach than had been intended. "The points of landing differed greatly from those intended, the craft touching down at points too widely dispersed and disposed too far to the EAST by about 400 yards. The positions of Teams 2 and 3 were reversed."[34]

The cross currents and strong following tide also made the job of keeping the craft nosed up on shore incredibly difficult, especially for the large and clumsier LCT's. Many broached sideways to the beach after their initial touchdown, which made it impossible for the vehicles to debark safely from them. The problem of course wasn't unique to Jig; it was a problem encountered to one degree or another on all the beaches. But the confusion that resulted on Jig was to have many ramifications for the work of the 82nd Assault Squadron, the engineer clearance teams, and the assault infantry battalions.

Jig Green East: Lane 6—Successful

LCT-(2030), with the assault team under the command of Capt. Frances John Burchall Somerset, carried two Crabs and three A.V.R.E.'s (Pusher, Bobbin, and Fascine). It landed almost alongside LCT-(2029) on the far left boundary of Jig Green Beach. Somerset reported:

Loading

Loading of AVREs was completed in good time and with no incidents.

Voyage

During the voyage and prior to sailing the Bobbin bolts had to be tightened every two hours to prevent them from shearing. Before sailing the Bobbin was secured from the top angle iron to either side of the LCT to counteract some of the swaying.

Landing

The LCT reached the beach without coming into contact with any obstacles. The leading AVRE had to wait for approximately four mins in the doorway, as the ramps were far from being properly down, after numerous efforts to try to contact somebody to lower them, I went off. The Roly Poly dropped down under the ends of the ramp and I went straight over the top.

The Roly Poly AVRE made for the most likely gap in the obstacles ahead and on seeing some bad ground pulled off and called up the Bobbin AVRE to lay its mat. This worked perfectly. The flails then crossed over and were followed immediately by the Roly Poly AVRE.

The Bobbin AVRE experienced no difficulty in shedding the Bobbin at the top of the beach—it then returned to beach clearance.

The flails then flailed a path from the edge of the beach to the roadway, turned to the right and engaged enemy MG positions on the rising ground to the left of MEUVAINE.

Markers were placed at the entrance to the lane, and green smoke hurled out immediately the lane was through.

The fascine AVRE (32166) on Lane 6, dropped its fascine prematurely in Lane 5 due to faulty split pins. The Commander immediately blew the binding ropes and put the bundles into some marsh in the lane which was proving troublesome.

Having got off the beach, the troop was rallied as soon as released from filling in craters etc and we proceeded in the direction of LE HAMEL, but were unfortunately not allowed to proceed straight through owing to one way traffic; had we been able to get through at that time the snipers and pillboxes in LE HAMEL could have been quite easily neutralized.

As soon as possible three AVREs were sent down to deal with snipers in LE HAMEL, by a round about route.

Sergeant Manning in the Fascine A.V.R.E. *Leopard* reported:

Nothing unusual until touch down, and then after drawing up to doors of LCT found that Field Coy were slow in fixing boats which I had to tow out. Whilst they were fixing boats LCT appeared to drift out and I was told by my driver that he thought we should be swamped if we went in from our position.

Owing to fascine I was unable to see forward and check this, I signaled the bridge of LCT and then to go further in to the beach. Whilst this was going on the Field Coy Sjt told me they were ready to move. I gave the order to advance and started to move off the LCT. The jolt as the AVRE left the ramp sheared the pins of the blow plates holding the fascine but the fascine did not drop. When we got off the ramp the AVRE seemed to stick and the driver accelerated hard. In doing so I found on looking back that the boats had broken loose and were still on the LCT.

On reaching the beach proper the driver could not see the Bobbin, nor any AFVs from our lane, & immediately drove for cover besides a lane which had been opened. During this time my periscope extension was partially shot away thus leaving me completely blind forward. After trying to find my exact position from the lane commander who could not help me, I was told to remain in a hull down position and await orders. Some time later I was told to use the first available lane (lane 5) and to go down the rd towards the village. Unfortunately whilst crossing the dune the fascine was shaken off, thus blocking the lane. It was blown apart and used to make good the lane which was becoming torn up. I withdrew from the lane to allow passage of traffic. Some hours later I joined Capt Somerset outside ASNELLES SUR MER and followed him into the town to clear up snipers. We found the infantry in possession.[35]

No report was made by Lance Sergeant Williams in A.V.R.E. *Loyal*.

Jig Green East: Lane 5—Successful

LCT-(2029), with the assault team under the command of Lt. George Raymond Ellis, carried three Crabs and three A.V.R.E.'s (Pusher, Bobbin, and Fascine). Captain Stanyon of the Westminster Dragoons, the breaching squadron commander for Jig Green East, was also aboard. They landed on the lef: boundary of Jig Green Beach, apparently on time. Lance Sergeant Tosh in the Bobbin A.V.R.E. *Leviathan* reported:

Embarkation carried out without incident.

On craft device (Bobbin) became unstable due to constant roll of boat. By use of wedges device was held secure enough to disembark without incident. Found beach firm and did not use the device.

Reached sand dunes, and was told by Lane Comd to retain device in case needed elsewhere.

Retained and returned to waters edge for beach clearance.

Immediately struck clay patch under water, and could not pull out. Rapid rise of tide caused abandonment of tank. Tank was rapidly submerged and was then rammed by incoming LCT.

On beach, crew assisted in laying of chespale bundles for marking up of flailed lane. One member of crew Spr Owen was standing at head of lane when a Sherman tank came off the beach, swung too far left of track, thus hitting a mine. Spr Owen caught the blast and received injuries to his right foot. He was left on beach under care of Red Cross.

At end of day, reached ASNELLES, remained there without incident until recalled to Unit HQ.

Lance Sergeant Morgan in the Fascine A.V.R.E. *Lemur* reported:

Embarked without incident. During voyage split pin of fascine blow plates partially sheared through movement of fascine. It was renewed.

During disembarkation was delayed in LCT doorway by length of time Field Coy

The abandoned A.V.R.E. (68309) on Jig Green. Note the Roly-Poly discarded in the foreground. THE TANK MUSEUM

took to load boats. When AVRE left ramp boats broke loose. Probably caused by weight of fascine taking AVRE off ramp with a jolt.[36]

The "Field Coy" referred to were elements of the 73rd Field Company R.E., which were assigned to obstacle-clearance duties on Jig, supporting No. 9 and No. 10 L.C.O.C.U.'s The boats were engineer assault boats on which the engineer stores, including demolitions, were to be floated while the engineers did their work.

Fascine required to fill in crater in roadway. Neither bomb release or blow-plate worked, possibly due to contact with sea water. Fascine was dropped by jerking AVRE thus shearing split pins. Fascine then opened up to form carpet across crater.
  Moved into LE HAMEL to neutralize pillboxes but job completed on arrival.
  Harboured for night.

Captain Leytham reported:

Lane 5 was successful until a fascine from Lane 6 was dropped in the exit from the beach. This fascine was rapidly dismantled and used to improve the gap.

The initial lane to the lateral road was cleared quite quickly by the two Crabs and was open at H+15. The Crabs then followed the lateral road toward Les Roquettes until they were stopped by the large crater referred to by Lance Sergeant Morgan. The crater was successfully filled in by Morgan's fascine and the two from Lane 4, allowing the Crabs to get forward again. But the Crab commanded by Captain Stanyon was hit by a heavy mortar or artillery shell and immediately went up in flames.[37]

Jig Green East: Lane 4—Failed

LCT-(2028), with the assault team under the command of Capt. J. M. Leytham and Lt. P. Crofton, carried two Crabs and four A.V.R.E.'s (Pusher, Bobbin, and two Fascines). It landed over 300 yards east of

their planned touchdown point, but on time. Crofton in Bobbin A.V.R.E. *Lifeguard* reported:

D-2 4 Jun 44: Loaded onto LCT. Successful—no difficulties with Bobbin.
  D-1 5 Jun 44: On LCT. Rough seas—no trouble with Bobbin which was held secure with chains.
  D 6 Jun 44: Coming off LCT. No difficulties.
  Following Roly Poly: Difficult as Roly Poly carpet came off on an a curved rather than straight due to tide etc.
  Approaching mud patches: Roly Poly AVRE crossed beach with no apparent difficulty as did Bobbin (my) AVRE. Therefore I decided beach was OK. This however was wrong as succeeding Sherman Crabs got bogged on lane. Either the rule should be always lay Bobbin (in which case if the distance between end of Roly Poly and HWM is greater than 75 [yards] with Mk II Bobbin this may not solve the problem) or devise some more positive way of determining presence of mud dangerous to Shermans.
  I don't like principle of Roly Poly and Bobbin—It is too nice and liable to go wrong—Land as many AVREs and flails as possible and in most cases at least 50% will get through. Roly Poly and Bobbin did not increase this proportion. DDs should make high water mark by learning from mistakes of unlucky AVREs, flails and thus see where mud lies.
  Bobbin technically: OK (with luck), Puff pins—OK.
  Beach Clearance: AVRE very unsuitable on muddy beach with fast moving tide. Those that got back for beach clearance got bogged (except one) early on. Bulldozer (eight, broad track) is ideal veh for beach clearance on mud.

Lance Sergeant Gale in the Fascine A.V.R.E. *Lynx* reported:

Sun 4 Jun 44: AVRE and crew embarked.

Mon 5 Jun 44: Sailed 0830 hrs. Bomb release broke free, probably due to heavy seas at 2330 hrs. Fascine and bomb release replaced using LCTs adjustable shackles.

Tues 6 Jun 44: Beached 0730 hrs, drove forward up beach, and lay under cover of rise for approx 10—25 mins. Passed forward and dropped fascine in crater; remained at crater on Beachhead 4 assisting maintenance on this section of road for 4 hrs. Proceeded under troop leader's instructions, to assist R Hampshire Regt. Welding on elevating gear broke on Petard.

Lance Sergeant Pearson in the Fascine A.V.R.E. *Leveret* reported:

We disembarked on the 6 Jun 44. On coming off craft we made straight for our lane. On arriving at point had to wait a few minutes on the flails making a path through minefields. Then we were called on to drop our fascine in a crater a few yards up the road from the beach which was holding our armour up. With the help of other two AVREs the road was soon passable. We stood by the road for a while repairing it after every six or seven tanks passed through until the Aslt Field Sqn came up to take over and let us carry on to deal with any pillboxes further ahead. After the Field Sqn arrived we moved off with the rest of our AVREs and later went along to LE HAMEL to deal with some pillboxes, but on arriving the job had been done by another AVRE with his petard. We then returned to harbour and to do maintenance.[38]

When the Crabs began to flail forward, they immediately hit soft sand and both bogged before they even reached the edge of the minefield. Leytham reported:

Lane 4 was a failure, the flails failing to make an exit through the minefield, one having been bogged on the beach.

A crater on the lateral road prevented movement of all tracked vehicles proceeding via Lane 5 & 6, as these two lanes had become the exit for all tracked vehicles all available fascines were used to fill in the crater and the AVREs employed to tow any tracked vehicles that became bogged in crossing. This work was continued until a party of Beach Group RE took over.

All AVREs then rallied at Bde HQ in MEUVAINES. Three AVREs u/c Lieut Ellis then proceeded to LE HAMEL to deal with snipers in the Sanatorium and various pillboxes. On arrival the task had been completed by No 2118916 L sjt [Herbert Matthew] Scaife who was assisting a joint party of survivors from 2 Coys [companies] of the Hampshires. The party then reformed and proceeded to CABANE in readiness to assist the Hampshires in their advance on a position to the east of CABANE. No assistance was required.

This party then rallied at BUHOT for the night.[39]

The mopping up at Le Hamel by Lieutenant Ellis with the three A.V.R.E.'s as well as some DD tanks and a Crab was something of an anticlimax. The position had already been hammered by Lance Sergeant Scaife in A.V.R.E. *Loch Leven*, which had landed in Lane 2 on Jig Green West. Nevertheless, the Crab was destroyed by German antitank gun fire in the town, with two men wounded.

Jig Green West: Lane 3—Partially Successful
LCT-(2027), with the assault team under the command of Lt. S.V. Grant and Lt. N. W. Greene, carried two Crabs and three A.V.R.E.'s (Pusher, Bobbin, and Fascine). It landed just to the left of the intended touchdown point for Lane 3, but apparently close to the planned time.

Greene in Pusher A.V.R.E. *Loch Lomond* reported:

I was on Lane 3 and was in the leading vehicle in the LCT pushing a Roly Poly which after rolling down the ramp failed to unroll further and I found my AVRE driving over the central core. The Roly Poly became useless.

I then advanced up the beach to HWM [high water mark] avoiding all obstacles. There was no difficulty negotiating mud or peat so the Bobbin which was on AVRE No 2 was not required. All following vehicles were able to avoid the dumped Roly Poly by driving round it.

It was difficult to see as salt covered my periscopes so I proceeded in a straight line to the top of the beach and did not go up the small existing beach roadway as planned.

I then called up two flails (Nos 3 and 4 in the LCT) who flailed for about 200 yards from HWM to the lateral road. The grass was about 2 ft high which probably made flails partly ineffective. One flail struck a mine but the other got through and advanced inland. The lane was successful but narrow especially past the knocked out flail and passing this flail my AVRE struck a mine. Two bogies were damaged and two or three track plates broken. The AVRE had not run off the track so the crew immediately started to repair it.

The AVRE and Flail together were a good target and brought down heavy enemy fire and it was then that I was hit by shrapnel in the arm. During this time the lane was being cleared completely and widened by Div RE and used as the heavy track exit.

I went down to the BDS [Battalion or Brigade Dressing Station?] and noticed several tanks on Lane 2 bogged in the peat which was covered by the tide.

I embarked on the morning of D+1 having spent the afternoon of D on the beach which was then still under fire from enemy snipers. Lt Grant (82 Sqn) apparently took over my tank in the evening as his own was waterlogged.

The DDs landed about 30 mins after us. Of the LCT (A)'s about 3 out of 8 were present to give support.[40]

The LCT(A)'s that Greene refers to were two of the eight assigned to the 108th LCT(A) Flotilla carrying the 1st Royal Marine Armoured Support Battery of four troops, each troop consisting of four

Centaurs and one Sherman tank. Only LCT(A)-2233 and 2442 arrived on time, carrying two Centaurs each and possibly one Sherman and one Crusader AA tank.[41]

Corporal Shampshire in Pusher A.V.R.E. *Loch Lomond* reported:

0725 hrs. Touched down. Ramp lowered. Roly Poly obstructed. AVRE proceeded over it. Ran up beach fairly easy. All obstacles avoided. Reached HWM. Flails late in following.

0730 hrs. Went to assistance of Lt Grant whose AVRE had become bogged. Pulled him out and made for lame AVRE hit by HE shell. Splined-spigot retaining plate damaged but AVRE still mobile.

0800 hrs. Lane reported clear for single line traffic.

0810 hrs. Prepared to advance through 1 Lane. Struck mine when passing mine-disabled flail. Left track broken, four plates missing, also two bogies. Started to clear path by prodding method on our right. Tried to contact mine-clearing party by wireless. No success. Lt Greene sent gunner back to beach to contact them and later followed him. Wireless op [operator] unable to contact control to report situation. Notified all stations in Lane 3 that lane was blocked.

0820 hrs. Lt Greene and gunner returned from beach. Later followed by clearing party.

0840 hrs. Lane cleared for single-lined traffic. We prepared to mend track. Under fire all the time.

1100 hrs. Lt Greene hit by shrapnel in upper left arm. Wound did not appear to be very serious. We bandaged the wound and Lt Greene went off to report to casualty station and I took over. Carried on mending track. Returned to beach to salvage spare track plates from bogged AVREs. Removed broken springs & replaced track & were on the road by approx 1700 hrs. Meanwhile Lt Grant decided to take over our AVRE as his was bogged on beach.

2145 hrs. Moved off to RV under command of Capt Somerset.

Lieutenant Grant in Bobbin A.V.R.E. *Lancer* reported:

No 32159 was Bobbin AVRE on craft 2027. When the craft beached at H hour the leading AVRE u/c Lt Greene pushed the Roly Poly off successfully but shortly after clearing the ramp it stuck and the AVRE mounted it and proceeded up the beach.

When No 32159 left the craft it turned and avoided the RP [Roly Poly] and followed up the beach behind the Lane Commander. The beach was sand and there were no orders from the Lane Commander to lay the Bobbin and his tracks gave no indication of soft ground.

I then turned right at HW [high water] mark and prepared to contact 73 Fd Coy on Lane 1. I could see nothing of Lane 1 or Lane 2 and turned back to lane 3 again in preparation to lay the Bobbin in any soft place which might appear.

I was waiting and found that in turning I had bogged down: I actually was not aware of this until told by Maj Elphinstone who climbed to my turret. I got out of the AVRE and contacted Lt Greene who then towed me out after I had blown the Bobbin. Every portion of the Bobbin functioned including the "Puff Pins".

I remounted and moved again towards Lane 1. There still was no sign of the lane being even attempted. I learned over the R/T that Lane 1 craft had failed to land. I saw that several DDs had advanced along the beach towards where Lane 1 should have been and were bellied in the clay under the sand. I too became bellied and before I could get a tow the tide came up and I gave orders for the crew to abandon the vehicle.

We took the Bren gun and two mags and also a small quantity of food and water and I also removed the binoculars and the maps.

The beach was under fire and the crew took shelter in the dunes.

The shelling increased so I gave orders to move East along the dunes to a safer spot intending to get off the beach entirely and go inland through Lane 3. My orders were not passed successfully along from man to man and after proceeding a few yards I found that only one member of the crew was with me. I sent this man back to repeat my orders and he came back with the other members. In the meantime Cpl Dafnis the demolition NCO was wounded in the nose. A field dressing was applied and we then proceeded along the beach.

Near Lane 3 I saw Lt Greene on the beach and his arm was wounded. He asked me to contact his AVRE in Lane 3 and see if it could be made mobile as it had been hit by a HE on the splined support and had lost 2 bogeys on the near side. The spigot support was good enough for movement and I ordered the remains of the bogeys below the fulcrum to be removed. I also instructed the crew to collect spare track plates from 32159 in the beach and also one from another AVRE on the beach.

I then contacted Lt Crofton on the East beach and under his orders I collected all spare personnel and AVREs and held them off the collateral road at the end of Lane 3. Then with Lt Crofton's permission I placed myself and available AVREs u/c of Capt Somerset. We harboured for the night in ASNELLES SUR MER.

Lance Corporal Phillips in Fascine A.V.R.E. *Loch Ness* reported:

After leaving LCT No 2027 we advanced up the beach to high water mark receiving several hits on the way. We were ordered to wait at the end of lane 3 until the signal of lane clear was given. We waited approximately 5 mins and then we received a message to say the lane was blocked by the lane commander's AVRE.

The tank commander was then asked to retrieve the immobile Sherman and we started advancing right of Lane 3 along high water mark. After proceeding about 50 yards we had some gear trouble and the commander got down into the driver's seat to try and rectify same. After doing so he opened the driver's visor and we then received a direct hit on the front of the tank which killed the commander [Lance Serjeant George] and injured the driver [Sapper A.W.L. Rawlinson]. Shortly after this we advanced and eventually our AVRE turned over on its side. On inspecting this later we discovered our blow plates had been hit and our fascine had dropped and not knowing this one track had started to climb the fascine thus turning us over. We then got out of the AVRE and took up a defensive position beside it with our Bren gun. Two of the crew assisted with the wounded.[42]

Two of the Crabs had bogged down, and one of those was later struck by shellfire. *Loch Ness* had taken a hit and then overturned and was a total loss, while *Loch Lomond* had been hit by shellfire and then disabled by a mine.

Captain Leytham reported:

Lane 3 was successful until a flail blocked the entrance to the lateral road, having been hit by a mine. On this lane L sjt George was detailed to report to Lane 1, owing to gear trouble he was driving the AVRE, as he was carrying a fascine the driver's vision port was open. A direct hit on the front of the AVRE killed L sjt George and slightly injured the driver Spr Rawlinson A.W.L. He took over the controls and advanced: unknown to him the fascine had dropped to one side having been hit by shell fire causing one track to ride up the fascine and then overturn the AVRE.[43]

A.V.R.E. *Loch Ness* after it turned over in Lane 3. THE TANK MUSEUM

Jig Green West: Lane 2—Failed

LCT-(2026), with the assault team under the command of Major Elphinstone, carried two Crabs and four A.V.R.E.'s (Pusher, Bobbin, Command, and Fascine). It landed incorrectly east of Lane 3 and about five minutes early. Lance Sergeant Scaife in Pusher A.V.R.E. *Loch Leven* reported:

> Embarked approx 0430 hrs 3 Jun 44. LCT Serial 2026.
>
> Stayed aboard until disembarking on beach 0725 hrs 6 Jun 44. Sea voyage rough, crew all seasick in various stages. Left LCT pushing Roly Poly. Roly Poly not a success, sticking at the bottom of ramp and AVRE advancing over top of it. Advanced up beach to HWM and stood aside to make room for Crabs to advance. Lane not a success due to flail sticking in boggy land.
>
> Unable to help on other lanes so assisted 73 Coy RE in smashing beach obstacles, mainly by running over hedgehogs. At approx 0845 hrs made way off beach by way of lane 300 yds East of Lane 3. Lane was blocked by wood obstacle which I smashed by running over it. I attempted to turn West along lateral road but had trouble with steering brake owing to sea water entering transmission compartment. Managed to get clear of road to enable anything else to pass and brakes improved after short time.
>
> Was under spasmodic machine gun and mortar fire all the time from leaving LCT but only very minor damage inflicted on AVRE.
>
> Was unable to maintain contact with other AVREs by wireless so moved off West in company with four Sherman DDs. Turned South and passed through ASNELLES SUR MER and stopped in field where I reported to the officer IC Shermans (Sherwood Rangers). He could give me no information regarding rest of my formation so told me to stick with them for time being. I followed them for half a mile West until they started to look for an A-tk gun that was causing trouble. Not having suitable guns to assist I

> returned to ASNELLES SUR MER and found HQ of Hampshire Regt. I was asked to assist them in some clearing operations and did so.
>
> The time was approx 1500 hrs when I first went into action against large building on sea front (I think it was a hospital being used as a German HQ). After firing two rounds from Petard at emplacements and building the infantry cleared it without further opposition, taking about 20 prisoners.
>
> A large pillbox containing an A-tk gun and MGs was next objective and I attacked from rear. The first Petard round entered through opening and shattered the inside and set it on fire. More Germans then came out of surrounding small buildings and were taken prisoner.
>
> I then fired on emplacements slightly to the East and again the enemy surrendered.
>
> I then followed the infantry to the West and assisted them to clear emplacements along the sea front. Had just cleared last in vicinity when we were joined by more AVREs under command of Lt Ellis.
>
> The Hampshire Infantry body I worked with appeared to consist of 2 Majors, 1 Captain and 2 Subalterns and approx 2 WOs, 50 NCOs and men.
>
> I then came under command of Lt Ellis and moved West to assist infantry of needed. We were joined by Capt Leytham in another AVRE and he took over command and, not being required to assist infantry, we moved to harbour area for the night.

Lance Sergeant Cassap in Bobbin A.V.R.E. *Lightning* reported:

> AVRE No 31097 landed from craft LCT No 2026 on Lane 2 carrying the Bobbin. On the run up the beach no soft ground was encountered. We then turned right. As we had not used the Bobbin the wireless operator sent out a call to control. As no reply to the calls was received I dropped the Bobbin. I also blew the puff charges but owing to the

twist on the Bobbin the pins would not blow out. I then asked for one volunteer to help me free the Bobbin from the AVRE. L/cpl Long then volunteered. We then jumped out of the AVRE and tried to pull out the pins without any success. We then blew the Bobbin supports with a charge of PE [probably Plastic Explosive]. We then proceeded in AVRE to Lane 2 to report to the Offr IC beach clearance. As no beach group was to be seen I then turned to come back to Lane 2. I then encountered the Major of the beach group with a party of sappers blowing up the Hedgehogs. He then gave me orders to crush down the Hedgehogs which I proceeded to carry out. I was then ordered by the Major of the beach group to take him up to each of the lanes. On reaching Lane 4 I was ordered to help to pull out other AVREs stuck in the clay. Owing to getting stuck ourselves we were forced to leave the AVRE as the sea was ris-

ing very quickly. After the tide had receded again we secured the help of a bulldozer and had our AVRE pulled out. We then received orders from our troop Offr to report to a beach group busy removing type C elements. We left the beach at 2330 hrs and proceeded to the village of BUHOT on the morning of the 7 Jun 44.

Lance Sergeant Bright in Fascine A.V.R.E. *Lough Neagh* reported:

Embarked 0400 hrs 4 Jun 44 (Lane 2). On Landing Craft all day 5 Jun 44. Beached at 0725 hrs 7 [sic, 6] Jun 44 and made for Lane 1 as ordered, which was not identified owing to Lane 1 not being started as landing craft had been hit before Assault Vehicles could be disembarked. Ran into concentrated fire from enemy pillbox, to which it was impossible to reply owing to fascine and fittings being in way of armament. Turned about and

A Crab of the Westminster Dragoons knocked out on Gold. It is difficult to make out the LCT loading number, but this appears to be the Crab from LCT-2026 that was mined. In the right background, a knocked-out DD can also be seen. THE TANK MUSEUM

made for lane 3 in case required. 0800 hrs Gears jammed in reverse; unable to move approximately 150 yds from enemy pillbox. Unable to effect immediate repairs. Comd and Co-driver left AVRE and were brought under fire by enemy. Returned to AVRE and attempted repairs from inside being pinned down until 1400 hrs (approx). Left AVRE. Unable to effect repair. Left AVRE on beach and reported to RV just off beach through Lane 3 on Lt Crofton's orders. Returned to AVRE on morning 8 Jun 44 when temporary repairs were effected by Sjt Mackintosh (Fitter Sjt).[44]

There is no report from the Command A.V.R.E, as Major Elphinstone was killed by a gunshot wound to the neck shortly after his A.V.R.E. disembarked when he exposed himself in the turret hatch to engage pillboxes with his machine gun. His demolition NCO handed over command to Captain Taylor, the second in command of B Squadron of the Westminster Dragoons.

Both Crabs were disabled, one bogged down in a marshy minefield between the beach and the lateral road and the other mined, while *Lough Neagh* was immobilized by a mechanical defect.[45] Leytham reported:

> Lane 2 also failed as craft 2026 touched down to the left of Lane 3. Major H. C. A. Elphinstone of craft 2026 was killed after disembarkation whilst exposing himself through the turret hatch.[46]

Jig Green West: Lane 1—Failed

LCT-(2025), with the assault team under the command of Capt. K. M. Wilford, carried two Crabs and three A.V.R.E.'s (Pusher, Bobbin, and General Purpose). It touched down in the correct spot at 0720 hours, ten minutes early, just east of the German strongpoint at Le Hamel (WN 37). Leytham reported:

> Lane 1 u/c Capt Wilford failed completely— LCT 2025 came under direct enemy fire from battery in LE HAMEL, a direct hit was

scored on the bridge, wounding Capt Wilford. The AVRE pushing the Roly Poly became jammed behind the Roly Poly and prevented any disembarkation before 1330.

Corporal Southby in Pusher A.V.R.E. *Lough Corrib* reported:

> Roly Poly failed to run straight off ramp, went into crater. Pusher failed to make contact and AVRE would not mount obstacle because only one track was making contact. With this Capt Wilford told driver to reverse then to go forward. Gear jammed in neutral and AVRE could not get off LCT which was by now disabled.
> Driver's vision port opened and water came in flooding AVRE. Crew had to abandon AVRE and returned to LCT. Capt Wilford went along deck towards bridge and was wounded by shrapnel. LCT drifted until low tide when crew got ashore and reported to Lt Grant.
> AVRE still on beach all papers removed and destroyed. AVRE is half full of water at low tide.

Lance Sergeant Stephenson in Bobbin A.V.R.E. *Lucifer* reported:

> Embarkation
> Quite smoothly. No difficulty in getting AVRE on LCT.

> Voyage Across
> It was found that 1 hr after sailing operationally the Bobbin began to sway pretty badly owing to a choppy sea. It was feared that the pin on the front brackets would shear; also the swaying affected the brakes and we had great difficulty in preventing the whole carpet from unwinding. We eventually overcame all this by chaining the Bobbin down from either side and driving wedges between the drum and the uprights to stop it from turning.

The core of a Bobbin, quite possibly the one from Sergeant Stephenson's *Lucifer*.

79TH ARMOURED DIVISION
MEMORIAL ALBUM/DANNY LOVELL

Approach to the Beach

Approaching the beach it was obvious that we were not going to be dropped down in front of Lane 1, instead we were dropped approx 50 yds to the left. Whilst the ramp was being dropped down the craft 2025 had a direct hit on the bridge, consequently we never managed to beach correctly. The Roly Poly on running into the water struck a hedgehog and prevented Capt Wilford from getting off the craft. I was ordered to try and push him off but it was quite hopeless as his AVRE by this time was nearly submerged. I waited about two minutes and then decided to get out of the AVRE. I went straight up to the bridge and found Capt Wilford wounded also Lt Browning IC of 73 Field Coy Section and naval personnel of the craft. I was able to get my AVRE off the craft about 1330 hrs and laid my carpet in a specified place given to me by OC 73 Field Coy. I then assisted in beach clearance and then on to the rally, after this I came under Capt Somerset's command and was detailed to assist infantry in clearing

up BAYEUX and finally finished up at BUHOT where we rallied for the night and from then on we joined Sqn.

Lance Sergeant Pinks in Bridge A.V.R.E. *Lough Swilly* reported:

When proceeding off sand bank at the hard offside leg came away from anchor. Orders received from Capt Wilford to go forward about 200 yds along hard, then lower.

Whilst lowering, anchor and nearside leg bent.

Further orders received from Major Elphinstone to disband it, which was done.

Owing to craft being hit, unable to proceed in Lane 1. Came off craft at approx 1330 hrs. From there until 1800 hrs beach clearance, after which we were under Capt Somerset's comd.[47]

Only one of the A.V.R.E.'s, the Pusher *Lough Corrib*, had managed to barely get off the LCT. The awkward Roly Poly had gotten stuck, trapping the

A.V.R.E. at the end of the ramp, where it blocked the exit of the other vehicles and the dismounted engineer team from the 73rd Field Company. As the tide came in, the LCT was then broached to and became the target of the 75-millimeter gun in the strongpoint at Le Hamel, which hit the craft a number of times, at least once in the engine room and once on the bridge, effectively knocking it out of the battle for the beach. Eventually, the LCT managed to retract, abandoning *Lough Corrib*, which by that time was nearly underwater, and withdrew to deal with its casualties. The rest of the men and vehicles were not landed until the afternoon; well after the initial assault was over.

Altogether, the assault had cost the 82nd Squadron four of its twenty A.V.R.E.'s[48] and B Squadron, Westminster Dragoons, one of its twelve Crabs knocked out by mortar or artillery fire and another six bogged or mined. Personnel casualties had been relatively light considering the heavy vehicle losses, with just two killed and five wounded in the 82nd Squadron, plus another four wounded in B Squadron, Westminster Dragoons.

THE ASSAULT BY 231ST INFANTRY BRIGADE GROUP

The problems encountered by the gapping teams of the assault squadrons were mirrored in the experience of the engineer clearance teams and the assault infantry battalions. It had been planned that a total of fourteen demolition teams, including the L.C.O.C.U., would land on Jig. However, on the left of the brigade sector, on Jig Green East, only three sections from the 73rd Field Company R. E. landed (the rest landed later, never landed, or landed farther east in Jig Red West) and were able to begin demolition of the obstacles. Six other sections, one without its equipment, landed farther to the left (east) on Jig Red West. On Jig Green West, only two sections, one from the 73rd Field Company and the other from No. 10 L.C.O.C.U., managed to get ashore, while two remained on LCT-(2025) after it was disabled and landed in the afternoon. As a result, some clearance was done on Jig Red West, while Jig Green remained virtually untouched, except for the few lanes opened by the gapping teams.

By H hour the water level had already risen up the vertical stakes and had crept round the sandbank and was washing the concrete tetrahedral. The first parties attacked the timber and concrete obstacles over lengths of 250 yards. By H plus 60 mins a lane of varying dimensions was made through Jig Green EAST. (N.B. This lane was apparently on Jig Red WEST . . .). A large number of stakes and Element 'S's remained on Jig Green WEST. The tide with a following wind had covered the obstacles area by H plus 60 mins, except for the hedgehogs, to which attention was directed, while the LCOCUs under command carried on under water, with charges on the timber stakes. Demolition continued until the tide rose above the last obstacle and at about H plus 2 hrs. 3 AVsRE arrived to assist. One was bogged in soft ground almost immediately but the other two did sterling work crushing hedgehogs under water.[49]

The landing of the assault infantry companies was also confused by misplaced landings.

Jig Red

The 1st Dorsets were also swept eastward and instead of landing on Jig Green East as intended, they landed on Jig Red. The assault companies of the 1st Dorsets, A and B, touched down at 0725 and 0737 hours respectively, without the expected DD tanks in support, and east of their intended position opposite WN 36. A Company landed and "pushed forward to the line of the lateral road without opposition. . . . The Coy Comd, Major A. A. E. JONES. Lt. ELLIS, and C.S.M. HOWELL were all wounded soon after landing by shell and mortar fire."[50]

B Company landed to the left of A and also encountered shell and mortar fire, which caused a considerable number of casualties. They reached Les Roquettes at 0915 hours only to find that C Company from the second assault wave was already there. C Company had landed at 0745 hours over the same beach as A Company, but encountered nearly zero opposition. D Company touched down at 0750 hours behind B Company and suffered heavy casualties from shell and mortar fire and the loss of an LCA on one of the mined obstacles. Overall losses in the battalion for the day were severe—4 officers and 17 other ranks killed, 10 officers and 88 other ranks wounded, and 9 other ranks missing, for a total of 128.[51]

Jig Green

A and B Company, 1st Hamps, were supposed to land on Jig Green West and seize their initial objective, Dart (WN 37 at Le Hamel), with the support of the DD Tanks of the Nottinghamshire Yeomanry (Notts Yeo). However, they instead landed on Jig Green East at H+05, 0730 hours, without the DD tanks, which came in somewhat later. It seems that the 1st Hamps didn't realize that they had landed in the wrong place, since no mention of that was apparently made in their report:

The aerial bombardment did not seem to have been so effective as expected. Enemy machine gun nests survived the aerial, naval and artillery bombardment and made the fullest use of their underground, well concealed and well built positions. The narrowness of the beach and the presence of mines added to the difficulties of the battalion's task. In spite of heavy casualties, however, the battalion drove the enemy from the beach . . . inflicting heavy casualties.[52]

The position they had attacked was actually WN 36, which was intended to be the initial objective of the 1st Dorsets. They then turned west and advanced on Le Hamel and Asnelles-sur-Mer. The reserve companies, C and D, began landing at 0745, about the same time that the battalion commander, Lt. Col. David Nelson-Smith, was wounded. Maj. David Warren of C Company, who took over command, left a vivid account of the battle.

During the last half mile of the run-in there was mortar and light artillery fire coming down on the sea, together with limited small arms fire, which in the last hundred yards could be heard striking and passing over the LCA. Mortar fire burst close to the craft but it seemed to be on fixed lines and not observed, for at this stage the beach would have been a more effective target.

Typ SK casemate with 5-centimeter gun on Gold, probably at St-Come-de-Fresné, WN 38, west of Le Hamel. The photo was taken on 13 June 1944. NARA

It is apparent that the craft were heading for the extreme eastern edge of Jig Green WEST, instead of the extreme western edge as planned. The obstacles were no real trouble and the LCA beached on a runnel about thirty yards from the waterline. Small bursts of small arms fire coming from the direction of LE HAMEL and LES ROQUETTES were seen on the surface of the water, which at first came well up to the thighs. There were some casualties. Machine gun fire from LE HAMEL EAST swept the beaches during disembarkation and mortar fire fell around the water's edge.

About twenty British troops could be seen fighting near some pillboxes in the dunes. This was the left hand platoon of A Company dealing with two pillboxes at the edge of LES ROQUETTES. The enemy were not offering much opposition and, although some continued to fight on, many gave themselves up to the troops running up the beaches from their craft.

With this platoon was the second in command of A Company, who said that his company had landed well down to the eastern end of the beach and that the two other platoons were last seen working toward LE HAMEL against stiff opposition.

The fire from LE HAMEL showed no sign of decreasing . . . and fire was coming onto the beach from the southern end of Asnelles. Movement of any kind was becoming well nigh impossible on the beach owing to the heavy machine gun and mortar fire. A Flail was standing about 20 yards down the beach, and by throwing pebbles at the turret the attention of the driver was attracted and he was asked to fire at the hospital in LE HAMEL, from which most of the fire seemed to be coming. As he opened fire, movement down the beach towards LE HAMEL was possible, although not without casualties, for the fire from the tank appeared to neutralise the enemy fire to some extent. The tank commander, however, decided to bring his Flail further up the beach towards the enemy and was immediately hit by an 88 mm firing from LE HAMEL. The tank was soon burning fiercely and, as soon as the covering fire from the tank stopped, intense machine gun fire was resumed immediately. Casualties began to occur very rapidly and it was necessary to hold up the advance. Machine gun fire was now coming from several slit trench positions as well as from the hospital and buildings in LE HAMEL EAST, and if the enemy were to be reached in any strength it was clear that mortar fire as well as gunfire from tanks would have to be laid on.

A runner from battalion headquarters came forward to report that the battalion commander had become a casualty and that the support company commander had taken over command, until such time as I could reach battalion headquarters. I handed over to the coy 2 i/c and went to battalion headquarters in the LES ROQUETTES position. The support company commander explained that the CO had been wounded again and was unable to continue; I took over command pending the arrival of the battalion second in command who was still at sea in the LCH [Landing Craft Headquarters]. Unfortunately, he was killed by a sniper when landing two hours later.

Information on the battalion situation at the time I took over command was extremely scanty. D Company, beaching well down on the DORSET beach (Jig Green EAST) had landed quite easily and were working round without much difficulty to the forming up position for their attack. B Company, who had landed with A Company, had little difficulty in getting ashore and by 'reading the battle' it appeared that they were in ASNELLES, according to plan. Of A Company there was no news except about the platoon I had met when I landed. The mortar platoon had been seen trying to get across to ASNELLES.

No wireless communication with the LCH containing the second in command, or with A or B Company, was possible. Contact

was maintained with D Company, however, through the FOO working with them. As the battery commander of the SP regiment who landed with the battalion commander had become a casualty, the FOO with D Company was moved to battalion headquarters, leaving that company with only the FOO signal party.

The beach and LES ROQUETTES position were being mortared heavily at this period and there was frequent Nebelwerfer fire on the road junction 879859 [about 600 meters inland at Asnelles at what is now the intersection of the Rue du Magasin and the Rue de L'Eglise]. The DORSETS and DEVONS could be seen moving across country West of MEUVAINES and meeting a certain amount of mortar fire.

D Coy reported [at about 1400 hours] the half-troop gun position at 860863 [WN 39] captured with about 30 prisoners and only slight casualties, so they were sent to the Radar Station 855864 [just east of Arromanches]. . . . While the mopping up of LE HAMEL EAST was going on, C Company with the AVRE was sent to deal with the position at LE HAMEL WEST 870864 [WN 38]. Again the enemy fought it out until the end, but a frequent application of Petard bombs to fortified houses allowed the infantry to close with the enemy. Another 20 prisoners were taken and LE HAMEL was reported clear at 1600 hours.[53]

Losses for the battalion on D-Day are not known, but the two day total for 6 and 7 June was given as 144.[54]

As was noted above, two LCT(A)'s did manage to beach at about 0730, but the effect of the four Centaurs, one Sherman, and one Crusader AA tank was apparently nil (it is known that the Sherman was burnt out and the Crusader AA got bogged,[55] while two of the six Centaurs landed on Gold are known to have broken down). Additional armor support for the two assault battalions, the DD tanks of B and C Squadron, Notts Yeo, finally were beached at 0758. C Squadron lost five of their twenty tanks swamped in the heavy seas, while B Squadron lost three of twenty tanks to swamping. Four more tanks were knocked out by gunfire, attributed to 88s on the high ground between Asnelles and Meuvaines, although one or more 75-millimeter guns of the 14th Tank Destroyer Company of the 916th Grenadier Regiment in WN 40, 4Ca, or 40b were the more likely cause. A Squadron landed at H+90 to support of the 2nd Devon and apparently did not suffer any losses.[56]

The Assault Reserve Lands

The brigade reserve battalion, the 2nd Devons, was scheduled to land at H+45, 0810 hours, on Jig Green West behind the 1st Hamps. Unfortunately, unlike the 1st Hamps, they landed only slightly east of their intended beach and so encountered an intact German defense, WN 38 at Le Hamel. The first two companies touched down at H+45 and the remaining two just ten minutes later. "The beach was under spasmodic gunfire and mortar fire. It was found that the 1 HAMPS had failed to clear the immediate beach defences and thus the battalion was held up on the beach unable to go forward to the pre-arranged assembly area."[57]

As a result, C and D Companies were unable to get off the beach until 0915 hours, while A and B did not move inland until 0955 hours. For more than an hour, the battalion attempted to reorganize and deal with the German strongpoint that had already done so much damage to the three breaching teams of the 82nd Assault Squadron, especially with its well-sited 75-millimeter gun. By the end of the day, after Le Hamel and Asnelles had finally been cleared, it was found that the battalion had lost two officers and twenty other ranks killed and six officers and sixty other ranks wounded, for a total of eighty-eight casualties.[58]

The delay kept the 2nd Devons from reaching their main objective, the battery at Longues on D-Day. By that evening, they had only reached the high ground northwest of Ryes, spending the night there except for C Company, which attempted to advance to Masse de Cradalle, but was stalled by resistance at

La Rosiere. It wasn't until the morning of 7 June at 1053 hours that C Company captured the Longues Battery and ninety prisoners, while suffering the loss of just one officer killed during the mopping up.[59]

The last major assault element to land on Jig was No. 47 (RM) Commando, at 0950 hours. Unfortunately, they lost three of their LCA's to mines on the run in causing forty-three casualties (initial reports were that four officers and sixty-eight other ranks had been lost). They reorganized on the beach and then moved off toward their primary objective, Port-en-Bessin, reportedly losing another twelve men en route.

The Reserve Brigades Land

At around 1100 hours, the 151st Brigade began to land on Jig Red. The brigade encountered no opposition on the beach at all and quickly moved inland. By evening, the 6th Durham Light Infantry (DLI) had advanced through Crépon and Villiers-le-Sec to Esquay-sur-Seulles. The 9th DLI advanced to Sommervieu on the outskirts of Bayeux. The last battalion, the 8th DLI, remained in the rear in division reserve.

By the time the 56th Brigade began to land, just after noon, the opposition on the beaches had practically evaporated, except on Jig Green West, where sporadic mortar and sniper fire continued to hamper operations. However, the 56th Brigade successfully diverted its landing to the east as well and so had no major trouble.

> 2 Glosters landed from LCIs on Jig Red Beach at 1200 hrs and "quickly cleared the beach area", and advanced to the battalion concentration area. By 1600 hrs the battalion had suffered only two casualties wounded.
>
> 2 Essex beached at 1230 hrs east of Le Hamel (i.e. Jig Green) without casualties and proceeded inland.
>
> 2 SWB landed on Jig beach, there being mention of neither opposition nor casualties.[60]

GOLD ASSESSED

Unfortunately, although the narratives by the assault engineers on Gold were quite extensive and often very vivid, certain of the events that occurred are less clear than on the other beaches. We know that gapping operations on Jig were a disaster—only one gap was opened by the end of the assault phase (of six that were planned). King was somewhat better, but only relatively so. As best can be made out from the accounts, the Crabs were either knocked out (Lane 2) or bogged down. The A.V.R.E.'s had similar problems getting bogged or were occupied in attempting to extricate the bogged Crabs. Eventually, one Crab, commanded by Lieutenant Pears, managed to get off the beach at Lane 1, possibly as late as 1120.[61] Lane 6 was not opened until 1100. The result was a major traffic jam on the beaches as vehicles and men attempted to make their way through the narrow cleared lanes or pick their way through partially cleared gaps that were slowly opened by the field companies.

GAP CLEARANCE ON GOLD

81st Assault Squadron—King

Lane	6	5	4	3	2	1
Touched Down	0730	0725	0730	0730	0725	0730
1st Obstacle	0750	Failed	Failed	Failed	Failed	0750
1st Gap	1100					

82nd Assault Squadron—Jig

Lane	6	5	4	2	3	1
Touched Down	0720	0730	0730	0725	0730	0720
1st Obstacle	0752	0745	Failed	Failed[a]	Failed	Did not beach
1st Gap	1120	0830				

a. The lane was open sporadically throughout the morning, but was ultimately blocked by bogged Crabs.

CASUALTIES IN THE GOLD ASSAULT, 68TH INFANTRY BRIGADE AND ATTACHED UNITS

Unit	Killed		Wounded		Missing		Total
	Off.	OR	Off.	OR	Off.	OR	
5th East Yorks							161
6th Green Howards							117
7th Green Howards							50
4th/7th RDG							26
1st (RM) Armd. Spt. Regt.							5
81st Assault Squadron R.E.	0	1	0	8	0	5	14
89th Fd. Coy. R.E.							4
233rd Fd. Coy. R.E.							21
280th Fd. Coy. R.E.	0	8	1	26	0	0	35
No. 3 and No. 4 L.C.O.C.U.	0	1	1	4	0	0	6
86th Fd. Regt., R.A.	1	2					5
Miscellaneous							45
Total							489

Curiously enough, given the attention that Jig Beach has generally received because of the battle for Le Hamel, losses in the 69th Infantry Brigade, on the "easier" King Beach, were about the same. About 202 of the 489 casualties reported or estimated for the units of 69th Infantry Brigade on D-Day were calculated as having occurred "on the beach." The most severe loss on the beach was to the 5th East Yorks, who lost an estimated 91 officers and other ranks, mostly in storming WN 33 and 34.[62] It seems likely that it was the resistance of La Rivière (WN 33) and especially the 88-millimeter gun there that created so much havoc among the Crabs, A.V.R.E.'s, and tanks—at least two Crabs and two of the A.V.R.E.'s were lost to it—that was to blame.

About 223 of the 534 casualties reported or estimated for the units of the 231st Infantry Brigade on D-Day were calculated as having occurred "on the beach." The most severe loss was incurred by the 1st Hamps, most of whose loss was caused by the intense fire coming from Le Hamel and in the assault on that position.[63] Another 41 casualties were incurred later in the day in the 56th Brigade and the units of the 104th Beach Sub-area, but no casualties were recorded for the 151st Brigade.

By the measure of casualties, it could be assumed that resistance on Jig and King were roughly the same. Given that the defenses were fairly similar and spread evenly along the front that should come as no surprise. However, it is interesting that the beaches that saw the most disastrous performance by the 1st Assault Brigade R.E.—in terms of opening gaps, at least—were also the beaches where the lowest casualties were incurred. In part, that seems to be a direct consequence of the outstanding actions of Lieutenant Pears in silencing the 88 millimeters at La Rivière and the magnificent exhibition of gallantry and initiative by Sergeant Scaife and the crew of *Loch Leven* at Le Hamel.

CASUALTIES IN THE GOLD ASSAULT, 231ST INFANTRY BRIGADE AND ATTACHED UNITS

Unit	Killed		Wounded		Missing		Total
	Off.	OR	Off.	OR	Off.	OR	
1st Hamps							144
1st Dorset	4	17	10	88	0	9	128
2nd Devon	2	20	6	60	0	0	88
82nd Squadron Total	1	1	2	3	0	0	7
B Sqn., Westminster Dragoons	0	0	0	4	0	0	4
Notts Yeo							21
No. 47 (RM) Commando[a]							55
73rd Fd. Sqn., R.E.							26
90th Fd. Coy., R.E.							10
295th Fd. Coy., R.E.							15
1st Bty, 1st (RM) Arm. Spt. Regt.							10
90th Fd. Regt. R.A.							9
147th Fd. Regt., R.A.							8
120th LAA Regt., R.A.							4
50th Div. Prov. Coy.							5
Total							534

a. Postwar Royal Navy casualty reports account for 2 officers and 16 other ranks killed and 4 other ranks missing, presumed killed.

LANDING CRAFT IN THE GOLD ASSAULT			
Total Craft engaged in Assault	Number known sunk	Number lost or damaged	Percentage lost or damaged
144 LCA		52	36
12 LCP(L)		3	25
148 LCT (all types)	3	34	23

The naval commander of Force G noted:

The beach obstacles were considerably thicker than air photographs had led me to expect, and they were also heavier than the experimental types made in England. The tide was higher than had been forecast, possibly due to the strong westerly wind, and the vertical posts with mines at the top and bottom caused damage to a considerable number of landing craft. In addition, there was reluctance in the heat of the assault to use kedge anchors, and this, combined with the considerable surf, caused many craft to broach to, fill with water, and so encumber the beaches.[64]

The number of landing craft lost and damaged was almost exactly the same as on Juno, a total of eighty-nine as opposed to ninety. Like Juno, it was about less than half the loss incurred on Sword, in terms of an average brigade front. However, it may be that the number sunk was perhaps highest on Gold, at least with regards to LCT's. After the war, the Royal Navy identified LCT(A)-2039 and LCT(IV)-809 and 886 as sunk on Gold. LCT(A)-2039 was part of the 109th LCT(A) Flotilla that attempted to land the 2nd Royal Marine Support Battery on Jig Green off Le Hamel and was probably lost there. However, the other two were both lost off King Beach.[65]

CHAPTER 8

Assault Force Omaha: The U.S. 1st and 29th Infantry Divisions

WHAT OCCURRED ON THE BEACHES of Omaha on D-Day has become the stuff of legend and, unfortunately, a bit of myth as well. That what occurred there was so different from all the other beaches is undeniable, but recognizing that it was different gives little clue as to why it was different. Furthermore, accounts of what happened are innumerable—and too many of those are at best woefully inaccurate or at worst simple mythology. This sketch is not intended to be a complete record of events, but is rather an outline so that what happened and why it happened may be discerned. The four best accounts of what occurred on Omaha—although they conflict in a few points—are used for this overview. They are the classic *Cross-Channel Attack* by Gordon A. Harrison, which itself built on the earlier *Omaha Beachhead (6 June–13 June 1944)* prepared by the 2nd Information and Historical Service of the First Army; Joseph Balkoski's *Omaha Beach: D-Day, June 6, 1944*; and Steven Zaloga's *D-Day 1944, Omaha Beach*. These authors and the anonymous authors of the 2nd Information and Historical Service have done much to eliminate some of the confusion and mythmaking surrounding the events on Omaha, and I am deeply indebted to their scholarship.

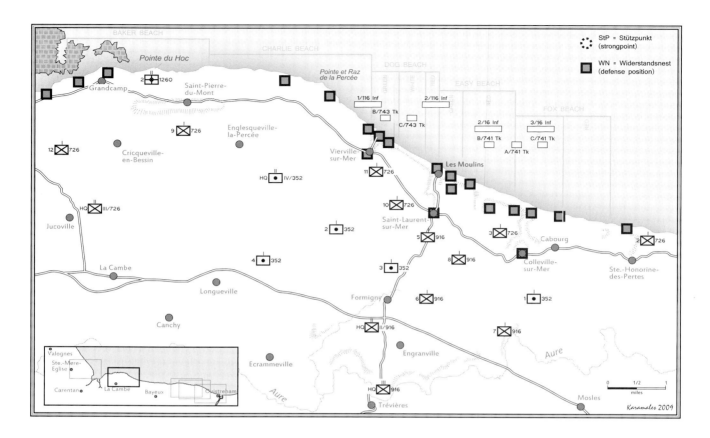

The assault on Omaha.

THE GAPPING TEAMS

Of the sixteen gapping teams that landed initially, most were able to make some progress preparing charges, but only five of them are known to have managed to detonate their charges with complete success. Few records remain of what happened to the teams, given the heavy casualties they suffered, so only a partial picture of the events can be given.[1]

Team 16 disembarked near the E-3 Draw on Fox Green, apparently at 0633. However, just as the team cleared the boat, a shell struck it, destroying the LCM and taking most of the team's explosives with it. Nevertheless, the few remaining unwounded set what charges they had only to have mortar fragments cut the primacord. The rising tide prevented the team from making repairs and trying again.

Team 15 landed on Fox Green about ten minutes late at 0640, so it had little time to attempt to set charges as the tide came in. In any case, a mortar round struck their explosive-laden rubber boat, killing three men and wounding several. Only four team members were left combat effective when they reached shore.[2]

Team 14 had a rough passage, but was actually the first reported to touch down, landing on Easy Red about 25 yards to the left (east) of a large fortified house and about 150 yards to the right (west) of

WN 62 at 0625—well before the infantry or tanks since the commander of its LCM thought that H-hour was 0620. The army team members got off the LCM just as a shell hit the rubber raft loaded with explosives, destroying the LCM and killing three of the navy team and leaving another four missing and presumed dead. The remaining team members were unable to set charges as more infantry and wounded sheltered behind the obstacles.[3]

Team 13 also had a rough passage in their over-loaded LCT(A). Most of the explosive packs were soaked from the sea washing over the sides and couldn't be dried out. They landed about 30 yards to the right (west) of Team 14 on Easy Red. Its LCM was hit by artillery or mortar fire as they were unloading and suffered heavy casualties. Enough army team members survived to set the few remaining charges, but arriving infantry prevented them from being set off.[4]

Team 12 landed shortly afterwards, also on Easy Red. They wired the sector they were in but, when finished, found it was impossible to set off the charges because of the infantry sheltering behind the obstacles. They began to make for shore when a shell set off the primacord, setting off the charges, killing ten members of the team, wounding nine

Fox Red just east of the Colleville (E-3) Draw at 0730. A few of the troops that landed here can be seen as well as possibly three tanks. The Cabourg (E-1) draw is at bottom center, and WN 60 is at lower right. NARA

Heading inland for Easy Red. These are men of the 16th Infantry in an LCVP. NARA

others, and killing or wounding many of the infantrymen. Staff Sgt. Bertram Husch of Team 12 was interviewed on 16 July:

Craft came in with its MG blasting away at shore installations. 0630 [midway between] E-1 and E-3, As soon as ramp down, MGs opened up. First group to get off. Ten men tried to get the pre-loaded rubber boat off the LCM but couldn't move it. The 6-man demolition crew took off for the beach and rest of the crew went to work on obstacles. In the first band [of obstacles] were saw horse ramps 10 feet high. It was necessary for one man to boost another on his shoulders to get the mine at the peak off (3 belts of obstacles). Men managed to bring up charges to blow a gap of about 30 yards using ring main with a 3-minute fuse. Tetratol was used since the C-2 had been left in the rubber boat. Fire heavy—work was done spasmodically. As the men were taking off for the protection of the shin-

gle pile, a mortar shell came over, struck the primacord, and set off the charges. Six Army team members were killed, 2 wounded. Four Navy team killed, 2 wounded. A number of infantry killed and wounded 0700. Explosion left few obstacles standing. Room for boats to come in, and many did. About 0800 the infantry managed to start moving out.[5]

Team 11 had a rough crossing. The LCT(A) carrying them and towing their LCM began to take in water about 20 miles off the beach and was abandoned. They managed to transfer to their LCM but lost most of their Tetrytol (22.5-pound high-explosive) packs and all their bangalore torpedoes in the process. They landed on the far left of Easy Red at 0635 without any infantry support and were immediately suppressed by German fire. By the end of the day, over half the team had been lost, killed, or wounded.[6]

Team 10 landed on Easy Red and managed to open a gap nearly 100 yards wide but was slowed by casualties and the continued arrival of landing craft and infantry.

Team 9 landed in the center of Easy Red, but their LCM took a hit just as the ramp was drawing. One man was killed and three wounded, but the remainder set their charges and after two attempts at setting them off managed to clear a partial gap.

Support Team H, with Capt. William J. Buntline of the 299th Engineers aboard, landed on Fox Green just to the west of the bluffs. The heavy German fire prevented any gapping attempts until the infantry began working up the hillside between 0800 and 0900.[7]

The LCM carrying Gapping Support Team F was hit by several shells. The first struck on the ramp, blowing three men into the water and throwing the craft out of control. The second burst in the bow, killing most of the men aboard. A total of fifteen of the twenty-five men aboard were killed, and only five members of the army team reached shore.[8]

Two more teams meant for the 116th Infantry sector landed on Easy Green, directly in front of the defenses at Les Moulins. Despite suffering heavy casualties, Team 8 managed to open a gap nearly fifty yards wide.

Team 6 landed on Easy Green, east off Les Moulins draw. They were faced with only two rows of ramps and a single row of hedgehogs that were sparsely distributed in this sector. They too had problems clearing infantrymen from their area, but succeded in clearing an effective gap fifty yards wide. Later, as the tide rose, two LCT's missed the few markers indicating the clear lane, struck mined obstacles, and sank, blocking about half the lane.

Team 7 was about to set off its charges when an LCM loaded with infantry crashed into the stakes. The landing craft set off at least seven Teller mines on the obstacles, wrecking it and killing many of the infantrymen aboard. The explosion also cut the primacord to the team's demolitions, preventing them from clearing the gap. With the rapidly rising tide making another attempt impossible, they moved ashore.

Teams 2 through 5 all had little success. Team 2 arrived late on Dog Green, and the rising tide made work impossible. Team 3 landed on Dog White on time, but was hit by artillery fire as the ramp was lowered, detonating all the explosives in the LCM, and killing or wounding all but one man. Team 4 suffered heavy casualties and was unable to set

	Team 6	Team 8	Team 9	Team 10	Team 11	Team 12	Team 13	Team 14	Team 15	Team 16
GAPPING IN THE 16TH INFANTRY ZONE										
Landed					0635	0630	0630	0625	0640	0633
Gap Open	0650	0700	Partial	0700	Failed	0700	Failed	Failed	Failed	Failed

	Support E		Support F		Support G		Support H		Command 2	
Landed	0640		0700		0650		0710		0714	

	Team 1	Team 2	Team 3	Tean 4	Team 5	Team 7
GAPPING IN THE 116TH INFANTRY ZONE						
Landed	0635	0730	0630	0630	0630	0630
Gap Open	0650	Failed	Partial	Failed	Partial	Failed

	Support A	Support B	Support C	Support D	Command 1
Landed	UNK	UNK	UNK	UNK	UNK

Above: What the Americans saw. An LCVP from the USS *Samuel P. Chase* landing men of the 1st Battalion, 16th Infantry on Easy Red at 0730. The vehicle directly ahead on the beach is Tank A-9 of A Company, 741st Tank Battalion, which was knocked out by a Teller mine that blew off the left center bogie assembly. NARA

This surrealistic scene is a detail from one of Robert Capa's famous photos taken on Easy Red on 6 June 1944. NARA

enough charges to clear a gap. Team 5 arrived on time on Dog Red and managed to set its charges by 0655, but arriving infantry taking cover behind the obstacles forced them to delay setting them off. When they finally managed to clear the area, they were only able to get an incomplete detonation that only partially cleared the gap.

Team 1 landed at 0635 at the boundary of Dog White and Dog Red well east of their planned landing on Dog Green. They worked rapidly to set its charges. After about fifteen minutes of work, they set them off, clearing an initial gap that they worked to widen in the afternoon. However, the team reported

that no craft used the gap on D-Day, even though they managed to widen it to 150 yards before night-fall.

Gapping Support Team B landed with C Company, 2nd Ranger Battalion, and elements of the 116th Infantry at the extreme western end of the beach at 0710. They prepared their charges within fifteen minutes of landing, but for an unknown reason, the detonation failed.

The other five gapping support teams—A, C, D, E, and G—all landed considerably later than scheduled because of difficulties in transferring from their LCT's to the LCM's for the trip into the beach.

Their landings were between 0640 and 0745. The turning tidal current pushed them all farther east than the assault teams they were intended to support. All were reprtedly met by heavy machine-gun, mortar, and artillery fire and suffered heavy casualties. The LCM of Team F was hit at 0700 hours and promptly sank; only four of the team members eventually made it to shore.

The two command craft also landed late. Command Team 1, leading the teams supporting the 116th Infantry on the western end of the beach, landed at 0700 hours after being bracketed by gunfire.

Command Boat 2, leading the teams supporting the 16th Infantry on the eastern end of the beach, was swept eastward and had to reverse course to come in on Easy Red as intended. Maj. Milton Jewett, commander of the 299th Engineer Combat Battalion, was in command of the Special Engineer Task Force teams on the eastern end of the beach supporting the 16th Infantry. He was interviewed on 16 July:

> Considerable difficulty in landing LCMs, causing delay. Went in too far west—FOX Beach—and had to pull along shore. Had to estimate beach—got in 0711. Water just coming up to the hedgehogs in inside of sandbars. Water waist deep. Easy Red Beach at point designated. Infantry and men from 37th C

Bn on shingle. Two assault tank and 1 dozer. AA guns and vehicles coming in and one of their LCTs beached and blocked the beach.[9]

The sixteen tank dozers intended to support the teams, one per gap, also fared poorly. Only six were known to have gotten ashore, where they did yeoman service, earning high praise from the engineers, but eventually, all but one were disabled.

The sixteen assault teams managed to clear five complete (the navy report says six) and three partial gaps by 0700. However, none of the gaps was adequately marked and one was not even used on D-Day. Later in the afternoon, four more gaps were opened, and the three morning gaps were completed, and all were widened.[10]

Even that partial result had been incredibly costly. The men of the Special Engineer Task Force suffered some of the highest casualties of any unit on D-Day. The navy teams lost 4 officers and 20 enlisted men killed, 3 officers and 29 enlisted men wounded, and 15 enlisted men missing—a total of 71 casualties of the 126 officers and men that were the nominal strength of the 21 N.C.D.U.'s present.[11] The 146th Engineers reported estimated losses of 31 killed, 79 wounded, and 3 missing on 10 June, but later a total of 145 casualties. The 299th Engineers reported 50 wounded and 52 missing in their estimated loss report of 19 June, but it seems clear that all the missing were in fact killed.[12]

THE ASSAULT BY THE 16TH REGIMENTAL COMBAT TEAM

On the left (east) end of Omaha, the landing by the 16th Infantry RCT began to unravel early. As on the Commonwealth beaches, the final decision on launching the DD tanks had been left as a joint decision between the naval commander of the LCT group and the army commander of the DD tanks embarked in the LCT. The decision to launch was made by Captain Thornton, the ranking officer of the 741st Tank Battalion, with the tacit concurrence of Lt. (Junior Grade) J. E. Barry, the commander of the LCT flotilla. At 0535, the tanks of B and C Companies began driving off the ramps of the LCT's some 5,000 to 6,000 yards from the beach.[13] The result was catastrophic. Of the twenty-nine DD tanks launched, twenty-seven were sunk in the run-in to the beach. On one, LCT-600, the first tank into the water immediately sank and the other three aboard aborted their launch. C Company was annihilated, losing all sixteen of its tanks. All five of the survivors were from B Company, but the company fared little better, losing eleven tanks during the swim in. The two remaining operational DD tanks landed at 0630 and were joined a few minutes later by the three from LCT-600, which were landed directly onto the beach.

The five tanks did yeoman service trying to support the initial waves of infantry, but they were too few to make a significant difference against the weight of German fire. Another was knocked out by an antitank gun early in the morning and another was lost to unknown causes, quickly reducing the survivors of B Company to just three tanks. Worse, the strong lateral currents off Omaha made a shambles of the infantry and obstacle-clearance team landings they had been intended to support.

Above: A medic among the wounded under the bluff below WN 60. A tank, probably a DD, can be seen in the water center left while to the left of that is the stern of LCI(L) 83. NARA

LCI(L) 83 lands Company B, 20th Engineers. WN 60 was immediately up the slope to the left, just west of where LCI(L) 83 landed. NARA

Two battalions of the 16th Infantry were intended to land abreast on the eastern end of Omaha Beach, the 3rd on the left and the 1st on the right. Each led with two assault companies, with the third assault company, weapons company, and battalion headquarters following thirty minutes later—theoretically after the gap clearance teams had done their work.

On Fox Green, the first wave of the 16th Infantry was supposed to consist of L Company on the left (east) and I Company on the right (west). Instead, L Company—minus one of its six LCA's that had been swamped—landed on the right edge of Fox Red directly in front of WN 60, where no landings had been intended. I Company was swept over a mile eastward toward Port-en-Bessin and had to work their way back, landing four of six boat sections—two of their LCA's had swamped and the men had been taken back to the assault ship by rescue boats—at 0800 hours, an hour and a half late.

Where L Company landed on Fox Red, they had a 200-yard wade under heavy fire from WN 60, which caused heavy casualties. What they were then confronted with was a narrow strip of beach along the edge of twelve-foot-high cliffs, above which was WN 60. Fortunately for the men of L Company, the steep cliffs prevented the Germans from getting a direct shot at them, so they were reduced to lobbing occasional grenades at the Americans. But otherwise, the Americans were equally unable to get to grip with the Germans—and the tide was coming in, inexorably shrinking the beach they stood on.

The actual landing on Fox Green turned into chaos. Elements of three infantry companies in fifteen LCA's and LCVP's—none of which was supposed to be there, including six boatloads of E Company, 116th Infantry, which had come ashore more than 3,000 yards east of its intended landing site—were intermingled under the fire of WN 60, 61, and 62. About 465 men landed there, and it is impossible to know how many fell. In a report that included all casualties incurred up to 1200 hours 8 June, E Company, 16th Infantry, accounted for one officer and six enlisted men killed, one officer and seventy-eight enlisted men wounded, one officer missing, presumed dead, and forty-two enlisted men presumed to be stragglers. F Company, 16th Infantry,

fared little better; they also had one officer and six enlisted men reported killed, two officers and sixty-four enlisted men wounded, no less than four officers missing, presumed killed, and thirty-six enlisted men missing, presumed to be stragglers. It may safely be presumed that most of the dead and wounded were incurred on Fox Green.

On Easy Red, only slightly less chaotic conditions reigned. Just one boatload from E Company, 16th Infantry, and two more errant LCA's from E Company, 116th Infantry, landed there. The section of E Company, 16th Infantry, under Lt. John Spalding, lost twelve of its thirty-two men crossing the beach, but managed to find a sheltered position among some demolished beach houses and then, almost immediately, began to explore ways of getting up the bluffs and behind the German positions dominating the beach exits.

At 0640 hours, the troops and five operational tanks on the beach were joined by twelve more tanks and six tank dozers of A Company, 741st Tank Battalion. One A Company LCT(A) had struck a mine and sunk at 0200, taking two more tanks and a tank dozer down with it, while yet another had broken down and was unable to land until D+3, also taking two tanks and a tank dozer out of the fight.

Of the six tank dozers landed, one was hit and destroyed within minutes, reportedly by the 88-millimeter gun in WN 61, another had its bulldozer blade blown off by the explosion of a mine, and two others were lost to unknown causes. The remaining two, with the help of the gapping teams, managed to enlarge the four partial lanes into a single large gap nearly 600 yards wide later in the morning.

One LCT(A) of the 741st Tank Battalion landed on Easy Red just east of the E-1 Exit at 0635 hours, and Sergeant Coaker's and Ball's tanks and Lieutenant Klotz's tank dozer immediately began engaging WN 64 and WN 65. Sergeant Beetson, commanding Klotz's tank dozer, reported:

At 2,000 yards from shore, we began firing, expending about 50 rounds, HE Amm [high-explosive ammunition]. Landed on beach at approximately 0630 hours continued firing at definite targets approximately ten, both large gun and machine gun emplacements, using

A panorama of the Colleville-sur-Mer area taken at about noon on 6 June. At upper left is Easy Red, upper center is Fox Green, while upper right is Fox Red. The large white blotch in the center is the heavily pummeled WN 62, with WN 61 to its right at the end of the antitank ditch. WN 60 is at the far right edge of the frame. NARA

Below: Easy Red later in the morning. The bend in the road at left is at the juncture with East Green. In the center is a damaged and smoking LCT, with the wreckage of what is probably an LCVP next to it. The many whitecaps in the water are caused by the waves breaking over the obstacles. NARA

A damaged and smoking LCVP from the USS *Samuel P. Chase* heads toward Easy Red at 0700 hours on 6 June. NARA

At the juncture of Fox Green and Fox Red, two sunken LCVP's are crowded with men attempting to get to shore while men on shore attempt to rig a lifeline. NARA

Below: The raft reaches shore with at least seven men. NARA

about 90 rounds HE amm. It is reasonably sure that hits were scored. During this time, we were also engaged in the removal of beach obstacles. At about noon, we reloaded with amm. in order to continue our work. At this time Lt. Klotz became casualty due to enemy fire. The remainder of the crew continued the work of clearing the beach. It was necessary for the crew to dismount under fire to facilitate the removal of obstacles which were dragged by means of cables. From time to time the crew assisted in the evacuation of wounded to the landing boats also while under fire. In the early afternoon, Sgt. Daum became a casualty due to enemy fire. The remainder of the crew continued operating the tank dozer clearing the beach of obstacles, and the removal of wrecked and burning vehicles, in order to expedite the movement of traffic. This work was continued until the tide rendered further operations impossible.[14]

At 0700 hours, the reserve companies of the assault battalions began to land. The usual plan was that the reserve rifle company landed first, followed ten minutes later by the weapons company and battalion headquarters.

On the left, K Company landed just slightly west of WN 60 and was caught in the crossfire between it and WN 62. Its losses as reported on the morning of 8 June were three officers and seven enlisted men killed, another thirty-eight enlisted men wounded, and twenty-two missing, most of those almost certainly being incurred during the assault. With nearly half the company down, it was out of the fight as an organized unit. However, M (Weapons) Company was more fortunate, landing farther east, where they were somewhat less exposed. They reported no one killed and just twenty wounded, with another twenty-four missing but believed to be stragglers. The 3rd Battalion Headquarters also landed intact, with none killed and just a few wounded and missing.

Farther west, G Company arrived nearly intact and close to where Lieutenant Spalding's small group from E Company had landed. It suffered some wounded getting off the landing craft and across the beach, but was the largest organized body of troops that had landed in that quiet area. The weapons company, H, was also fortunate, suffering just three enlisted men killed, with one officer and twenty-two enlisted men wounded, and eight missing. The 2nd Battalion Headquarters was even more fortunate, losing no killed or wounded and just twelve enlisted men missing.

Meanwhile, also at around 0700 hours, under the inspired leadership of two officers, Capt. John Armellino and Lt. James Monteith, L Company,

A soldier being given artificial respiration. NARA

16th Infantry, on Fox Red slowly began to work its way into the E-1 Exit. Armellino was wounded early on, but Monteith was able to contact the two DD tanks of B Company that had swum ashore and directed them to open fire on the German strongpoint. One, commanded by Sergeant Geddes, was credited with knocking out the two 75-millimeter guns in WN 60 and effectively suppressing its fire at around 0745 hours. The other, commanded by Sergeant Sheppard, claimed to have knocked out a "75mm or 88mm gun" that may well have been the one in WN 61; Colonel Ziegelmann's account states that it was reported to have been silenced at 0720 hours.[15] Sergeant Sheppard's tank was knocked out a few minutes later.

Monteith then scrambled up the cliff side with bangalore torpedoes, blew a hole in the wire entanglement, and personally led an assault that seized the German position at around 0900 hours. It was the first of the German strongpoints on Omaha to fall to the American assault. The loss of WN 60 drove a wedge into the German defenses at the eastern end of Omaha and began the unraveling of the German position. For his part in the action, Lieutenant Monteith was awarded the Medal of Honor, one of only two awarded on Omaha Beach.

Farther west, on Easy Red, Lieutenant Spalding's twenty men had started to gnaw away at the German defenses at the Colleville Draw. S/Sgt. Curt Colwell managed to blow a small gap in the wire entanglement at the base of the bluffs just west of WN 62 with a bangalore torpedo. Then, a lone man, Sgt. Philip Streczyk, exploited the gap, guiding Lieutenant Spalding and the rest of the tiny group through the gap and up the bluffs, where they seized one of the machine-gun positions and captured their first prisoner, a Pole. Spalding's men were supported by frontal attacks on WN 62 by the remnants of Company F, 16th Infantry, which knocked out one of the pillboxes and by one of the tanks, probably from B Company, 741st Tank Battalion, which knocked out one of the antitank guns on the bluff. Then G Company, under Capt. Joseph Dawson, joined the fight, penetrating the wire just east of Spalding's gap and fighting their way to the top of the bluffs. By about 0845, the group of perhaps 200 men, joined by the misplaced men from E Com-

The 4.2-inch mortars of the 81st Chemical Mortar Battalion attached to the 1st Division firing on D-Day. They are firing toward the east from positions somewhere on Easy Red between WN 62 and 64. NARA

Below: Fox Red and Fox Green, with one of the half-tracks of the 467th Anti-Aircraft Battalion standing parallel to the beach. The prominent fortified house in front of WN 65 is easily seen. NARA

pany, 116th Infantry, was poised to exploit the narrow opening they had opened in the German defenses between Colleville and St. Laurent.

Between 0740 and 0800 hours, the small groups on Easy Red received a powerful reinforcement when the reserve 1st Battalion, 16th Infantry, began to land. It landed nearly intact as an organization, although not without casualties. After assembling on the beach, the companies began to follow the torturous paths blazed by Spalding and Dawson's men, and by 0930, they were formed at the top of the bluff, ready to exploit the breach in the German line.

Although it did not appear so at the time, the situation had already tipped in the favor of the beleaguered American assault teams. WN 60 had fallen, WN 61 had been isolated, and its heaviest weapon, the 88-millimeter antitank gun, had been knocked out. The defense of the Colleville Exit was still holding, as WN 62 continued to resist attacks to front and flank, but the penetrations by L Company to the east, Spalding's and Dawson's gallant bands, and the 1st Battalion to the west had effectively isolated it.

At 1030 hours, the 2nd Battalion, 18th Infantry, was landed in LCVP's on Fox Red just west of WN

Easy Red just east of the E-1 Draw at 1100 hours after the landing of the 1st and 2nd Battalions, 115th Infantry. Tanks of the 741st Tank Battalion are lined up on the shingle firing inland. LCI(L) 553 is to the left. NARA

Below: The crew of an LCI(L) watching a large explosion on Easy Red. It is likely the explosion was part of the engineer operations to clear the beach obstacles. NARA

65. Supported by two tanks of the 741st Tank Battalion, some half-track mounted guns of the 467th Antiaircraft Battalion,[16] and the destroyer USS *Frankford* standing close offshore, the battalion overwhelmed the position, opening Exit E-1, the St. Laurent Draw, at about noon. The 2nd Battalion was followed by ten LCI(L)'s that landed the bulk of the

18th Infantry on Fox Red at about 1100 hours.[17] That finally ended the stalemate in the 16th Infantry sector, although it was the next day before the last German strongpoints surrendered.

The fate of the 741st Tank Battalion well illustrates the strength of the German position. Of twelve gun tanks reported landed by A Company, one was swamped on the beach as the tide came in, and five threw tracks in the heavy going on the shingle. Three more were lost to antitank gun fire, two to mines, and one to unknown cause, leaving none in action at the end of the day. B Company landed five tanks and quickly lost two more, but at the end of the day, just one was operational; two of the three surviving tanks were knocked out attempting to finally subdue WN 62 around 1100 hours. C Company was lost at sea. Four of six tank dozers landed were lost. Four more reserve 741st Tank Battalion tanks landed between 1300 and 1630 hours, but by the end of the day, just five tanks and two tank dozers were left operational ashore with the battalion of the twenty-three that had landed, while thirty had been lost at sea.[18]

THE ASSAULT BY THE 116TH REGIMENTAL COMBAT TEAM

On the right (west) end of Omaha, the 743rd Tank Battalion initially fared somewhat better than the 741st to the east. The commander of the LCT flotilla, Lt. D. L. Rockwell, decided that the sea was too rough for the DD tanks and decided to land them directly on the beach.[19]

C Company landed with eight tanks on Dog White and eight on Easy Green, instead of on Dog Green as had been intended, at 0624 hours in "unusually rough water." When the tanks began to cross the beach, they also encountered considerable fire from German antitank guns, but only one tank was disabled when it lost a track in the heavy shingle. It appears that observation from WN 68 may have been obscured by a grass fire that had been caused by the naval bombardment, while the guns of WN 70

apparently concentrated on B Company on Dog Green. However, the infantry the eight tanks on Dog White had expected to team up with, G Company, 116th Infantry, didn't appear—they had been swept eastward to the far eastern boundary of Easy Green. The swiftly returning tide was forcing the tankers steadily inland, so they shifted westward in search of infantry to support. Eventually, the fifteen operational tanks concentrated near the D-1 Exit where they joined the survivors of B Company in hammering WN 68, 70, and 71 in turn with gunfire. In return, the life raft stowed on one of the DD tanks was hit and caught fire, eventually setting the tank ablaze and destroying it. But by the end of the day, fourteen tanks were still operational and only one officer and four enlisted men had been wounded.[20]

This is Dog Green Beach at about 0930, with the tide nearly in. Eleven DD tanks of the 743rd Tank Battalion can be counted along the beach promenade road and on the beach. The multitude of small black dots on the beach are men of the 116th Infantry sheltering among the beach obstacles. NARA

B Company landed intact on Dog Green at 0630 with all sixteen tanks, but was met by a storm of fire from the 88-millimeter and 50-millimeter guns at WN 72 and the two 75-millimeter guns in WN 70. Within a few minutes, tanks began to get hit, and by the end of the day, seven had been lost, with three officers and six enlisted men killed and one officer wounded.[21]

A Company, 743rd Tank Battalion, with the wading tanks landed at about the same time as the DD Companies, on Dog Red, directly in front of the defenses at Les Moulins. Two of the LCT(A)'s were hit by German gunfire before beaching. As a result, only one M4 tank they carried was able to get to shore; three other M4 tanks and two M4 tank dozers were lost. The remaining thirteen tanks and six tank dozers attempted to advance through Exit D-3, but failed, so they shifted west toward Exit D-1 and the other two companies of the battalion. The battalion commander, Lt. Col. John S. Upham, landed at H+90 with six reserve and headquarters tanks. He was mortally wounded after dismounting from his tank in an attempt to direct fire on the 88-millimeter gun at WN 72. By the end of the day, another five tanks and all but one of the tank dozers had been swamped or lost to unknown causes, five enlisted

men were wounded, and two officers and fifty-eight enlisted men were missing.[22]

The infantry landings that commenced at about the same time were as confused as those of the 16th Infantry. On Easy Green, none of E Company was present as planned. Instead, G Company, intended for Dog White, and F Company, intended for Dog Red, landed there. Even though both units landed intact, confusion was inevitable as the landings of the two companies became intermingled, two boatloads of G landing on the far left, then two boatloads of F to their right, four more of G to their right, and then four of F on the far right, straddling Easy Green and Dog Red.

No troops landed initially on Dog White, while, on Dog Green, only A Company landed more or less as intended, but unsupported. Twelve to sixteen tanks of B Company, 743rd Tank Battalion, were supposed to be there as well as well as two LCA's with C Company of the 2nd Ranger Battalion. However, the tanks had drifted eastward, while the Rangers had deviated slightly westward, leaving A Company alone. Their five remaining LCA's—one had foundered in the heavy seas during the run in—grounded nearly astride the Vierville Exit and about 300 yards offshore. The troops gallantly filed off the

A detailed low-level shot of Easy Green Beach at about 1000 hours. Vehicles are crowed along the beach unable to go forward, but there are few troops visible. By this time, men of the 116th Infantry had begun to work their way inland over the bluffs. NARA

LCA's and were mercilessly machine-gunned into oblivion by the concentrated fire from the intact and nearly unengaged defenses of WN 71 and 72. Of the roughly 160 men in the five craft, it is estimated that nearly 100 died and most of the rest were wounded—a casualty rate of nearly 100 percent. Nineteen of the dead, including two brothers, were from the tiny town of Bedford, Virginia, which is now the site of the U.S. D-Day Memorial.

Despite fifty-one medium tanks landing on the beaches with the 116th Infantry, the situation was, if anything, worse than in the sector of the 16th Infantry farther east. Only one complete and one partial gap in the German obstacle belt had been cleared for the landing of the follow-on forces. The tanks were unable to maneuver effectively on the narrow beach and were under constant fire that slowly whittled away their strength. Nonetheless, the reserve companies of the assault battalions began to land at about 0700 hours.

On Easy Green, Dog Red, and Dog White, the 2nd Battalion, consisting of E, F, and G Company, Headquarters Company, and H (Weapons) Company were to land at 0700 hours, neatly aligned with their leading waves. Instead, none of the waves was where it was supposed to be, and the reserves became scattered as well. At H+50, the 3rd Battalion was to land, also dispersed between the beaches, but for once, the tendency to drift east was to their advantage. The entire battalion was landed at about 0730 hours between the E-1 Exit at St. Laurent and the D-3 Exit at Les Moulins, a position that was partly sheltered by smoke from grass fires.

The rest of the 1st Battalion, 116th Infantry—A Company Headquarters, B, C, and D (Weapons) Company, and Battalion Headquarters—were supposed to follow A Company onto Dog Green in three distinct waves at H+30, H+40, and H+50. Instead, they were scattered along the length of the 116th Infantry sector. The current, the smoke obscuring reference points, and a simple desire by the landing craft coxswains to land at a point where there was a reasonable chance of some of the infantry aboard getting ashore all added to the confusion.

Three boatloads from B Company, one with A Company headquarters, and three with battalion headquarters landed more or less in the same spot as

Dog Green looking west. A knocked-out DD tank of B Company, 743rd Tank Battalion, can be seen in the distance. A number of unrecovered American dead are also visible, 7 June 1944. JULIUS SHOULARS

The DD tank of B Company, 743rd Tank Battalion, that was knocked out trying to cross the shingle and seawall on Dog White. This view is looking east toward Les Moulins, 7 June 1944. JULIUS SHOULARS

A Company—and met much the same fate. The boat section carrying company commander Capt. Ettore Zappacosta was wiped out; only one man, Captain Zappacosta's radioman, Pvt. Robert Sales, managed to reach shore alive.

One LCA from B Company veered right away from Zappacosta's group and landed near C Company of the 2nd Rangers, where they were a welcome reinforcement. Three other LCA's of B Company, 116th Infantry, turned left (east) and landed on Dog White. More importantly, C Com-

The landing of the 5th Ranger Battalion and 116th Infantry just west of the D-3 Draw, looking toward Dog White and Dog Red, at about 0900. Drowned vehicles from earlier waves can be seen in the water while in the background a Rhino ferry prepares to land engineer equipment. In the background is a large white beachfront house that was a prominent landmark. Many of the beach obstacles are still intact. NARA

Tank C-13 (*Ceaseless*) of C Company, 743rd Tank Battalion, on Dog White amid other debris on the evening of 6 June. NARA

pany, 116th Infantry, landed nearly intact just to their left, with D (Weapons) Company, 116th Infantry, to their right; somewhat later, the entire 5th Ranger Battalion and Company A and B of the 2nd Ranger Battalion followed in behind them.

As a result of some good fortune, the reserves had landed in some strength, with fewer losses, and a more intact organization, right where they were needed, if not where they were planned. Between St. Laurent and Les Moulins, the 3rd Battalion, 116th Infantry, and scattered elements of the 2nd

Battalion began to work their way up the nearly undefended bluffs between WN 65 and WN 68. By 0830 hours, they were moving inland, and by noon, they were on the outskirts of St. Laurent.

Farther west, the mass of troops from the 1st Battalion, 116th Infantry, the 2nd and 5th Ranger Battalions between WN 68 and WN 70, east of Vierville, had also gotten organized under the steady hand of the assistant division commander, Brig. Gen. Norman Cota, and the commander of the 116th Infantry, Col. Charles Lanham, and began to work

What the Germans saw looking east from the 88-millimeter bunker in WN 72 at the E-1 Draw on Dog White. In the immediate foreground is the remaining rubble from the antitank wall that was blasted by the 121st Engineers on the afternoon of D-Day. NARA

Outside the bunker at WN 72, looking southeast, with the muzzle of the 88-millimeter gun in the foreground. Just beyond it can bee seen the remnant of the antitank wall left after it was cleared. NARA

their way up the bluffs against scattered German resistance. By 0830, they too had begun to crest the bluffs and turned westward toward Vierville, overrunning WN 70 from the flank and rear. By 1000 hours, Vierville had fallen, and at about noon, General Cota and a small party of men approached the Vierville Draw—from inland—only to be nearly killed by American naval gunfire.

A little after WN 70 fell, at about 0900 hours, C Company of the 2nd Rangers and the single boat section of B Company, 116th Infantry, also began to work their way inland. The Rangers had moved west to clear the line of fire of WN 73 and then began to stealthily climb the cliff face. In a hard-

A close-up of the embrasure. "Doc" Hall was a member of the 7th Naval Beach Battalion. JULIUS SHOULARS

fought action, about thirty Rangers managed to clear WN 73 and then, reinforced by the men from B Company, forced the Germans to withdraw from WN 72. At about 1000 hours, the defenses at both German positions had collapsed.

Thus, by 1100 hours, the situation at the western end of Omaha had stabilized, at about the same time as it had farther east. Although neither the 16th or 116th Infantry had reached their assigned D-Day objective line, they had achieved the primary goal of Operation Neptune; they had established a beachhead in France, however tenuous, that could be exploited by the follow-on forces of the V Corps. The 26th Infantry of the 1st Division, in corps reserve, began landing at 1830 hours at Colleville. The 175th Infantry of the 29th Division began landing at Les Moulins at 1200 hours on 7 June and were followed shortly thereafter by the entire 2nd infantry Division. By midday on 7 June, Omaha Beach was secure.

The final coda to the Omaha assault occurred at the Vierville Draw and, appropriately enough, was orchestrated by the engineers. One of the thorns in the side of the 116th Infantry and 743rd Tank Battalion had been the massive antitank wall abutting WN 71 that extended nearly the width of the draw and left only a narrow chicane open for vehicles to carefully back and fill through. At 1300 hours, the position was finally silenced, and two platoons of engineers of C Company, 121st Engineers, went to work demolishing the wall. For nearly an hour, 1,100 pounds of explosive, in the standard twenty-pound satchels, were carefully positioned against the eight-foot wall. At 1400, Colonel Ploger, the commander of the 121st, gave the order to fire. The resulting explosion cleared the entire wall from WN 72 to its end, leaving a two-inch depression in the roadway. The Vierville Exit was open.[23]

OMAHA ASSESSED

Losses in the 16th Infantry were simply horrific. The initial reports counted 36 officers and 935 enlisted men as casualties out of the 185 officers and 3,475 enlisted men who were present for duty on the morning of 6 June—more than 26.5 percent. Later reports filed with the regimental combat report for June were nearly identical, as was a report filed by the regimental medical detachment.[24] The losses in the units attached to the combat team were nearly as bad. Of the 9,850 men embarked, at least 1,697 were casualties—a loss of 17.2 percent.

The 116th Infantry as a regiment did not suffer as severely as the 16th Infantry. However, the losses in the combat team as a whole were just as staggering. Of the 10,497 officers and men recorded as having embarked as part of the 116th RCT and Ranger Reserve force, at least 1,799 were casualties—over 17 percent of the total force embarked.

There is simply no way to avoid the conclusion that Omaha was a fiasco that was saved from becoming a complete disaster by the bravery and initiative of the officers and men that were dumped into that maelstrom. There is also much to be criticized in some of the decisions made during the Neptune planning process that had such dire results on Omaha. However, as has been seen, many of those

CASUALTIES OF THE 16TH INFANTRY RCT AND ATTACHED UNITS ON D-DAY

	Killed		Missing Believed Killed		Missing Believed Straggler		Wounded		Total	
	Off.	Enl.	Off.	Enl.	Off.	Enl.	Off.	Enl.	Off.	Enl.
16th Infantry	5	44	9	26	3	354	19	510	36	934
7th Field Artillery Bn.	1	1	1	32	0	0	3	3	5	36
A Co., 1st Medical Bn.	0	5	0	0	0	6	0	11	0	22

	Killed		Missing		Wounded		Total	
			Off.	Enl.				
741st Tank Bn.[25]	45[a]		0		60		105	
62nd Armored Field Artillery Bn.[26]	0	2	0	0	2	11	2	13
1st Engineer Combat Bn.[27]	4		6		27		37	
20th Engineer Combat Bn.[28]	3		0		10		13	
197th AAA Bn.[29]	5		0		12		17	
Provisional Bttry 397th AAA Bn.[30]	9		35		16		60	
A and C Co., 81st Chemical Weapons Bn.[31]	5		0		10		15	
5th Engineer Special Brigade[32]	13		59		106		178	
299th Engineer Combat Bn. (SETF)[33]	0		52		50		102	
6th Naval Beach Bn.[34]	4	14	0	10	4	34	8	58
Naval Demolition Units[35]	3	16	0	12	2	23	5	51
Total	179		605		913		1,697	

a. Except for the 16th Infantry; 7th Field Artillery Bn.; A Co., 1st Medical Bn.; 62nd Armored Field Artillery Bn.; 6th Naval Beach Bn.; and Naval Demolition Units, casualty figures are not broken down by officers and enlisted and include both categories.

CASUALTIES OF THE 116TH INFANTRY RCT AND ATTACHED UNITS ON D-DAY

	Killed		Missing		Wounded		Total	
	Off.	Enl.	Off.	Enl.	Off.	Enl.	Off.	Enl.
116th Infantry[36]	341[a]		26		241		668	
111th Field Artillery Bn.[37]	3	11	1	13	1	3	5	27
112th Engineer Combat Bn.[38]	3	5	0	64	1	29	4	98
121st Engineer Combat Bn.[39]	2	30	1	65	6	56	9	151
5th Ranger Bn.[40]	30		18		70		118	
2nd Ranger Bn. (-)	23		9		70		102	
743rd Tank Bn.[41]							70	
467th AAA Bn.[42]	8		0		31		39	
Provisional Btty, 397th AAA Bn.[43]	8		16		36		60	
B and D Co., 81st Chemical Weapons Bn.[44]	5		0		10		15	
58th Armored Field Artillery Bn.[45]	2	7	1	9	5	14	8	30
6th Engineer Special Brigade[46]	23		111		70		204	
146th Engineer Combat Bn (SETF)[47]	1	30	0	3	8	71	9	110
7th Naval Beach Bn.[48]	0	23	1	6	4	23	5	52
Naval Demolition Units[49]	1	4	0	3	1	6	2	13
Total	560		347		756		1,799	

a. Casualty figures for the 116th Infantry; 5th Ranger Bn.; 2nd Ranger Bn.; 467th AAA Bn.; Provisional Btty, 397th AAA Bn.; B and D Co., 81st Chemical Weapons Bn.; and 6th Engineer Special Brigade are not broken down by officers and enlisted men and include both categories.

LANDING CRAFT IN THE OMAHA ASSAULT

Total Craft Engaged in Assault	Number Known Sunk	Number Lost or Damaged	Percentage Lost or Damaged
268 LCVP & LCA	55	25	29.9
24 LCS(S)	1	0	4.2
166 LCM	8	?	?
54 LCP(L)	0	0	0
148 LCT (all types)	11	35	23.6

same decisions were made on the Commonwealth beaches and on Utah without consequences so dire.

Some were a consequence of inadequate resources, although it is difficult to see how additional resources would have changed things very much. For example, the lack of sufficient LCT's led to the 7th and 11th Field Artillery Battalions going ashore with towed howitzers in DUKW's. However,

as it turned out, conditions on Omaha were such that even the two armored field artillery battalions that were deployed had problems. At 0830 hours, the decision was made to close the beach to landing craft carrying vehicles, so the two battalions were delayed some two hours in landing. That led to one of the LCT's carrying the 58th Armored Field Artillery striking a mine and sinking, taking four of

Easy Red on the afternoon of D-Day. On the crest of the ridge is WN 64, which was taken by E Company, 16th Infantry, attacking from left to right (east to west) through the tree line. The opening of the St. Laurent (E-1) draw is just to the right.
NARA

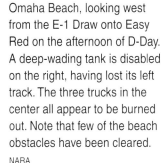

Omaha Beach, looking west from the E-1 Draw onto Easy Red on the afternoon of D-Day. A deep-wading tank is disabled on the right, having lost its left track. The three trucks in the center all appear to be burned out. Note that few of the beach obstacles have been cleared.
NARA

the battalion howitzers down with it, but that was *not* a consequence of the lack of LCT's.

On the other hand, it seems to be clear that additional LCT's carrying additional tanks in to support the assault in its initial stages might have been beneficial. However, that is a subject that is better left to the general conclusions that may be drawn from the experience of D-Day.

One thing that is noticeably different between the Omaha and the Commonwealth beaches is the number of LCT's reported sunk. The total for all three Commonwealth beaches was just eight, three fewer than the number lost at Omaha alone.[50]

Easy Red as seen from the bluffs where WN 65 was. The LCT in the center is LCT-305 of Flotilla 18. NARA

Exit E-1 between WN 64 and 65 looking inland. NARA

Exit E-1 looking seaward. NARA

Below: The work at improving the exits at Exit E-1 went on for some time. This photo of a D7 bulldozer improving the road was taken 15 June. NARA

The result of striking a mined obstacle. This is LCT-332. The mine has torn the loading ramp and right front bow off.
JULIUS SHOULARS

CHAPTER 9

Assault Force Utah: The U.S. 4th Infantry Division

THE EVENTS OF D-DAY on Utah are inextricably linked with a series of chance occurrences that had unexpected, far-reaching, and—for the American landing force—fortunate consequences. The first was the loss to a mine at 0525 hours of the Primary Control Vessel, PC-1261, marking the left boundary of Task Force Uncle Red during the approach to the beach. The second was the loss of PC-1261's backup, secondary control vessel LCC-80, which fouled her propeller on the cable of a buoy dropped by the minesweepers to indicate a clear channel. The third was that PC-1176, the Primary Control Vessel of Task Force Tare Green, had been sent at 0430 hours to guide the eight LCT's carrying the DD tanks of A Company, 70th Tank Battalion. Then, when PC-1261 sank, PC-1176 was signaled to take over, but all was thrown into confusion again at 0552 hours when LCT-593 hit a mine and sank at 0557 hours. LCC 60, one of the two secondary control vessels for Task Force Tare Green, then arrived to take over for PC-1176. Finally, the second Task Force Uncle Red secondary control vessel, LCC 90, was busy guiding the approach of the LCT(A)'s to the beach. That left one secondary control vessel, LCC 70 of Task Force Tare Green, available to attempt to correct the leftward (southern) drift of Task Force Uncle Red, an attempt that was completely unsuccessful. With control lost, Task Force Tare Green conformed to the movement of Task Force Uncle Red, with the result that the entire assault landed some 2,400 yards south of its intended landing place.[1]

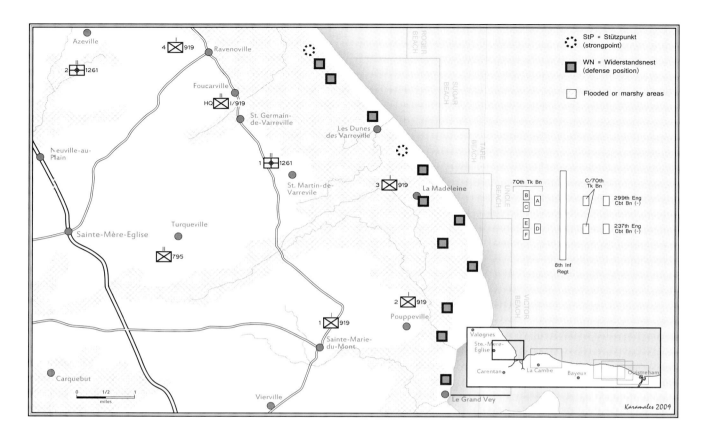

The assault on Utah.

THE ASSAULT BY THE 8TH INFANTRY

On Utah, the DD tanks of the 70th Tank Battalion were launched at 3,000 yards instead of at 5,000 yards as planned. A Company lost four tanks before they launched in the loss of LCT-593, and one other that was rammed by a landing craft and swamped on the run in. B Company had no losses though, so twenty-seven M4 medium tanks came ashore more or less at the same time. However, the confusion caused by the sinking of LCT-593 and then LCT-592—albeit, in that case, after it had launched its tanks—delayed the arrival of the DD tanks to a few minutes after the leading assault waves of the 1st and 2nd Battalions of the 8th Infantry had touched down.

A few minutes before the first assault troops landed, 277 B-26 medium bombers of the Ninth Air Force dropped a total of 4,414 250-pound instantaneous-fuzed bombs with devastating accuracy on top of WN 5. Another sixteen aircraft of the 322nd Bomb Group dropped the 32 2,000-pound delay-fuzed bombs intended to clear the four gaps in the beach obstacles, but conditions weren't good enough for the precision required, and they were apparently

Wheeled vehicles are pulled ashore by D7 bulldozers. NARA

Men of the 4th Division landing from an LCT. NARA

dropped inland; none of the intended lanes were cleared by bombing.[2]

On the left (south), the 2nd Battalion landed with F Company on the left and E Company on the right. To the right (north), the 1st Battalion landed with C Company on the left and B Company on the right. The resistance they encountered was minimal, although hardly nonexistent.

E Company headed straight for WN 5 at La Grand Dune and quickly overwhelmed it. The defenders had been nearly buried alive by the accurate medium-bomber strike, and all its heavy weapons had been destroyed or disabled except for a single 8-centimeter mortar. F Company landed and encountered no resistance, and the two then drove on to La Dune, where they found WN 4 deserted except for a few stragglers. From there, they turned left to follow a secondary road leading to Causeway 1, although it seems likely, given the confused landing, that they may have thought it was Causeway 2.

C and B Company also met minimal resistance and quickly overwhelmed WN 7 and turned right toward Causeway 3. They may have believed they were approaching Causeway 4.

C Company, 70th Tank Battalion, the wading tank company, lost one LCT(A) that capsized during the crossing on the night of 4 June and one LCT(A) that struck a mine on the morning of 6 June. They took four M4 tanks and two M4 tank dozers down with them, leaving twelve tanks and four tank dozers to reinforce the twenty-seven already on the beach. They landed at 0645 hours.

The gapping teams were also late and began to touch down at about 0645 hours as well. They quickly went to work. Unfortunately, the army engineers and navy demolition units suffered some

Above: Troops landing on Utah. Note the densely clustered craters from the successful Ninth Air Force bombing mission. NARA

The 4th Division streams ashore. NARA

The French-built 4.7-centimeter PaK 183a(f) antitank gun of WN 5. Engineer bulldozers are hard at work and a heavily loaded Rhino ferry is about to touch down on the beach. NARA

Below: The greatest threat on Utah was German artillery fire. NARA

bad luck. One of the LCM's suffered a direct hit from German artillery the moment it grounded, killing four and wounding thirty-nine army engineers and killing four and wounding eleven navy demolition men.

However, not all the luck was bad; it was found that the beach obstacles were a minor problem on Utah. The shallow water and extensive beach gave the men plenty of time to do their work. The relative paucity of obstacles and their light weight made it easier to clear them than on other beaches. Many were simply cabled together, linked to one of the tank dozers, and then hauled away in a single mass. Within a half hour, significant gaps were opened in the beach obstacles, but problems and bad luck continued to bedevil the operation. By 0800 hours, the 1st Engineer Special Brigade reported that the gapping teams had fired their first set of charges and, in some cases, second or even third sets, and the entire beach in the assault area was clear of obstacles.[3]

A Company, 531st Engineer Shore Regiment, 1st Engineer Special Brigade, on Uncle Red lost all the equipment of one platoon and the two company bulldozers when one of its LCT's struck a mine and sank. At the same time, C Company had the LCT carrying its bulldozers shelled while landing, and both of them were disabled. The losses delayed planned gapping of the concrete seawall that ran along the beach and blocked vehicle traffic inland for some time. Something similar appears to have occurred on Tare Green since photographic evidence reveals that as late as 0930 hours, tanks, DD tanks, and other vehicles were lined up on the beach waiting to get inland. Matters were not improved when it was discovered that five other LCT's, carrying elements of the 1106th Engineer Combat Group, had been forced to turn back during the rough weather of the crossing.[4]

Troops take shelter along the seawall. NARA

One of the defenders of WN 5 lying dead outside his bunker. NARA

At least once they were on land, the tanks had little trouble suppressing the German defenses. However, mines, guns, and other hazards disabled seven more tanks once ashore—three from A Company, 70th Tank Battalion, two from B, and two from C.

After four reserve tanks were landed during the afternoon, the battalion had forty operational medium tanks ashore, plus five others that were landed from the reserve 746th Tank Battalion. Losses in the 70th Tank Battalion were recorded as three enlisted men killed, one officer seriously wounded, two officers and five enlisted men lightly wounded, and one officer and sixteen enlisted men missing and presumed drowned in the loss of the A Company LCT.[5]

Despite the loss of some key equipment and landing far south of the planned locations, by about 1000 hours, the landings on Utah could be generally described as a success. Bad luck had caused delays in getting vehicles off the beach. Mines on the causeways leading inland from the beach had hindered movement as well. And the general confusion caused by landing on the wrong beach had slowed movements as various units backed and filled, attempting to figure out where they were and where they needed to be. By the evening of 6 June, the bulk of the 4th Division and its attached units were ashore and had made firm contact with elements of the 101st Airborne Division that had secured the causeways leading inland.

UTAH ASSESSED

There does not appear to be much more that needs to be said about Utah. It was an operation simultaneously plagued by some very good luck as well as some very bad luck. The misplaced landing was a result of a chain of events so unlikely as to be almost unbelievable, but which proved to be very fortunate. The 1st Engineer Special Brigade S-2 was said to have called it "an act of providence." The beach defenses farther north were found to be well fortified and heavily mined, while at the actual landing site the fortifications were minor and mines were only encountered on the causeways leading inland.[6]

The assault benefited from the very accurate bombing by the U.S. Ninth Air Force. The report of the 1st Engineer Special Brigade noted they had found "many craters, particularly between the dunes and the inundated area, a belt 200 to 500 yards wide. . . . Brigade officers feel that the Ninth Air Force did its job and did it well."[7]

The naval bombardment was also considered to be very effective, and the state of Jahnke's men seems to bear that opinion out. The bombardment disabled the remote-controlled Goliath demolition vehicles, all but one of which was found in their "garages" after the battle, while the sole "doodle bug" that had sallied out was overturned by a blast before it could complete its mission. In another piece of good luck, it was found that, just as on Juno Beach, the firing switchboard for the six to eight batteries of *Wurfgerät* launchers just inland had been damaged by the naval bombardment, making it impossible for the defenders to fire them.[8]

It was the loss of LCT's sunk that was extraordinary on Utah. It was a greater loss even than at Omaha and nearly 50 percent higher than all three of the Commonwealth beaches combined. However, again as at Omaha, the record of damage to the LCT's appears to have been incompletely and inconsistently reported, as was the record of damage and loss to the other landing craft.[9]

One of the German "doodle bugs" next to one of the casemates in WN 5. Note that a GI has appropriated some of the barbed wire as a clothesline to dry his socks on. NARA

CASUALTIES IN THE UTAH ASSAULT, 8TH INFANTRY RCT AND ATTACHED UNITS

Unit	Killed	Wounded	Missing	Total
8th Infantry	29	110	0	139
1st Engineer Special Brigade	18	96	3	117[a]
286th JASCO	5	10	1	16
70th Tank Battalion	19	10	0	29
87th Chemical Mortar Battalion	2	3	0	5
65th Armored Field Artillery Bn	2	22	0	24
29th Field Artillery Battalion	39	22	0	61
Total	114	273	4	391

a. Three of the wounded later died, and the three men reported missing were later confirmed as killed

LANDING CRAFT IN THE UTAH ASSAULT

Total Craft engaged in Assault	Number known sunk	Number lost or damaged	Percentage lost or damaged
220 LCVP	43		
12 LCS(S)	0		
80 LCM	0		
26 LCP(L)	7		
160 LCT (all types)	11	17	11.25

CHAPTER 10

Results

IT IS DIFFICULT TO OBJECTIVELY MEASURE and compare results in a military operation. In this case, it is even more difficult since, ultimately, all of the Allied landings were successful in their primary goal, which was establishing a beachhead in France.

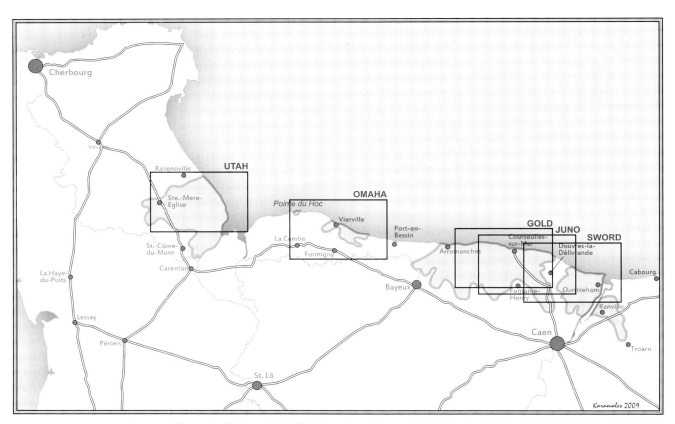

The end of D-Day, with Allied beachheads shown as shaded areas.

German prisoners being herded to the rear as an M4 tank advances. The wading stacks have been removed from the tank, which has had the nickname *The End* whimsically chalked to its rear. NARA

The victors enjoying a well-deserved cup of Norman cider from a *barriquot* inland from Omaha, probably around 7 June. The four on the left are from an engineer special brigade; the four on the right are probably from the 2nd Infantry Division. NARA

Cpl. Victor Deblois of the Régiment de la Chaudière poses with German prisoners in front of the seawall at Bernières. NATIONAL ARCHIVES CANADA

OBJECTIVES

One theoretically objective measure of the results achieved on the various beaches is the depth of the penetration inland gained by the Allies on D-Day and the number of assigned objectives they reached. On Gold, that was done after the war by comparing the 50th Division, objectives as they were planned with what was achieved.

56 Bde

The two forward battalions, 2 ESSEX and 2 SWB, were at ST SULPICE (8181) and VAUX-SUR-AURE (7882) respectively 3,500 yards and 3,000 yards from BAYEUX [the brigade objective].

151 Bde

Of the leading battalions, 9 DLI was in the area just NORTH of VILLENEUVE (8279) 1,500 yards short of the road BAYEUX—CAEN and 6 DLI was in the area ESQUAY-SUR-SEULLES (8479) 2,500 yards short of the road [the brigade objective].

231 Bde

The three battalions 1 HAMPS, 1 DORSET and 2 DEVON were established along the coast from LE HAMEL (8786) to ARROMANCHES-LES-BAINS (8586), at Pt 54 (8585) and at RYES (8483) respectively, the first two (assault) battalions having progressed as planned, but 2 DEVON having achieved only the first of their four objectives.

69 Bde

The most forward elements of 69 Bde, which were from 7 GREEN HOWARDS, were NORTH of COULOMBS (at 887773) and about 3,000 yards from the road BAYEUX-CAEN.

Thus of the four brigades, 3 were 2,000 yards to 4,000 yards from their objectives, whilst the fourth was up to schedule, except one battalion, which was held up at its first objective.[1]

Unfortunately, it is not a very practical measure. Using that scale, the 3rd Division on Sword achieved virtually none of its objectives either, nor did the 50th Division on Gold, the U.S. 1st and 29th Divisions on Omaha, or the U.S. 4th Division on Utah. In each case, the division failed to reach as far inland or seize the final D-Day objectives they were assigned. It could be said that the 3rd Canadian Division and 50th Division came closest, but the simple truth is that none of the many objectives deep inland that were planned for D-Day were achieved. Caen and Bayeux were still in German hands on 7 June, and neither American beachhead had achieved the depth or width expected. Neither Sword nor Juno were linked nor were Omaha and Gold.

Quite simply, by such measures, Neptune could be assessed as a "failure." However, common sense tells us it was not since it achieved its primary objective: establishing a viable Allied beachhead on the continent of Europe.

CASUALTIES

The 5th Assault Regiment was hard hit on D-Day, suffering sixty-five casualties, including its commander, Lieutenant Colonel Cocks. Of eighty-one A.V.R.E.'s that the regiment had embarked in England, as of D+4, fifty-three were reported fit, eight were in second-line repair, sixteen were in third-line repair or written off, and four were "missing." That seems to be odd wording to use in describing a forty-ton vehicle; in fact, the four were simply unaccounted for at the time of the report, but it is unclear if they were lost, damaged, or simply out of contact with the regiment.[2] What is immediately noticeable is the evident intensity of the resistance on Sword: ten of the fifteen officer and thirty-seven of the fifty other-ranks casualties were incurred there—nearly 75 percent of the total casualties lost by the 5th Assault Regiment R.E. on D-Day. Another measure is that the personnel of the 77th and 79th Squadrons were collectively awarded a total of two Distinguished Service Orders, four Military Crosses, and three Military Medals for actions on Sword on D-Day.[3]

From these casualty figures, it seems clear that the intensity of the fighting on Juno and Gold was much less than that on Sword, with Gold somewhat more severe than Juno. Overall, the casualties of the 6th Assault Regiment R.E., not including the detachment of the Westminster Dragoons, totaled twenty-

Above: Men of the 16th Infantry killed in action on Fox Red in front of WN 60. NARA

Looking eastward along Dog White. Crossed rifles in the sand pay tribute to a fallen soldier. NARA

CASUALTIES OF THE 5TH ASSAULT REGIMENT, R.E. ON D-DAY

	Unit	KIA Off.	KIA OR	WIA Off.	WIA OR	MIA Off.	MIA OR	Total Off.	Total OR
	5th Assault Regiment Total								
	(not including 22nd Dragoons)	6	17	9	29	0	4	15	50
Sword	5th Regiment HQ	1	1	0	0	0	0	1	1
	77th Squadron Total	1	6	3	10	0	2	4	18
	1 Troop	1	1	0	0	0	2	1	3
	2 Troop	0	4	0	6	0	0	0	10
	3 Troop	0	1	2	2	0	0	2	3
	4 Troop	0	0	1	2	0	0	1	0
	79th Squadron Total	2	8	3	10	0	2	5	20
	1 Troop	0	7	0	0	0	0	0	7
	2 Troop	1	0	1	3	0	2	2	5
	3 Troop	1	0	1	4	0	0	2	4
	4 Troop	0	1	1	3	0	0	1	4
Juno	**26th Squadron Total**	1	2	1	3	0	0	2	5
	1 Troop	1	2	0	3	0	0	1	5
	2 Troop	0	0	1	0	0	0	1	0
	3 Troop	0	0	0	0	0	0	0	0
	4 Troop	0	0	0	0	0	0	0	0
	80th Squadron Total	1	0	2	6	0	0	3	6
	1 Troop	0	0	1	1	0	0	1	1
	2 Troop	0	0	0	2	0	0	0	2
	3 Troop	0	0	0	0	0	0	0	0
	4 Troop	1	0	1	3	0	0	2	3
	22nd Dragoons Total	1	8	9	25		43		
	Grand Total								93

CASUALTIES OF THE 6TH ASSAULT REGIMENT, R.E, AS OF D+2 (8 JUNE)

	Unit	KIA Off.	KIA OR	WIA Off.	WIA OR	MIA Off.	MIA OR	Total Off.	Total OR
Gold	**6th Assault Regiment Total**								
	(not including Westminster Dragoons)	1	2	2	11	0	5	3	18
	81st Squadron Total[4]	0	1	0	8	0	5	0	14
	82nd Squadron Total	1	1	2	3	0	0	3	4
	B Sqn, Westminster Dragoons Total	0	0	0	4	0	0	0	4

one officers and other ranks—just less than 45 percent of those incurred on Sword by the 5th Assault Regiment and only 24 percent greater than those incurred by them on Juno.

Commonwealth Casualties by Beach
Sword

The Victory Campaign states that the only figures found for the 3rd British Infantry Division were those given in AORG Report No. 261—a total of 630.[5] That statement is inexplicable, given that the losses for most of the units are generally very well known—in some cases very accurately known—and simply adding them together reveals a very different and much more sanguinary total.

Losses in the 8th Brigade were fairly completely reported and have already been recounted. A recapitulation by battalion indicates that the 2nd East Yorks lost 5 officers and 60 other ranks killed, 4 officers and 137 other ranks wounded, and 3 other ranks missing, a total of 209.[6] The 1st South Lancs lost 5 officers and 13 other ranks killed, 6 officers and 83 other ranks wounded, and 19 other ranks missing, a total of 126 officers and men in the beach assault and possibly another 2 later in the day. The 1st Suffolks lost 2 officers and 5 other ranks killed and 25 other ranks wounded. The assault engineers also suffered their heaviest losses on Sword: 47 casualties—19 killed, 24 wounded, and 4 missing, plus possibly 42 more in the 22nd Dragoons. As we have seen, the losses of the 8th Brigade and its supporting units actually totaled as many as 1,063 on D-Day.

Losses for the rest of the division are not quite as clear. Those in the intermediate 185th Brigade are fairly well known: the 2nd Battalion the King's Shropshire Light Infantry Regiment (2nd KOSLI) lost 2 officers killed and 4 wounded, and 107 other ranks killed and wounded, for a total of 113 casualties.[7] The 2nd Battalion the Royal Warwickshire Regiment (2nd Royal Warwicks) lost 3 killed and 35 wounded. Finally, although the record for the 1st Battalion of the Royal Norfolk Regiment (1st Norfolks) seems to be incomplete, they appear to have suffered 20 killed and at least 44 wounded. In the reserve 9th Brigade, the 2nd Battalion of the Royal Lincolnshire Regiment (2nd Lincolns) suffered just 13 casualties, the only battalion to report losses on D-Day in that brigade. The brigade headquarters group had 6 killed and 7 wounded for another 13, including the brigade commander. Those losses total another 241.

Thus, it is inconceivable that the figure given in *The Victory Campaign* is correct. Instead, it seems clear that the total casualties incurred on Sword for D-Day were—at a minimum—1,304 and may have been greater.[8] This appears to indicate that, at least in broad outline, the fighting on Sword was nearly as intense in some respects as the fighting on Omaha.

Juno

Of all the participants on D-Day, only the casualties of the Canadians are precisely defined and have usually been accurately reported in various histories. That helps to establish a lower limit for the casualties incurred on Juno.[9] The losses of the 3rd Canadian Division and attached Canadian (but not other nationalities) units were 275 killed, 65 died-of-wounds, 539 wounded, 35 injured-in-action, and 47 prisoners of war, for a total of 961. Of those, 39 were killed, 1 died of wounds, 49 wounded, and 4 injured among Canadian units attached to the 3rd Canadian Division.[10]

These postwar totals are 17 percent higher than those reported after the landing in September 1944, although it is likely that earlier figures may have excluded some 26 who died of wounds between 7 and 28 June and the injured in action. *The Victory Campaign* also references AORG Report No. 261, which reported 805 total casualties "on the beaches" for the 3rd Canadian Division. *The Victory Campaign* also references another AORG report that gives the casualties of No. 48 (RM) Commando on Juno as 243, which is probably excessive and which may actually be the total for the 4th Special Service Brigade as a whole on 6 June.[11] The assault engineers reportedly suffered 16 casualties—4 killed and 12 wounded—while the 22nd Dragoons lost just 1 other rank wounded. Overall, it appears that the total loss on Juno for the entire day was 961 Canadians and about 286 others, for a total of about 1,247.

Gold

The Victory Campaign states that "the only figure found for this [50th Infantry] division is in a compilation in a report of the (British) Army Operational Research Group [likely Report No.261], which concludes on the basis of examination of war diaries that there were 413 casualties on the beaches." However, it is evident that that figure was meant quite literally as the number of men calculated to have been lost in the assault phase "on the beaches" and actually excluded nearly 600 casualties lost in that sector on D-Day.

For example, according to Capt. John Forfar, the medical officer of No. 47 (RM) Commando, the Commando mustered 276 men against its establishment strength of 420 as of 9 June. Of the 144 men he counted as casualties, 46 were killed or drowned, 65 were wounded, 6 were captured, and 27 were missing. Most of the missing men were apparently from four LCA's that had been sunk with 4 officers and 68 men initially reported missing, including the commander of No. 47 (RM) Commando. Thus, about 45 of the missing were subsequently picked up by landing craft making their way back from the beaches and returned to England, from which they rejoined No. 47 (RM) Commando later in the month. However, since most, if not all, of the casualties incurred by the Royal Marines occurred later at Port-en-Bessin—except the 43 known losses in the LCA's and the 12 lost en route to Port-en-Bessin—only those 55 are added to the 50th Division's casualties.

Hence, the total minimum casualties in the Gold sector were about 1,023 on D-Day.

Total Beach Losses

The casualties for the three divisions and their attached units on D-Day as derived above total about 3,644. Of those, the 5th Assault Regiment suffered 63 casualties and the 22nd Dragoons 43 casualties while supporting the 3rd Division on Sword and the 3rd Canadian Division on Juno, while the 6th Assault Regiment suffered 21 casualties and the Westminster Dragoons 4 casualties on Gold. The total casualty figure is 42 percent higher than the total calculated in "British Casualties during the First Month of Operation Overlord,"[12] which gave D-Day casualties as

British: 420 killed, 869 wounded, and 405 missing—total 1,694
Canadian: 222 killed, 490 wounded, and 109 missing—total 821
Commonwealth Total: 642 killed, 1,359 wounded, and 514 missing—total 2,515

However, that report carefully notes that the totals excluded

Airborne Troops and RM [Royal Marine] personnel . . . in order to give a fair basis of comparison with the [pre-invasion] estimated casualties which did not include these arms." That estimate was 7,750, which total included 1,500 drowned—a figure [7,750] that was 3.1 times higher than the figure actually reported. . . . It is striking and perhaps co-incidental that the US estimate was approximately 3.1 times their actual reported figure. . . . These figures must of course be linked to the 'D' Day operational picture. Opposition on the British beaches was *less than anticipated* [emphasis added] and at the same time, the rate of advance was, in many cases, slower than planned.

Yet another source for D-Day casualties is the collected "A" SITREP reports found in the 21 Army Group recorded filed in duplicate copies with the SHAEF records at the U.S. National Archives.[13] However, although the earliest report of any of the units engaged in D-Day was for the "24 hours ending 0600 hours 7 June," the majority were as of 8 June. Those losses were recorded as

3rd Canadian Division (as of 0600 8 June)—89 killed, 256 wounded, 297 missing*
3rd British Division (as of 0600 8 June)—124 killed, 635 wounded, 237 missing
6th British Airborne Division (as of 0600 7 June)—61 killed, 349 wounded, 612 missing**
50th British Division (as of 0600 8 June)—123 killed, 557 wounded, 315 missing
1st Special Services Brigade (as of 0600 7 June)—13 killed, 189 wounded, 87 missing
4th Special Services Brigade (as of 0600 8 June)—34 killed, 126 wounded, 219 missing

* In examining the records for the days after D-Day, it is notable that excessive numbers of wounded appear to have been reported on 10 June: 368 wounded to just 43 killed—nearly a nine-to-one wounded-to-killed ratio when the expected norm is between three-to-one and six-to-one. That may indicate that a "catching-up" of wounded reports from D-Day had occurred.
** As many as 259 missing may have returned as early as 7 June.

1 Corps (as of 0600 7 June)—14 killed, 56
  wounded, 106 missing
30 Corps (as of 0600 8 June)—13 killed, 33
  wounded, 2 missing
Total, 4,547

From all this, it can be concluded that in terms of casualties incurred in the assault phase, Sword was by far the most intense of the Commonwealth beaches, closely followed by Juno. On Sword, an estimated 630 casualties were incurred "on the beach" by the assault brigade and attached units, while overall casualties were about 1,304 for the day. On Juno, at least 721 casualties were suffered "on the beaches," and the total in that sector for the day may have been as many as 1,247. Finally, on Gold, only about 425 casualties were incurred "on the beaches," although the total for the day there was at least 1,023. However, it also must be recalled that there was but a single assault brigade on Sword, while there were two each on Juno and Gold. By that benchmark, the "average" assault brigade loss on Sword was 1,063, but only about 360 on Juno and 210 on Gold. On the other hand, Juno was probably—by a slight margin—the most intense in terms of casualties incurred by an assault division and its attachments.

Of course, it may be fairly asked why, for so many years, such wildly inaccurate casualty figures were accepted as correct. The British Army's official history, *Victory in the West*, made no attempt to clarify the casualty figures, stating that "casualties among troops landed from the sea are believed to have been in the region of three thousand."[14] It seems clear it was a simple case of an initial misunderstanding of the nature and intent of the reports given in AORG Report No. 264, *Opposition Encountered on the British Beaches in Normandy on D-Day*, which was simply repeated over and over again without question.

American Casualties by Beach
Omaha
The actual number of losses that were incurred by the Americans at Omaha on D-Day is possibly one of the greatest mysteries of that day. Estimates over the years have ranged from the 2,000 given in *Cross Channel Attack* to the 4,385 given by Balkoski in *Omaha Beach*.[15] The actual total probably fell between the two extremes.

The 1st Division recorded 1,190 casualties in the V Corps' history. However, the 1st Division G-1 recorded losses for D-Day and D+1 as 1,036 on 8 June and the after-action report for June recorded 186 killed, 620 wounded, and 358 missing, for a total of 1,164. In the same report, the number of missing returned-to-duty in June was given as 70. Internal evidence suggests that the "actual" number missing on 6 June was about 312. (Postwar accounting shows only 60 men actually captured between 6 June and 24 July.) Thus, the likely total casualties for the 1st Division on 6 June were 1,118. The most recent detailed history of Omaha, by Joseph Balkoski, gives a total of 1,346 for the 1st Division.[16]

Figures for the 29th Division are even more difficult to puzzle out. The V Corps' history recorded 743 total casualties for the division, while Joseph H. Ewing in his *29 Let's Go: A History of the 29th Division* reported 390 killed, 511 wounded, and 27 missing, for a total of 928.[17] The somewhat fragmentary reports made by the infantry regiments give a total of 366 killed, 265 wounded, and 27 missing, for a total of 658, while Balkoski gives a total of 1,272.

The V Corps' history recorded an additional 441 casualties for the V Corps' troops. However, those reported apparently were only for units assigned to the corps and so did not include many additional casualties suffered on Omaha by troops attached to the corps by the First Army.* It appears that most of those were suffered by the 741st and 743rd Tank Battalions, which reported cumulative casualties as of 15 June of 14 killed, 20 wounded, and 154 missing, with the remainder mostly being incurred by the two engineer battalions attached to the 1st and 29th Divisions.

The losses of the 5th and 6th Engineer Special Brigades and the 2nd and 5th Ranger Battalions do not appear to have been included as part of the V

---

* In the U.S. Army, a unit was normally either assigned or attached to another, the first designating a more or less permanent condition and the other a temporary one.

Corps' casualties; technically, they were only attached to the V Corps, but were assigned to the First Army. And yet their losses were substantial. As of 15 June, the 5th Engineer Special Brigade reported casualties of 13 killed, 106 wounded, and 59 missing; the 6th Engineer Special Brigade reported 23 killed, 70 wounded, and 111 missing. The 2nd Rangers' incomplete report gave 255 total casualties, while the 5th Rangers reported 30 killed, 70 wounded, and 18 missing. The "final" accounting of the casualties in the two Ranger battalions done in July 1944 reported 98 killed, 211 wounded, and 39 missing, although it is impossible to tell now how many were lost on 6 June and how many in the few days immediately after D-Day. Unfortunately, only the losses of HQ Detachment and D, E, and F Companies of the 2nd Rangers—along with the attached detachments from the 293rd Joint Assault Signal Company and 165th Signal Photo Company, which together made up the Pointe du Hoc force—appear to be firmly established. They suffered 42 killed (including 1 who died of wounds on 14 June), 43 wounded (including both Lieutenant Colonel Rudder and Lieutenant Colonel Trevor, a British Commando attached to the Ranger Force), 22 missing (all of whom but 3 survived and rejoined later), and 1 captured. Overall, it appears that as many as 550 additional casualties may have been incurred by the engineer special brigades and Rangers on D-Day.

Finally, the NCDU lost 24 killed, 32 wounded, and 15 missing, while the two naval beach battalions attached to the 5th and 6th Engineer Special Brigade suffered 41 killed and 87 wounded.

Overall, the highest casualty figure is the 4,385 given by Balkoski. However, it appears that he may have overcounted the divisional casualties by about 572, mainly because of the use of higher missing-in-action figures, the inclusion of the casualties at Pointe du Hoc with those on Omaha "proper," and other possible duplications or overestimates. If so, that would still gave a total of 3,686—significantly higher than the losses on any of the Commonwealth beaches and, in fact, slightly greater than the assumed total of Commonwealth casualties on all three of those beaches as found above (3,644).

Utah

The 4th Division reported 12 killed, 125 wounded, and 60 missing, for a total of 197 casualties on D-Day. That figure has long been accepted as indicating how weak the German opposition on Utah was, but it was in fact just the estimated loss report for the day and not the final casualty report.[18] Individual units of the 4th Division reported a total of 311 casualties, including 81 killed, 166 wounded, 4 missing (most of those men initially reported missing were apparently drowned), and about 60 undefined casualties. In addition, the units attached to the VII Corps and 4th Division also suffered significant casualties. The 1st Engineer Special Brigade lost 18 killed, 96 wounded (three of whom later died), and 3 missing (all later reported as killed), for a total of 117 casualties.[19] VII Corps troops lost 38 killed, 111 wounded, and about 10 other undefined casualties for a total of 159. Finally, elements of the 4th Cavalry Group on the Isles St. Marcouf lost 2 killed and 17 wounded, for a total of 19 casualties (although, like the casualties incurred by the airborne troops, they probably should not be counted toward the total casualties incurred "on the beach"). The 90th Infantry Division liaison party with the 4th Division suffered 1 killed and 1 wounded.[20]

That is a total of about 608 casualties, including 140 killed, 391 wounded, 7 missing, and 70 undefined casualties, which makes Utah very comparable to the Commonwealth beaches in terms of losses. However, it must be considered that the density of defenses, obstacles, and defenders was probably lower than at any of the other beaches. Furthermore, the only strong defensive position on Utah, WN 5, was possibly the only German position that was effectively surpressed before the assault troops landed. But overall, that appears to indicate that only Omaha may have been anomalous.

CHAPTER 11

The Funnies' Impact on D-Day

HOW EFFECTIVE WERE THE A.V.R.E.'S? This has proven to be a difficult question to answer. For example, there is a tendency by some to say that the Commonwealth forces had greater success than the American forces on D-Day, with regards to achieving their objectives. On the other hand, it is also possible to say that the realistic differences are minor, since none of the major D-Day objectives was achieved except for the paramount one "to secure a lodgment on the Continent from which further offensive operations can be developed."[1]

It has also been claimed that it was the Funnies that mitigated the Commonwealth casualties on 6 June. However, there is little cause-and-effect evidence for that assumption, and as we have seen, in some circumstances such as on Queen Beach, those Commonwealth casualties appear remarkably similar to those on Dog, Easy, and Fox Beach at Omaha. Nor does it explain why the American troops on Utah, facing defenses similar to Gold and Juno but possessing no Funnies, suffered the fewest casualties incurred by the assault troops on D-Day.

EVALUATION OF THE A.V.R.E.'S, CRABS, AND THE "DEVICES"

A firsthand evaluation of the various devices as they were used in the invasion was compiled shortly after D-Day by Captain Leytham of the 82nd Assault Squadron.

Roly Poly—a futile device, more of an obstacle to ourselves than a help to anybody. In no single case was it successfully employed. On a beach covered with obstacles there is always the risk that the RP will jam against an obstacle thus causing the AVRE to overrun the RP and expose the belly of the AVRE. A potential danger to the remaining vehicles on the craft.

Bobbin—this appeared to be partially successful. It is not built to withstand a passage in rough sea. If employed, it should not be left to the discretion of any commander when to start unrolling. If required then the only sure policy is to use it for the complete length of the lane.

Petard Fuze 289 definitely unreliable
    Fuze 291 100% reliable
    It is considered that the Petard is an ideal weapon used in support of the infantry provided that they themselves are supported by tanks capable of providing covering fire against anti-tank guns.

There appears to be considerable ignorance amongst the infantry as to the methods of employing an Assault Sqn RE.

A more comprehensive evaluation was also included in the report of the invasion compiled by the chief engineer of the 21st Army Group, Maj. Gen. Sir John D. Inglis.[2]

Of the nineteen assault bridges taken to Normandy by the 1st Assault Brigade, eleven were laid successfully. Another three were taken inland up to four miles to planned bridging sites, but then were found to be unneeded because the bridges they were to replace hadn't been demolished. Of the others, one never beached and four were disabled in one way or another—two that deployed prematurely, one that was knocked off by being rammed by an LCT as it waded in, and one that fell off when it became unbalanced while trying to cross the dunes.

Of the twenty-four fascines taken to Normandy, fourteen were used successfully, three were not needed, three were jettisoned on the beach for one reason or another, two fell off when the A.V.R.E. was damaged, and two were on A.V.R.E.'s that were drowned on the beach.

Of the eleven log carpets taken to Normandy, five were placed successfully, four weren't needed, one was on an A.V.R.E. that drowned, and one was on an LCT that did not beach.

Of the twenty-four Bobbin carpet-layers taken to Normandy, eleven were laid successfully, five were not required, two were jettisoned on the beach, two were on A.V.R.E.'s that drowned, two were on an LCT that did not beach on D-Day, one was on an

A.V.R.E. disabled by mines, and one broke up on the LCT before it was unloaded.

Of the ten bullshorn plows taken to Normandy, only one was used successfully, but it encountered no mines. Simply enough, the only German mines below the high-tide line were mounted on obstacles where the plow had no effect; none were emplaced on the beach itself because of the threat of the tidal action moving them and the seawater rendering them inert. (It was found that many of the mines fixed to the obstacles were duds, even though they were usually submerged only at high tide.)

The Petard was found to be highly effective in the right circumstances, especially against light field fortifications, unfortified buildings, and when it could be fired into the vulnerable entrance or firing slit of some stronger fortifications. However, the Petard was very short-ranged and so couldn't be used near accompanying dismounted personnel without threat of injury to them from the blast. Furthermore, it was neither a "wall-buster" round as was then being developed in Britain and which later became known as HESH (high-explosive squash head) nor was it a HEAT (high-explosive anti-tank) round and so had no advanced armor or concrete-defeating capabilities designed into it. Rather, it was a simple twenty-six-pound charge of high explosive—destructive, but not very effective against heavily reinforced concrete fortifications.

An unknown number of the twin-bangalore torpedo was employed on D-Day, but there is little evidence that any of them actually worked. And one, at least, did more harm than good on Sword when it exploded prematurely, killing Cocks and his Signals sergeant.

LIEUTENANT COLONEL REEVES'S REPORT

Another fascinating, but frustratingly incomplete evaluation of the A.V.R.E.'s and special devices was written by Lt. Col. G. C. Reeves, Denovan's boss in the Special Devices Section, shortly after D-Day.[3] Reeves had managed to convince the officer commanding the 8th Armoured Brigade, Brig. Hugh John Bernard Cracroft, in support of 50th Division on Gold, to arrange to have Reeves attached as a supernumerary officer with the 104th Beach Sub-area so that he could observe the landing and the effectiveness of the special devices. Reeves arrived at Concentration Camp C21 at 1600 hours on 29 May 1944 and made the crossing on the night of 5–6 June on LST No. 264. They arrived off the beach at Ver-sur-Mer at 0700 hours, and Reeves embarked on a DUKW of the 536th Company R.A.S.C. and at 0845 headed for the beach. He remained on the beach investigating wrecked craft and vehicles, interviewing troops, and taking photographs (at least forty of them, which were included as part of the original report), until 2100 hours, when he hitched a ride on an LST transporting wounded back to England, arriving at Southampton at 1100 hours on 7 June.

Reeves began his report with a general description of the passage, complaining—like so many—of the rough seas but noting that the seasickness pills issued to the troops reduced the incidence of severe seasickness to about 20 percent of the men. He also gave a general description of the obstacles and terrain, noting the problems with the "blue clay" that underlay the shingle and sand that had led to the development of the Carpet-Layer Marks II and III. Unfortunately, the remainder of his report is uninteresting—except for some of his photographs. He catalogued the vehicles he found on the beach, destroyed, damaged, or abandoned, but didn't always actually evaluate their performance.

For example, Reeves noted that the DD tanks did not swim in because of the roughness of the water and described their passage as a "super deep wade." He further remarked that he found six of the tanks abandoned along the beach, two of which had been swamped when their screens had failed after the struts fractured and four of which had bogged in "blue clay" patches. He noted that all the tanks had become obstacles and had suffered further damage from being run into by landing craft; in one remarkable photograph, he captured the moment when one of the derelict tanks was run into by LCT-883. However, he failed to give an evaluation of how well they performed on D-Day in terms of their effectiveness against the enemy.

His comments about the Crabs were the same; he merely noted that of the four he found, two had been bogged and abandoned and two had broken tracks on mines. On the other hand, he did remark that the "Porpoises appeared to have been a success."

At least his comments regarding the A.V.R.E.'s were somewhat better focused, if ambiguous. First, Reeves noted that few appeared to have been used on the beach he examined. Then he made the somewhat cryptic remark that

a sloping sea wall protected the concrete defences at Hable de Heurtot and two breaches passable to tracked vehicles had been made in this. In addition, the concrete pillboxes (in one of which there was a 75mm A/Tk gun) had received severe damage. Some of this had plainly been done with the Petard.

It was impossible to assess, however, how much was done by this and how much from support fire from craft. The two breaches were almost certainly made by the former, since a blind [unexploded] dustbin was found just behind one of them.[4]

All in all, it is difficult to draw any substantial conclusions from Reeves's report.

CONCLUSION

There appears to be two extremes of opinion that are generally voiced regarding the usefulness of the A.V.R.E.'s on D-Day. One is expressed in the *79th Armoured Division Final Report*:

> There is no doubt that the troops of the Division were of inestimable value on 'D' Day and thoroughly justified the time and material that had gone into their specialist training and equipment. . . . It was the overwhelming mass of armour in the leading waves of the assault, the specialist equipments coming as a complete surprise, that overwhelmed and dismayed the defending troops and contributed a large part to the combination of strategic and tactical surprise which resulted in the comparatively light casualties suffered by our troops on 'D' Day.[5]

The other is from the history of the 1st Assault Brigade R.E.: "It is idle now to speculate how the D-Day assault would have fared had we not been able to land tanks early. That we did so was largely made possible by the contribution of the Assault R.E. and the Flails."[6]

The viewpoint of the 79th Armoured Division—albeit expressed in a somewhat torturous fashion—was that it was the mass of armor and the surprise they and the specialized equipment engendered that were decisive. But somehow over the years, that has been modified into the opinion that it was the A.V.R.E. and the devices that were solely responsible. That is the opinion that has been repeated over and over again since D-Day, from the Australian war correspondent Chester Wilmot in 1952 to the British historian William Buckingham in 2004, usually in conjunction with a criticism of the U.S. Army for "failing" to make use of the full panoply of Funnies.

On the other hand, an alternate position is that the A.V.R.E. was an over-engineered solution to a problem that did not really exist. That point of view is supported by the simple fact that there is actually little evidence that the "specialist equipments" were as great a surprise to the Germans as was later claimed by the 79th Armoured Division. As far as

can be found, only the Royal Winnipeg Rifles on Juno are known to have claimed that the Germans were surprised by the Funnies. Furthermore, as we have seen, many of the special devices simply didn't work, didn't work well, or don't appear to have been needed. It also could be speculated that the hasty organization, training, and equipping of the 1st Assault Brigade hampered their effectiveness on D-Day; certainly, the lack of sufficient practice acting as part of an all-arms team was highlighted by the action at Douvres on 7 and 12 June.

However, it seems most likely that the truth falls somewhere between those two extremes. In some circumstances, the A.V.R.E.'s were a very valuable asset; in other circumstances, their shortcomings made them less so. In retrospect, it seems that the fascines and bridges were valuable on D-Day on some of the Commonwealth beaches, where they saved time for the troops and vehicles moving inland. At the same time, we also know that savings of time was purely relative and did not truly affect the final outcome of the battle on the beaches. And yet it was on those beaches where the A.V.R.E.'s and the devices were least successful that the greatest success getting inland and off the beach occurred. That contradiction highlights the problem of assessing such a complicated series of occurrences and decisions.

In the right place, the A.V.R.E.'s and the other Funnies rendered invaluable service. They did provide valuable armored engineering support to the infantry assault on D-Day. They also at times supplied welcome fire support when no other armored vehicle was available for the job. But they cannot be shown to have been the sole difference between success and failure on any of the Commonwealth beaches.

And it must always be remembered that the A.V.R.E.'s, the devices, the Crabs, the landing craft, and all the other clever implements developed by the Allies to defeat the Germans were merely tools of war. The real achievements were not gained by those inanimate tools, but by the brave men who wielded them on that day. The victors of D-Day were Colonel Cocks, Sergeant Weightman, Lance Sergeant Scaife, Colonel O'Neill, and the thousands of others like them.

Epilogue

DOUVRES-LA-DÉLIVRANDE

One of the thorniest problems for Commonwealth forces after D-Day was the unexpected resistance put up by the *Luftwaffe* radar station complex near Douvres-la-Délivrande. On D-Day, the Canadian North Shore Regiment got caught up in the battle at the chateau near Tailleville that housed the headquarters of the Germans' 2nd Battalion of the 736th Grenadier Regiment, and so they were only able to send some patrols to scout the area of the radar station before night fell. Unfortunately, the position gave the Germans there a good view of much of Juno and Sword, while a deeply buried communications cable kept them in contact with the German command.

On 7 June, another reconnaissance was made by Captain Essery, commanding No. 3 Troop of the 80th Assault Squadron with three unsupported A.V.R.E.'s. Two of the three were quickly knocked out for no result.

On 12 June, a more serious attempt was made by twelve A.V.R.E.'s of the 26th Assault Squadron, supported by elements of No. 41 (RM) Commando, again unsuccessfully. No Crabs had been allocated to clear the extensive minefields, and the bangalore torpedoes that were placed had little effect, so the A.V.R.E.'s were unable to penetrate the perimeter and were reduced to a desultory and ineffective bombardment of the position with their Petards that lasted into the night.[1]

Finally, on 17 June, a carefully planned and well supported attack was executed. A total of 17 A.V.R.E.'s of the 26th Assault Squadron, 28 Crabs of the 22nd Dragoons, and 160 Commandos were committed to the attack, supported by machine-gun, mortar, and artillery fire. In addition, two troops of the 77th Assault Squadron staged a diversion from the west and the south. Once the Crabs breached the minefield, the A.V.R.E.'s and Commandos were able to get into the perimeter and successfully suppress the defenders. Then each position was reduced with Petard fire and Beehive charges. Total losses to the 26th Assault Squadron were three killed and seven wounded, while three of the A.V.R.E.'s were write offs and three were damaged.[2] The detachment of the 22nd Dragoons suffered no casualties, and neither, apparently, did the Commandos.[3]

From then until 14 August, the mission of the 6th Assault Regiment R.E. was succinctly described as follows:

> Since D day Sqns have been in action on 30 occasions. Petard fire has been used against houses and pillboxes on 20 occasions. 27 fascines have been used successfully.
>
> The petard in conjunction with bulldozers has been repeatedly used for breaching "Bocage Banks" [the famous hedgerows of Normandy], rly [railway] embankments etc, as a "Pick and Shovel" combination. It [the bulldozer] has also been used in river crossings for ramping far banks to make tk exits.[4]

The war diary entries for the 5th Assault Regiment show little more activity. They played a minor role in operations against the German airfield at

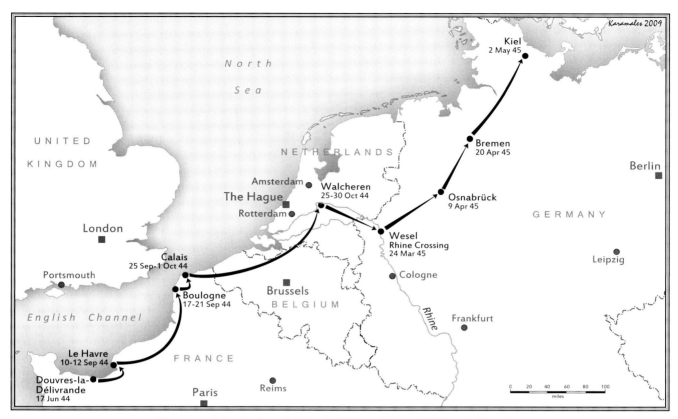

The route of the 1st Assault Brigade RE from D-Day to VE-Day, 8 May 1945.

Carpiquet on 4 July, supporting the Canadians, but suffered only two men wounded. Otherwise, there were no other significant activities remarked by the regiment in July, and August was quiet as well, although one officer, Lieutenant David of the Royal Engineers, was killed by shellfire on 7 August.

Most of the activities of the 1st Assault Brigade R.E. in July and August were confined to reorganization and training. Brigadier Watkinson, with the forward echelon of brigade headquarters, arrived in Normandy on 13 July. On 14 July, the main elements of the brigade headquarters began to arrive, and an order was given to reorganize the assault squadrons on a three-troop basis, reducing the total number of A.V.R.E.'s authorized in the squadron from twenty-six to twenty.

In early August, the 87th and 284th Squadrons of the 6th Assault Regiment landed in Normandy along with the 557th Squadron from the 42nd Assault Regiment, the remainder of which was still in England. However, it was decided that the special training required for the A.V.R.E.'s meant that the regular Royal Engineer training establishment was unsuitable for the brigade requirements, so the 557th was reorganized as the 557th Assault Training Regiment and sent back to England. Finally, on 17 August, the 16th, 222nd, and 617th Assault Squadrons, and headquarters of the 42nd Assault Regiment landed in France, finally completing the deployment of the brigade.[5]

THE CHANNEL PORTS

The Allies began to break through the German cordon around the Normandy beachhead beginning on 25 July with Operation Cobra in the U.S. First Army's sector. That was followed in late July and early August by Operations Bluecoat, Tractable, and Totalize in the Commonwealth sector, where the 21st Army Group now had command of both the British Second Army and the newly activated Cana-

A 79th Armoured Division column—including A.V.R.E.'s, Crocodiles, Petards, Flails, and armored bulldozers—being briefed before the attack on Boulogne Boulogne in September 1944. NATIONAL ARCHIVES CANADA

dian First Army. By 12 August, the German lines in Normandy had shattered; by 21 August, most of the German 7th Army had been encircled and largely destroyed in the Falaise Pocket. By the end of the month, the Seine had been crossed and Paris liberated, and by mid September, the Allied forces were approaching the frontier of Germany.

However, the pursuit of the German armies out of France and back to Germany had a downside for the Allies: the immense distances covered steadily put the Allied spearheads farther and farther from their logistical base in Normandy. That made the opening of the French and Belgian Channel ports an urgent priority and also brought the 1st Assault Brigade R.E. to the forefront again; the assaults on the heavily fortified ports were tailor-made for them.

The first to fall was Le Havre, which was attacked on 10 September by the 49th and 51st Divisions, supported by the three squadrons of the 42nd Assault Regiment R.E. By midnight on 12 September, it was over; the German garrison capitu-

lated under the relentless assault. Next was Boulogne. At 0825 hours on 17 September, the 3rd Canadian Division and the 81st and 87th Assault Squadrons, under the command of the 6th Assault Regiment R.E., attacked the ring of fortifications around the town, and by the morning of 21 September, the last German garrison on the harbor mole had surrendered. The 3rd Canadian Division quickly redeployed again and, by 25 September, was ready to attack Calais and the massive German coast artillery fortifications at Cap Griz Nez and Sangatte—again supported by the 6th Assault Regiment R.E., this time commanding the 81st and 284th Squadrons. By 1 October, the German defense again had collapsed.

Thus, in the space of just twenty-two days, including fourteen days of combat operations, the A.V.R.E. had played a major role in capturing three heavily fortified port cities—an extraordinary achievement by any measure and a suitable finale to the 1st Assault Brigade operations in France.[6]

Amid A.V.R.E.'s, men from the 79th Armoured Division are briefed before the attack on Boulogne, September 1944.

WALCHEREN

By late September, the 1st Assault Brigade was supporting operations of the Canadian First Army at Breskens on the River Scheldt, aimed at opening the great port of Antwerp in Belgium to Allied shipping. Three interlinked operations were executed by the brigade: in order, they were Switchback, Vitality, and Infatuate. Those operations were heavily dependent on a new brigade capability created by the conversion of the 5th Assault Regiment and parts of the 6th Assault Regiment to Buffalo and Terrapin amphibious assault vehicles.*

Switchback was an amphibious assault intended to destroy the German forces remaining in the Breskens Pocket. Vitality and Infatuate were two-part operations designed to annihilate the German forces on the Beveland Peninsula and the island of Walcheren. All were successful.

WINTER

During late fall and early winter, the units of the brigade provided general support for the 21st Army Group's operations along the German frontier. In the soggy, flooded fields of the north German plain, amphibious vehicles were again at a premium, and few opportunities for massed use of A.V.R.E.'s were found. In December, with the outbreak of the Germans' Ardennes offensive, operations in the 21st Army Group's zone were curtailed, and the 1st Assault Brigade was given a welcome rest and re-equip.

THE RHINE CROSSING

In early January 1945, the brigade participated in Operation Blackcock to clear a small area of the Dutch-German border. On 16 January, at the end of the operation, the brigade shifted northeast to pre-

---

* Buffalo was the British name for the American amphibious tractor (amtrac or LVT). Terrapin was a British-designed and -built vehicle similar to the American DUKW amphibious truck.

Churchill tanks, equipped with bridges and fascines to cross antitank ditches, wait to support an attack by units of the 3rd Canadian Infantry Division near Keppeln, Germany, February 1945. NATIONAL ARCHIVES CANADA

pare for operations intended to take the 21st Army Group across the Rhine and into Germany. Almost the entire brigade was used to support Operation Veritable, beginning on 8 February. By 23 March, the brigade had closed up on the Rhine River, and at 0600 on 24 March, it began crossing operations.

VICTORY

By 9 April, the 21st Army Group had broken out of its Rhine bridgehead and had reached Osnabrück. By 20 April, the outskirts of Bremen had been reached. On 29 April, the 1st Assault Brigade assisted in an assault crossing of the River Elbe. A few days later, elements of the 1st Assault Brigade were at Kiel on the Baltic Sea, and then on 7 May, operations halted as the Germans opened surrender negotiations. On 8 May 1945, the war in Europe was over.

By that time, considerable changes had occurred in the 1st Assault Brigade. Brigadier Watkinson had left just before the opening of Veritable to become

the chief engineer of the 30 Corps. He was replaced by Brig. P. St. B. Sydenham.

By that point, the brigade organization had changed to reflect the hard-won experience gained on D-Day and after. Brigade Headquarters included the 149th Armoured Engineer Field Park Squadron, which was equipped with twelve D7 armored bulldozers as before, as well as the 87th Squadron, now styled as an "Armoured Engineer Dozer Squadron." It was equipped with thirty-six bulldozers converted from turretless Centaur tanks. Headquarters was rounded out by the 557th Armoured Engineer Training and Experimental Establishment, which prepared replacements for the arduous service in the brigade and trained personnel in the complex workings of the various A.V.R.E. devices. It was equipped with twenty-six A.V.R.E.'s. Each of the three regiments now consisted of only three squadrons. The 5th Armoured Engineer Regiment—as such units were now called—consisted of the 26th, 77th and

79th Armoured Engineer Squadron; the 6th Armoured Engineer Regiment of the 81st, 82nd, and 284th Armoured Engineer Squadron; and the 42nd Armoured Engineer Regiment of the 16th, 222nd, and 617th Armoured Engineer Squadrons. Each squadron, except for the 77th, consisted of three troops with twenty A.V.R.E.'s. The 77th Squadron was equipped with twenty-five Buffaloes. Brigade strength was nominally 158 officers and 3,611 other ranks.[7]

The 1st Assault Brigade R.E. had matured into a sophisticated combat engineer tool—a far cry from its hurried and somewhat ad hoc creation barely two years earlier when it had no doctrine, none of its critical equipment, and little idea what its requirements were.

A sad coda to the brigade's war occurred on 9 February during the opening stages of Veritable. Capt. Thomas Wyllie Howie Fairie of the 77th Squadron—a survivor of the horror onboard LCT-947 (109) on Queen Red when Lieutenant Colonel Cocks was killed and one of the best officers in the brigade—was killed along with the commander of the Canadian Scottish when the Buffalo they were riding in was hit by two *Panzerfaust* rounds. He was just twenty-three years old.

AFTER THE WAR
The British Army continued development of the A.V.R.E. after World War II. By 1946, a new Mark VII A.V.R.E. was put through trials with a new 6.5-inch demolition gun replacing the Petard; it entered service in 1954. It was eventually replaced by A.V.R.E. designs based upon first the Centurion and then the Chieftain tank. The Centurion A.V.R.E. soldiered on for nearly thirty years before being retired in 1992, making them the longest-serving A.V.R.E. in British service. The last A.V.R.E.'s ordered were forty-six CHAVRE's (Chieftain A.V.R.E.'s) built by Vickers between 1991 and 1994.[8]

At the end of the war, the 1st Armoured Engineer Brigade was disbanded along with all units except the 42nd Assault Regiment. It too was disbanded when a new 32nd Assault Regiment was formed in 1948 with the 26th, 59th, and 81st Assault

Squadrons and 31st Park Squadron, but by 1957, only the 26th Assault Squadron was still active. Then the 32nd Assault Regiment was reformed in 1963 around the 26th Assault Squadron for service with the British Army of the Rhine in Germany. That lasted until 1977, when defense spending cuts forced the disbandment of the 32nd Assault Regiment, again leaving the 26th Assault Squadron as the only active A.V.R.E. unit in the British Army. Yet another defense policy change resulted in the reforming of the 32nd Assault Regiment in 1980, which lasted through the Gulf War, where the armored engineers supported the 1st U.S. Infantry Division, until 1993, when it was disbanded for the last—although perhaps not final—time.[9]

Finally, in the twenty-first century, the A.V.R.E. is to be replaced in the British Army by a new generation of engineering vehicle that will not be designed for direct assault. It will no longer be fitted with a demolition gun, but instead will incorporate a mine plow and bucket arm and will be solely an obstacle-clearing vehicle, taking the role filled in World War II by the Crab and bulldozer.

POSTSCRIPT
Whatever became of Lt. John James Denovan?

Shortly before D-Day, he was posted away from England to Italy, and thereafter, information on his career becomes spotty. I would like to be able to report that he was lionized for his contributions, but unfortunately, that doesn't quite seem to be the case. He eventually reached the rank of major, but it is unclear when. It is known that on 12 May 1953, he received an award of 1,500 pounds—a not insubstantial amount at that time—in recognition for his work in the development of the A.V.R.E. And in 1993, he was the last recipient of the Commemorative Medal for the 125th Anniversary of Confederation. Finally, in July 1998, just two years before his death, the 5e Regiment de Génie du Canada dedicated its armored engineer building to him. It would be nice to report that the awards and dedication were accompanied by appropriate fanfare and ceremony, but they seemed to have been quiet affairs.[10]

D-Day Roll of Honor

THIS LIST WAS COMPILED from the graves registries kept by the Commonwealth War Graves Commission for fatal casualties incurred by the 1st Assault Brigade on 6 June. It is probably incomplete and contains some oddities when compared to the regimental casualty reports. For example, a total of eight other ranks were reported killed in the 79th Squadron, but the names of only four—all listed with those whose bodies were never identified—can be found. However, there are four other ranks of the

80th Squadron buried, and yet there was no report of any other ranks being killed on D-Day. Given the hurried organization of the 1st Assault Brigade, it may be possible that some men from the 80th Squadron were used to fill vacant positions in the 79th Squadron, but that is just supposition. It also appears that the report of one officer and two other ranks killed made by the 26th Squadron may have been in error, since the names of only three other ranks can be found in the graves register.

Le Pont A.V.R.E. on display at Graye-sur-Mer. It is the fascine carrier of the 1st Troop, 26th Assault Squadron, that had been submerged in the flooded crater and then used as a support for an SBG bridge. It was excavated in 1976 and put on display. STEVE ZALOGA

1ST ASSAULT BRIGADE ROYAL ENGINEERS

5th Assault Regiment Royal Engineers

Headquarters
Lt. Col. Arthur Denis Bradford Cocks
Sgt. James "Jock" Wingate

77th Squadron
Capt. George Alastair McLennan, No. 1 Troop
Sgt. Albert Edward Myhill
L/Sgt. Arthur Frederick Spender
L/Cpl. Frederick Ronald Shea
L/Cpl. Walter Craig Fairlie (body not identified)
Sapper John Kenneth Manuel
Sapper William Henry Tredrea

79th Squadron
Capt. William Henry Beedom Ayers, No. 3 Troop
Capt. Geoffrey Cecil Desanges, No. 2 Troop
Cpl. Edgar Ronald Roberts (body not identified)
Sapper Richard Sidney Lawson (body not identified)
Sapper George Lorimer (body not identified)
Sapper Ray Askew Marsden (body not identified)

26th Squadron
L/Sgt. Cecil Robert Ashton
Sapper Alfred Charles Battson
Sapper Roy Manly

*80th Squadron**
Lt. Jack Harold Hornby, No. 4 Troop
Sgt. Robert Gall Martin
L/Cpl. Leslie Henry Porter
Sapper Bernard Paul Cordwell
Sapper Albert Gunning

6th Assault Regiment, Royal Engineers

81st Squadron
L/Sgt. Harold Walter Cosham (body not identified)
L/Cpl. William Turner Morgan (body not identified)
Sapper James Graham
Sapper James Richard Huxley
Sapper Edward William James Jones (body not identified)

82nd Squadron
Maj. Harold George Almond Elphinstone
L/Sgt. Eli George

Attached

*22nd Dragoons (all on Sword)***
Lt. John Allen
Sgt. Joseph Gibbs (drowned when LST was bombed and sunk)
Sgt. Nathaniel Turner
Cpl. Robert Aird
Cpl. Ernest "Bob" Brotherton
L/Cpl. James James
L/Cpl. Fred Johnson (drowned when LST was bombed and sunk)
Trooper Thomas Healey (drowned when LST was bombed and sunk)
Trooper John Hogg
Trooper Leonard Kemp
Trooper William McShand
Trooper Robert Thomas

★ There is no record of any other ranks killed on D-Day in the accounts of the 80th Assault Squadron.
★★ Raymond Birt, *XXII Dragoons 1760–1945: The Story of a Regiment* (Aldershot, England: Gale & Polden, 1950), 335.

A Footnote to History: The "Offer" of A.V.R.E.'s to the U.S. Army

IT HAS LONG BEEN ACCEPTED as fact that the U.S. Army's resistance to using specialist assault vehicles on D-Day led to the severe casualties suffered by American troops on Omaha Beach. Furthermore, the inference has been made that if the Americans had utilized such vehicles, those casualties would inevitably have been less. For example, Chester Wilmot stated:

> There might have been some justification for the policy of direct assault if the Americans had accepted Montgomery's plan for landing armour en masse at the start of the attack, and for using the specialized equipment of Hobart's 79th Armoured Division to deal with the fortifications and the underwater obstacles. When Montgomery first saw this equipment he ordered Hobart to make one-third of it available to the Americans, and set himself to interest Eisenhower and Bradley in its revolutionary employment. Hobart's account of the reaction of the three generals is illuminating.
>
> "Montgomery," he says, "was most inquisitive. After thorough tests and searching questions he said in effect: 'I'll have this and this and this; but I don't want that or that.' Eisenhower was equally enthusiastic but not so discriminating. His response was, 'We'll take everything you can give us.' Bradley appeared to be interested but, when asked what he wanted, replied, 'I'll have to consult my staff.'" Bradley and his staff eventually accepted the "DDs" but did not take up the offer of "Crabs", "Crocodiles", "AVREs" and the rest of Hobart's menagerie.[1]

The commonly accepted view, however, appears to misstate both the circumstances and the consequences of the American actions. For one, there seems to be some confusion about what the Americans actually did and didn't want. For another, there is little evidence that the "policy of direct assault" was uniquely American. Finally, there is little real evidence that the lack of specialized engineering vehicles would have resulted in reduced casualties on Omaha.

Eisenhower's papers contain two or possibly three references to a demonstration on 27 January by the 617th Assault Squadron R.E. On 29 January 1944, Eisenhower wrote a personal note to General Hobart thanking him for the demonstration, stating that he was, "much impressed with all your work and the training you are doing" and that he "should like some of my senior officers to see what I did as I know how much they would profit by it."[2] At that

---

1. Chester Wilmot, *The Struggle for Europe* (New York: Harper & Brothers, 1952), 265. The paragraph was footnoted "This account was given to me by General Hobart on November 10th, 1946."
2. *The Papers of Dwight David Eisenhower*, vol. 3, *The War Years*, Alfred D. Chandler, Jr., ed. (Baltimore, MD: The Johns Hopkins Press, 1970), entry 1522, Eisenhower Mss. to Percy Cleghorn Stanley Hobart, January 29, 1944.

time, he did not mention any of the Funnies specifically, although later, on 7 February, in a note to Nicholas Straussler, Eisenhower specifically mentioned Straussler's invention, the DD tank, and commented that he was "looking forward to the day we can use them to good effect."[3] Then, in a letter on 9 February to General Marshall, Eisenhower again mentioned the demonstration, but only commented that the "visit was for the purpose of inspecting special items of equipment that are designated to help us through that type of defensive organization."[4]

Alan Brooke's diary entry for 27 January 1944 shows that he was present at the demonstration with Eisenhower, although he is not mentioned in the Hobart/Wilmot account:

> Eisenhower met me at the station last night and we traveled up by special train through the night. Hobart collected us at 9 am and took us first to his HQ where he showed us his models, and his proposed assault organization. We then went on to see various exhibits such as the Sherman tank for destroying tank mines, with chains on a drum driven by an engine, various methods of climbing walls with tanks, blowing up of minefields and walls, flame throwing Churchill tanks, wall destroying engineer parties, floating tanks, teaching men how to escape from sunken tanks, etc, etc. A most interesting day, and one which Eisenhower seemed to enjoy thoroughly. Hobart has been doing wonders in his present job and I am delighted that we put him into it.[5]

Brooke's account confirms that the Sherman Crab mine-clearing vehicle was demonstrated to Eisenhower, and it is evident that the demonstration also included various bridging vehicles, probably prototypes of the SBG assault bridge, demolition vehicles, Crocodiles, hand-emplaced demolitions, and DD tanks and their associated escape gear. Note that

Hobart also displayed "models" and a "proposed" organization, implying that at that time, only a few of the vehicles and crews were ready, an assumption that, as we have seen, was confirmed by the account of the organization and equipping of the brigade found in their history, the various postwar remarks of some of the brigade members, and the actual production records for the A.V.R.E.'s.

Patrick Delaforce mentions an incident that apparently occurred at the 27 January demonstration that shows at least some A.V.R.E.'s were also demonstrated:

> Major Roland Ward of 617 Assault Squadron relates: 'Dick Stafford's AVRE fell over upside down off an Assault bridge in trying to climb over a wall in the Orford battle area. Eisenhower ran forward quite concerned for the crew, but 'Hobo' said 'Don't worry—they do it every day. . . .'"
>
> Although Eisenhower was impressed with 'Funnies' and Montgomery offered them to the American forces on D-Day, General Bradley turned the offer down.[6]

Mention is made of the 27 January demonstration in the 79th Armoured Division Final Report as well.[7] It states that in a meeting following the demonstration, it was agreed that the U.S. First Army's technical representatives were to see the new equipment on 11 February, after which they were to inform the British of their requirements. It also explicitly stated that General Bradley was at that post-demonstration meeting on 27 January, so presumably, he also witnessed the demonstration.

Although the meeting with the First Army's technical representatives is not mentioned in Bradley's papers or in the Historical Report of the First Army Armor Section, it does appear that the U.S. Army representatives did see the new equipment, since on 16 February 1944, Brig. Sir Edwin Otway Herbert, a General Staff officer with the 21st

---

3. Ibid., entry 1537. Eisenhower specifically mentioned riding in a DD at the demonstration at Fritton, Norfolk, so it is clear it was not the 27 January demonstration, which was at the Orford Battle Area, Suffolk. The Fritton demonstration did result in the decision to convert DD tanks in the U.S. although no U.S.-built DD tanks were used in the invasion.

4. Ibid., entry 1539.

5. Alan Brooke, *War Diaries, 1939–1945: Field Marshal Lord Alanbrooke* (Berkeley, CA: University of California Press, 2001), 516–17.

6. Patrick Delaforce, *Churchill's Secret Weapons: The Story of Hobart's Funnies* (Barnsley, England: Pen & Sword, 2007), 87.

7. TNA WO 205/1159, 79 Armoured Division Final Report, 1943 Apr.–1945 July.

Army Group, sent a memo on the subject of "US Requirements for British Devices—OVERLORD" to the British Under Secretary of State at the War Office, with copies to the U.S. First Army headquarters, British Second Army, 79th Armoured Division, SHAEF, and various staff sections in the 21st Army Group.[8] He noted that

1. Equipments as shown in the attached Appendix are required by First US Army for operation OVERLORD. They will be operated by US personnel. In the event of the US Army being equipped with similar equipment from US sources, or suitable substitutes, the equipments will be returned to the British.
2. "DD tanks" and "Porpoises" dealt with separately.

What is intriguing is that the requirements list included twelve items, four of which were specifically mounted on Sherman-based chassis: Crab, Sherman Bullshorn Plow, Sherman OAC Mark III Plow[9], and Sherman Crocodile. Two others, Harrow and Centipede, were mine-clearing devices designed to be adaptable for towing or mounting on either American or British vehicles. Of the remainder, four were strictly British-based vehicles (the A.V.R.E., the ARK, and the SBG Mark II, all based on the Churchill, and bridgelayers, which in this context probably referred to the Valentine bridge-laying tank that was then being distributed to Commonwealth armored units), and two were "devices" (special charges and snakes).

Significantly, it is the latter six items that the First Army did not place a requirement for. The primary reasoning given was that they did not want to further complicate their already complex training program and add to their logistical burden by accepting into inventory four non-standard British vehicles based on the Churchill and Valentine tank chassis just three and a half months before the projected date of the assault. (Commonwealth units had no such qualms; they had been using American tanks since August 1941 and Sherman tanks since August 1942.)

Similarly, the special charges were more or less standard engineer shaped charges, while the snake was essentially a giant bangalore torpedo comprised of twenty-foot lengths of three-inch pipe that could be assembled into as much as a 400-foot length, towed to the edge of a minefield by a tank that then pushed it into place. In the case of snake, the requisition specifically identified that an "order [was] placed and supply promised from USA."

That left six items that were actually requested. Of those, the twenty-five Crabs actually requested must simply not have been available over and above the Commonwealth requirements, since none were provided. That was probably also the case for the forty Bullshorn Plows, forty OAC Mark III Plows, and fifty Harrow Plows that were requested, which also were not supplied.[10] Neither was the Centipede, which was a device that was specifically designed to clear antipersonnel mines more quickly than the Crab was capable of doing. Few Centipedes were ever built, and there is little evidence that it was ever used in combat.

The memo further specifically noted that the Sherman Crocodile was "understood to conflict with Churchill Crocodile"—a statement that was quite correct and also illustrated some of the basic problems that the Allies faced. In this case, the Churchill Crocodile prototype had been demonstrated in March 1943 and had immediately attracted the interest of the Americans. On 16 July 1943, the European theater of operations of the U.S. Army recommended that the British-designed flamethrower should be adapted to fit in the Sherman and that 100 conversions and 25 extra trailers should be procured through a combination of British and American resources. Unfortunately, the adaptation did not prove to be as simple as was originally thought, and although an initial prototype was completed in February 1944, delays dogged the project. In the end, despite all plans to the contrary, only four were ever completed, and they were not issued to units in the field until November 1944.[11]

8. I am indebted to Stephen Zaloga for reminding me of this document.

9. OAC was the Obstacle Assault Centre, which was created by the Royal Engineers at Hankley Common, near Farnborough, and was where many of the devices were invented and tested.

10. The fact that only ten of the Bullshorn Plows were utilized (not very successfully) by the 1st Assault Brigade on D-Day seems to reinforce the notion that there simply were not many of them available.

11. R. P. Hunnicutt, *Sherman: A History of the American Medium Tank* (Novato, CA: Presidio Press, 1978), 418.

Finally, unstated in the memo was a little-known fact that may have been affecting the American decision: the U.S. Army Corps of Engineers and Ordnance Department were also developing their own assault engineer vehicle based upon the M4 medium tank. At about the same time that Denovan's two prototype A.V.R.E.'s were being completed in February 1943, U.S. Army Ground Forces authorized a Corps of Engineers study to investigate new and innovative ways to clear beach and underwater obstacles at the Amphibious Training Base at Fort Pierce, Florida.[12] The tests resulted in a recommendation that an armored engineering vehicle, based upon the Sherman tank, be developed. That recommendation was approved in August 1943.

The result was a prototype that replaced the Sherman's 75-millimeter gun with twin access doors in the turret, a side access door in the right sponson, and mounted a 7.2-inch T40 (later standardized as the M17) "Whiz Bang" multiple rocket launcher in a sturdy armored box above the turret. It was completed and had undergone preliminary testing, but did not arrive at Fort Pierce for operational testing until 20 March 1944. The tests resulted in further modifications and a second pilot, but by then, of course, it was too late for any production to reach Britain in time for the invasion, and in any case, there would have been no time to train crews and integrate the vehicles into the assault plan. Eventually, although 1,000 conversion kits were authorized, only two conversions were ever completed. That delay, and the refusal of the Army Ground Forces and the Operations Division of the War Department General Staff to authorize creation of a new engineer organization to operate such units, doomed the project.[13]

That U.S. Army Ground Forces was resistant to unique organizations intended for specific tasks is incontrovertible.[14] In this case, however, it made little difference. There simply weren't sufficient British-made specialist vehicles to support the American operations, whether they were American- or British-manned. The American projects to develop similar equipment, begun in a similar timeframe as the British projects, simply were delayed too late for them to have been available in time. Those delays were, of course, unforeseen in mid-1943 when the projects were begun and in early 1944 when the equipment requests were made.

So although an "offer" of the special equipment developed by the 79th Armoured Division was made to the U.S. Army, it was not "refused," and in fact, a large number of various types were asked for but, for various reasons, were not supplied. The "refusal" of some of those items was for perfectly logical reasons—the difficulty associated with issuing brand-new, unique, and complicated items so close to the invasion date, as well as the mistaken belief that similar equipment, on standard American vehicles, would be supplied from the U.S.

The truth appears to be that no matter how hard Hobart tried to "sell" the Funnies, and no matter how many of the Funnies the Americans were willing to "buy," the simple fact was that any such offer was premature, since the concepts were still being worked out and the production was barely adequate to fulfill Commonwealth requirements, let alone American ones.

The incident, however, does highlight one major advantage that the British Army enjoyed over the Americans. The British Army decision to centralize the development, organization, and use of specialized vehicles and equipment under a single command, the 79th Armoured Division, was much wiser than the decentralized approach of the Americans, where the varying concerns and priorities of the Engineers, Armor Force, Ordnance, Army Ground Forces, and the Operations Division of the General Staff all contributed to the inability of the U.S. Army to procure more than a handful of specialized vehicles during the war.

---

12. U.S. Army Ground Forces was the headquarters organization in the U.S. Army responsible for organizing and training all ground forces units of the four combat arms (cavalry, infantry, field artillery, and coast artillery) and the new "quasi-arms" (armor, tank destroyer, and antiaircraft artillery). See Kent Roberts Greenfield, et al., *The Organization of Ground Combat Troops* (Washington, DC: Historical Division, Department of the Army, 1947).

13. Hunnicutt, *Sherman*, 435–36. There was further development of the armored engineer vehicle as a concept, but none ever got past the prototype stage, and all were much too late for D-Day.

14. See Greenfield, et al., *Organization of Ground Combat Troops*, for the controversies in the U.S. Army over the creation of specialized units.

The Funnies and Omaha Beach

DISCUSSIONS REGARDING THE OFFER of A.V.R.E.'s to the American army seem inevitably to lead to the next logical question: would the presence of A.V.R.E.'s on Omaha Beach have had a difference to the outcome there?

In fact, most of the controversy surrounding the A.V.R.E.'s seems to revolve around that question. Of course, the simple answer is that there was little chance that A.V.R.E.'s *could* have been available for Omaha Beach since there simply were not enough to go around or enough LCT's available to transport them even if more A.V.R.E.'s had been available. Furthermore, it is clear that the U.S. Army would have used them had they been available. However, that does not answer the perennial question about what would have happened *had* they been landed as part of the Omaha assault.

For that question to be fairly answered, a few parameters must be established. For one thing, it has to be decided whether the A.V.R.E.'s would have been deployed on the LCT's that were available or whether additional LCT's would have been available.

The first—no additional LCT's—implies that the number of regular tanks or other heavy equipment loaded for the assault troops would have been reduced, and that is problematic. As has been seen, the numbers of LCT's and the loads they carried were already finally calculated. Reducing the number of gun tanks landed would have been a very risky gamble since it appears there were few enough that actually were landed. Take the five from the 741st Tank Battalion that were successfully landed on Omaha away from the 16th Infantry and it seems

certain that WN 60 and 62 would have held out for even hours longer than they did. Reducing the number landed in support of the 116th Infantry seems equally problematic.

Assuming the second, though, requires an even more torturous twisting of history. Additional LCT's simply weren't available, and even the number actually made available for the invasion required an extraordinary effort by shipyards in England, which managed the feat of getting over 95 percent of the mass of landing craft operational for D-Day. Furthermore, if Omaha was given an allotment of A.V.R.E.'s, the logic of the assault organization required that Utah would have required some as well, which would have required that many more LCT's. More LCT's were in service, in the Pacific or working up, but priorities in allotments had been given to Europe for months, so it is very questionable if even the additional twenty to thirty required could have been provided.

However, if it was simply assumed that A.V.R.E.'s were deployed with the Omaha force what might have been their effect? In other words, ignoring everything else, what was the possible utility of the A.V.R.E. for dealing with the particular defensive strengths of Omaha?

One major problem with Omaha was simply the geography of the area and how the Germans made use of that geography to improve their defenses. In turn, that related to weapons effectiveness, survivability, and maneuverability of the A.V.R.E.'s as it applied to the geography of Omaha.

In terms of weapons effectiveness. it should be recalled that the use of the A.V.R.E. as a "gun" platform was limited by the range and accuracy of its Petard. That simple fact limited its engagement range to targets within a radius of about eighty yards of its firing position. Otherwise, its armament was limited to its hull-mounted Besa machine gun, the Bren machine gun carried inside the vehicle, and the various explosive charges that could be hand-carried from the vehicle and emplaced by the sappers. Thus, the effectiveness of the A.V.R.E. on Omaha, as on the other beaches, would have been limited by its ability to engage targets—an ability itself determined by what and where the targets were relative to where the A.V.R.E. could engage them from.

In terms of survivability, the Churchill-based A.V.R.E. was much better protected than the M4 medium tank—from the front, at least. However, in the operational environment encountered on D-Day, that made it only marginally superior to that of the M4 or almost any other armored vehicle given the threats that were encountered. Bogging and swamping were responsible for a large percentage of all of the vehicles that were disabled on D-Day. And those actually knocked out by gunfire were in a classic antiarmor trap where the guns firing on them were able to engage them from enfilade, while turning the A.V.R.E. to present its better protected front simply exposed its flanks and rear to other guns. For example, the A.V.R.E. and other armored fighting vehicles at Jig Green knocked out by a 75-millimeter gun at Le Hamel were lost to enfilading fire; it was fortunate that the only other German antitank gun positioned to hit them was the 5-centimeter gun at WN 36, which became fully occupied with the 1st Dorsets and their supporting tanks.

In terms of maneuverability, the Churchill was possibly the best Allied tank at the time. It was found capable in tests of mounting a thirty-degree slope (i.e., a 58 percent grade), although attempting such a slope in combat could be problematic. Nonetheless, that performance was spectacular compared to the roughly twenty-three-degree slope that could be traversed by most of its contemporaries. But it still faced some practical limitations. The critical slopes found on Omaha, from Pointe et Raz de la Percée in the west to Colleville in the east, were the bluffs behind the beaches, and those varied from forty to nearly ninety degrees along much of their length, impassable to any vehicle, which is why the five exits from the beach were so critical. However,

even then, only three of those, the Colleville Draw, (Exit E-3), the Les Moulins Draw (Exit D-3), and the Vierville Draw (Exit D-1), were truly practicable for tracked vehicles, while only the road through Exit D-1 was paved and fully trafficable to all vehicles without improvement.

That meant that most of the defenses simply weren't within the limited engagement envelope of the Petard. For example, at the Colleville Draw, WN 62 was at the crest of the bluff and was completely inaccessible to the direct approach of any vehicle except from inland. The configuration of the slope and the position of the emplacements simply made it impractical for an A.V.R.E. to get within the Petard's range. WN 60 was also on the bluff, but was somewhat more practicable in that there was a slightly less steep approach from northwest to southeast that might have been negotiated, although that would have meant driving headlong into the 75-millimeter guns there while exposing the A.V.R.E.'s rear to fire from the 5-centimeter gun in WN 62. On the other hand, WN 61 between them inexplicably was placed on the beach, but the approach to the Petard's eighty-meter zone was covered by an extensive antitank ditch that ran entirely across the front of WN 62, blocking the exit, and extended beyond the front and flank of WN 61, while the flat beach between WN 61 and WN 60 was heavily mined. So an approach would have required the successful deployment of an assault bridge, fascines, and mine-clearing flails, all under the close-range fire of the guns of the three positions.

Each of the other exits enjoyed similar advantages conferred upon them by the terrain. The positions at Les Moulins were also atop the bluff, and maneuver across the flats leading to the lower tier of defenses was through marsh, antitank ditches, minefields, and seawalls. Vierville was perhaps the most difficult. The massive bunker housing the 88-millimeter gun there could only be targeted at the close range required by the Petard if the A.V.R.E. was first able to cross the shingle without bogging—it is notable that it was similar shingle at Dieppe that caused so many problems for the Churchill tanks there during Jubilee— get across the four to eight-foot high seawall, span an antitank ditch cutting access inland on the paved coast road, and survive the fire of the 88-millimeter gun itself.

It could be argued that that was what the A.V.R.E.'s were designed to do. But that rather misses the point: would they have been any more successful by attempting a headlong rush into the teeth of such defenses than was the American armor? Would a choreographed assault with a Bobbin laying carpet over the shingle, a SBG laying a bridge up the seawall, a Fascine filing in the antitank ditch, and then a close frontal assault with Petard have worked any better than did the longer-range sniping by the 743rd Tank Battalion? It seems doubtful.

Nor does it appear that the Crab would have been much more useful on Omaha. Except in a few places, such as the Colleville Draw in front of WN 62, the minefields employed by the Germans were emplaced on the slopes controlling access to the flanks and rear of the positions, in some areas of the marshy flats at the foot of the bluffs, and on the footpaths that led up the bluffs. However, few of those areas were accessible to any vehicle, let alone a Crab, so with the exception of the area of the Colleville Draw, their presence also may have been moot.

It may be significant to this analysis that on Sword, where personnel casualties on the beach were very high in comparison to the other Commonwealth beaches, casualties to armored vehicles of all types were also very high. Only thirty-one of an expected forty DD tanks landed (77.5 percent), and of those, another nine were lost to swamping by the unexpectedly swiftly returning tide. Ten of the remaining twenty-two tanks were lost to gunfire, leaving twelve operational before additional ones began to arrive.

That seems very similar to what occurred on Omaha, especially in the 16th Infantry sector, where even fewer tanks arrived and the casualties were even greater than on Sword. The more difficult terrain and obstacles found at the western end of Omaha in the 116th Infantry sector may then explain why casualties there were as bad as at the eastern end even though more operational tanks had gotten ashore there than in either the 16th Infantry sector or on Sword.

That observation appears to hold at all the beaches. At Juno, the 8th Canadian Brigade landed nearly forty DD tanks to support the assault waves and suffered fewer casualties in the assault than did the 7th Brigade, which encountered various problems and only managed to get fewer than half that number of tanks ashore in the initial stage of the assault, even though they did manage to get them ashore before the infantry. On Gold, the number of tanks gotten ashore was similar on both King and Jig, and the casualties incurred were nearly identical as well.

On the other hand, it cannot be said that there is a significant correlation between the successful gapping of the beach obstacles and the casualties that ensued. On Sword, six of eight of the gaps attempted succeeded, and none were significantly late. On Juno, eight of eight were completed, and only one was significantly later than the others. On Gold, though, only two gaps were completed in the assault phase, and only one of those could be considered to be more or less "on time." And yet Gold witnessed the lowest casualties and almost the greatest mission effectiveness, in terms of the advance inland and objectives achieved, of any of the five beaches on D-Day— matched only by Juno, where the gapping effort was possibly the most successful. That is the exact opposite of Omaha, which was closer to Gold in terms of lack of gapping success (at best, eight of sixteen planned gaps) but farthest from it in terms of casualties. Nor does gapping effectiveness explain Utah, where gapping was much more effective than on Gold but where casualties were similar in relative terms.

Based on that, and given that one of the primary tasks assigned the A.V.R.E.'s and Crabs was gapping, it may be fairly asked what their actual effect on D-Day was. They did provide additional armored support to the assault infantry, which may actually have been their critical role. Indeed, it may in some cases have been better to eschew the complex and marginally useful "devices" and simply employ the A.V.R.E. as a tank. In the final analysis, it seems clear that that was the critical shortfall on Omaha—a simple lack of armored vehicles of any kind rather than a lack of armored engineer vehicles. And yet it also seems to be an inescapable conclusion that some form of armored engineer vehicle may have been a critical missing ingredient on the western end of Omaha Beach, where a mass of armor was impotent for so long simply because they were unable to get inland. However, that would have been no true guarantee of earlier success or of fewer casualties given the immense boost the unique combination of terrain, obstacles, fortifications, and firepower gave the Germans.

Notes

CHAPTER 1: CONCEPTION

1. M. E. Orsbourn, *The Shortest Gap: Story of the Armoured Engineers Vehicles of Royal Engineers*, (NP, ND), 9.

2. Ibid., 4–5.

3. I am greatly indebted to Ken Holmes, a researcher affiliated with the Canadian Engineers Military Museum, Canadian Forces School of Military, Mitchell Building, CFB Gagetown, Oromocto, New Brunswick, Canada, for discovering Denovan's Christian names. Much of the information on Denovan has come from four sources: Joyce Singer, "Tanks for the Memories," *Today's Seniors* (August 1994); Canadian Military Engineers, *Customs and Traditions of the CME*, A-JS-007-003/JD-001, Annex A—Canadian Military Engineer Memorials; Sgt. P. Little, CD, "History of the Armoured Vehicle Royal Engineers (AVRE)," *SITREP, 2 Canadian Field Engineers Newsletter* 5, no. 3 (June 2005); and an unpublished monograph by David Fletcher, historian at the Tank Museum, Bovington, "The Armoured Vehicle Royal Engineers." It is notable that even the photo caption in Singer's otherwise excellent article misspells his name as "Donovan."

4. Orsbourn, *Shortest Gap*, 5.

5. Canadian losses at Dieppe were recorded on 24 August 1942 as 161 killed, 584 wounded, and 2,650 missing, out of of 4,984 embarked. See The National Archives of the United Kingdom (hereafter TNA), WO 162/297, Dieppe Casualties, dated 28 August 1942 and Canadian Section, G.H.Q. 2nd Echelon 99/15/STATS/1/A3, Casualties—Enemy Action.

6. John P. Campbell, *Dieppe Revisited: A Documentary Investigation* (London: Frank Cass, 1993), 222; and Orsbourn, *Shortest Gap*, 10.

7. Orsbourn, *Shortest Gap*, 10.

8. Ibid.

9. U.S. Army Command and General Staff College, Combined Arms Research Library Digital Library (hereafter CARL), Conference on Landing Assaults, Vol. 1 and 2, 1 July 1943, "Discussion Following Lecture by Lt. Col. C. R. Kutz."

10. Singer, "Tanks for the Memories."

11. It has been implied that had Denovan's experiment failed, he would have left himself wide open for charges of destruction of government property and misuse of issued equipment. See Orsbourn, *Shortest Gap*, 11; and Little, "History of the Armoured Vehicle Royal Engineers (AVRE)."

12. Blacker's fascinating story can be found in Barnaby Blacker, *The Adventures and Inventions of Stewart Blacker, Aviation Pioneer and Weapons Inventor* (Barnsley, England: Pen & Sword, 2006). Maj. (later Maj. Gen.) Millis Jefferis, the mercurial leader of the Ministry of Defence establishment known as MD1 (nicknamed "Churchill's Toyshop") and concerned with the development of special weapons, later claimed to have been behind the development of both the Petard and the A.V.R.E., but the evidence is against him.

13. Orsbourn, *Shortest Gap*, 12.

14. Ibid.

15. Ibid., 13.

16. One modification introduced to the conversion was the retention of the turret basket, which was kept in all later conversions. See Peter Chamberlain and Chris Ellis, "Churchill and Sherman Specials" in Duncan Crow, ed., *British and Commonwealth AFVs, 1940–46* (Garden City, NY: Doubleday, 1972).

17. There appears to be some confusion about when the first "production" model of the A.V.R.E. was produced. Mention is made in a number of sources to the first Cockbridge & Company "prototype" being completed 9 December 1943, but that actually appears to have been a "one-off" demonstration of their conversion kit. M. G.'s records clearly show that they completed the first actual conversion on 20 November 1943. From then until 26 April 1945, M. G. recorded completing 518 A.V.R.E. conversions. Other records indicate that a total of 532 conversions were completed in 1944 and 32 more in 1945, for a total of 564. See "Calling All Arms!! Experience at M. G. during Wartime" at www.mgcars.org.uk/mgcc/sf/000101.htm. For total A.V.R.E. production, see TNA, AVIA 22/456, Armoured fighting vehicles: conversions and modifications, 1942–1945; AVIA 22/469, Armoured fighting vehicles: monthly returns of deliveries, 1939–1941; AVIA 22/576, Blacker Bombard (297 mm Spigot-Mortar) weapon: requirements, 1941–1943; AVIA 22/511–514, Monthly Statistical Summaries nos. 1–46, 1942–1946; and AVIA 22/515–519, Statistical Summaries nos. 1–16 and Statistical Abstract, December 1940–1945.

To make things even more confusing, the 79th Armoured Division R.E.M.E. apparently completed only 43 conversions, while the 59 A.V.R.E.'s used in Italy were converted in theater from worn-out gun tanks and apparently were not included in the total number reported converted. Orsbourn, *Shortest Gap*, 12–13. If the total of 564 completed conversions is correct, then it seems likely that the figures may have been 518 completed by M. G., 43 by R.E.M.E., and the three prototype conversions (Denovan's first, the second authorized in February 1943, and the third completed by the 79th Armoured Division R.E.M.E.)

On D-Day, the actual availability of A.V.R.E.'s in the 1st Assault Brigade was 34 on Sword Beach, 47 on Juno, and 40 on Gold, for a total of 121. See TNA, WO 171/1797, No. 1 Assault Brigade War Diary, June–December 1944; WO 171/1800, No. 5 Assault Regiment War Diary, June–December 1944; WO 205/1120, Report by Brig. Watkinson on Work of Assault RE in the Invasion; WO 205/1160, The Story of the 1st Assault Brigade Royal Engineers, 1943–1945; and WO 205/1170, Chief Engineer 21 Army Group, R.E. Report on the Battle of Normandy, 6th June–5th July 1944. These numbers can be compared to the distribution given in the *Abridged Second Army Engineer Plan*, which allocated 30 to Sword Beach, 28 to June, and 44 to Gold, for a total of 102. In other words, there were 19 more A.V.R.E.'s actually landed than were originally planned for. The original engineer plan also called for the arrival of the "residue" of the 5th and 6th Assault Regiments by D+27, with an additional 104 A.V.R.E.'s and the arrival of the reserve 42nd Assault Regiment with 104 more on D+30 or later.

These planning figures must be balanced against a number of hard realities. For one, by D-Day, only about 180 A.V.R.E. conversions had been completed, meaning that exactly two-thirds of those available were committed to the assault. For another, at that time, manufacture of the conversion kit and the actual conversion work were averaging about 250 hours per A.V.R.E. to complete. See Orsbourn, *Shortest Gap*, 13. The record is not clear whether it was the production of the kits or the time required for the conversion that created the major bottleneck.

Finally, the theoretical war establishment for the squadrons was intended to be 26, which would have meant that the six squadrons deployed on D-Day, should have had 156 A.V.R.E.'s and the full brigade (12 squadrons), 312. By that measure, the squadrons landed on D-Day were actually 35 short of establishment, while the 180 actually produced left the brigade 132 short of establishment. It is also problematic whether or not all of the A.V.R.E.'s produced up to D-Day had been delivered to the brigade.

18. Maj. Kenneth J. Macksey, *Armoured Crusader: A Biography of Major-General Sir Percy Hobart* (London: Hutchinson, 1967).

19. Maj. Michael J. Daniels, *Innovation in the Face of Adversity: Major-General Sir Percy Hobart and the 79th Armoured Division (British)*, MMAS Thesis (Fort Leavenworth, KS: U.S. Army Command and General Staff College, 2003), 5.

20. See Lord Alanbrooke, *War Diaries, 1939–1945: Field Marshal Lord Alanbrooke* (Berkeley, CA: University of California Press, 2001), 155–56. Brooke was Chief of the Imperial General Staff (CIGS).

21. Alanbrooke, *War Diaries*, 319–20. To be fair, since there has long been intimation of a concerted anti-Hobart cabal in the War Office, Brooke specifically recorded discussing the matter with Churchill on 9 September 1942. The prime minister was pressing to send Hobart with his division to North Africa, but Brooke remarked that the "doctors and

medical board [considered Hobart] as being a very doubtful medical case."

22. Hobart was given the news by Brooke personally, but the CIGS did not record Hobo's reaction in his diary. Alanbrooke, *War Diaries*, 328.

23. It appears that Brooke actually meant self-propelled flamethrowers when he referred to "self-propelled guns" since that is how he referred to them in later meetings with Hobart on 1 April and 17 June 1943. Alanbrooke, *War Diaries*, 388, 391, 421.

24. Canadian Army Headquarters (AHQ) Report No. 42, *The Preliminary Planning For Operation "OVERLORD": Some Aspects of the Preparations for an Allied Re-entry to North-West Europe, 1940–1944*, 171.

CHAPTER 2: ORGANIZATION, TRAINING, AND EQUIPPING

1. TNA WO 205/1160, The Story of the 1st Assault Brigade Royal Engineers, 1943–1945, 8–9.

2. Ibid., 9.

3. Ibid., 8–9.

4. Orsbourn, *Shortest Gap*, 14.

5. See the list of equipment used in the 5 Assault Regiment War Diary, June 1944, TNA WO 171/1800, and in the 21st Army Group Engineer Report, TNA WO 205/1170. Additional descriptions of the design and function of the various devices and other equipment of the 79th Armoured Division can be found in Chamberlain and Ellis. "Churchill and Sherman Specials," and N. W. Duncan, "The 79th Armoured Division" in *British and Commonwealth AFVs 1940–46*, Duncan Crow, ed. (Garden City, NY: Doubleday, 1972).

6. See for instance the War Diary of 341 Battery of the 8th Field Regiment R.A., which landed at 0845 to support the 69th Infantry Brigade of the 50th Division on Gold King Beach. Benjamin S. Beck, web.nkonline.co.uk/benjaminbeck/batterydiary.htm.

7. Daniels, *Innovation in the Face of Adversity*, 23.

8. Orsbourn, *Shortest Gap*, 13.

9. Each regiment nominally consisted of twelve five-Crab troops, four troops in each of three squadrons, so sixty Crabs per regiment. But it was also supposed to have three "pilot" troops, one per squadron. However, the "pilot" tanks, specially designed to mark cleared routes, were not completed in time for the Normandy landings and so regular Sherman gun tanks were substituted, but none are known to have landed on D-Day. Yet various documents indicate that the 22nd Dragoons deployed eight troops in the assault waves, four each on Sword and Juno, plus five more as follow-on forces (three on Sword and two on Juno). It is possible that an ad hoc thirteenth troop was organized, or the documents may simply be referring to the regimental headquarters troop. See Raymond Birt, *XXII Dragoons 1760–1945: The Story of a Regiment* (Aldershot, England: Gale & Polden, 1950); and TNA WO 179/409, 3rd British Infantry Division Operation Order No 1, OVERLORD, dated 14 May 1944. Westminster Dragoons reported fifty-six Crabs fit along with twenty-six Sherman gun tanks and six obsolete

Valentine Scorpions on 30 May. See WO 171/864, 2 County of London Yeomanry (Westminster Dragoons), Jun.–Dec. 1944. The strength report for the two regiments in France was seventy-eight "fit" as of 0600 hours on 1 July. See WO 205/636, A.F.V. States, Summaries at HQ 21 Army Group, June–July 1944.

10. Chamberlain and Ellis, "Churchill and Sherman Specials"; Duncan, "The 79th Armoured Division."

11. Peter Chamberlain, "Armoured Recovery Vehicles" in *British and Commonwealth AFVs 1940–46*, Duncan Crow, ed. (Garden City, NY: Doubleday, 1972).

12. Much of the following, unless otherwise indicated, is from *Allied Landing Craft of World War II* (1944; reprint, Annapolis, MD: Naval Institute Press, 1985), originally as *ON1226—Allied Landing Craft and Ships*.

13. TNA ADM 179/506, Operation "NEPTUNE," Report by Naval Commander, Eastern Task Force, Enclosure "E," Report of Proceedings of Force "J," Enclosure No. 3 "Lessons Learnt," 5.

14. TNA WO 171/102. 21 Army Group G.S., January–April 1944.

15. TNA ADM 179/458, Western Task Force, 1944 Mar–May, 7.

16. See Gordon A. Harrison, *Cross-Channel Attack* (Washington, DC: Center of Military History, United States Army, 1951), 191–93, for the organizational changes. For various criticisms of the assault planning, see William F. Buckingham, *D-Day, the First 72 Hours* (London: Tempus, 2004); and Adrian R. Lewis, *Omaha Beach: A Flawed Victory* (Chapel Hill, NC: University of North Carolina Press, 2001), 10–11.

CHAPTER 3: ALLIED PLANNING AND PREPARATION

1. Forrest Carlisle Pogue, *The European Theater of Operations*, vol. 4, *The Supreme Command* (Washington, DC: Office of the Chief of Military History, United States Army, 1954), 108.

2. Charles Lamb, *Montgomery in Europe, 1943–1945* (New York: Franklin Watts, 1984), 59.

3. Carlo d'Este, *Decision in Normandy* (New York: Dutton, 1983), 62–64. There is some controversy about the exact dates and who objected first. See Chester Wilmot, *The Struggle for Europe* (New York: Harper & Brothers, 1952), 172–76; Lamb, *Montgomery in Europe*, 61–67: and Harrison, *Cross-Channel Attack*, 165–66.

4. Harrison, *Cross-Channel Attack*, 72, 182.

5. Ibid., 72.

6. Ibid., 182.

7. CARL, "Appendix 1 to Annex C and Appendix 4b to Annex G", Operation Plan No. 2-44 of the Western Naval Task Force, Allied Naval Expeditionary Force, 21 April 1944, cgsc.leavenworth.army.mil/carl/contentdm/home.htm.

8. Campbell, *Dieppe Revisited*, 224.

9. TNA ADM 179/504, Operation "NEPTUNE," Report by Naval Commander, Eastern Task Force, Enclosure "C," Report of Proceedings of Force "S," 7.

10. AHQ Report No. 42, 266.

11. Ibid., 261.

12. War Department, Military Intelligence Service, *German Coastal Defenses*, Special Series, No. 15 (Washington, DC: War Department, 1943), 1–3, 17–18.

13. Ibid., 2.

14. CARL, *Conference on Landing Assaults*. The Assault Training Center had been authorized in April, but except for the conference training operations, it did not begin there until September. Harrison, *Cross-Channel Attack*, 162.

15. CARL, *Conference on Landing Assaults*, 6.

16. CARL, *Conference on Landing Assaults*, 12.

17. CARL, *Conference on Landing Assaults*, 5.

18. U.S. National Archives and Records Administration (hereafter NARA), RG 407, Entry 427, Records of the Adjutant General, Pre-Invasion Planning, Box 24309, Folder 209, Overlord Conference, 21 December 1943. Participants included Gen. Omar Bradley, commander of the U.S. First Army; Maj. Gen. Harold R. Bull, ETOUSA G-3; Maj. Gen. Leonard T. Gerow, commander of the U.S. V Corps; Maj. Gen. Charles H. Gerhardt, commander of the 29th Infantry Division; Brig. Gen. William Hoge, commander of the Provisional Engineer Special Brigade Group; Brig. Gen. William B. Kean, chief of staff of the U.S. First Army; Col. Benjamin A. "Monk" Dickson, the First Army's G-2; and Col. Benjamin B. Talley, the V Corps' G-2.

19. James Douglas O'Dell, "Joint-Service Beach Obstacle Demolition in World War II", *Engineer* (April–June 2005), 38.

20. See Alfred M. Beck, et al., *The Corps of Engineers: The War Against Germany* (Washington, DC: Superintendent of Documents, U.S. Government Printing Office, 1985), 301–8; and Sid Berger, *Breaching Fortress Europe: The Story of U.S. Engineers in Normandy on D-Day* (Dubuque, Iowa: Kendall/Hunt Publishing Company, 1994), 152–156.

21. In February 1944, seventy-one sappers from the Royal Marine Engineer Commando were assigned to the L.C.O.C.U. See Nicholas van der Bijl and Lee Johnson, *The Royal Marines, 1939–93*, Elite Series, 57 (London: Osprey, 1994), 15. Each L.C.O.C.U. nominally consisted of an officer, a petty officer, and eighteen other ranks, but see TNA WO 291/246, 9, 111, which indicates that the teams on Gold consisted of one officer and fifteen other ranks each, while it reports that the two teams on Sword totaled one officer and twenty-one other ranks between them. Thus, they may have averaged between thirteen and fourteen officers and men each.

22. Tim Kilvert-Jones, *Sword Beach: British 3rd Infantry Division/27th Armoured Brigade* (Barnsley, England: Pen & Sword, 2001), 109–10.

23. TNA ADM 179/505, Operation "NEPTUNE," Report of the Naval Commander, Eastern Task Force, Enclosure "D," Report of Proceedings of Force "G," Appendix "E," 1.

24. Operations Order No. 1-44, Western Naval Task Force, Assault Force "O" (Task Force One Two Four), Naval Combat Demolition Group, 31 May 1944.

25. Berger, *Breaching Fortress Europe*, 152–53.

26. Ibid., 78–80.

27. AHQ Report No. 42, 262.

28. TNA WO 179/409, 3rd British Infantry Division Operation Order No. 1, OVERLORD, dated 14 May 1944.

29. AHQ Report No. 54, 51.

30. TNA WO 291/246, 5.

31. Unlike the other assault divisions, the 3rd apparently grouped all four of its M10 troops under the 105th as a "composite" battery. It appears that the 105th's two troops of towed 6-pounder guns arrived on D+1, after which the regiment returned to its normal organization. See TNA WO 171/155, Appendix 'A' to R.A. Branch Headquarters 21st Army Group War Diary May 1944; and TNA WO 171/234, Second Army R.A. Landing Tables. But the heavy surf caused considerable difficulties. The 105th Battery was not actually ashore until sometime in the afternoon, and the 248th Battery of the 62nd Antitank Regiment did not come ashore until 1700. See AHQ Report No. 54, 115.

32. TNA WO 291/246, 77–78.

33. Ibid., 4.

34. Ibid., 62.

35. Ibid., 80.

36. TNA ADM 179/506, Part I, 6.

37. TNA WO 291/246, 7.

38. Ibid., 4.

39. Ibid., 42–43.

40. Ibid., 4.

41. TNA WO 291/246, 9.

42. Ibid., 43.

43. NARA, RG 319, Records of the Army Staff, Historical Division, Background Files-Study "American Forces in Action", 1943–1946, "Navy Notes", Omaha Beachhead, Boxes 1 and 2.

44. Andreas Parsch, *Directory of U. S. Military Rockets and Missiles*, www.designation-systems.net/dusrm/index.html.

45. I am indebted to Steve Zaloga for the information of the tests by the 79th Tank Battalion. See his *U.S. Armored Funnies: U.S. Specialized Armored Vehicles in the ETO in World War II* (Hong Kong: Concord Publications, 2005), 5–6.

46. NARA RG 498, ETOUSA Historical Division Files, Box 73, Folder 359A, Notes on Utah Beach and the 1st Engineer Special Brigade (compiled 20 October–7 November 1944), 58.

CHAPTER 4: GERMAN PLANNING AND PREPARATIONS

1. Prior to his new appointment, Rommel had been in command of Army Group B in Italy from June through August 1943, where he organized the forces intended for the occupation of Italy in the event the Italians defected from the Axis. After 8 September, when Italy capitulated to the Allies, Army Group B was to occupy and organize the defenses of northern Italy. Erwin Rommel and Basil Henry Liddell Hart, *Rommel Papers* (New York: Da Capo, 1982), 447. Hitler had made the decision to give Rommel this task on 30 October 1943, after briefly considering appointing him commander in chief of the German forces in Italy, an assignment he gave to Field Marshal Albert Kesselring on

25 October. AHQ Report No. 40, The Campaign In North-West Europe, Information From German Sources, 28 April 1951 and AHQ Report No. 41, The German Defences in the Courseulles-St. Aubin Area of the Normandy Coast, 20 July 1951; and Harrison, *Cross-Channel Attack*, are indispensible for understanding the background of the German command organization and decision-making in the West.

2. It was noted that the reason Omaha and Gold were so "heavy" was because considerable use of Element C, the heaviest obstacle, was made there, while fewer of those obstacles were employed on other beaches. For example, none were found on Utah or Sword. See Army Operational Research Group Report (AORG) No. 292, Comparison of British and American Areas in Normandy in terms of Fire Support and its Effects, 14 August 1945. On Gold, the engineer reports counted the obstacles on Jig Green and the adjacent Item Red (which was not assaulted), so that particular count, unlike the others, was actually a composite of a beach that was assaulted and one that was not. However, given that the sample represented a 2,700-yard wide stretch of Gold, it probably was representative of the average density encountered on that beach. The count by type of obstacle was done on Juno, but apparently was not recorded, so only the raw count of the number of obstacles and their estimated total weight is available now. The count on Sword is complete in all particulars for the obstacles encountered on Queen Beach. See AORG No. 292 and AORG Report No. 264 (TNA WO 291/246), Opposition Encountered on the British Beaches in Normandy on D-Day.

3. Maj. Gen. John D. Inglis, "The Work of the Royal Engineers in North-West Europe" *R.U.S.I. Journal* (May 1946): 180.

4. See AORG Report No. 261 Casualties and Effects of Fire Support on the British Beaches at Normandy, 21 April 1945; and AORG Report No. 292 for contemporary analyses of the German defenses. More modern analysis can be found in Georges Bernage's *Gold, Juno, Sword* (Bayeux, France: Editions Heimdal, 2003) and *Omaha Beach* (Bayeux, France: Editions Heimdal, 2002); Joseph Balkoski's *Omaha Beach: D-Day, June 6, 1944* (Mechanicsburg, PA: Stackpole Books, 2004) and *Utah Beach: The Amphibious Landing and Airborne Operations on D-Day, June 6, 1944* (Mechanicsburg, PA: Stackpole Books, 2005); and Berger, *Breaching Fortress Europe*. The best general source for German defensive doctrine and fortifications design and construction is J. E. Kaufmann and H. W. Kaufmann, *Fortress Third Reich* (Cambridge, MA: Da Capo Press, 2003). The German viewpoint can also be found in AHQ Reports No. 40 and No. 41.

5. Ian Hogg, *German Artillery of World War II* (London: Greenhill Books, 1997), 42.

6. For unit compositions, see Niklas Zetterling, *Normandy 1944: German Military Organization, Combat Power and Organizational Effectiveness* (Winnipeg, Canada: J.J. Fedorowicz Publishing, 2000).

7. TNA WO 291/246, 92–93.

8. The FK 16 n.A. was a World War I vintage piece, the "n.A." indicated *neuer Art*, which meant the piece had been mod-

ernized between the wars. See Hogg, *German Artillery of World War II*, 38.

8. AHQ Report No. 54, The Assault and Subsequent Operations of 3 Cde Inf Div and 2 Cdn Armd Bde, 6–30 June, 42. Note that this is a later and more "refined" version of CMHQ Report No. 147.

9. TNA WO 291/246, 93.

10. AORG Report No. 292.

11. Ibid., 2.

12. Hogg, *German Artillery of World War II*, 202.

13. Overall, about 200,000 mines had been laid along the eighty-kilometer front of the German LXXXIV Corps—about 2,500 per kilometer. But by the second Battle of Alamein in North Africa, the German and Italian engineers had emplaced a half-million mines on a seventy-kilometer front, almost three times the density in Normandy. See U.S. Army Engineer Agency for Resources Inventories, *Landmine and Countermine Warfare: North Africa, World War II* (Washington, DC: U.S. Government Printing Office, 1972), 45.

14. AORG Report No. 292 identified just two 88-millimeter, six 75-millimeter, ten 50-millimeter and 37-millimeter guns, six mortars, and eighty-five machine guns.

15. Fritz Ziegelmann, "The 352nd Infantry Division (MS B-432)" in David Isby, ed., *The German Army at D-Day* (London: Greenhill Books, 2004), 123–28, 192–220. Ziegelmann was Ia (operations officer or G-2) of the division, and his report, written soon after the war for U.S. Army interrogators, is the most complete account of events on the German side by any of the participants.

16. NARA RG 498, Box 73, Folder 359A, Notes on Utah Beach and the 1st Engineer Special Brigade (compiled 20 October–7 November 1944), 61.

17. Ibid., 50–51.

18. For that reason, some of the figures for mortars and machine guns differ substantially from those often given in other sources. Those usually rely on AORG Report No. 261 Casualties and Effects of Fire Support on the British Beaches at Normandy, 21 April 1945, and No. 292, Comparison of British and American Areas in Normandy in terms of Fire Support and its Effects, 14 August 1945. However, those reports used a count of fixed weapons only for the Commonwealth beaches but relied on an estimate of the number of weapons with units on the American beaches, so exaggerated the differences even more so than they actually were.

CHAPTER 5: ASSAULT FORCE SWORD: THE 3RD BRITISH INFANTRY DIVISION

1. The lack of sufficient assault craft was also the reason the U.S. 4th Infantry Division assault on Utah was in a similar column of regiments. The best general narratives of the assault on SWORD are Maj. Gen. Michael Reynolds, *Eagles and Bulldogs in Normandy, 1944* (Havertown, PA: Casemate, 2003); and Norman Scarfe, *Assault Division: A History of the 3rd Division from the Invasion of Normandy to the Surrender of Germany* (London: Collins, 1947), 61–92.

2. Another three troops of Crabs from A Squadron of the Westminster Dragoons were in direct support of the 27th Armoured Brigade, which was also under command of the British 3rd Infantry Division, but the number of Crabs they employed is unknown. Birt, *XXII Dragoons 1760–1945*, 147–48.

3. Of the six that were not launched, one became stuck on its LCT when the chains supporting the ramp broke, while the other five on a second LCT were unable to launch because the lead DD tank tore its skirt. Rather than jettison it and launch the others the LCT commander elected to beach his craft, which he did at H+40. See TNA ADM 179/504, 24.

4. There is some confusion as to the number of DD tanks sunk and the number of crewmen who drowned. On 17 July, SHAEF reported that only one was sunk with all five crewmen drowned. But the naval reports and the 13/18 Hussars War Diary mention two sinking and one being run down by the LCT, with only the commander of that one being saved. See TNA WO 291/246, 109.

5. TNA ADM 179/504, 22.

6. Ibid., 35.

7. Ibid.

8. Ibid.

9. Birt, *XXII Dragoons 1760–1945*, 147. Birt was the regimental signal officer and landed later in the day.

10. TNA WO 171/1800.

11. TNA WO171/1800, No. 5 Assault Regiment War Diary, June–December 1944.

12. Birt, *XXII Dragoons 1760–1945*, 171.

13. TNA WO171/1800.

14. Birt, *XXII Dragoons 1760–1945*, 171–72.

15. TNA WO171/1800.

16. Birt, *XXII Dragoons 1760–1945*, 171.

17. TNA WO171/1800.

18. Ibid.

19. Ibid.

20. TNA WO 171/1800.

21. Lambton Burn, *"Down Ramps!": Saga of he Eighth Armada* (London: Carroll & Nicholson, 1947), 213–14.

22. Burn, *Down Ramps*, 214.

23. Ibid.

24. There are other fleeting references to *Nebelwerfer* rocket launchers being encountered on Sword, but unlike Juno, Gold, Omaha, and Utah, they were not reported in WO 291/246 or any of the other postwar operations research analyses done of the landing.

25. TNA WO171/1800.

26. Birt, *XXII Dragoons 1760–1945*, 168.

27. TNA WO171/1800.

28. TNA WO171/1800.

29. Kilvert-Jones, *Sword Beach*, 111–13. Sergeant Kilvert was a relative of Kilvert-Jones.

30. TNA WO 291/246, 105.

31. Ibid., 107.

32. Ibid.

33. P. R. Nightingale, *A History of the East Yorkshire Regiment (Duke of York's Own) in the War of 1939–1945* (East Riding, England: Mr. Pye, 1952).

34. Tony Chapman, "D-Day from Landing Craft," www.combinedops.com/LCT_PAGE.htm#The%20Fallen.

35. Burn, *Down Ramps*, 215.

36. Kilvert-Jones, *Sword Beach*, 93–98.

37. Robin McNish, *Iron Division: The History of the 3rd Division, 1809–1989* (London: Ian Allen, 1990), 100.

38. Ibid.

39. The French contingent numbered 177 officers and men and was supported by six Royal Signal Corps radiomen and two Royal Army Medical Corps (R.A.M.C.) medical orderlies. K Troop was formed for the invasion to man four Vickers Type K machine guns. Nicholas van der Bijl, *No. 10 (Inter-Allied) Commando 1942–45: Britain's Secret Commando* (Oxford, England: Osprey, 2006) 25–26.

49. TNA WO 291/246, 108.

50. TNA DEFE 2/40, War Diary, No. 4 Commando.

51. Van der Bijl, *No. 10 (Inter-Allied) Commando*, 25–26.

52. TNA WO 291/246, 108.

53. Derek Mills-Roberts, *Clash by Night: A Commando Chronicle* (W. Kimber: London 1956), 93–95

54. TNA WO 291/246, 111.

55. Ibid., 112.

56. Ibid., 108.

57. TNA WO 291/246, 112. Casualties are from *The Story of 45 Royal Marine Commando*, as transcribed at www.combinedops.com/45%20Royal%20Marine%20Commando.htm.

58. Kilvert-Jones, *Sword Beach*, 113–15.

59. TNA ADM 179/504, 39.

60. For additional details of the events later in the day, which are outside the scope of this work, see Michael Reynolds.

61. TNA WO291/246, 109–12. See also the previous casualty references in this text. Note that none of these totals include Royal Navy or Royal Air Force losses incurred in the invasion, which were substantial. Royal Navy losses alone accounted for at least another 134 killed, died of wounds, or missing/presumed killed. See Don Kindell, *Casualty Lists of the Royal Navy and Dominion Navies, 1922–Present*, www.naval-history.net/xDKCas1003-Intro.htm.

62. *War Diary of No. 6 Commando* at www.pegasusarchive.org/normandy/frames.htm.

63. Birt, *XXII Dragoons 1760–1945*, 176.

64. *No. 3 Commando Roll of Honour* at www.pegasusarchive.org/normandy/frames.htm.

65. TNA WO291/246, 116.

66. The *War Diary of No. 3 Commando* gives a complete account of their casualties. See www.pegasusarchive.org/normandy/frames.htm.

67. NARA, RG331, Allied Operational and Occupation HQ, World War II, SHAEF, General Staff G-1 Division, Administrative Section Decimal Files. 21st Army Group Casualty ('A' SITREPS) Reports, Vol. I (10 June–22 July 1944).

68. Royal Navy ship and craft loses may be found in *British Vessels Lost at Sea, 1939–45* (London: HMSO, 1947).

69. TNA ADM 179/516, Operation NEPTUNE—Report of Naval Commander, Eastern Task Force, 8.

CHAPTER 6: ASSAULT FORCE JUNO: THE 3RD CANADIAN INFANTRY DIVISION

1. The narrative of the assault in TNA ADM 179/506, Part I, 6, caustically remarked that "subsequent survey has NOT confirmed" that the late arriving intelligence was correct. In fact, it actually appears the original depth assessment had been correct all along, and the delay was unnecessary.

2. TNA ADM 179/506, Part I, 7–8; and TNA WO 291/246 79.

3. TNA ADM 179/506, Part I, 9.

4. TNA WO 291/246, 87.

5. TNA WO 171/1800.

6. TNA ADM 179/506, Enclosure No. 4, Gunnery, 2.

7. TNA WO 171/1800.

8. Ibid.

9. Ibid.

10. King and Martine were apparently the only two wounded in the troop. See Patrick Delaforce, *Churchill's Secret Weapons: The Story of Hobart's Funnies* (Barnsley, England: Pen & Sword, 2007), 159.

11. TNA WO 291/246, 79–80.

12. TNA WO 171/1800.

13. TNA WO 291/246, 87.

14. Ibid., 88.

15. Ibid.

16. Ibid.

17. Ibid.

18. Ibid., 87.

19. Ibid., 89.

20. Ibid., 88.

21. Ibid., 89–90.

22. Ibid., 90.

23. Ibid.

24. Ibid., 80.

25. Ibid., 81.

26. Ibid., 84.

27. Ibid., 81.

28. Ibid., 81.

29. Ibid., 81. The 76-millimeter guns referred to were probably two of the three 7.5-centimeter PaK 40 of the 2nd Company, 716th Tank Destroyer Battalion, located south of Berniéres.

30. TNA WO 291/246, 82.

31. TNA WO 205/636, A.F.V. States, Summaries at HQ 21 Army Group, June-July.

32. TNA WO 291/246, 82.

33. Ibid., 82–83.

34. Ibid., 84.

35. Ibid.

36. See Terry Copp, *Fields of Fire* (Toronto: University of Toronto Press: Toronto, 2003), 53, for a lengthier account of this incident. Copp says that fifty-five Germans were captured at the battery, but that may have been the total captured for the day by the Chaudières.

37. TNA WO 291/246, 85.

38. The reports by 5th Assault Regiment gave the strength of each of the detachments of the 22nd Dragoons as fifty, but it

seems clear that nine Crabs of B Squadron were with the 26th Squadron and eleven of C Squadron were with the 80th Squadron. With five-men per crew, that works out to forty-five men with the B Squadron detachment and fifty-five with the C Squadron detachment. See TNA WO 171/1800.

39. TNA WO 171/1800.
40. Ibid.
41. Birt, *XXII Dragoons 1760–1945*, 162.
42. TNA WO 171/1800.
43. Ibid.
44. Birt, *XXII Dragoons 1760–1945*, 160–61.
45. TNA ADM 179/506, 7. Curiously, the Royal Navy account says that the decision to launch was made when the LCT were just "1,000 yards off the beach"; a direct contradiction of the accounts given by A and B Squadron, the CAR, which reported the distance as 2,500 and 4,000 yards respectively. It seems likely that the Royal Navy was correct in this case.
46. By the end of the war, Powell had been awarded both the DSO and an MC for his bravery.
47. The rather complicated tale of the 6th CAR on D-Day is told, with some contradictory elements, by Brandon Conron, *A History of the First Hussars Regiment: 1856–1980* (London, Canada: np, nd).
48. TNA WO 291/246, 71.
49. Ibid., 67.
50. Ibid., 71–72.
51. Conron, *History of the First Hussars.*
52. TNA WO 291/246, 65–66.
53. Ibid., 67.
54. Ibid., 62.
55. Ibid.
56. Ibid., 65.
57. Ibid., 63.
58. Ibid.
59. Ibid., 84.
60. Ibid., 63.
61. Ibid., 67.
62. Conron, *History of the First Hussars.*
63. TNA WO 291/246, 84.
64. AHQ Report No. 54, Appendix D.
65. TNA WO 291/246, 83.
66. Ibid., 85. In addition to casualties suffered by the infantry battalions in the 9th Canadian Brigade, the attached 27th CAR had one killed and three wounded.
67. AHQ Report No. 54, Appendix D and TNA WO 291/246, 97–98.
68. Ibid.
69. In the summer of 2008, the remains of the two Centaurs and two D7a armoured bulldozers from LCT (A)-2428 were found off the British coast at a depth of twenty meters, where they had fallen after the LCT had capsized. See "Divers Solve D-Day Tanks Mystery," www.southsea-subaqua.org.uk.
70. TNA ADM 179/506, 9–10.
71. Ibid., Part I, 10, and Part II, p4.
72. Ibid., Part I, 11.

CHAPTER 7: ASSAULT FORCE GOLD: THE BRITISH 50TH INFANTRY DIVISION

1. TNA ADM 179/505, 5.
2. Ibid.
3. TNA ADM 179/505, Appendix C, 3.
4. Ibid., 1.
5. TNA WO 171/1797.
6. Ibid.
7. Ibid..
8. Ken Ford, *D-Day 1944*, vol. 4, *Gold & Juno Beaches* (Oxford, England: Osprey, 2002), 45.
9. TNA WO 171/1797.
10. Ibid.
11. Ibid.
12. TNA WO 291/246, 46. Initial reports counted one killed, four wounded, and eleven missing.
13. TNA WO 291/246, 45.
14. Ibid., 46.
15. Ibid.
16. Ibid., 49.
17. Ibid., 47.
18. Ibid.
19. Ibid., 49.
20. Ibid.
21. Ibid.
22. Ibid.
23. Ibid., 50.
24. Details of Hollis's exploits on D-Day can be found at www.greenhowards.org.uk/html-files/vcgc-hollis.htm.
25. Ibid.
26. TNA WO 291/246, 47.
27. Ibid., 50.
28. Ibid., 47, 50.
29. TNA ADM 179/505, Enclosure 1, "Report by Captain, Group G.1", p. 2 gave the landing time as 0725, which was exactly as scheduled, TNA WO 291/246 gave the time as 0730, and Captain Laytham of 82nd Squadron gave 0720, TNA WO 171/1797.
30. TNA WO 171/1797.
31. It may seem odd that in every case where the decision was made to land the DD directly on the beach from their LCT, their arrival was even later than planned. That apparently was due to the increasing congestion of landing craft in the waters immediately off the beaches and also, perhaps, some indecision about whether to launch or land.
32. TNA ADM 179/505, Enclosure No. 12, Report of Work of L.C.O.C.U. No. 9, 1.
33. TNA ADM 179/505, Appendix E, 1.
34. TNA WO 291/246, 10.
35. TNA WO 171/1797.
36. Ibid.
37. TNA WO 291/246, 11.
38. TNA WO 171/1797.
39. Ibid.
40. Ibid.
41. Only three of the sixteen LCT(A) assigned to Gold managed to get ashore at H+06, two on JIG and one on KING, carry-

ing six Centaurs, two Crusader AA, and one Sherman. It is not entirely certain, but it appears that the Sherman and one of the Crusader AA tanks landed on JIG. Of those tanks that did land two Centaurs broke down and the Sherman was hit and burned. Four more LCT (A) arrived between D and D+2, while four returned to England and the fate of five was unknown. TNA WO 291/246, 48 and TNA ADM 179/505.

42. TNA WO 171/1797.
43. Ibid.
44. Ibid.
45. TNA WO 291/246, 11.
46. TNA WO 171/1797.
47. Ibid.
48. *The Story of the 1st Assault Brigade* says twenty-one A.V.R.E.'s were landed, but it seems clear that was incorrect.
49. TNA WO 291/246, 13.
50. Ibid., 22.
51. Ibid.
52. TNA WO 291/246, 21.
53. TNA WO 291/246, 3–40.
54. Ibid.
55. Ibid., 48.
56. Ibid., 23.
57. Ibid., 21.
58. Ibid., 23.
59. Ibid., 30.
60. Ibid., 26.
61. AORG Report No. 261 gives the first gap on King as one and a half hours after touchdown, but the time on Gap 6 was definitely reported as 1100 hours. From that it may be surmised that Pears managed to open Gap 1 at the later time.
62. TNA WO 291/246, 57–58.
63. TNA WO 291/246, 35–36.
64. TNA ADM 179/505, 6.
65. TNA ADM 179/516, 8.

CHAPTER 8: ASSAULT FORCE OMAHA: THE U.S. 1ST AND 29TH INFANTRY DIVISIONS

1. The primary original source for the operations of the gapping teams on Omaha is NARA RG 498, ETO Historical Division Files, Box 117 and 117A, Folder 493, Operations Report Provisional Engineer Special Brigade Group, 84–90; and Interview, 299th Engineer Battalion, Background Files-Study, "American Forces in Action," 1943–1946, Omaha Beachhead.
2. Interview, 299th Engineer Battalion, Background Files-Study.
3. Ibid.
4. Letter, Sgt. Harrison A. Werble to R. A. Winnacker, Chief, Historical Division, War Department, 12 August 1946, RG 319, Records of the Army Staff, Historical Division, Background Files-Study "American Forces in Action," 1943–1946, Omaha Beachhead, Boxes 1 and 2.
5. Interview, 299th Engineer Battalion, Background Files-Study.

6. Ibid.
7. Ibid.
8. Ibid.
9. Ibid.
10. Ibid.
11. NARA, RG 498, ETO Historical Division Files, Box 44, Folder ADM 220, Commander Assault Force "O" Western Naval Task Force Action Report Assault on Colleville-Vierville Sector Coast of Normandy, 145.
12. Pogue Material, Background Files-Study, "American Forces in Action," 1943–1946, Omaha Beachhead. Balkoski, *Omaha Beach*, 351, notes casualties for the 299th as 71 killed and 75 wounded, but speculates that the losses of B Company on Utah might have been included.
13. The navy action report condemns Thornton's decision as unsound, but also lays some of the blame on Barry for failing to object to the decision. Action Report, Commander Group 35, LCT-6 Flotilla 12, 14 July 1944. The navy account gives the distance as 5,000 yards; the army account gives 6,000 yards. 741st Tank Battalion Unit Journal, June 1944. See also Pederson, *Armor in Operation Neptune*, 79, which gives the time of launching as 0540 hours.
14. "S-3 Journal, 741st Tank Battalion, June 1944," RG 407, Entry 427, Box 16703, ARBN-741-0.1 to ARBN-741-0.16, 741st Tank Battalion Unit Journal June–August 1944.
15. Ziegelmann, "The 352nd Infantry Division," 212.
16. The half-tracks each mounted twin .50-caliber machine guns as well as one 37-millimeter automatic cannon. They were capable of producing a hail of small-caliber fire. The 5-centimeter gun in the casemate at WN 65 was destroyed by thirty-five rounds of 37-millimeter.
17. The story that it was the courageous actions of LCT-30 and LCI(L)-554 that broke the deadlock by crashing directly through the obstacles on Fox Green appears to be apocryphal. There was no LCI(L)-554 in action during Operation Neptune and no mention in the action report of such occurring with LCT-30. She actually landed elements of the 467th AAA Battalion on Easy Red at about 0830 hours and then was hit by a German shell that knocked out the engine room and flooded her. See the 11 July 1944 Action Report, 18 LCT Flotilla. There also was an LCT-544, but she landed on Fox Red, not Fox Green, and there is nothing in the eyewitness account of Bill O'Neill, one of her crew, to support the story either. See *D-Day, June 6, 1944, as Seen from US LCT (6) 544*, ww2lct.org/history/stories/lct544.htm. The story may be based on the actions of Cmdr. L. C. Leever, who commanded the 7th Naval Beach Battalion. He landed from LCI(L) 90 onto Easy Green at 0740 hours with elements of A and B Companies of his battalion, and shortly afterward, he ordered the rest of the battalion to stand off. See the eyewitness account of Julius Shoulars at Witness to War Foundation, www.witness-to-war.org.
18. "S-3 Journal, 741st Tank Battalion, June 1944," RG 407, Entry 427, Box 16703, ARBN-741-0.1 to ARBN-741-0.16, 741st Tank Battalion Unit Journal June–August 1944.
19. Action Report, LCT "O-2", Commander, LCT-6 Flotillas 12 and 26, 29 June 1944.

20. S-3 Journal—History, Company "B", 743rd Tank Battalion, 6 June 1944.

21. Ibid.

22. By evening, six reserve and headquarters tanks had been landed, raising the total battalion strength to thirty-seven operational M4 medium tanks and a single tank dozer.

23. Berger, *Breaching Fortress Europe*, 181–83.

24. NARA RG 407, Entry 427, Box 5931, 301-INF (16) 6-0.1, "History Medical Det." "DAGWOOD Daily Casualty Report for Period from 0630 hours 6-6-44 to 1200 hrs 6-8-44," RG 407, Entry 427, Box 5909, 301-INF (16)-0.3, Report of Operations, June 1944. DAGWOOD was the code for the 16th Infantry. The "History of the 16th CT Invasion of France, S-3 Combat Report," NARA RG 319, Records of the Army Staff, Historical Division, Background Files-Study "American Forces in Action," 1943–1946, Omaha Beachhead, Box 2 changed one officer wounded in action to killed in action and added one enlisted man killed in action. The medical detachment report was identical to that in the S-3 Combat Report.

25. Ibid.

26. Balkoski, *Omaha Beach*, 351.

27. Pogue material, NARA RG 319, Records of the Army Staff, Historical Division, Background Files-Study "American Forces in Action," 1943–1946, Omaha Beachhead, Box 2.

28. Balkoski, *Omaha Beach*, 350.

29. Pogue material.

30. Balkoski, *Omaha Beach*, 350.

31. Ibid.

32. Estimated as one-half the battalion's total casualties in Balkoski, *Omaha Beach*, 350–51.

33. Pogue material.

34. Ibid.

35. NARA RG 498, ETOUSA Historical Division Files, Box 44, Folder ADM 220, Commander Assault Force "O" Western Naval Task Force Action Report Assault on Colleville-Vierville Sector Coast of Normandy, 145.

36. Joseph H. Ewing, *29 Let's Go: A History of the 29th Division* (Washington, D.C.: Infantry Journal Press, 1948), 306.

37. Pogue material.

38. Ibid.

39. Ibid.

40. Casualties of the 2nd and 5th Ranger Battalions are extrapolated from other totals. The losses of the 2nd Ranger Battalion detachment that assaulted Point du Hoc are known; see JoAnna M. McDonald, *The Liberation of Pointe du Hoc: The 2nd Rangers at Normandy: June 6–8, 1944* (Redondo Beach, CA: Rank & File Publications, 2000), 164–73. A total was reported for the battalions on 15 June by the First Army. NARA RG 331, Allied Operational and Occupation HQ, World War II, SHAEF, General Staff G-1 Division, Administrative Section Decimal Files, Box 41, 704/5 First US Army Casualty Reports, Vol. I (15 June–19 July 1944).

41. Balkoski, *Omaha Beach*, 351.

42. Ibid.

43. Estimated as one-half the battalion's total casualties in Balkoski, *Omaha Beach*, 351.

44. Estimated as one-half the battalion's total casualties in Balkoski, *Omaha Beach*, 350–51.

45. Pogue material.

46. As of 15 June 1944. NARA RG 331, Allied Operational and Occupation HQ, World War II, SHAEF, General Staff G-1 Division, Administrative Section Decimal Files, Box 41, 704/5 First US Army Casualty Reports, Vol. I (15 June-19 July 1944).

47. Pogue Material.

48. RG 498, ETOUSA Historical Division Files, Box 44, Folder ADM 220, Commander Assault Force "O" Western Naval Task Force Action Report Assault on Colleville-Vierville Sector Coast of Normandy, p. 145.

49. Estimated as 20 percent of the total reported for the NDUs in the Western Naval Task Force Action Report, 145. The totals given were 4 officers and 20 enlisted men killed, 3 officers and 29 enlisted men wounded, and no officers and 15 enlisted men missing.

50. Commander U.S. Naval Forces, Europe, *The Invasion of Europe, Operation Neptune, Administrative History, United States Naval Forces in Europe 1940–1946*, vol. 5 (London: n.p., n.d.), 530, reported only one LCT sunk (LCT-294) and seven damaged. However, collected action reports indicate that eleven sank, although attempts were made to salvage some of them, See "Larry Noel's Paper" at ww2lct.org/main.htm. The Report of the Western Naval Task Force counts eleven LCT's sunk and one damaged (and later destroyed by the June storm). A large number of those damaged were reported as probably being unrepairable. RG 498, ETO Historical Division Files, Box 44, Folder ADM 220, Commander Assault Force "O" Western Naval Task Force Action Report Assault on Colleville-Vierville Sector Coast of Normandy, 72–76.

CHAPTER 9: ASSAULT FORCE UTAH: THE 4TH U.S. INFANTRY DIVISION

1. The rather complex explanation for why the loss of just two of six control vessels caused such confusion can be inferred from the account given by John Suozzo, commanding officer of LCT(A)-2310, after the war. See ww2lct.org/history/stories/JSuozzo_report.htm.

2. NARA RG 498, ETOUSA Historical Division Files, Box 73, Folder 359A, Notes on Utah Beach and the 1st Engineer Special Brigade (compiled 20 October–7 November 1944), 58.

3. NARA RG 498, ETO Historical Division Files, Box 73, Folder 359A, Notes on Utah Beach and the 1st Engineer Special Brigade (compiled 20 October–7 November 1944), 63.

4. Berger, *Breaching Fortress Europe*, 214–71.

5. The LCT flotillas were especially unlucky on Utah. In addition to the two LCT(A)'s lost, the six other LCT(A)'s were damaged by gunfire, and nine other LCT's were sunk, mostly by mines.

6. Notes on Utah Beach, 60.

7. Notes on Utah Beach, 58.

8. Notes on Utah Beach, 61.

9. "Larry Noel's Paper" at ww2lct.org/main.htm.

CHAPTER 10: RESULTS

1. TNA WO 291/246, 7–8.
2. The sources for the 5th Assault Regiment conflict at different points, indicating that the 26th Squadron had 25 A.V.R.E., the 80th Squadron 22 A.V.R.E., and the 77th and 79th Squadrons each 17 A.V.R.E., a total of 81 for the regiment, but it is assumed that the more detailed breakdown given by gapping team (also totaling 81) is correct.
3. Kilvert-Jones, *Sword Beach*, 113.
4. The 81st Squadron's casualties probably included three reported by C Squadron, Westminster Dragoons.
5. C. P. Stacey, *The Victory Campaign*, 651–52. Note that the official British Army history, *Victory in the West*, does not give precise casualty figures for any of the divisions on D-Day. See L. F. Ellis, et al., *Victory in the West*, vol.1, *The Battle of Normandy* (London: HMSO, 1962).
6. The three other ranks missing are noted in P. R. Nightingale, *History of the East Yorkshire Regiment*.
7. Maj. G. L. Y. Radcliffe and Capt. R. Sale, *History of the 2nd Battalion, The King's Shropshire Light Infantry (85th Foot) in the Campaign in N.W. Europe 1944–1945* (Oxford, England: Basil Blackwood, 1947).
8. For example, in the 27th Armoured Brigade, the Staffordshire Yeomanry reported two officers and five other ranks killed, three other ranks wounded, and six other ranks missing—a total of 16. See TNA WO171/863, Staffordshire Yeomanry War Diary, Jan.–Dec. 1944. Providing further evidence is the case of 41st Royal Marine Commando, where the number of casualties incurred "on the beach" is exactly the same as their number of killed and missing; given the example of other units it seems inconceivable that the number wounded would have been less than 100. Thus, the total could easily be greater by another 116 or so.
9. Stacey, *Victory Campaign*, 650.
10. The 1st Canadian Parachute Battalion attached to the 6th British Airborne Division incurred an additional 19 killed, 6 wounded, 4 missing, and 84 captured for a total of 113, but they are not considered here as part of the "beach" casualties.
11. The actual total casualties in 48th RM Commando were 149. As of 0600 hours on 8 June, the 4th SS Brigade reported a total of 379 casualties.
12. TNA WO 205/405, 21st Army Group G (Operations), August, September 1944. This document was undated, except for the penciled notation "unofficial, produced by Lt.Col. Trencher [?] another paper to follow, 12 Sep." The follow-up, if it ever existed, has not been found.
13. NARA RG 331, Allied Operational and Occupation HQ, World War II, SHAEF, General Staff G-1 Division, Administrative Section Decimal Files, Box 41, 704/5 First US Army Casualty Reports, Vol. I (15 June–19 July 1944), 21st Army Group Casualty ('A' SITREPS) Reports, Vol. I (10 June–22 July 1944).
14. Ellis, et al, *Victory in the West*, vol.1, *The Battle of Normandy*, 222.
15. Harrison, *Cross-Channel Attack*, 330; Balkoski, *Omaha Beach*, 350–52.
16. Balkoski, *Omaha Beach*, 350–52.
17. Ewing, *29 Let's Go*, 306.
18. NARA RG 407, Entry 427, 4th Infantry Division G-1 File, June 1944.
19. RG 498, Box 73, Folder 359A, Notes on Utah Beach and the 1st Engineer Special Brigade, 58.
20. The most concise discussion on this subject is Joseph Balkoski, *Utah Beach*, 330–31.

CHAPTER 11: THE FUNNIES' IMPACT ON D-DAY

1. Harrison, *Cross-Channel Attack*, 450.
2. See the list of equipment used in TNA WO171/1800 and the evaluations made in the 21st Army Group Engineer Report, TNA WO205/1170.
3. The following section is largely drawn from Reeves's report, which can be found in TNA WO 171/153, 21 Army Group AFV (T) Technical Report No. 9.
4. TNA WO 171/153, 21 Army Group AFV (T) Technical Report No. 9, 7.
5. TNA WO 205/1159, 79 Armoured Division Final Report, 1943 Apr.–1945 July, 62.
6. TNA WO 205/1160, 25.

EPILOGUE

1. TNA WO171/1800, War Diary, HQ 5 Ast Regt R.E., 12 June.
2. TNA WO171/1800, War Diary, 17 June.
3. TNA WO171/1800, Report of operations against Radar Strongpoint at Douvres-la-Deliverande.
4. TNA WO171/1797, Activities of ARE on and since D Day.
5. TNA WO205/1160, 29–30.
6. The operations at Boulogne and Calais were analyzed in AORG Report No. 16, Air and Ground Support in the Assault of Boulogne.
7. 1st Assault Brigade R.E., 76.
8. Orsbourn, *Shortest Gap*, 14.
9. Ibid., 33–36.
10. An inquiry at the Canadian Military Engineers Museum yielded some more information from one of their researchers, Ken Holmes. It seems that Denovan may have been a very private person. Holmes noted that after Denovan's death in 2000, he had attempted to contact a family member who might have had knowledge of Major Denovan's wartime history, but without success. Sadly, it appeared that his personal papers had been destroyed. E-mail correspondence, Ken Holmes to the author, 11 April 2008. Because of the Canadian Privacy Act, Denovan's military file cannot be accessed by the public until twenty years after his death.

Bibliography

PRIMARY

Allied Landing Craft of World War II (originally published in 1944 with a subsequent supplement as ON1226-Allied Landing Craft and Ships). Annapolis, MD: Naval Institute Press, reprint 1985.

Army Operational Research Group. Report No. 261, *Casualties and Effects of Fire Support on the British Beaches at Normandy*. 21 April 1945.

———. Report No. 292, *Comparison of British and American Areas in Normandy in terms of Fire Support and its Effects*. 14 August 1945.

Canadian Army Headquarters (AHQ). Report No. 40, *The Campaign In North-West Europe, Information from German Sources*. 28 April 1951.

———. Report No. 41, *The German Defences in the Courseulles-St. Aubin Area of the Normandy Coast*. 20 July 1951.

———. Report No. 42, *The Preliminary Planning For Operation "OVERLORD": Some Aspects of the Preparations for an Allied Re-entry to North-West Europe, 1940–1944*. 5 March 1952.

———. No. 54, *The Assault and Subsequent Operations of 3 Cde Inf Div and 2 Cdn Armd Bde, 6–30 June*. 30 June 1952.

Canadian Military Engineers. *Customs and Traditions of the CME*. A-JS-007-003/JD-001, Annex A—Canadian Military Engineer Memorials, n.d.

Canadian Military Headquarters (CMHQ). Report No. 147, *The Assault and subsequent Operations of 3 Cdn Inf Div and 2 Cdn Armd Bde, 6–30 Jun 44*. 3 December 1945.

Commander, U.S. Naval Forces Europe. *The Invasion of Normandy, Operation NEPTUNE, Administrative History, United States Naval Forces in Europe 1940–1946*. vol. 5. London: n.p., n.d.

Commonwealth War Graves Commission. www.cwgc.org.

The London Gazette, various.

National Archives and Records Administration (U.S.) RG 38, Records of the Office of the Chief of Naval Operations,

Operations Order No. 1-44, Western Naval Task Force, Assault Force "O" (Task Force One Two Four), Naval Combat Demolition Group, 31 May 1944.

Operations Order No. 3-44, Western Naval Task Force, Assault Force "U" (Task Force One Two Five), Naval Combat Demolitions Group, 15 May 1944.

RG 319, Records of the Army Staff, Historical Division, Background Files-Study "American Forces in Action", 1943-1946, Omaha Beachhead, Boxes 1 and 2.

RG 331, Allied Operational and Occupation HQ, World War II, SHAEF, General Staff G-1 Division, Administrative Section Decimal Files, Box 41, 704/5 First US Army Casualty Reports, Vol. I (15 June–19 July 1944) 21st Army Group Casualty ('A' SITREPS) Reports, Vol. I (10 June–22 July 1944).

RG338, ETO Secretary General Staff, Statistics Section, Historical and Statistical Reports, 1944-1945, Box 3, D-Day Studies and Statistical Reports.

RG 407, Entry 427, Records of the Adjutant General, Pre-Invasion Planning, Box 24309, Folder 209, Overlord Conference, 21 December 1943.

RG 498, ETOUSA Historical Division Files. Box 8, Folder 44, Beaches.

———. Box 44, Folder ADM 220, Commander Assault Force "O" Western Naval Task Force Action Report Assault on Colleville-Vierville Sector Coast of Normandy

———. Box 73, Folder 359A, Notes on UTAH Beach and the 1st Engineer Special Brigade (compiled 20 October-7 November 1944).

———. Box 117, Folder 493, Operation Report NEPTUNE, OMAHA Beach, Provisional Engineer Special Brigade Group, 30 September 1944.

———. Box 117A, Folder 493, Operation Report NEPTUNE, OMAHA Beach, Provisional Engineer Special Brigade Group, Photographs 30 September 1944.

The National Archives (UK) ADM 179/504, Operation "NEPTUNE", Report by Naval Commander, Eastern Task Force, Enclosure "C", Report of Proceedings of Force "S".

ADM 179/505, Operation "NEPTUNE", Report of the Naval Commander, Eastern Task Force, Enclosure "D", Report of Proceedings of Force "G".

ADM 179/506, Operation "NEPTUNE", Report by Naval Commander, Eastern Task Force, Enclosure "E", Report of Proceedings of Force "J".

AVIA 22/456, Armoured fighting vehicles: conversions and modifications, 1942–1945.

AVIA 22/469, Armoured fighting vehicles: monthly returns of deliveries, 1939–1941.

AVIA 22/576, Blacker Bombard (297 mm Spigot-Mortar) weapon: requirements, 1941-1943.

AVIA 22/511–514, Monthly Statistical Summaries nos. 1–46, 1942–1946.

AVIA 22/515–519, Statistical Summaries nos. 1–16 and Statistical Abstract, December 1940–1945.

DEFE 2/40, War Diary, No. 4 Commando.

WO171/102, 21 Army Group G.S., January-April 1944.

WO 171/155, Appendix 'A' to R.A. Branch Headquarters 21st Army Group War Diary May 1944.

WO 171/234, Second Army R.A. Landing Tables.

WO 171/863, Staffordshire Yeomanry War Diary, Jan.–Dec. 1944.

WO 171/864, 2 County of London Yeomanry (Westminster Dragoons), Jun.–Dec. 1944.

WO 171/1797, No. 1 Assault Brigade War Diary, June-December 1944.

WO 171/1800, No. 5 Assault Regiment War Diary, June–December 1944.

WO 179/409, 3rd British Infantry Division, Operation Order No. 1, OVERLORD, 14 May 1944.

WO 205/405, 21st Army Group G (Operations), August, September 1944.

WO 205/636, A.F.V. States, Summaries at HQ 21 Army Group, June–July.

WO 205/1120, Report by Brig. Watkinson on Work of Assault RE in the Invasion.

WO 205/1159, 79 Armoured Division Final Report, 1943 Apr.–1945 July.

WO 205/1160, The Story of the 1st Assault Brigade Royal Engineers, 1943–1945.

WO 205/1170, Chief Engineer 21 Army Group, R.E. Report on the Battle of Normandy, 6th June–5th July 1944.

WO 291/246, AORG Report No. 264, Opposition Encountered on the British Beaches in Normandy on D-Day, ND, but apparently 1945.

Royal Navy. *British Vessels Lost at Sea, 1939–45*. London: HMSO, 1947.

U.S. Army Command and General Staff College, Combined Arms Research Library Digital Library. *Conference on Landing Assaults*. 1 July 1943.

———. *Headquarters V Corps, Operations Plan NEPTUNE*. 26 March 1944.

———. *Notes on German Obstacles and Field Works*. August 1943.

———. *Operation Plan No. 2-44 of the Western Naval Task Force, Allied Naval Expeditionary Force*. 21 April 1944.

War Department, Military Intelligence Service. *German Coastal Defenses*. Special Series, No. 15. Washington, D.C.: War Department, 15 June 1943.

SECONDARY

Alanbrooke, Lord. *War Diaries, 1939–1945: Field Marshal Lord Alanbrooke*. Berkeley, CA: University of California Press, 2001.

Arsicaud, Thierry. "The Modified British System," www.echodelta.net/mbs/eng-welcome.php.

Balkoski, Joseph. *Omaha Beach: D-Day, June 6, 1944*. Mechanicsburg, PA: Stackpole Books, 2004.

———. *Utah Beach: The Amphibious Landing and Airborne Operations on D-Day, June 6, 1944*. Mechanicsburg, PA: Stackpole Books, 2005.

Beck, Alfred M., et al. *The Corps of Engineers: The War Against Germany*. Washington, D.C.: Superintendent of Documents, U.S. Gov. Print. Off. 1985.

Beck, Benjamin S. "War Diary 341 Battery, 8th Field regiment, R.A. web.ukonline.co.uk/benjaminbeck/batterydiary.htm.

Berger, Sid. *Breaching Fortress Europe: The Story of U.S. Engineers in Normandy on D-Day*. Dubuque, Iowa: Kendall/Hunt Pub. Co, 1994.

Bernage, Georges. *Gold, Juno, Sword*. Bayeux, France: Editions Heimdal, 2003.

———. *Omaha Beach*. Bayeux, France: Editions Heimdal, 2002.

Bijl, Nicholas van der. *No. 10 (Inter-Allied) Commando 1942–45: Britain's Secret Commando*. Oxford, England: Osprey, 2006.

Bijl, Nicholas van der, and Lee Johnson. *The Royal Marines, 1939–93*. London: Osprey, 1994.

Birt, Raymond. *XXII Dragoons, 1760–1945: The Story of a Regiment*. Aldershot, England: Gale & Polden Limited, 1950.

Blacker, Barnaby. *The Adventures and Inventions of Stewart Blacker Aviation Pioneer and Weapons Inventor*. Barnsley England : Pen & Sword, 2006.

Buckingham, William F. *D-Day: The First 72 Hours*. London: Tempus, 2004.

Burn, Lambton. *"Down Ramps!": Saga of the Eighth Armada*. London: Carroll & Nicholson, 1947.

Campbell, John P. *Dieppe Revisited: A Documentary Investigation*. London: Frank Cass, 1993.

Canadian Forces, Department of National Defence. *Customs and Traditions of the CME*. A-JS-007-003/JD-001, Annex A—Canadian Military Engineer Memorials.

Chamberlain, Peter, "Armoured Recovery Vehicles" in Duncan Crow, ed., *British and Commonwealth AFVs, 1940–46*. Garden City, NY: Doubleday, 1972.

Chamberlain, Peter, and Chris Ellis, "Churchill and Sherman Specials" in Duncan Crow, ed., *British and Commonwealth AFVs, 1940–46*. Garden City, NY: Doubleday 1972.

Conron, Brandon. *A History of the First Hussars Regiment, 1856–1980*. London, Canada: B. Conron, 1981.

Copp, Terry. *Fields of Fire: The Canadians in Normandy*. Toronto: University of Toronto Press, 2003.

Daniels, Maj. Michael J. *Innovation in the Face of Adversity: Major-General Sir Percy Hobart and the 79th Armoured Division (British)* . MMAS Thesis, Fort Leavenworth, KS: U.S. Army Command and General Staff College, 2003.

Delaforce, Patrick. *Churchill's Secret Weapons: The Story of Hobart's Funnies*. Barnsley: Pen & Sword Military Books, 2007.

D'Este, Carlo. *Decision in Normandy*. New York: Dutton, 1983.

Duncan, N.W. "The 79th Armoured Division" in Duncan Crow, ed., *British and Commonwealth AFVs 1940–46*. Garden City, New York: Doubleday & Company, 1972).

Eisenhower, Dwight D. *The Papers of Dwight David Eisenhower*, vol. 3, *The War Years*. Alfred D. Chandler, Jr., ed. Baltimore, MD: The Johns Hopkins Press, 1970.

Ellis, L.F., et al. *Victory in the West*, vol.1, *The Battle of Normandy*. London: HMSO, 1962.

Ewing, Joseph. *29 Let's Go: A History of the 29th Division in World War II*. Washington, DC: Infantry Journal Press, 1948.

Fletcher, David. "The Armoured Vehicle Royal Engineers." Unpublished monograph.

Ford, Ken. *D-Day 1944: Gold & Juno Beaches*. Oxford, England: Osprey, 2002.

French, David. "Colonel Blimp and the British Army: British Divisional Commanders in the War against Germany, 1939–1945." *The English Historical Review* 111, no. 444 (November 1996): 1,182–1,201.

Greenfield, Kent Roberts, et al. *The Organization of Ground Combat Troops*. Washington, D.C.: Historical Division, Department of the Army, 1947.

Harrison, Gordon A. *Cross-Channel Attack*. Washington, D.C.: Center of Military History, United States Army, 1951.

Hogg, Ian V. *German Artillery of World War II*. London: Greenhill Books, 1997.

Hunnicutt, R. P. *Sherman: A History of the American Medium Tank*. Novato, CA:

Presidio Press, 1978.

Inglis, Maj. Gen. John D. "The Work of the Royal Engineers in North-West Europe" *R.U.S.I. Journal* (May 1946).

Kaufmann, J. E., and H. W. Kaufmann. *Fortress Third Reich*. Cambridge, MA: Da Capo Press, 2003.

Kilvert-Jones, Tim. *Sword Beach: British 3rd Infantry Division/27th Armoured Brigade*. Barnsley, England: Pen & Sword, 2001.

Kindell, Don. *Casualty Lists of the Royal Navy and Dominion Navies, 1922–present*, www.naval-history.net/xDKCas1003-Intro.htm.

Lamb, Richard. *Montgomery in Europe, 1943–1945*. New York: Franklin Watts, 1984.

Lee, David. *Beachhead Assault*. London: Greenhill Books, 2004.

Lewis, Adrian R. *Omaha Beach: A Flawed Victory*. Chapel Hill: University of North Carolina Press, 2001.

Little, Sgt. P. "History of the Armoured Vehicle Royal Engineers (AVRE)." *SITREP, 2 Canadian Field Engineers Newsletter* 5, no. 3 (June 2005).

Macksey, Major Kenneth J. *Armoured Crusader: A Biography of Major-General Sir Percy Hobart*. London: Hutchinson, 1967.

McNish, Robin. *Iron Division: The History of the 3rd Division, 1809–1989*. London: Ian Allen, 1990.

M.G. Cars. "Calling All Arms!! Experience at M.G. During Wartime." www.mgcars.org.uk/mgcc/sf/000101.htm.

Mills-Roberts, Derek. *Clash by Night: A Commando Chronicle*. London: W. Kimber, 1956.

Nightingale, P. R. *A History of the East Yorkshire Regiment (Duke of York's Own) in the War of 1939–1945*. East Riding, England: Mr. Pye, 1952.

O'Dell, James Douglas. "Joint-Service Beach Obstacle Demolition in World War II" *Engineer* (April–June 2005).

Orsbourn, M. E. *The Shortest Gap: Story of the Armoured Engineers Vehicles of Royal Engineers*. NP, ND.

Parsch, Andreas. *Directory of U. S. Military Rockets and Missiles*. www.designation-systems.net/dusrm/index.html.

Pogue, Forrest Carlisle. *The European Theater of Operations*, vol.4, *The Supreme Command*. United States Army in World War II. Washington, DC: Office of the Chief of Military History United States Army, 1954.

Radcliffe, Maj. G. L.Y., and Capt. R. Sale, *History of the 2nd Battalion The King's Shropshire Light Infantry (85th Foot) in the Campaign in N.W. Europe 1944–1945*. Oxford: Basil Blackwood, 1947.

Reynolds, Maj. Gen. Michael. *Eagles and Bulldogs in Normandy, 1944*. Havertown, PA: Casemate, 2003.

Rommel, Erwin, and B. H. Liddell Hart. *The Rommel Papers*. New York: Da Capo Press, 1982.

Scarfe, Norman. *Assault Division: A History of the 3rd Division from the Invasion of Normandy to the Surrender of Germany*. London: Collins, 1947.

Singer, Joyce. "Tanks for the Memories." *Today's Seniors* (August, 1994).

Slee, Jeff. "The Story of 45 Royal Marine Command." combinedops.com.

Stacey, C.P. *The Victory Campaign: The Operations in North-West Europe, 1944–1945*. Ottawa, Canada: Cloutier, 1960.

The Story of 45 Royal Marine Commando. www.combinedops.com/45%20Royal%20Marine%20Commando.htm.

War Diary of No. 3 Commando. www.pegasusarchive.org/normandy/frames.htm.

War Diary of No. 6 Commando. www.pegasusarchive.org/normandy/frames.htm.

Wilmot, Chester. *The Struggle for Europe*. New York: Harper & Brothers, 1952.

World War II Landing Craft Tanks. ww2lct.org/main.htm.

Blegen Robert D. "LCT (5) Flotilla 18 at Omaha Beach, D-Day, June 6, 1944."

Kaufmann, Edwin L. "LCT (A)s At Normandy on D-Day."

Noel, Larry. "LCTs and LCT (A)s in Normandy D-Day, June 6, 1944."

O'Neill, Bill. "D-Day, June 6, 1944 as Seen from US LCT (6) 544"

Suozzo, Joe. "LCT's at Normandy, Force 'U'"

Zaloga, Steven. *US Armored Funnies, US Specialized Armored Vehicles in the ETO in World War II*. Hong Kong: Concord Publications, 2005.

Zaloga, Steven, and Howard Gerrard. *D-Day 1944. 1, Omaha Beach*. Oxford, England: Osprey, 2003.

Zetterling, Niklas. *Normandy 1944, German Military Organization, Combat Power and Organizational Effectiveness*. Winnipeg, Manitoba: J.J. Fedorowicz Publishing, 2000.

Ziegelmann, Fritz. "The 352nd Infantry Division (MS B-432)" in David Isby, ed., *The German Army at D-Day*. London: Greenhill Books, 2004.

Acknowledgments

THIS WORK WOULD NOT have been possible without the help of the many kind members of the staff at The National Archives, Kew, Richmond, Surrey. In the course of my four visits there, in 1999, 2000, 2004, and 2006, I have always been overwhelmed by their professionalism and good cheer. Their efficient and user-friendly operation is an inspiration for what a government organization should be.

There are also many individuals whom I would like to thank personally for their help in getting this work to completion:

Jay Karamales translated my vague instructions into finished maps and graphics—and also put up with my badgering, abrupt changes of mind, and harebrained notions of what was possible.

Jon Sowden tirelessly—and patiently—slogged his way through various drafts of this work, providing me with comments and well-deserved criticisms, most of which are now embodied herein.

Ken Holmes of the Canadian Military Engineers Museum cheerfully sent me much of the crucial background history of J. J. Denovan.

David Fletcher, the well-known author of *The Great Tank Scandal* and historian at the Tank Museum, Bovington, kindly lent me a copy of his monograph *The Armoured Vehicle Royal Engineers*, which was invaluable for understanding the mysterious beginnings of the A.V.R.E. He also responded promptly to my many cries for help with photographs.

M. E. "Ossie" Orsbourn, a member of the Royal Engineer Association Armoured Engineer Branch, generously shared his unpublished history of the Royal Engineers and the Assault Vehicle Royal Engineers with me. His dad, E. J. Orsbourn (6353662)

was the driver of *Lifeguard* (A.V.R.E. 2F, 82nd Assault Squadron R.E.) from September 1944 and served with the 77th and 557th Assault Squadrons before that.

Rich Boylan, military archivist at the U.S. National Archives and Records Administration, Archives II, College Park, Maryland, shared his encyclopedic knowledge of sources pertaining to the Overlord and Neptune planning and operations.

Steven Zaloga, preeminent historian of American armored forces in World War II, encouraged me to complete this work. Steve also gently reminded me of a vital document that I had run across in my explorations in the U.S. National Archives some years ago and then promptly forgotten.

Mike Johnson provided a fascinating and thought-provoking online discussion regarding the possible derivation of some of the more esoteric code words and designations associated with Operation Neptune.

Bill Buckingham has given me many enjoyable hours of argument and more than a few keen insights, and he also kindly agreed to review this book in its final form.

Thomas Lane generously allowed me to use some of the photographs taken on Omaha by Lt. Stuart L. Brandel, who was a naval gunfire liaison officer with the 16th Infantry on D-Day.

Stanley Galik Jr.'s father, Stanley Galik, enlisted in the U.S. Navy on 29 June 1942 at the age of nineteen. He served on LCI(L) 35 through three major invasions—Salerno, Anzio, and Normandy. On D-Day, LCI(L) 35 was part of U.S. Navy LCI(L) Group 4 of Flotilla 2 and was attached to the Royal Navy

"I" LCT Squadron under Lt. Cmdr. M. O. W. Miller, Royal Navy. LCI(L) 35 was part of Intermediate Group S2 assigned to carry troops of the British 185th Infantry Brigade. In addition to the American LCIs, Miller's squadron was comprised of the Royal Navy 251 and 263 LCI(L) Flotillas in company with the 40th, 42nd, and 48th LCT Flotilla. Stan and Joe Logan Jr., whose father Joe Logan served on LCI(L) 219 and 216, both kindly allowed me to reproduce some of their photos from Sword.

Julius Shoulars, a member of the 7th Naval Beach Battalion, landed on Omaha on 7 June, and Tom Beaty founded the Witness to War Foundation (www.witness-to-war.org). Shoulars provided unique photographs—some I believe never before published—taken by members of the 7th Naval Beach Battalion that contribute some unique views of Omaha. Beaty's foundation is preserving the oral history of combat veterans through video interviews, written statements, and photographic memorabilia.

Michel Saberly helped guide me through the *London Gazette* in the neverending search for complete names to go with the cryptic initials usually found in British reports.

Danny Lovell contributed a number of hard-to-find and unique photos from his personal collection.

Kevin Tucker shared the fruits of his research identifying the names of the various A.V.R.E.'s that were used on D-Day.

Sam Wren shared a copy of the 22nd Dragoons history with me that proved to be a goldmine of information, filling in some of the gaps in the engineers' accounts.

Chris Evans and David Reisch of Stackpole Books guided me through publication with patience and good humor, accepting excuse after excuse from me while I struggled to add photographs and maps, tweaked the text in version after version, and then had the gall to badger them about the delay in publication.

My very special thanks and love to Jolly, who pushed me to complete this, refused to listen to my excuses when I said it was too tough, and has driven me to do my very best..

Finally, posthumous thanks to my Dad for the extraordinary generosity he displayed by taking my two eldest sons and me along with him to Normandy in 2000 for his first visit there since the breakout in August 1944. He had landed in Normandy on 14 June 1944 as a twenty-two-year-old second lieutenant in A Battery, 537th Antiaircraft Automatic Weapons Battalion (Mobile), earned two Bronze Star Medals and five Campaign Stars in Europe, ended the war near Pilsen on 8 May 1945, and went on to a distinguished twenty-six year career in the U.S. Army. That wonderful visit sparked my desire to write books about the Normandy campaign. Sadly, although he was the picture of health at age seventy-nine when we visited Normandy in 2000, he recently slipped away from us just before his eighty-fifth birthday.

A NOTE REGARDING THE PHOTOGRAPHS

Some of the best photographic records of the Funnies are not still photographs, but motion pictures. Many of the pre-invasion tests of the A.V.R.E.'s and other vehicles were filmed and are now available on the internet at www.limelighthd.tv/WorldWarII.

Index